PENGU

THE GERM

'Strong sane and valuable . . . one of the amazing features of *The German Trauma* is its ability to inspire the reader with horror and incredulity after all these years of bombardment by details of the atrocities, moral and actual, of the Third Reich'
Paul Binding, *Independent on Sunday*

'Gitta Sereny is, surely, our stellar investigative journalist . . . When Sereny has cornered her quarry, be he politician, academic or sadistic butcher, she closes in with uncompromising acuity, but with a seriousness, an intimation of personal vulnerability which establish a revealing trust'
George Steiner, *Observer*

'For over forty years she has been applying the cool steel scalpel of questioning to humanity's least tractable moral problems: the nature of evil, of complicity in evil and the fearsome process by which individuals inch their way towards wickedness' Gillian Glover, *Scotsman*

'The only real defence of a civilized society against such outrages is education. As our experience over the past decades shows, it offers but an imperfect cure. It is, however, one to which Gitta Sereny has made an invaluable contribution'
Joachim Whaley, *The Times Literary Supplement*

'Her fairness, charity, knowledge, industry, lucidity and conscientiousness shine from every page' Andrew Gimsom, *Evening Standard*

'Gitta Sereny [has] illuminated our understanding not just about Germany under Nazism but also, and perhaps more importantly, the reactions of those brought up in its aftermath'
Trevor Royle, *Sunday Herald*

'Puts into context her extraordinary life's work on the subject of evil and moral responsibility' Antony Beevor, *Independent*, Books of the Year

ABOUT THE AUTHOR

Gitta Sereny was born in Vienna in 1923 and educated in Austria, England and France. She is trilingual. Her journalistic work, which is published all over Europe, has mainly been for the *Daily Telegraph Magazine*, the *Sunday Times*, the *Independent on Sunday Review* and *The Times*. In the United States she has written for *The New York Times Magazine*, the *Atlantic Monthly*, *Harper's Magazine* and the *Readers Digest*. Her previous books include *The Case of Mary Bell* (1972 and 1995), *Into that Darkness* (1974 and 1995), *The Invisible Children* (1984), *Albert Speer: His Battle with Truth* (1995) and *Cries Unheard* (1998). She lives in London with her husband, the photographer Don Honeyman. They have two children and two grandchildren.

GITTA SERENY

The German Trauma

EXPERIENCES AND REFLECTIONS 1938–2001

PENGUIN BOOKS

PENGUIN BOOKS

Published by the Penguin Group
Penguin Books Ltd, 80 Strand, London WC2R 0RL, England
Penguin Putnam Inc., 375 Hudson Street, New York, New York 10014, USA
Penguin Books Australia Ltd, 250 Camberwell Road, Camberwell, Victoria 3124, Australia
Penguin Books Canada Ltd, 10 Alcorn Avenue, Toronto, Ontario, Canada M4V 3B2
Penguin Books India (P) Ltd, 11 Community Centre, Panchsheel Park, New Delhi – 110 017, India
Penguin Books (NZ) Ltd, Cnr Rosedale and Airborne Roads, Albany, Auckland, New Zealand
Penguin Books (South Africa) (Pty) Ltd, 24 Sturdee Avenue, Rosebank 2196, South Africa

Penguin Books Ltd, Registered Offices: 80 Strand, London WC2R 0RL, England

www.penguin.com

This collection of extended and revised essays
first published by Allen Lane The Penguin Press 2000
Published with further revisions in Penguin Books 2001

017

Printed and bound in Great Britain by Clays Ltd, Elcograf S.p.A.

ISBN 978-0-14-029263-3

www.greenpenguin.co.uk

Contents

Acknowledgements

I owe thanks to all the editors I name in the Introduction, who made it possible for me over the past thirty-odd years to spend weeks and sometimes months working on the subjects now covered in this book. This is my first book published by Penguin, and the help I received from the Penguin staff and, above all, from the Publishing Director of the Penguin Press, Stuart Proffitt, now my editor there, has been exceptional in my experience. I want to thank here, too, Drs Tim Ladbrooke and Simon Davies, and the Royal Brompton Hospital, whose combined efforts over the past year enabled me to return to work. My gratitude, as ever, to my agent Rachel Calder, for her never-failing support. My love and thanks to Mandy Honeyman for her help with 'Stolen Children', and, as always, to my husband Don, without whom I would not like to be.

List of Illustrations

Unless otherwise stated in parentheses, all photographs are in the collection of the author. Every effort has been made to contact all copyright holders. The publishers will be glad to make good in future editions any errors or omissions brought to their attention.

Introduction

How does one describe, not one's circumstances or what one did at any particular time of one's life, but what one was? Certainly, looking back at what has now been a long life, my most important years, which decisively affected everything I have done and perhaps have become since, were my late teens and early twenties. Like most people who have been marked by experience of war, everything I have written that is most important to me, about the unheard cries of suffering children, and about Germany during and after Hitler, basically evolved from my impressions and feelings during those formative years.

The nineteen chapters in this book, all intimately concerned with Germany before, during and since the end of the Third Reich, describe more or less sequentially what I saw and learned from 1938 to 1999, thus almost over a lifetime. They represent what I like to think of as a kaleidoscope of discovery.

My first awareness of Nazism as evil was at the time of the Anschluss – the annexation of Austria to Germany – and continued when, still in my teens in the early 1940s, I worked for two years as a nurse under the, at first, comparatively benevolent German occupation of France, where I had been studying until they approached Paris.

But it was not until my two immediate post-war years working with displaced persons, Hitler's slave workers, and – still now to my mind one of his worst crimes – the young children the Nazis stole in Eastern Europe, that I really began to understand the full impact of the Nazi ideology's contempt for human beings. During those two years, however, living in the comparative cocoon of an occupation job in Allied uniform, my work and thoughts were focused on the millions of slave workers and concentration camp inmates who had been Hitler's most obvious victims, not the Germans, old and young, who had been left angry, morally confused and entirely adrift about their past, present and future.

During many stays over subsequent decades in what formally became from 1949 until 1989 West Germany (I managed to spend only one week in East Germany, in 1983), I made close friends with some of the leading figures of the post-war decades, spoke at length with men and women from Hitler's close circle – almost all now dead – and with a few of the perpetrators of his worst crimes. Over the years I have also talked with many ordinary Germans of my own generation and older – the Third Reich and war generation – and probably hundreds of the post-war young, heavily weighed down by Hitler's crimes though entirely innocent of them.

As I planned this book, I realized that the reader would need some explanations of how – and more than that, why – I sought out the people I wrote about. And so, the links between these accounts of different aspects of German life that my publishers and I have selected from the many I have written over the past fifty years, have, almost unintentionally, taken on an autobiographical character. For what has always motivated me, as it has many other writers of my generation – a generation which has seen the two most catastrophic dictatorships in the history of the world – is the search for what it is that leads human beings so often and so readily to embrace violence and amorality. For me the answer to this fundamental question lies in a personal and human rather than a theoretical or intellectual realm. It was as a result of the many relationships I describe in the pages which follow that I began to understand both the idealism and the capacity of a tyranny to pervert human instincts from good to bad. It is, as I hope to show, the fatal combination of the two which led to – what I now call this book – the German trauma.

The character of one's reaction to the German invaders in the Second World War was largely dependent, I think, on where one was geographically, and what one was by nationality, religion, education, language, knowledge, profession and conviction. But as far as the profoundly demoralized French were concerned (very differently from the peoples of other countries the Germans occupied), the decisive factor was probably one's age. While a great many – surely too many

– middle-aged Frenchmen and women were bored with rather than tired of an unfought war and were prepared to make do with the Germans, there was, curiously enough, a degree of consensus between the quite old and the young about defeat. In the old, for whom the glory of France had been the core of their lives, it was shame; in the young it was fury. In the particular circumstances in which France found herself, the two were not far apart.

There can be no comparison whatsoever between the experience of the young in Western occupied countries and that of their peers in the East. The German occupation of Poland and Russia was swiftly accompanied by acts of almost unbelievable savagery. While particularly vicious against Jews, gypsies and 'communist commissars', millions of Christian Poles, Ukrainians and Russians were murdered too because of their religion, or their intellectual and social standing. This was not the case in Western Europe, where on the whole – certainly during the first period of occupation – German troops fairly conscientiously obeyed their orders to behave with restraint. More than any Frenchman ever did, German soldiers invariably stepped aside politely in the street or in the Métro for us in our nursing uniforms, and the German officers with whom (as I will later recount) I had to negotiate for food, clothes or documents were always courteous and often extremely helpful. Nevertheless, for many of us young people there was little that was normal or ordinary about our lives from the moment the invaders arrived, and the daily sight of well-dressed, laughing Germans in possession of France was enough to fuel our resentment to continuous boiling point.

So what was I, and what were we – in our late teens, at the most confusing and impressionable age, on the cusp between childhood and adulthood – we, who became part of a conflict that would leave its imprint on the world for the rest of the century and beyond?

We were – I remember it well enough to sense it again in my bones and the beating of my heart as I write this down nearly sixty years later – creatures of emotion. We could love (love, in my case specially for children, became very intense) and we could even, obstinately rather than with reason, hate. But more than that – an important component of wars – we found ourselves intoxicated by the excitement of fear and we deliberately provoked opportunities to be afraid. That love of danger would later kill a number of my friends, but in the circumstances of our lives then, it was impossible not to court it. What we could not be, what no one I knew of my generation in occupied Europe could be, was indifferent.

Two years before the Nazis invaded France, I had seen them march into Vienna, the city of my birth and childhood. As Austria was the country I unquestioningly considered my own despite my Hungarian parentage, I deeply resented its invasion. Though not immune to the immense enthusiasm for the Anschluss that surrounded me in the streets and at school that March of 1938, I very quickly became aware – as any Viennese was almost bound to be – of the Nazis' behaviour towards Jews. Certainly for me, who had, like most Viennese children with an intellectual or artistic family background, grown up (without being particularly aware of it) in an entirely mixed society where Jews, many eminent in their field, were a majority, this discovery no doubt had a decisive influence on my later development. Even so, nothing I saw, heard or had read by spring 1938, abominable though I felt it was, could have predicted the horrifying events which began in the summer of 1941 in Eastern Europe. Looking back on it now, and on our lives in France under the Germans after June 1940, the fact that we knew or guessed nothing of what the future held for this huge group of Europeans of all nationalities, demonstrates yet again how effective the Nazis were, well before and indeed after they embarked on genocide, in keeping their intentions secret. Reading over what this book contains, I have been struck and – I say it frankly – somewhat disturbed by how much of it came to revolve around the murder of the Jews.

It is worth summarizing what took place. The winter of 1940, with severe shortages of food, clothes and coal, most of which were taken by the conquerors, was the coldest, hardest in French memory. Though we were intensely aware of the risks we took when we chose to oppose the invaders in small ways (this was a time when the later famous Maquis was in its infancy, so these were always individual decisions made from one occasion to another), between May 1940 and the onset of winter in 1941 we knew nothing of forced deportations of Jews from Germany, from Belgium, from Holland or from France. The

French media, totally controlled by the German occupation authorities, refrained from any mention of measures against Jews and even the Vichy government's deplorable Statut des Juifs of 4 October 1940, depriving refugee Jews of their civil rights (it was, as I would discover only much later, like the Nuremberg Laws between 1935 and 1938, published only in the official gazette), was not mentioned in the national press; nor was that next tip of the iceberg, eight months later, on 14 May 1941, the internment of 3,000 naturalized Jews. With increasing arrests of (both Catholic and Jewish) public figures we knew in Paris, we did become aware of German concentration camps, though without knowing any of their locations or names. But I do not recall anyone in that early period of the occupation – Jews or non-Jews, people of my age or older – ever mentioning a threat to the *lives* of Jews, in France or elsewhere. The term 'extermination camp' had not been coined at that point, for of course the four designated extermination camps in Poland (as well as the labour-cum-death installations like Auschwitz and Majdanek) did not yet exist. Indeed, as we now know, the decision for genocide was not taken until – so it is now believed – shortly before the invasion of Russia in June 1941. So while we certainly soon learned of the economic threats to Jews, heard of academics losing their university appointments and the arrest of Jewish politicians, that was as far as it went. It was not the fate of the Jews that was on our minds, but that of France and, for a few of us who had connections there, of Britain, now standing alone.

I emphasize this because even now, as I write, many people still believe that the fatal threat to Europe's Jews – which, if it had been understood, would have confronted us with a moral imperative – was obvious almost from the start and startlingly unopposed, not only by 'all Germans' (as has recently been wrongly claimed in one much-discussed book, of which more later), but in the United States and Britain, and in all the countries occupied by the Germans, that is, most of Europe.

The truth is that even after July 1941, although huge numbers of *Wehrmacht* soldiers and of civilians – including of course neutral diplomats in Eastern Europe – became fully aware of the killings in the conquered areas of the Baltic countries and the Soviet Union, the world did not realize that this was the beginning of a planned genocide of the Jews of Europe. They preferred to accept the German interpretation of 'acts of war', a psychological attitude of denial which (except in Germany, as I will presently show) was to endure, at least in legal semantic terms, for the rest of the century.

Oddly enough, it was the Nazis themselves, with their fanatical *Ordnungsliebe* ('passion for order'), who informed the world, after their era had passed, of what they had done. For in the West German archives in Koblenz, in the Institute for Contemporary History in Munich, in the Wiener Library in London and now in the spasmodically opening Russian archives in Moscow, there are a number of documents which contain 'action reports' from SS *Einsatzgruppen* commanders in the East, and provide meticulously precise figures for the murders.

Viciously anti-semitic Lithuanian police units, set up by the SS within days of conquering the country, had started the killings there on 4 July 1941, and for the first time killed women and children: the SS, anxious to demonstrate the fervour of nationalists in the conquered East, soon afterwards made a film of the proceedings for use in their orientation courses in Pretzsch near Leipzig. (Students of the Third Reich learned this from the post-war denazification trial of a one-time SS recruit who, seeing the film, had managed to get himself transferred to the front.)

One of many examples is the infamous 'Jäger Report' dated 10 December 1941 by SS Colonel Karl Jäger, the commander of SS/SD Einsatzkommando 3 in charge of the killings in half of Lithuania, in which he announced that thanks to the work of his *Kommando* (which included the Lithuanian police units), Lithuania was the first country in Eastern Europe that could be considered *judenfrei* ('cleared of Jews').

As was the rule, Jäger presented the day-by-day listings of those shot between 4 July and 17 October 1941 in four categories: male Jews, female Jews, 'Jew-children' (*Judenkinder*) and *Sonstige* ('others'). Of 137,422 Jews killed there in those three months, 55,556 were women and 34,464 children. The 1,851 'others' – the minute proportion corresponding to that in all other command reports from occupied Eastern regions – included 1,064 Lithuanian and Russian communists, 653 mentally sick, 44 Poles, 5 gypsies, 1 Armenian and 28 Russian POWs. Three other commanders of *Einsatzgruppen* – SS Generals

Jeckeln, Stahlecker and Ohlendorf – reported the killings of hundreds of thousands of Jews by their commands as meticulously as did Colonel Jäger. Otto Ohlendorf, the only SS general to testify at Nuremberg, confirmed there the figures and the authenticity of the reports.

But as angry young people in occupied France, we knew nothing of this, nor of the killings by the SS or indeed by the German *Wehrmacht* in obedience to Hitler's famous 'Commissar Order', of communist officials and, by extension, of untold tens of thousands of Jews and gypsies further east, in Ruthenia and the Ukraine.

The fact that the Russians, who lost 50 million people to Stalin, Hitler, and the war, feel both bitter and puzzled by the West's almost exclusive concentration upon the Nazis' genocide of the Jews is not surprising. Even so, if their post-war literature reports both Stalin's murder of about 20 million, and 10 million murdered by the Germans (aside from those who were killed in the war), without specifically citing the number of murdered Russian Jews, it is not a reflection of their traditional anti-semitism, but a demonstration of their post-war public policy of considering all the victims, whatever their religion or national origin, as Russians. By the same standard, the official Polish figure for Poles murdered by the Nazis is cited as 6 million, which includes almost 3 million Jews.

Many people, myself included, have come to feel that the particularism accepted by the Western world over the past fifty-five years, in so entirely identifying Hitler and national socialism with the genocide of the Jews, virtually ignoring the millions Hitler murdered elsewhere and concentrating the historic and emotional memory of that period so exclusively on this one aspect of it (including by the appropriation of the – capitalized – word 'Holocaust'), is both historically incorrect and psychologically unwise. It is incorrect because it diminishes Hitler's megalomania, which, going beyond even the horrible destruction of this one 'race', envisioned and came terrifyingly close to achieving a future where Germany would have dominated a world in which, after grotesque mass killings, huge 'racially inferior' populations such as Slavs and blacks would merely have existed as labouring vassals. And it is unwise, because it has risked creating new resentment against Jews for their part in shaping this one-sided image. We need to accept and acknowledge, without diminishing in any way the fate and pain of *any* group of victims, that death came to so many: death is death, whether by hanging, shooting or gassing. Loss is loss, whether suffered by Jews, Christians of many denominations, or by any others.

None the less, after thousands of books, films and documentaries on the subject over the second half of the twentieth century, the Nazi infamy of the factory-killing of the Jews in gas chambers is seen by most of the West (though, understandably as I have said, not by the Russians and Poles) as the key crime of the century, the defining event of unique horror that will brand the Nazis for eternity. What is still insufficiently recognized is the fact that outside the Jewish world community, it is in Germany that this has been most deeply felt for fifty-five years, and where the most effective legal and educational measures have been introduced to confront this terrible past. Many of the events and reactions described in the following pages germinated in this history, which therefore inevitably threads through this book.

Running concurrently after the end of the war with an increasing preoccupation in Germany about the murder of the Jews, were the effects of the separation of the country into East and West. In May 1945 when the war in Europe ended, Germany was divided into four zones of occupation: the Americans in the south, the French in the west and the British in the north. The Russians, who would soon extend the territory they controlled in the east across Poland to the Baltic states, held the largest area of Germany (including half of the former capital, Berlin), access to which was forbidden to West Germans and from which East Germans were prohibited to leave. East Germany, renamed the German Democratic Republic (DDR), became a communist dictatorship controlled and exploited by the Soviets, while the Western Federal German Republic (Bundesrepublik Deutschland), its seat of government moved to the small spa of Bonn, was politically reformed by the three Western Allies and economically restored by America's Marshall Plan, which laid the foundation for its prodigious recovery, the *Wirtschaftswunder* of the 1950s. The central part of the former capital – or 'West Berlin' as it was referred to at the time – was an island surrounded by Soviet-occupied territory in which the three Western Allies, determined to demonstrate their resolution to keep the city free, maintained garrisons and headquarters. The historic 'airlift' in 1948–9 when, following the closing of all ground-access routes by the Russians, hundreds of Western Allied planes landed perilously day and night at the small Tempelhof Airport in the centre of the city, ferrying in food, medicines and clothes for the isolated population, emphasized their resistance to the Russians in the by then bitter 'cold war'. Their determination to maintain the symbolic status of the city led to a fundamental change in attitude towards the Western Allies by the West Germans.

The recovery of real political and psychological independence and civic responsibility was slow. One must not forget that every aspect of German life had been controlled by the party, and every civic function, whether the administration of the *Länder* ('federal states') or of the schools, universities and courts was held by those who could be trusted by the regime. Not surprisingly, the Allies assumed almost all of these responsibilities in the immediate aftermath of victory. It took almost a decade to train new German teachers, new German lawyers, new German judges. For example, for ten years after the end of the war, German courts could only deal with misdemeanours or crimes committed by Germans against Germans. Though this included individual criminal acts associated with the *Kristallnacht* in November 1938, with various concentration camps, and with the euthanasia programme – the killing of the mentally ill and handicapped between 1939 and 1941 – German courts did not have jurisdiction over crimes committed by members of the SS or the *Wehrmacht* in occupied countries or concentration and extermination camps abroad.

Such proceedings, usually – and, as we shall see, incorrectly – referred to as 'war crime trials', were reserved to the Allies in their four zones. The record has never been clearly established as to who did what to whom in the Soviet zone. But the Western Allies, particularly the Americans, not only carried out so-called 'denazification investigations' of all adult West Germans between 1945 and 1950 – an impossible task, not surprisingly ineffectually executed – but between them tried 50,000 to 60,000 Germans accused of 'war crimes', sentencing 806 of them to death and executing 486. By 1950, however, when the increasing tension between West and East increased the Allies' political dependence on West German support, German public demands for an end to the Allied trials resulted in the release of most of those who had been tried – and were still alive – who, thanks to an Allied ruling imposed before the trials began, could never again be brought to trial. Indeed, a number of those released who had been highly placed Nazi officials soon found themselves re-employed either by the American or British authorities, or by the West German state.

It was in the autumn of 1958, three years after full jurisdiction had been returned to German courts, that the Conference of Ministers of Justice of the West German *Länder* set up in Ludwigsburg near Stuttgart the Central Agency for Investigations (*Aufklärung*) into National Socialist Crimes. For the four decades since, around 130 prosecutors and judges, assisted by 300 police officers, have investigated almost 100,000 people suspected of having committed Nazi (NS) crimes. A number of the resulting trials lasted for many months, even years. They have been a landmark in the process of West Germany's taking issue with, and beginning to come to terms with, its own past. It is noteworthy too, that, keenly aware of the difference between a 'war crime' (committed in the course of war actions) and an 'NS crime' (unrelated to war and committed mostly against innocent civilians), neither the Central Agency nor the German media reporting on the trials ever referred to these proceedings as 'war crimes trials', the term used so misleadingly first by the Allies, and ever since by various countries, including Britain.

There were 6,494 individuals tried and convicted by West German courts, 13 receiving the death sentence, 166 imprisonment for life. As of 1 January 1996, 4,002 proceedings initiated by Ludwigsburg were still pending in German courts. As of the end of the century, the Ludwigsburg agency, now with a staff of twenty-five, is still handling fifty-two judicial inquiries they expect to hand over to the courts where the accused persons are residing.

Despite considerable public opposition – the agency's officials at first found themselves virtually ostracized by the local population – the media and educational authorities have over the years fully supported the 'NS' trials, which were attended by thousands of secondary school and university students.

To many people of my generation in Europe – those born in the 1920s, whether in Britain or the continent of Europe, north, south, west or east, and, above all, in Germany – some of the accounts in this book may recall the intensity of their own feelings, not only during the war – whichever side they were on – but when they discovered the nature and consequences of tyranny. In Germany, that discovery goes beyond the war generations. In millions of people there, including the young of today as I write this, it has caused and left a deep wound with which they are still trying to come to terms. The fact that, as I try to demonstrate in this book, this wound exists and has been felt so deeply for what is now half a century, has altered what has usually been thought of as 'the German character'. And if today Germany (in a quite different manner from the one Hitler planned) has become not the ruler, but the heart of Europe, it is precisely, I believe, because this wound is still being constantly confronted by Germans of all ages.

Each chapter bears the date of its original composition.

I
Beginnings

Autumn 1995

My father, who died when I was two, was a passionately Anglophile Hungarian, whose greatest ambition for me was that I receive an English education. And so it happened that in 1934 I was travelling back to my boarding school in England from my home in Vienna when the train broke down in Nuremberg. I was an eleven-year-old girl, on my own, wearing my English school uniform – brown, as it happened, though I don't really think it influenced subsequent events. The German Red Cross, or its equivalent Nazi organization, quickly took charge of me; within an hour, to my amazement and, it must be said, pleasure, I found myself in a spectator's seat at the Nazi Party Congress.

I was overcome by the symmetry of the marchers, many of them children like me; the joyful faces all around; the rhythm of the sounds; the solemnity of the silences; the colours of the flags; the magic of the lights (these, though I didn't know it, Speer's creation). One moment I was enraptured, glued to my seat; the next, I was standing up, shouting with joy along with thousands of others. I saw the men on the distant podium and heard their hugely amplified voices. But I understood nothing; it was the drama, the theatre of it all that overwhelmed me. (Forty-four years later, Albert Speer described to me his own feelings that day and said, resignedly, 'To think that when I'm gone, *that's* what I will be remembered for: not the buildings I designed but that – *theatre*.')

A few days later, back at my peaceful school near the Kentish downs, we were given the subject for our first essay of the new term – not surprisingly, 'The Happiest Day of my Holiday'.

What else could I, not yet twelve, have described other than that experience in Nuremberg? Although my essay was not chosen to be read out to the class (that honour fell to a lovely description of the birth of a foal), my teacher, Miss Hindley, told me that it was 'a very good piece of work'. She had a strangely formal way of speaking which I found very beautiful, and I thought her a marvel of erudition and adulthood. In fact she was in her early twenties, a slight, delicate, rather shy young woman, with a fine English complexion. She had a quiet sense of humour, was passionate about books and drama and had the wonderful gift of imparting that passion to her pupils, however cloddish.

'I think you need to understand what you were seeing,' she told me. 'Anyone who comes from your part of the world needs to understand.' And she handed me a book. 'Read this, or as much of it as you can.'

The book was *Mein Kampf*, and I did read as much of it as I could. Years later, when people told me they had found *Mein Kampf* unreadable (in Speer's case, he said Hitler had told him not to bother, that it was outdated), I never understood what they meant. It was hard going, true enough; I skipped large portions, and certainly I wished that it had more paragraphs. But I understood what Hitler was saying and, above all, that his vision of a new Germany, a new Europe, could not be realized without war.

Was I particularly prescient? I don't think so. Throughout those hundreds of densely written pages, he repeated, again and again, Germany's need for *Lebensraum* in 'the East'. I knew nothing about politics and very little about the geography and tortured history of Eastern Europe, but it seemed to me obvious that no country would voluntarily give away any of its territory. How could anyone doubt that?

I also knew very little about anti-semitism. 'Why does he keep talking about "the Jews"?' I asked Miss Hindley when I returned the book.

'He hates them,' she said. And, as she so often did with all of us, she left me to think it out on my own.

I did not succeed. I knew, of course, that there were, in the school of my early childhood in Vienna, three classes of religious instruction – Catholic, Jewish and, my own class, Protestant – but I was not really consciously aware of who among my classmates belonged to which group. This must sound strange, but I have since asked Viennese friends of my own age, from similar backgrounds, about this, and they too, I found, had little awareness of religious difference – which is perhaps a tribute to our schools.

For a privileged child like me, Vienna was paradise. I lived with my mother, who was beautiful and much courted, in a large flat overlooking St Stephen's Cathedral. She had been an actress when she was young, and her life revolved around the theatre, actors, playwrights and drama. Was St Stephen's Cathedral, with its powerful smell of incense, its monotonous singing and its silences, its bleeding or smiling statues, just drama to me? I don't know, but until I was sent to England, I went in there every day on my way to or home from school, leaving my irritated governess outside while I knelt there in a curious pretence of – or perhaps wish for – religious fervour.

My other passions were more prosaic: my mother, for her looks; a few of her gentleman friends, for their charm and elegance; the countless books I read, many on the sly by torchlight under my bedclothes at night; teachers – there was always a special one – for their cleverness and, as I was mostly lucky, kindness; the theatre, which obsessed me from my first visit at the age of four; and Vienna, because it was Vienna.

By the time I was fourteen, I had left my English boarding school and was back in Vienna, studying at the Max Reinhardt Drama School. Although I had not inherited my mother's looks – I was a little girl with puppy fat – I somehow never doubted that they would give me a place, and for some reason I was accepted on the spot, as was another girl my age. She was delicate, with a cloud of silky, dark hair, and was most appropriately named Elfie. We were inseparable from that moment on.

The Max Reinhardt Drama School was a wonderful place, housed in the extraordinary setting of the Imperial Palace of Schönbrunn. Reinhardt, the greatest producer-director of his time, who had had to leave Germany and his school in Berlin because he was Jewish, made a speech on the day the school opened in Vienna which was reprinted in a brochure we were given: 'Use this place. Walk in the park on your own, think on your own, speak on your own, dream on your own: before you can know anyone else, in life or on the stage, you must know yourself!'

These were powerful words for young minds, and both Elfie and I followed his advice, conscientiously taking long walks on our own, speaking aloud as he advised, expressing our thoughts, our longings, our anger, on occasion, and our dreams.

Most of Elfie's and my life was spent together. We would meet every day half-way between our homes, by the statue of Johann Strauss in the Stadtpark. We would go together to our fencing or dancing lessons close by, or attend rehearsals at Reinhardt's theatre, the Josefstadt. Later on, we would take the tram to Schönbrunn and most nights – often very late, because many of our teachers were directors and could only take classes in the evening – we would walk home past the palace park, down the immensely long Mariahilfer Strasse and finally along the Ring with its beautiful trees and baroque buildings. When we reached the Opera, we parted, Elfie turning right and I left. No one ever bothered us; despite its many political conflicts and frequently violent demonstrations, Vienna was – and still is – a strangely safe city for children.

This innocent, or insouciant life ended shockingly and quickly in March 1938, when Hitler invaded Austria. At about nine-thirty in the evening on 11 March, Elfie telephoned me. 'Meet me at the statue,' she whispered.

'Why are you whispering?' I asked.

'Just come,' she said, and hung up.

While I waited for Elfie in the dark, deserted park, I heard for the first time a sound that was to echo around Vienna for weeks: the rhythmic chant of many voices shouting words I had never heard before: *'Deutschland erwache! Juda verrecke!'* – Germany awake! Jewry perish!

When Elfie arrived, we stood stiffly in the darkness, listening. Then she said, 'My father –'

'What's the matter with your father?' I asked, and then, to my own surprise, added, 'Is he a Jew?'

Elfie looked at me helplessly. 'A Jew?' she said, confused, her voice tight. 'He is a Nazi. They told me tonight. He's been an illegal for years. He said I was never to speak to any Jews at school, and that anyway' – her voice sounded dead – 'the whole place will be . . . *disinfected* from top to bottom. What shall I do?' She sobbed, holding on to me. 'How can I not talk to Jews?' Then, for the first time, she put into words the subject that had never touched us, reeling off the names of four of our teachers whose criticism or praise had dominated our lives for over a year.

I was almost speechless. 'But why?' I asked, and then, immediately, 'How do you know they are Jewish?'

'*He* knows,' she said, tonelessly. 'He says they are *Saujuden* and that they will all be got rid of.'

'Got rid of?' I repeated stupidly, and she cried out then, furiously, 'Didn't you hear what I said? *Disinfected*, he calls it, the schools, the theatres, everywhere' – she spat out the word – '*disinfected*.' The chanting from the street went on and on as we stood there under the trees. 'What shall I do?' she said. 'How can I live with them?'

She could do nothing, of course; well-brought-up teenage girls in Vienna did not leave their families. (In the end, happily, she did manage to escape; by the time she was sixteen, she had become a star.)

Three days later, I stood in a crowd underneath the Imperial Hotel balcony and heard Hitler speak.

I had become terribly, achingly aware of wrong, wrong in my small world and in the world beyond it. But I don't remember Hitler saying anything outrageous: he was just lauding the Austrians for welcoming the Germans. And indeed, huge numbers of Viennese, and Austrians all over the country, did welcome them, and the air was full of excitement and joy. What I remember most clearly – to my horror – is how excited I felt myself as, part of this seethingly emotional crowd, I listened to that man. Four years earlier, in Nuremberg, I had sat high up in the stands and found myself shouting with joy. Small as I was, I was aware that my pleasure derived not from any person or words but from the theatrical spectacle. But now? I had heard the Austrian chancellor Kurt von Schuschnigg announcing the plebiscite of 13 March, his voice breaking at the end: 'Austrians, the time for decision has come.' I had heard Elfie crying about her father's betrayal. I had heard those raucous voices, '*Deutschland erwache, Juda verrecke*'. And here I was, standing before this man whose orders had sent troops into Austria and who had followed those troops to seal the deed with his presence. What was it that made me join the mindless chorus around me, welcoming this almost motionless figure to our Vienna?

What was it in him that drew us? What was it in us – in me too, that day – that allowed ourselves to be drawn?

The next day, Elfie and I went for a walk around the city. On the Graben, one of Vienna's loveliest streets, we came across a band of men in brown uniforms, wearing swastika armbands, surrounded by a large group of Viennese citizens, many of whom were laughing. As we drew near, I saw that in the middle of the crowd a dozen middle-aged people, men and women, were on their knees, scrubbing the pavement with toothbrushes. I recognized one of them as Dr Berggrün, our paediatrician, who had saved my life when I was four and had diphtheria. I had never forgotten that night; he had wrapped me again and again in cool, wet sheets, and it was his voice I had heard early that dawn saying, '*Sie wird leben.*' (She will live.)

Dr Berggrün saw me start towards one of the men in brown; he shook his head and mouthed, 'No,' while continuing to scrub with his toothbrush. I asked the uniformed men what they were doing; were they mad?

'How dare you!' one of them shouted.

'How dare *you*?' I shouted back, and told him that one of the men they were humiliating was a great physician, a saver of lives.

Stunningly beautiful, her trained voice as clear as a bell, Elfie called out, 'Is this what you call our liberation?'

It was extraordinary: within two minutes, the jeering crowd had dispersed, the brown guards had gone, the 'street cleaners' had melted away. 'Never do that again,' Dr Berggrün said to us sternly, his small, round wife next to him nodding fervently, her face sagging with despair and exhaustion. 'It is very dangerous.' They gassed them in Sobibor in 1943.

(When I told Speer, forty years later, that I was in Vienna in March 1938 when he too, as he had told me, was there to prepare a hall for a rally at which Hitler was to speak, I asked him whether he had seen the shop windows marked in white paint with the word 'Jew', or noticed Nazi brutalities. He said no: 'I saw nothing like that; I wasn't there long. I did my work . . . I stayed at the Hotel Imperial. I strolled along the Ring and the old streets of the inner city, and had a few good meals and lovely wine. And I bought a painting – that was nice. That's it.' He hadn't known that people, Catholic and Jewish patriots, were being arrested in droves by then and that the first wave of suicides, mostly elderly Jews, had started? 'No, I knew nothing about that. I still know nothing about that. Suicides?')

The schools and colleges reopened within days. I have tried to recall the changes in our lives. The main one, at least for me, was a sudden awareness of feelings I had not felt before, an excitement that I didn't understand, and didn't really want to feel.

Though Hungarian by nationality, I loved Austria and above all Vienna; even now, having lived in cities all over the world, I cannot recall ever having been so joyfully aware of the changing of the seasons as I was there. Is there another city in Europe where the scent of lilac lingers so heavily over the streets in May, or the leaves of the trees in the parks turn so golden and red in October, or the snow lies so thickly on roofs and streets in winter? I remember as if it were yesterday the hard, clean feel of the pavement under my shoes once the galoshes were put away: childhood memories of unimportant things that mattered. All this probably didn't change, but my awareness of it did. It was a warm and beautiful March, but I don't remember the sun or the buds on the trees or the smell of the lilac later that spring. It is people I remember: the first day we returned to school, two students wearing swastika pins, and a few days later, the school administrator too, a man of great importance to us all, appointed by Reinhardt himself.

By now, we knew of course that there were three categories of people who were in real danger: Jews, communists and Austrian patriots. For the rest, life could go on more or less as usual, although foreign embassies sent small pins in the national colours to their citizens, urging us to wear them. My mother and I received small Hungarian flags, and I wore mine not so much for protection as to separate myself from those at school who wore that other pin.

In the weeks that followed, people began, slowly, to disappear: one of my teachers, a small man of quite incredible kindness to fumbling young drama students, killed himself by jumping out of a fourth-floor window; two others left for the United States. Elfie and I no longer walked home; her parents and my mother forbade it. We no longer went to theatres, for rehearsals or performances. All of us came and went in groups, orderly, quiet and, in many cases, suspicious of each other.

A few months before the *Anschluss*, my mother had become engaged to Ludwig von Mises, one of the country's leading economists. He had been living and teaching in Geneva for several years, spending only his summer holidays in Austria, where he and my mother indulged their passion for hiking in the mountains.

Among my mother's many other admirers was a high-ranking German diplomat. Early one evening in May 1938, he appeared at our door and told her that the Nazis intended to arrest her and hold her as a hostage against von Mises's return; being both Jewish and a prominent intellectual with dangerous ideas, he was high up on their blacklist.

I don't know whether the Nazis would actually have taken my mother hostage, but she believed it, and so we had to go. By late that night, she had packed our cases and arranged for friends to send on to Switzerland my father's collection of paintings and other valuables. Austrians, by then, needed exit permits for travel abroad, but we had our Hungarian passports and we left the next day for Geneva.

I don't think I was bitter; just as Elfie could not leave her family and live on her own, I could not stay behind by myself in the political cauldron of Vienna. But having experienced the adult freedom of drama school, I was both sad and furious to find myself in a finishing school near Lausanne. I developed a particular loathing for the headmistress when, just weeks after my arrival, a little German Jewish girl was suddenly removed from the classes and our luxurious accommodation and sent to work in the kitchen; her parents, it transpired, had been sent to a concentration camp, and there was no money for her fees. My mother and my new stepfather, together with the mother of my co-conspirator, a wealthy New York socialite, came up trumps: they threatened not only our removal but the most unpleasant publicity for the school unless the child was immediately given a free place.

This incident, which demonstrated that the Nazi poison was not limited to Germany and Austria, along with Elfie's carefully phrased letters, which clearly conveyed her unhappiness, convinced me that an expensive finishing school was not the place for me. At dawn one lovely Sunday, when I knew my mother and stepfather were away for the weekend, I ran away. I confided in two slightly older American girls who thought the plan mad but romantic, and gave me a large sum from their considerable hoard of pocket money. I packed a small bag; my American friends agreed to lock the door behind me (they also promised to telephone my mother that night, having told the teachers at Sunday breakfast that I had joined my parents for the day); and without great difficulty I got to Geneva in time for the early-morning train to London via Paris.

I knew nobody in London, having only been there on brief excursions from my school in Kent years before, but I had a plan. Either I would obtain a place at the Old Vic Theatre School, where I would complete my training; or I would audition for Alexander Korda, Britain's top film producer, and get into films. Of course, neither plan worked. At the Old Vic, the suspicious school secretary, having seen the address I had written down of a fleapit hotel in a less than salubrious part of London, asked whom I was staying with and then added kindly, 'It's none of my business, but don't you think you should go home, wherever home is?' Fellow Hungarian Alexander Korda, upon learning my name and that I came from the Reinhardt school, granted me an audition and talked to me for a long time about what was happening in the world, about books and about music. By the time we got down to my audition, his wife, Merle Oberon, had joined us, and he had managed to extract a lot of information from me. 'You have some talent,' he said, after hearing my Juliet (I had played the part in Vienna in a special English performance for the Duke of Windsor and Mrs Simpson). 'I'll help you here if you really want, but I suspect this is the wrong direction for you. You are too young and you are uneducated. I advise you to go away, grow up, study – then come back and see me in a couple of years.'

Merle Oberon then took me to lunch, lent me a handkerchief when I cried and arranged for me to telephone my mother.

By early autumn 1938, I was living in Paris with two young academics, Jacqueline and Jean (Yani) Hubert-Rodier, sister and brother, in a wonderful old flat in the 16th arrondisement off the avenue Henri Martin. Following the example of their mother, a noted hostess who had recently died, Jacqueline and Yani were astonishingly well read and multilingual, and kept open house for thinking people of all ages, colours and nationalities. I had a pass for lectures at the Sorbonne, had signed up for a typing course at Pitman's and was taken on as a pupil by one of the most generous and awesome actresses in Paris, Madelaine Milhaud, the wife of the composer Darius Milhaud. Vienna, the *Anschluss* and the Nazis were suddenly very far away. I was caught up in a passion for all things French and above all Paris; my life was wonderful, and I was learning what it was to learn.

When war broke out on 3 September 1939, I was in Les Baux de Provence, at that time not even a village, more a settlement of about fifty people who lived in caves dug out of rock on top of a mountain. There was one extremely basic hotel, the Reine Jeanne, which the conductor Pierre Monteux took over for a few weeks every summer for a seminar to which, that year, thanks to the Milhauds, I had been invited. There were about a dozen of us, French and American. We had been immersed in music for two weeks when we heard on the wireless that the Germans had invaded Poland and that France and Britain had declared war. French mobilization was incredibly swift – the young men in the valley were gone within days – and a request arrived from the mayor at the foot of the mountain that the maestro's young students should come down and help with the grape harvest.

The weather was glorious; it was fun to wash our feet and legs with rough country soap, rinse them in a stinging, green disinfectant and then walk, jump and dance on the grapes. We held hands and made a ballet of our first war-work. On the last evening, Monteux conducted his student orchestra in a piece by Brahms; '*N'oubliez jamais*,' he said at the end, '*lui aussi était Allemand*.'

My mother and stepfather ordered me to return to Switzerland. When I refused to go, they stopped my allowance in an attempt to force me. But I was sixteen and in love – with an English boy, with France and with my studies. Nothing would have made me leave and, after a few weeks during which I slept on friends' sofas, ate very little and walked wherever I had to go, they relented, at least for the time being. I was not an easy daughter or stepdaughter; I suspect that they were almost relieved.

*

My return to Geneva soon became a moot point. Five months into 1940, the Germans, with almost unbelievable speed – their second blitzkrieg after Poland – occupied France. Thousands of refugees streamed into Paris, among them many children whose parents were dead or lost.

For the next year and a half I worked as a volunteer nurse for an aid organization called the Auxiliaire Sociale. It established reception centres for refugees in Paris and homes for abandoned children in châteaux all over occupied France. I went to Villandry, one of the great châteaux of the Loire, which belonged to the American mother of Isabelle de la Bouillerie, the president of our charity. There were two young volunteers and one paid nurse to look after about twenty children between the ages of three and fourteen in a hastily converted stable block. Downstairs was the kitchen with one tap, a huge, old, wood-burning stove and a long table with benches; upstairs was a dormitory with twenty-odd iron bedsteads. I had a tiny room off the dormitory; the other helpers and a number of refugees from Paris, Isabelle's friends and staff, some of them, incidentally, Jewish, were lodged in the château; we all ate together with the children.

My mother and stepfather had gone to the United States, and I had no money at all except for pocket money Isabelle sometimes gave me, particularly after I became her interpreter in negotiations with the Germans. It was an important function, given our desperate need for documents to facilitate the running of the centre and food for the children and, as a well-brought-up Viennese Hungarian, I was peculiarly qualified for it.

I was, of course, passionately Francophile and Anglophile and – mainly I suspect to give myself an identity – furiously anti-German. In those early years of occupation there were few opportunities for active opposition. There is, however, one occasion I remember which, involving us thrillingly in high-level diplomatic sabotage, illustrates the excitement of danger about which I spoke earlier.

A huge formal reception room at the Château de Villandry had been chosen by the fleeing French government as the repository for the Foreign Office files; shelves had swiftly been put up and two very elderly diplomats had been lodged at the castle and were nominally in charge of them. 'Nominally', because when the Germans arrived in the district, about twenty soldiers were quartered in the adjoining equally large room to guard the archive in ten-hour shifts. A few weeks after all of us had arrived there – it was, I recall, a sunny evening in June after the children had gone to bed – one of the diplomats, M. Gaston Hauchecorne, a charming man who had spent much of his working life in China and had come to look extraordinarily Chinese, told us in the by then quiet kitchen, that in that guarded locked room at the château there was a file that referred to certain negotations between France and Britain and which presented great danger to men who were named in it if the Germans got a hold of it. It was absolutely essential, he said, to remove it. There was, we learned then, a kind of dumb waiter hidden under the brocade wall coverings of that reception room, but to get into it would require supple young bodies. He and his colleague knew exactly where the file was on the shelves: he drew a map. But to locate it quickly demanded nimble minds and a good knowledge of English. The next night a case of excellent wine was presented to the German guards and by 2 a.m. when two of us youngsters climbed into the musty receptacle behind a door in the castle kitchens – with the two old gentlemen winding it up, stopping at every creak – and retrieved that file, they were audibly and merrily drunk. This was the first and certainly the most dramatic act of 'resistance' I was involved in, and I loved it: I was happy that night and Monsieur Hauchecorne presented me with a lovely small sculpture he had made in China: I found it after the war and it stands on a shelf in my study to this day.

For the remainder of my time in France then, aside from hiding a couple of shot-down British airmen (on both occasions in the children's beds, to their joy), the most I could do to demonstrate opposition was to treat the visiting Germans with disdain. Hundreds of – rather polite – Germans, mostly officers who came to see Villandry on their rounds of the châteaux of the Loire, were received very coldly indeed.

There were two in particular who came quite often, one an army doctor, the other a supply officer who had been a schoolmaster in civilian life. Both took an immediate interest in our children and helped us obtain medical supplies and food. They were – though I refused to see it at the time – good men and, I suppose because of that very fact, allowed themselves to be targets for my fury. For months, they accepted my railings and Isabelle's more elegantly phrased criticisms without demur. And then, without warning, they disappeared. The doctor, I later discovered, was soon sent to the Russian front, where he died within weeks; the former teacher, older and not very fit, was sent to a concentration camp. They had both been devout Christians and opponents of the regime.

We had never known. They hadn't told us; they had just tried to express it by showing affection to the children and helping us to care for them. Indulging our own feelings, we had abused their kindness. We had never sensed their pain and their dilemma, or that they desperately wanted to be – and indeed were – our friends. (Three years later, when France was liberated, the almost ethereally elegant Isabelle de la Bouillerie was imprisoned at the Santé prison accused of collaboration – principally on the basis of her friendly relationship with those two Germans. She wrote to me asking for help. I wrote and telephoned to everyone I knew in Paris. But in the belated anti-German hysteria of the time it was hopeless: she died there.)

It was another German who, some months later, undoubtedly saved my life. He was a Prussian aristocrat, head of military intelligence in the nearby city of Tours. He had helped me get assistance from official quarters for the children and had become something of a friend. I had suspected for some time that he was an anti-Nazi. One day, getting no reply when I knocked on his office door, I opened it. The room was empty, but the door to his living-quarters was open. As I walked across the room to announce myself, I heard the radio, tuned to the BBC. For the average German, listening to the BBC was a crime. Perhaps this rule didn't apply to officers, but even so, he was startled when he saw me.

'You see,' he said, raising his arms in a gesture of surrender, 'I'm in your hands now. Will you spare me?' He was a charmer.

One night, about six months later, Marie, the oldest of our children, who had appointed herself my friend and assistant, tiptoed up to my bed and whispered that there was an officer in a car at the gate who had asked for me by name.

It was just before dawn; the air was sweet. I ran out to the gate. 'You are going to be arrested this morning,' he said very quietly. 'Get dressed quickly. Don't say goodbye to anybody. Hurry.'

Not long before, we had hidden a British airman for a week or so, after which, disguising him with a nurse's cape and veil (he was very young and thin), I had driven him in a horse-drawn buggy Isabelle had lent me, to a rendezvous from where he would be taken to safety. I had been stopped by a German security patrol, but the Auxiliaire passes I carried – issued with the help of the officer who now waited for me at the gate of Villandry – plus my Hungarian passport, got us through, and wrongly, I had thought myself quite safe.

I sent Marie back to bed, swearing her to silence; dressed in my uniform; packed nothing except soap, a toothbrush, a change of underclothes, a spare shirt and my papers; and left. I had no money, but he gave me all the French currency he had and drove me to Orléans, where I got an early train to Paris.

It sounds dramatic, but it didn't seem so at the time. I was grateful, but not that surprised he'd come to my aid – I would have come to his, had the opportunity offered itself. As I rode on that train, it was a beautiful day; Paris, a few hours later, was still Paris; I had very good friends. Two days later, still in my nurse's uniform, I was taken over the Pyrenees by a mountain guide, and walked out of France and into Spain.

(When I told Speer about this German, I asked him, 'If it had been you, would you have helped a young girl like me?' He thought for a long moment before he answered. 'I don't know,' he said, finally – he always tried to be honest, though he often didn't succeed. 'I really don't know. Thank God, the question never arose.' I said that wasn't quite so, that a number of people at risk, for political or 'racial' reasons, had been offered a safe haven in his ministry. 'True,' he said, 'but that was my ministry, not me: I knew, but I didn't *have* to know or do anything myself.')

Although I was sad to leave, and quite determined to return as soon as possible, I was also glad. I had many friends of my age in the growing French Maquis who already knew of Gestapo cellars, particularly in Paris and Lyon, where people were subjected to appalling tortures. I fear I was not a heroine; I was afraid of physical pain.

2

My Friend, a Heroine of France

March 1997

But there were heroes among my friends.

Some of Jacqueline and Yani Hubert-Rodier's close friends in Paris before the war were Lucienne Schamash, French-born but of Iraqi origin, who would marry Yani, a judge, and become a leading political journalist; Max Dietlin, a writer at heart who after release from a German POW camp married Jacqueline; Max's sister Liliane, who, the war over, married art expert Jean-Paul Crespelle; and Stan Lasocki, born in France but a descendant of the loftiest Polish aristocracy.

The war, for a while, scattered us. When it was over, friends had died, others felt bitter because of political differences particular to France; also, we married, had children, worked. But through it all, this little group became and has remained my French family, giving the lie to the alleged xenophobia of the French bourgeoisie.

Liliane – my friend Lili, whose unsung heroism during the occupation of France is the subject of this story – died in February 1997 aged eighty-six. Although I saw her as often as I could until she died, I can barely think of Lili as old; to me she was always and remained throughout her life as I saw her when we first met – the epitome of the young Parisienne: small, slim, finely boned, with that very special elegance of speech, behaviour and of course dress that none of us adoptive Parisians could ever emulate.

It was a few days after her death that Lili's daughter Anne phoned me, sounding absolutely baffled. 'I rang Catherine Dior [Christian Dior's sister and Lili's closest friend] to tell her about the memorial mass,' she said, 'and she said, "You will see to it, won't you, that somebody speaks about what she did: that she was a heroine, a great heroine?"

'I told her I had no idea what she was talking about,' said Anne, 'and Catherine, who I knew had been in the resistance and was sent to Ravensbrück by the Germans, said, "She was in the same *réseau* [section] as I, but for much longer."'

'Did *you* know about this?' Anne asked me, sounding devastated.

Well, I did, but only since the early 1970s, when Lili read my book, *Into That Darkness* on the commandant of Treblinka and initiated a conversation about the evil in man, of which I then found she had more experience than most.

For the four years of occupation, she had a cover job at the Musée Carnavalet in Paris, but her real life was spent as a courier for Stan Lasocki, who was the chief of the section 'Massif Central' of Polish intelligence in France, responsible to the general staff in London. This élite organization of more than 2,000 agents – which suffered enormous losses – was later credited as one of the most dynamic intelligence movements in Europe. By the end of 1942, most of its leaders had been killed by the Gestapo.

One of the few who survived was Pierre Heinrich, another Frenchman of Polish descent, who now lives in London. 'We were not what is commonly thought of as "Résistance",' he said last week. 'We were a source for sabotage, but not active saboteurs. We were an operational intelligence unit collecting information about German troop and rail movements, and production, particularly of rockets in later years. It involved a huge amount of written information, which had to be carried by hand between sections – and this is what Liliane did.'

She was doubtless recruited by Lasocki, he said. 'What was so wonderful about her was that she made it all seem so easy, almost fun, and she never stopped being enchantingly beautiful and you know, in the midst of all that horror and, yes, all the risks, she never stopped laughing.'

When I think of Lili, I ponder on the incredible danger she faced carrying out Stan's orders. 'Oh, when I couldn't carry it in my head I'd just take it in my pocket,' she would tell me later, still laughing. 'What was the point of complicating matters? If they'd got me, they'd have got what they wanted anyway.'

'What would you have done?' I asked, and she answered lightly, patting my hand as if to console me retrospectively. Eaten a '*gentille petite pille que j'avais'* – a nice little pill. The incredible courage this veritable slip of a girl showed, the incredible things she did for her country.

After the defeat of France in May 1940, I gave up my studies to work for a charity, the Auxiliaire Sociale, looking after abandoned children at the Château de Villandry in the Touraine. I only came to Paris when my additional role as the charity's negotiator and interpreter with the Germans required me to travel there in search of *laissez passers* and extra ration cards.

But even if I had spent more time in Paris, I wouldn't have known what Lili was doing. Her father, the colonel, a straight-as-a-die army officer, probably guessed that her activities were not restricted to art research.

'*Please* don't stay out after curfew,' I heard him say one morning when I was staying briefly with them in 1941, and then, his voice a trifle sharp with worry, '*Must* you bicycle?' But nobody else within her family knew then, or it turns out, later. It was her nature not to talk about herself.

Once, in January 1941, when we had made a date for tea at a café on the Champs-Élysées on a cold and snowy afternoon, I questioned her choice of meeting place – the Right Bank was full of Germans, the Champs-Élysées worst of all. 'The safest places in Paris are those where they congregate,' she said in her light voice. It was a lesson I would vividly recall later.

She had come to the café on her bicycle – the bicycle on which she virtually lived during those years. She wore wool stockings, a straight dark skirt with one seam undone to give her space for riding her bike, a short fur jacket that had seen better days, passed on to her by her mother, and a knitted cap that hid her dark hair. She was twenty-nine then, but looked eighteen, and there wasn't a male eye that didn't follow her when she came through that terrace door and hugged me, rather tightly I thought.

(Thirty-five years later, recalling that occasion, she told me that day had been quite terrible: she had carried four messages, three to individuals in the morning and one to a group meeting that afternoon; eight people had been arrested that day, two in the morning and the six others that afternoon, just as Lili had turned into the streets on her bicycle. All would be executed, mostly hanged after being tortured. 'A bad day,' she remembered. Were there many like that? She shrugged. 'Ah oui.')

I was worried about endangering my friends and had hesitated to call anyone when I got to Paris, after fleeing from Villandry. But, having spent one night on a park bench – pretty unsafe, given the curfew – I decided I needed help. The first who, strangely enough came to my mind was Lili, whom many people I knew referred to as *une petite fleur*.

It was 7.30 a.m. when I rang her and, confronted by my refusal to come to the family flat, she met me in a corner café. It was a beautiful day and we sat outside drinking a cup of chicory. I told her I was looking for a route out and why. 'Bon,' she said, 'but first you need a bath and sleep, then we will think.'

My protests – probably not entirely heartfelt by then as I was tired and frightened – were shrugged off and I was taken home and put to bed.

Two days later, on a corner of the Place de la Concorde, she introduced me to a handsome young Swede called Bjorn (that was all I was ever told). To this day, I don't know how she knew him, but certainly she, or Stan Lasocki, knew exceptional people.

This was the last time Lili and I spoke until after the war; she wore a wide cotton skirt that day and a brilliantly white short-sleeved blouse I had watched her ironing that morning, no stockings, but sandals with, I think, wooden soles. After a brief hug, she cycled away from us across the Pont de la Concorde. Her shiny hair blowing in the gentle wind of that day, she raised her arm goodbye. 'Elle est bien belle,' said the Swede looking after her, nostalgically, and he was so right.

Ten minutes later, at the Café de la Madeleine, he told me how to reach the escape route out of France – ridiculously, it was by means of an Englishman at the Thomas Cook agency across the street. Bjorn pressed money into my hand – I had virtually none – and he manifestly knew the necessary amount. It was not his money, he said quickly, and added that he would wait for me while I made the arrangements.

Half an hour later, he led me to the servants' quarter on the top floor of an apartment block in the eighth *arrondissement* (which thoughtfully had four Agatha Christie novels on a rickety night table) and told me to rest until he came to pick me up for dinner at eight – I was leaving on the train to Marseilles at midnight.

Following Liliane's principle of safety where 'they' congregrated, he took me, wearing my nurse's uniform – the only clothing I had – to Maxim's, where we sat between two tables of German generals who stood up and bowed to my uniform as I passed. Three hours later, he dropped me outside the station in his small car. As he pulled away, I noticed he had a diplomatic licence.

An hour afterwards, when the train departed, I opened the window of the third-class compartment I was in and leaned out to look at Paris. Way back on the platform, under the palest of lights, almost only shadows, there was Bjorn, and next to him, Lili.

I mentioned this to her when we first met again after the war, when I still hadn't the slightest notion of her real role in the scheme of things. She airily dismissed my suggestion that breaking the curfew had surely been risky. 'Oh, he had some diplomatic paper or other. Helpful,' she laughed as always. 'And we had to be sure we were rid of you. Worth the risk.'

February 2000

Lili's wonderful house in Seillans, in the South of France, full of great modern paintings dedicated to her art historian husband, who died ten years before her, has now been sold. But in two weeks' time at Easter, her family and friends will attend a memorial mass in Seillans' small church, as they have every year since her death. She would, I think, have loved to celebrate the millennium, not because of the new century, but because she loved to honour occasions, welcome friends and cook: Lili's health (never mentioned when she phoned) was very delicate at the end of her life, but she remained what she had always been, a truly great French cook. Which reminds me of the miraculous omelette she produced for lunch for three of us that late spring day – my last day in Nazi-occupied Paris I have just described. It was miraculous because she had only two eggs, no butter, no cream and yet what appeared on the table was a golden herb-filled high-rise creation indeed worthy of Maxim's. 'How do you do it?' I asked, and as she smilingly shrugged in that inimitable French way, her father said, *'Elle coupe la verdure au jardin, fait couler un peu d'eau and quelques perles d'huile d'olives, ajoute, oh oui, sel et poivre et puis, le plus important, elle benit les petits oeufs, qui, évidemment, respondent en se multipliant.'* (She cuts greenery from the garden, adds a little water and a few pearls of olive oil and, yes, salt and pepper, and then, the most important, she blesses the little eggs which of course respond by multiplying.) Rather than the discomfiting dinner at Maxim's, it was Lili, our lunch, and my last glimpse of her at the station that remained on my mind during that train journey to Marseilles, and a day later, the long hike over the mountains into Spain.

I was part of a group of eight or ten refugees led by a small muscular mountain guide whose French *patois* was peppered with (to me) incomprehensible Spanish. I was young and without luggage, and was accustomed since early childhood to hiking in the mountains. So it was easy enough for me to keep up with him. But the others, mostly middle-aged and – despite the warnings they had received, as I had, to bring only the barest necessities with them – carrying an extraordinary amount of baggage, had a rough time, not least because our guide was anything but patient with their difficulties. 'Idiots', he kept murmuring as the group crashed through the bushes and frequently dropped belongings which with what seemed extraordinary noise plunged down the sharp inclines. 'Don't these *crétins* understand that there are German guards around here?' he asked me. He knew most of the 'Boches', he told me. He had a *coup* (a glass) with them quite often; they were good fellows who knew a man had to make a living. He thought he could get me across in my nurse's uniform. 'But that lot? With all that stuff? We'll all be shot.'

Strangely, and unjustifiably as it turned out, I wasn't worried: yet again it was that enjoyment of adventure, that so easily fatal excitement of fear. I did wonder, however, why he was quite so tense, given, as he told me, that he was doing these 'tours' about twice a week and 'knew his *boulot*' (his job). I found out when, at about 3 a.m., half-way to the Spanish border, we heard the sound of dogs. Within seconds he had shouted to the terrified group to disperse, sit on the ground and keep absolutely quiet. To my astonishment he then, quick as a monkey, climbed a tree and a moment later slid down it, without the rucksack he usually carried. They were going to be there very quickly, he told me; he would tell them he was taking me across to see my old grandmother who was dying. 'They are sentimental, the Boches,' he said. And he said he and I would retrace our steps to lead them away from the rest of the group. In fact, as I found out later, what he really needed to keep them away from was the rucksack, which was now lodged a good distance up a tree.

I told him then to let me talk to them and that I would tell a different story, nearer the truth, which was always best. The moon was bright and we could see the soldiers below us fairly clearly; luckily for us they were holding on to their two dogs. He was right: they were good fellows, Bavarian country boys to whom I introduced myself, in German of course, as a Hungarian nurse. I told them – it was true – that I was engaged to an Englishman whom I hadn't seen in two years; he had been able to get leave to meet me for a week in Madrid, I said, and the nice guide was helping me to get there. A week from that night (I said it on a sudden impulse, but am sure it was what saved us) he would help me get back across the mountains into France. 'You're coming back?' one of them said, sounding amazed (as he well might have been). 'Yes, of course,' I said, 'I am on duty in Paris.' It was a ridiculous story, but it worked; they had German rye bread and a bottle of wine and shared it with us; they told me about their homes, one near Passau, the other near Regensburg. They were happy to find that I knew where they lived, and that I was a girl, in love, and talking to them in soft Viennese German not so unlike their own language. We shook hands when we parted and I stroked their dogs.

The guide – totally against the rules of the escape route – was carrying letters. He shrugged when he told me; he needed the money he said. Twenty-four hours later in Madrid, I stayed with the president of the Spanish 'Auxilio Social', a friend of Isabelle de la Bouillerie, in his sumptuous town house and telephoned Ronnie Preston, the man who, true enough, I was engaged to and hadn't seen in two years. Ronnie was, alas, not in Madrid, but in Egypt, where he was stationed, but my host was rich and generous and allowed me the free use of his telephone. Twenty-four hours later, he put me on a train for Lisbon. Ten days after that I left on a ship for New York.

*

The next three years I spent in the United States. This period has never seemed quite real to me; amid the incredible plenty and – even in wartime – peace, I never stopped feeling guilty and ashamed: guilty for having left Europe, ashamed for being safe. Everyone tried to make me feel at home – I had never experienced such kindness and generosity – but the only way I could deal with my grinding homesickness, which wasn't for one particular place but for all the places in Europe I so loved, was to work at things connected with my life there and so remain a part of the struggle from which I would otherwise be excluded.

For my first eighteen months in the United States, I travelled across the country, lecturing in schools and colleges on the war and Europe's children. Still practically a child myself, and trained for the stage, it was not difficult for me to communicate with the thousands of young Americans I met. I gave, on average, three lectures a day, driving from town to town and city to city, travelling through about twenty states in all. It allowed me to get to know the country, and I grew to love it too. New York was electric and exciting, but it was the rest of America that touched, fascinated and also frightened me: that extraordinary mixture of innocence and chauvinism, kindness and incipient violence was utterly different from anything I had known before.

I learned, when giving my lectures, that the most effective way to engage people, whether they are children or adults, is through emotion. This was a great lesson. I often had to remind myself to hold back, to go easy when, standing on stage in an auditorium, I felt waves of emotion coming from my audience in response to my accounts of what was happening in Europe. Even in these circumstances, I grew to understand that people's need to feel must never be abused. Many years later, when Speer explained to me how Hitler had exploited people's emotions, I remembered my own temptations on stage in America, and was glad I had resisted them.

For most of the rest of my time in the States, I worked at the Office of War Information, writing anti-Nazi propaganda and broadcasting it, via England, to German troops.

Four months before the end of the war, I finally managed to return to Europe. I had joined the United Nations Relief and Rehabilitation Administration as a child welfare officer, to work in the displaced persons camps in what would become the American zone of Germany.

I had arrived in the States in the navy-blue uniform of an Auxiliaire Sociale nurse; I left just over three years later in the khaki uniform of UNRRA.

My very first assignment in the field, which lasted only two weeks, was the care of child prisoners from Dachau concentration camp. Arriving with only the shortest of briefings, I found it a traumatic experience. There was, I now know, no comparison between the condition of the prisoners at Dachau and those at Bergen-Belsen and Buchenwald (and of the camps in Poland we knew absolutely nothing, not even their names). But Dachau was bad enough those first few days – especially meeting those people who had been force-marched south for weeks from other camps, and then, of course, the children. Was it thinkable that they would have sent children to these places? It was: children of all ages, all religions, many nationalities, including Germans.

There were very few Jewish children – most of them, we found out later, had been killed – but many from Eastern Europe: young children who had been taken away from their mothers when they were sent for forced labour; older ones who, even during that last year of the war, had been taken away from their countries to work in Germany and who, at the end, had been marched south to end up in concentration camps. And then, strikingly, there were the German children who, curiously isolated from the others, looked less worn but were, if anything, the most helpless of all. These were victims of the *Sippenhaft*, the imprisonment of families accused of treason, frequently the children of high-ranking officers and diplomats who had been executed after the assassination attempt of 20 July. Heaven only knows how these children, many of whom had no doubt attended Nazi élite schools, coped with their reversal of fortune, with the brutalities of their gaolers, with their co-prisoners, almost all of them from 'races' and nations they had been taught to despise.

My job was to help the American army authorities to get all the children out of Dachau as quickly as possible, to their homes, if that was feasible (it almost never was), to hospitals if necessary but in most cases to the UNRRA reception centres and camps which were being set up all over Germany in expectation of many thousands requiring care.

Over the year and a half I then spent working with war-traumatized children in displaced persons camps and special children's centres, I became deeply immersed in the misery the Nazis had caused. My wish – indeed my need – to find out how it could have happened became more intense with every day.

3

Stolen Children

February 2000

It is strange that so little was ever written about UNRRA, the forerunner of the dozens of charities which in the last decades of the twentieth century so dramatically – and thanks to television so visibly – cared for the victims of war and natural disasters all over Africa, South America and Europe. Perhaps it was because television was still in its beginnings; perhaps because of that well-known resistance in all medias to so-called 'goodie-goodie' stories; perhaps also however because UNRRA's structure and the political problems between its (United Nations) members were too complex and its task too large for easy descriptions. There can be little doubt that the huge financial resources poured into it, above all by the United States, at that time the principal supporter of the United Nations, resulted in venality of all kinds. In a post-war atmosphere where millions of people were displaced, homeless, without means for anything approaching a normal life, the temptations presented by the immense amounts of material, above all food and medicines brought into Germany and elsewhere by UNRRA, were irresistible to black marketeers, and security, in the sense we know it now, barely existed. It is perhaps all the more remarkable that while we were of course aware of black-market activities in some of the camps we managed, in my nearly two years in UNRRA no one in the teams I worked with or knew, was ever accused, suspected or, I believe, even tempted into dishonesty.

The fact is that – very much as happens now, too, in the human-aid groups who rush to the rescue of populations threatened by disasters – most of us were young, idealistic and profoundly affected by both the human distress and the political-psychological problems which impinged upon us, during every day of the week and most of the hours of long working days.

About 5 million slave labourers, in concentration and labour camps and outside them, had confronted UNRRA upon the end of the war. Not unlike the Kosovan refugees in the spring of 1999 as I was writing this, the main goal for most of them was to return home by whatever means, and just under 4 million, it was thought, walked home or were rapidly repatriated, West and East. What remained by the autumn of 1945 – the time when the Soviets extended their political domination across Eastern Europe and the cold war had begun between them and the West – was a highly volatile mass of about a million and a half East Europeans, mostly devout Christians, who, subject to political pressure both from the left and the right and torn by conflicting fears and loyalties, did not know whether to go home or emigrate. This was the core group of our responsibility. And in order to contain and look after them, we had the obligation to assemble them in groups of houses or barracks – which they themselves guarded against the infiltration of communist liaison, that is to say, orientation officers from Russia – and to provide them and their children with counselling, medical care, educational opportunities and everything material necessary for a decent life. Although we could not buy German goods or take or accept any valuables from them, we had the authority to requisition German housing, cars, furniture, kitchen utensils and warm clothing if needed.

Additionally, however, those of us with special knowledge, of languages, history or the management of disturbed children, would soon be involved in two areas, at times closer to policing, detective work and psychotherapy than to welfare: as members of 'screening teams' we could recommand arrests of suspected war criminals, some of whom, we soon realized, were inevitably hiding out in the Displaced Persons (DP) camps. And as of early 1946, if appointed child welfare 'investigating' (or tracing) officers, we had the right of entry to any German institution or home where we had reason to believe an unaccompanied child resided. Eventually, some of us with experience in working with children, such as I had had in France, were posted to 'special children camps': I, then twenty-three years old, worked off and on in all of these functions.

My most difficult general DP posting was in early 1946 to the city of Regensburg, where UNRRA's largest displaced persons camp housed about 20,000 Ukrainian men, women and children, most of them genuine former slave labourers, but – a particularly worrying problem for both UNRRA and the US army authorities who were unequipped for dealing with investigating people who had committed crimes for the Nazis – hidden among them a number of men who had served as SS auxiliaries in the worst of Nazi camps.*

The Regensburg camp was an immense installation which would, over the years, turn into a loosely fenced-off township with its own highly politicized administration, its own churches, schools, playgrounds, meeting halls and thousands of barracks, where men and women lived, courted, married and had children. Most of them had been brought to Germany by force, and in a period when, under Stalin, any Russian who had survived either Nazi POW or forced-labour camps was considered a criminal or a traitor and risked either being shot or sent to the gulags, few of them wanted to go home.

There were of course numerous children in the DP camps, quite aside from recently born babies. (According to surviving UNRRA HQ documentation, 51,307 children under fourteen were living in DP camps in February 1946, 27,185 of them under six years old.) Poles, Ukrainians, Balts, but also Yugoslavs and Greeks who, when life became ever harder at home, had volunteered or not too strenuously resisted being sent to Germany to work on the land, had, in some cases, managed to bring young children with them – these were the relatively lucky ones. But there were others, who were, one might say, shanghaied out of their countries and into Germany with the parents because they looked to be somewhat near 'working age' and were put to backbreaking work in munition factories. Where they survived, the parents, from whom they were usually separated anyway, often did not; and, the war ended and the labour and concentration camps breaking up, many of them formed gangs and roamed the countryside

* This would provide me with specialized knowledge forty-odd years later when I became involved with researching and reporting on the case of John Demjanjuk, accused and eventually acquitted in an Israeli court of having been the Ukrainian guard the Treblinka prisoners called 'Ivan the Terrible,' see p. 309.

stealing and causing mayhem for both the Germans they hated and the Allies they did not trust, until finally tempted into the refuge of the UNRRA DP camps. And this also applied to yet another deeply angry category of pre-adolescent boys for whom UNRRA became responsible. According to surviving German documents, there were between 10,000 and 50,000 of them, twelve to fourteen years old. They had been selected in Poland – according to the record on Albert Speer's orders (though he denied responsibility to me) – in the spring and summer of 1944, to be brought to Germany to work on the land – it was called the 'Hay Action'.

Although there were Jewish children in Germany at the end of the war, compared to other groups, they were not many. Historically, no Jewish child is known to have survived the four specific extermination camps of Chelmno, Belzec, Sobibor and Treblinka. But a considerable number, mostly between twelve and fifteen years old, did, strangely enough, manage to survive the concentration and labour camps to which – caught in their hiding-places in gentile homes, or where they lived, wild, in the forests – they had been sent if they were strong and of working age (ten years old for Jews and Slavs), to work on exhausting and exacting armament and industrial tasks which required good eyes, small hands and nimble fingers. ('Extermination by work', it was called, and it applied not only to children or Jews, but to countless slave workers. 'If 10,000 Russian women die of exhaustion in digging an anti-tank ditch, this is of no interest to me except to the extent to which the ditch is readied for Germany,' said Heinrich Himmler on 4 October 1943 in Posen. 'We Germans, who are the only people in the world who have a correct attitude towards animals, also have a correct attitude toward these animal human beings.') These prematurely aged bitter youngsters, mostly boys, who for Himmler's SS as 'Jew-children' had been at the very bottom of the scale of 'animal human beings', for months refused all well-meant assistance, absconding from any shelter they were offered. More often than not, they vagabonded, again in gangs, around the Western zones of the country, spreading alarm wherever they went, and no one – UNRRA, the Western military, not to speak, of course, of the Germans – dared lay a hand on them. Presumed to be orphans after a traumatic childhood, they were as if hallowed by their recent fate: punishing them for misdeeds was taboo, and, as numerous UNRRA child welfare officers, including myself, were to find, attempts to subject them to the relative structure of DP camps proved impossible. While UNRRA retained administrative, that is, financial responsibility for them, it was not until the early summer of 1945, when Jewish youth workers from the United States and from the Jewish Agency for Palestine arrived to take over their care, that they began to accept help. It was less the fact that they came equipped with considerable material support, than that they offered them – and this goes for both national groups – a sense of purpose. And although these angry youngsters would also remain extremely difficult to deal with and almost impossible to hold in any kind of controlled environment, the Zionists (who, interestingly enough, almost immediately put them into scout-type uniforms), as well as the American youthworkers, eventually succeeded in eliciting a response in most of them to the special cohesion they were able to offer. Thus, fittingly enough, the first 'unaccompanied' children and adolescents to leave Germany, some for America, many for Israel, were young Jews.

The unaccompanied children in the DP camps generally attached themselves to adults who spoke their language and who, in the manifold fears which governed their lives and that passionate solidarity of religion, language and suffering which was almost all that was left to them, often concealed the fact that these children were not their own and indeed became quite possessive of them. The sorting out of this mass of chaotic humanity – the 'unaccompanied' children the most chaotic of all – into individuals with their own needs and desires, would remain one of the most difficult tasks to confront UNRRA. Especially since, when all countries soon raised strong demands for the return of their unaccompanied children, those living in DP camps under the influence of the politically bewildered displaced adults, fervently resisted attempts to persuade them to go home.

A dramatic demonstration of this chaos and the conflicts it produced occurred in the late spring of 1946 in Regensburg, where I was in charge of a 'Children's House' set up, under rather special circumstances, within one of UNRRA's biggest and most troublesome DP camps, for about 20,000 Ukrainians.

The children, about fifty 'unaccompanied' boys between eleven and fifteen, were all from the border regions between Poland and the Ukraine which the Soviets were now claiming as their own. UNRRA discovered not only that they were unaccompanied children, but that the UNRRA Central Tracing Bureau at Arolson, a small town in the British zone, had had communications from families in Poland and the Ukraine about missing boys whose descriptions fitted a number of them. But by this time, they had lived for nine months with DPs, all of whom, considering themselves lucky to be out of Soviet influence, were refusing to go home. A no doubt fairly arbitrary decision to move all the boys out of the camp into one of the special children's units, where they could receive individual care and from where they would, it was hoped, eventually be persuaded to go home, brought about a near riot in the camp which could only be assuaged by a compromise UNRRA offered. A Children's House would be set up within the camp, and if the boys agreed to live in it, attend a Polish-language school outside the camp and take part in an activity programme – sports and field trips with volunteers from the US army – UNRRA would promise that they would not be subjected to any meetings with Polish or Soviet liaison officers (a prospect all DPs passionately rejected), or for that matter to any political or emotional pressures from anyone else, including UNRRA, and that they could continue to see the families in the camp whom they had come to think of as their own. UNRRA hoped that the outside schooling and activities would sufficiently remove the boys from the constricting atmosphere of this particularly politicized community to open their minds and eventually help them to make individual and free decisions.

It is doubtful whether the measures would ever have affected the older boys in the group, but our optimism seemed vindicated when three of the younger ones, who knew their parents had contacted Arolson, came to see me one day with letters they had written to their mothers in which they said that they were longing to see them. The pleasure we felt for the children's parents was short-lived. In moving the boys into a house where they would be so readily identifiable, we had failed to take into account the anger of the Soviets, who were bound to learn of their existence and who passionately felt that all such children belonged to and in their countries of origin.

It was about three weeks after the Children's House had been opened that the Regensburg CIC (the US Counter Intelligence Corps) received a tip that the Soviets planned to raid the Children's House that night. Such a thing had never happened before in any zone, not only because the DP camps were off-limits to all military personnel, but because everyone, including the Soviets, had always been intent on avoiding any 'cold war' confrontations. It was decided in hurried US army–UNRRA consultations that afternoon to move the fifty children and all their belongings back to the families they had previously lived with, leaving the Children's House empty, only keeping intact the playrooms and schoolrooms which were in use for younger children in the camp. As was the rule for official occasions, or if, as often happened, trouble was brewing in the camp, MPs would be posted at the gate together with the permanent uniformed DP guards (and troops held discreetly at the ready in the vicinity), but it would be the UNRRA team director and staff of the camp who would talk with the Soviets, if they really came.

They did, just before 11 p.m., four liaison officers accompanied by security officers in uniforms we had never seen before. Two covered trucks which arrived with them were parked across the street.

They had been informed, they told us across the closed gate, that we were keeping fifty unaccompanied Soviet children in a Children's House, where they were being subjected to persuasive orientation with the purpose of dissuading them from returning home. They demanded to see them, now.

The camp, our director said, was, as they could see, asleep. (All lights were out by order, though it was doubtful that anyone was asleep.) There was indeed a so-called Children's House, with schoolrooms and playrooms, but we could not think, he said, what led them to believe that any children lived there: in UNRRA DP camps, children lived with their parents.

The spokesman for the group, pointing at the Children's House, quite near the gate, said, 'There it is. We do not believe what you are saying. We demand to see it.'

As we had always expected to show it to them, the final outcome was that the liaison officers, but not the accompanying military, were allowed in. UNRRA regretted such misunderstanding, our director said as we took them from one totally bare room to the next, and suggested that the liaison officers should return at a pre-arranged time the next morning, when we would be pleased to have them see the young children there, at school and at play.

It was a successful strategy, but morally it was a Pyrrhic victory. Not because the DPs, unable to restrain themselves, turned on all the lights and, laughing and applauding, streamed out of the houses as the Soviet cars drove off, and not even because, in the need to prevent violence, we had lied. The thing that those of us who believed that in the final analysis children belonged with their parents felt to be wrong, was that such an official act of deceit by UNRRA denuded us of any pretension of neutrality and could only confirm the Ukrainian children in the belief that they shouldn't, indeed couldn't, go home. We had created the Children's House to give them a chance of making a free decision. Our lie had defeated that chance.

One of the friendships I made during that UNRRA time, which became particularly important to me and has lasted all of my life, was with the Waldbotts, Hungarian aristocrats with six children, whose middle daughter, Isabella, became my secretary at UNRRA in 1945 and whose oldest daughter, Maria – 'Mädi' – my lifelong friend. Baroness Waldbott, a woman of exceptional beauty and distinction, was the Archduchess Alicia, who as a child was brought up in the Palace of Schönbrunn. She and Mädi's father, Baron Fritz, had been given refuge with their three girls and three boys by German relatives (much of central Europe's and Bavaria's aristocracy is interrelated) on the attic floor of a Bavarian castle, Schloss Moos, which in turn became my social and emotional refuge from the tensions of my life working with the DPs.

Fritz Waldbott soon claimed to have discovered some vague family link between my Hungarian ancestors and his, and although I suspected this find to be a charming protective gesture towards my youth and the stress of my life, I gladly accepted the comfort of this possible kinship and Mädi and I have called each other cousin ever since. After Mädi's marriage not many years later to a wealthy Bavarian, Count Hansibert Törring-Jettenbach, their palatial Schloss Seefeld, an hour from Munich, with its lake, its deer and lovely forests would become a retreat for me on many occasions. But in 1946, it was through the

Waldbott girls, who heard of a family on the estate who had some young children possibly not their own, that I first came into direct contact with the awful human problem of the 'stolen children', by comparison with which all other human conflicts confronting us daily paled.

November 1999

I have found countless times when talking to the people I have written about that it is dating the events of one's life that is most difficult. We recall the look of houses, of rooms, of landscapes, colours and temperatures and we remember faces, voices, movements and the feelings of others and ourselves, but more often than not it is impossible to put a day, a month, sometimes even a year to these memories.

Nevertheless, trying today to write about memories of my own, I'm almost sure it was in the pre-spring of that first post-war year – perhaps already March, perhaps still February – that I found 'Johann' and 'Marie', as I will call them. For as I write, I clearly recall that the fields barely showed colour and that it was cold and wet the evening I drove to the farm – a large peasant holding in southern Bavaria – where Hungarian refugees, former slave workers of the Nazis kindly disposed towards me as a one-time fellow Hungarian, had told me the peasants, formerly members of the Nazi party in good standing and parents of a son who had died in Stalingrad, had two young children who allegedly appeared out of nowhere as toddlers three years and a bit earlier, towards the end of 1942.

Though my visit was more than fifty years ago and the farm was of traditional Bavarian design, I think I might recognize it to this day, the elongated white-painted single-storey building with uncurtained small windows, attics in the roof, and – attached to it I thought on the left – a large wooden stable; I could hear the tramping and munching sound of cattle as I walked up to the house. And when no one answered my knock and I opened the unlocked door to find myself in the dark, I could smell, too, that slightly acid animal scent that was in past days always present in European peasants' homes.

Only two of the windows I had seen from outside had shown light;

Germans were sparing then with their use of electricity. And when, after knocking again, I opened the only door and stepped across the thresh-hold into the kitchen, there were – as expected, for I had examined the area records at the mayor's office in the district capital (*Kreisstadt*) that morning – six people in the room: the farmer and his wife, 46 and 45 (both had light-brown hair); his parents, 67 and 65, but looking a lot older; and, listed in the 1945 records as minor children, a husky boy with merry blue eyes and fair hair with a short circular home-cut, and an equally blue-eyed slim and somewhat smaller girl, with equally blonde but long hair, tightly braided who looked to me younger than the boy; oddly enough I remember being surprised when she immediately smiled at me. These two children, the registration papers had told me, had been born in 1940 and would thus both have to be six years old.

I had carefully planned this visit for a time when they would all be there together, for although I hoped the children would be sent to play or to bed before I started on my inevitably distressing questions, it was essential for me to see them first within the family circle. As I had expected, they were at table, the fare, manifestly meagre that first hard post-war winter even on a fine farm, was soup, rye bread and lard (rendered pork fat), beer for the men, water for the women and children. While reminding myself not to read too hasty an interpret-ation into their reactions – no one in occupied Germany in those days would have readily welcomed an unexpected, uniformed stranger – there was no mistaking the adults' unease at my appearance.

I went around the table holding out my hand to each of them. Though no one stood up, all but the old man took and shook it, albeit limply – again except for the little girl, who pumped it playfully up and down. The grandfather almost childishly hid his right hand behind his back and, justifiably gruff, asked, 'What do you want?'

'Just to talk to you for a bit,' I said and handed the children each a chocolate bar. It was when the little girl, beaming, said 'Danke' and I stroked her face, that the farmer's wife said, sharply, 'Gehts zu Bett' (Off to bed) and the two children shot up to obey. I said, 'Gute Nacht, Marie, gute Nacht, Johann.'

'Gute Nacht,' Marie whispered as she slipped by me, throwing herself into her mother's arms, at the same time stretching out one arm towards her father, now standing up next to her. 'Guat Nacht, Vater, guat Nacht Mutter,' said Johann in a strong Bavarian accent and, giving me a suspicious sidelong look, briefly rubbed his head against his grandfather's stubbly cheek while the farmer took the small girl out of her mother's arms and hugged her, once, tightly.

Children always sense atmospheres. 'Muatta?' Marie, stopping already on her way to the door, said suddenly, in Bavarian too, and in a questioning voice. The grandmother got up then and pushed them ahead of her out of the room.

It is strange how clearly I came to recall, once I searched my memory, that first sight of the two children and (given that I cannot possibly claim to remember much verbatim from so long ago) the words they spoke, their manifest loving ease within the family, but also the marked difference in their reactions, less due, I can remember feeling at once, to gender or intelligence than to development. Twins? I asked myself.

Ever since the establishment of a Central Tracing Bureau in Arolson, the small town in the British Zone of Germany where UNRRA HQ for Germany was located, information had come in from parents, relatives and even villages, mostly in Eastern Europe, of children, some as young as two years old or even less, who had been taken away by the Germans. And slowly, as information, reports and instructions to individual UNRRA teams followed high-level meetings, the word 'Germanization' crept into the vocabulary.

Two attempts had been made since September 1945 to achieve a census by requesting German agencies and institutions, as well as private individuals, to report the presence of any 'Unaccompanied children of United Nations and assimilated nationality'. Although reports did come in from institutions, and by January 1946 6,600 (8,500 by June) unaccompanied children had been identified in the three Western zones of occupation,* these were mostly illegimate and half German, some of them fathered by German occupation soldiers abroad, others the result of relationships between German girls and foreign slave workers in Germany. But the almost complete lack of response from German families tended to support the insistent claims from Eastern Europe and the Balkans, that many thousands of children

* The Soviet Union not having subscribed to UNRRA, the Soviet Zone would never be included in the search for children.

had been kidnapped by the Nazis with the dual purpose of depleting the population of the countries Germany was conquering, and to replenish her own population with 'racially valuable' children.

It was difficult for us to believe that this could have happened. Who would have taken babies or toddlers away from mothers? How could it be done? How could anyone, even bigots gone mad, believe they could tell 'racial value' and specifically that of young undeveloped children? Above all, how, in practice, could there now be large numbers of foreign children, at least some of whom would have to be old enough to have memories, living, basically in hiding, within the German community?

Over the months, as the Central Tracing Bureau received, above all from Poland, the Baltic borderlands and the Ukraine, tens of thousands of snapshots of babies, toddlers and older children, with descriptions of when and how they had disappeared from home and schools, the problem became ever more pressing. A house-to-house census was considered a last resort, as it was feared (as one UNRRA HQ notice we received said), 'it could panic both children and the adults caring for them and serve as advance notice to families who intend to conceal children', but UNRRA teams were directed to appoint 'child welfare investigating officers' and to seek and follow information from all sources. And the notice giving these instructions, which was publicly posted all over the Western-occupied zones, was specific:

> Any person who wilfully delays or obstructs a Child Welfare Investigating Officer in the exercise of any power under . . . this Notice . . . or who fails to give such information or to produce such documents or records as aforesaid, or conceals or prevents any persons from appearing before or being examined by a Child Welfare Investigation Officer, shall, upon conviction by a Military Government Court, suffer such punishment (other than death) as the Court may determine.

I remember clearly that I was certain, within moments of arriving at that Bavarian farm, that this family were aware of these orders and were afraid. None the less, while the grandmother was putting the children to bed, I had sat down across from the three others at the kitchen table and given them copies of the military government order to read.

It was after seven by the time the grandmother returned. 'Schlafen's?' (Are they asleep?) the farmer's wife had asked and the older woman nodded. I brought out a pad, on the top page of which were the notes about the family I had made that morning in the mayor's office.

I told them that I was a child welfare investigator from UNRRA; that UNRRA had the responsibility for all individuals who had been brought into Germany from territories forcibly annexed or conquered by the Germans, including any minor children who, with one or both parents possibly nationals of any of the fifty countries belonging to the United Nations, might have been brought into Germany and be living there now, either in institutions or in families.

'Our boy fell at Stalingrad,' the farmer said immediately, and his father added, angrily, 'The Bolsheviks killed him.' The loathing for the Russians was, during those immediate post-war years, the strongest sentiment one heard expressed by Germans. I cannot now recall the precise sequence of what followed, but I know I told them that everything they would say to me or to each other in my presence in the course of the talk we were about to have would be noted and later considered in the decisions that might have to be made. 'But always remember as we talk,' I said (as I would say repeatedly over the next months to other families we suspected of having been given kidnapped children), 'that none of us want the children to be hurt.' They sat stiffly looking neither at each other nor at me.

I told them I was sorry for them if their son had died in the war. I said that my understanding was that Johann and Marie had come to live with them less than four years ago. Was it after their son died that they had applied to foster or adopt a child or children? Continuing to sit motionless, they did not answer. I said I was sure they loved Marie and Johann and could see the children loved them, too. But it was necessary that they tell me everything they knew about them. Did they know who were their natural parents?

'They are dead,' the younger woman said at once, and added, what had I meant by 'children brought into Germany'?

How did she know the children's parents were dead, I asked.

'They told us,' she said.

'Who were "they"?' I asked.

'Die Leut' (The people), she answered vaguely, and then repeated her own question. I then told them that thousands of Eastern European parents were looking for missing children. 'East?' said the grandfather and, repeating it, virtually spat out the hated word, 'EAST! Our children have nothing to do with "East": they are German; German orphans. You need only look at them.'

And there it was: 'You need only look at them.'

At the end of 1939 by which time Hitler had conquered Poland in a two-week campaign, thereby winning the first of the six 'lightning wars' which in twenty-two months would give him control over virtually all of Western Europe and the Balkans, Himmler delivered a speech to a restricted audience of SS in which he announced the Nazis' plans for Poland.

'In the course of the next ten years,' he said, 'the population [of occupied Poland] will become a permanently inferior race which will be available to us for slave labour. A fundamental question is the racial screening and sifting of the young. It is obvious that in this mixture of people some very good racial types will appear from time to time.'*

The country had immediately been cut up into three parts, the most eastern part going to Germany's then Soviet allies; central Poland, dubbed the 'General Government' and containing the country's three main cities, Warsaw, Cracow and Lublin, with a population of 11 million, was occupied and run primarily as a supply area of human stock for Germany's labour requirements. The north-western rich agricultural part, which before the First World War had been mostly part of Germany and included West Prussia, Posen, a part of Silesia (awarded to the Poles by the Treaty of Versailles) and the port of Danzig (the possession of which had been Hitler's pretext for starting the war), was named the 'Warthegau' and reincorporated into the 'Reich'. Programmed to be cleared within a few short months of Poles (and, of course, all Jews), with the Polish language prohibited, street signs changed into German, and settled with 200,000 ethnic Germans, it would by the summer of 1941 be unrecognizable as ever having been a part of Poland. All children of 'Nordic appearance' found in orphanages or foster care would be presumed to be German and,

* *Denkschrift Himmler's über die Behandlung der Freundvölkischen im Osten*, quoted in Noakes and Pridham, *Nazism*.

with or without surviving families' agreement, would eventually be evacuated to re-educational institutions in Germany.

Between November 1939 and mid 1941, both Himmler and the Nazi Office for Race and Resettlement (RuSHA), which was to supervise the measures about to be undertaken, would time and again take up the theme of 'racially valuable' Warthegau and Polish children. The first condition for the management of 'racially valuable children . . .', announced RuSHA in a secret paper, 'is a complete ban on all links with their Polish relatives. The children will be given German names of Teutonic origin. Their birth and heredity certificates will be kept (filed) in a special department.'

'We have faith above all in this our own blood which has flowed into a foreign nationality through the vicissitudes of German history,' Himmler added in May 1940. 'We are convinced that our own philosophy and ideals will reverberate in the spirit of these children who racially belong to us.'

Eventually, he wrote a month later to Arthur Greise, Gauleiter of Danzig, an annual examination of *all* Polish children between two and twelve years old would segregate them into 'racially valuable or worthless'. Children found immediately to be racially worthless would either be sent home or, if old enough and capable, be sent to Germany to work. Those with racial potential would be taken to one of three centres to be set up in the Warthegau, where further tests would be carried out. Children between six and ten found there to be of racial value would be sent to suitable institutions in Germany to be Germanized, a process which was thought to be impracticable for any older than ten; those between two and six, who would eventually be given to childless or deserving German families for adoption, would first be sent for a period of observation to a *Lebensborn* home.

By 9.30 that night I knew the family's story. It wasn't the death of their son in 1942 that had led them to apply to be put on a list of potential foster or adoptive parents. It was the accidental death four years earlier – in 1938, in a motor accident – of their younger child, a daughter, then aged fifteen. Irmi was her name, and a photo was brought out to show me, a fine-looking young girl proudly in BDM uniform (*Bund Deutscher Mädel* – the girls' equivalent of the Hitler Youth). She had been on an outing in a BDM holiday camp that summer, the father said, when the brakes failed on a bus that was taking thirty-five girls down a mountain road: eighteen of the girls had died, the worst accident the BDM would ever have. His wife cried softly. Their boy, then seventeen, enthusiastic and bright, had just been accepted into ... (a momentary hesitation) ... a leadership school, he went on.

'An SS school?' I asked.

'A good school,' he answered sharply; he knew I wouldn't understand, but it had been a great honour for the boy, the family; yes, they could have asked to have him returned home after their daughter died, there were provisions for that; the party cared, he said, stubbornly, but Franz was so longing to go and in 1938 ... they themselves were still young, the parents were still able to work with them; at the end of that year they even thought they might be having another baby. It was when his wife miscarried at the end of that year and they were told it was the end of her child-bearing years that they first thought of adopting; and shortly afterwards, though without much hope of success because there was anything but a surfeit of babies in Germany then, they wrote out an application.

By the end of 1939, while Franz had fought in the victorious Polish campaign, they had had nothing except an acknowledgement from the authorities to whom they had applied for permission to adopt a baby girl. But early in 1940, the farmer told me, they had heard that many German children were being found in Polish orphanages with false Polish birth certificates issued – so they had heard – to rob them of their German past. And that was when they wrote again. 'And we said that, with the war and all and our boy in the service, we'd happily take two children, a boy and a girl; and that they could be twins.' Irmi had been a twin, he added – her brother had died at birth.

The role *Lebensborn* played in the theft and Germanization of possibly a quarter of a million largely East European children is abominable. Conceived in 1935 as arguably the most progressive of the Nazis' many social organizations, its excellent 'homes' dotted around Germany were set up to provide, not principally, as has often been claimed, 'breeding farms' for SS men, but periods of respite for overburdened mothers, and care for pregnant single girls and illegitimate children. It was no doubt not only because of these existing facilities, but because of the organization's sterling reputation, that the SS, always keen to protect its image, decided in the winter of 1941 to make *Lebensborn*, whose integrity no German soldier, whether SS or *Wehrmacht*, was likely to doubt, the executant of the Germanization project. By late 1941, large children's reception centres (used for first initial sorting by 'racial experts') had been set up in virtually all the conquered territories and in Germany. They were staffed with trained *Lebensborn* care personnel and reinforced by the dreaded 'Brown Sisters' (Nazi People's Welfare Association (NSV)) nurses, who, in an odious attempt at reassurance, played the 'good' cops when they accompanied the SS men who abducted the children from homes, schools, playgrounds and streets. There were also smaller homes, where selected children spent several months being taught German and Nazi ideals.

A secret order, No. 67/1, signed in the winter of 1941 (documentation differs as to the date) by SS Lieutenant-General Ulrich Greifelt, head of the Central Office of the SS and SD in Poland, was, after long preparations and a considerable number of first kidnappings in Romania, Yugoslavia and the Warthegau, the actual starting-point for the project in Poland, where most of the children would be taken.

There were, Order 67/1 said, 'a large number of children in Poland who by reason of their racial appearance should . . . as potential bearers of blood valuable to Germany, be Germanized'. 'My representative,' Greifelt continued, 'will inform the Lebensborn Society of the children aged between two and six who have been recognized as being capable of Germanization.' (After punitive actions against partisans or other resistants in Eastern Europe and the Balkans – the most infamous example of which was the town of Lidice in Czechoslovakia, which on a pretext of collective guilt was razed to the ground after the assassination of 'Reich Protector' Reinhard Heydrich in May 1942 – all men were usually killed and women sent to concentration camps while children between six months and twelve years were handed over to *Lebensborn* and older ones sent to work.) 'The Lebensborn Society,' continued the Greifelt Order, 'will in the first place transfer the children to one of its children's homes [and] from there . . . distribute them . . . to families with a view to subsequent adoption . . . These children are to be treated as German children even before the granting of

German nationality ... Particular care must be taken,' the Order concluded, 'to ensure that the term "Germanizable Polish children" does not come to the public's knowledge ... *The children should rather be described as German orphans from the regained Eastern territories* [my italics].'

'It is true,' the farmer's wife said not long after her father-in-law's outburst. 'They *were* found in the Eastern territories, but they were German orphans; they told us that very clearly.'

And of course, they might have been – there had always been many ethnic Germans in western Poland. Nor did I ask for any proof that the children, who, aside from colouring, appeared to have no physical traits in common, were really twins – it seemed immaterial for my purpose that evening, though it would turn out to be of great importance later. But I said that if they were now six, they would have been nearly three when they came to them. How did they seem to them after what must have been a big change in their lives? Shy? Happy? Did they speak well? (I meant, but didn't say so, in German.)

The grandfather, who would remain angry throughout, complained about the questions. They were just little kids then. What's shy? What's happy? If I wanted to know about happy, all I had to do was look at them. 'Happy as the day is long they are,' he said. What tricks was I playing?

But by that time, well into the second hour of my visit, as far as the farmer and his wife were concerned, the atmosphere had changed: somehow, without exchanging a private word and without any more encouragement from me than common courtesy, they appeared to have persuaded themselves that rather than attacking me they needed to get me on to their side. But, sadly for her – for I was sure she would be made to pay later for her ingenuous sincerity – the farmer's wife was an honest woman. 'I don't know how happy they were,' she said, thoughtfully. 'Marie wanted a lot of cuddling and Johann ...' she stopped and looked at her husband. 'Well,' he said, 'they were in a new place ...' 'He was often naughty at first,' she continued. 'Not for long,' the grandfather muttered and spread his right hand. 'He knew pretty quickly what was good for him.'

For the first time, the farmer's wife laughed. 'Come on, father,' she said, 'you make yourself out an ogre.' The truth she said was that

Johann particularly took to the grandfather, who almost immediately took him along on his chores. 'Still do,' the old man growled. I asked again whether they spoke a lot and she said that Marie, yes, spoke 'like a baby, you know, but Johann . . .' Again the grandfather interrupted. 'Silly question. He talks like a watermill now,' he said, firmly. 'What does it matter how they talked when they came from the orphanage?'

The grandfather was right, the younger woman then said, then was then and now was now. 'And you know now, don't you, Fräulein, that they are ours? That they were given to us?' Yes, I told them, I believed the children had been given to them. 'And that they are German,' the farmer said. They could be, I said. I'd be glad with them if they were. We would find out. But it was likely to take a long time and I hoped they could just go on being happy together.

Following that, a wooden plate with sliced rye bread, some rough country cheese, glasses and a bottle (precious I was sure) of red country wine had been produced and, more important, the farmer's wife had taken me to see the children asleep next to each other under their big featherbed. They were happy, loved and happy, and I felt vaguely ashamed when she handed me a photograph of them I asked for, taken just days after they had arrived, at Christmas 1942, with the family. I knew she thought I wanted it to remember the children who were so pretty.

It was the only time I saw these farmers. The photograph was sent to Arolson, where it was discovered that three families in different parts of Poland were searching for two- and three-year-old twins who had been taken from them. The photo was copied and sent to them. The ones who recognized the children as theirs – young farmers in a small village not far from Lodz – were able, as was required, to prove their identification, by a small birthmark Marie had on the inside of her right arm. (Bitterly ironic: had that tiny mole been any bigger, Marie would not have been thought worthy of Germanization.)

Happily for me, I had been transferred away from the area by then and it was someone else's painful task four months later, after verifying that Marie was this little girl who had the birthmark, to take the children away.

This task was, for whoever had to carry it out, never anything but traumatic. I only had to do it once, and I will never forget the inconsolable grief of the couple who loved the five-year-old I had to take away, and the uncomprehending wild anger of the child himself, who had no memory of his birth parents or native language and for whom the German parents were his world. In fact, in the four periods I was involved with different aspects of the identification of stolen children, I never met or ever heard of a single case where the German foster or adoptive parents treated the kidnapped child anything but lovingly or, whatever their politics might have been, were aware, as far as we could determine, of the methods by which the child came to them.

So in the final analysis, the Nazis committed here, as in so many other respects, a double infamy: that of stealing children from their parents in conquered lands, and that of grievously deceiving their own people about the integrity of their actions.

By the early summer of 1946, by which time (even where the Nazis had ordered records destroyed) a good many German documents had been discovered and quite a number of older kidnapped children had been found who could help us with information, we had learned a great deal about the process of Germanization. Seven Nazi organizations and one ministry were involved in this wicked programme, which, doubtlessly conceived by Himmler (though, as the documentation shows, it was, as for all major decisions, approved by Hitler) and planned and operated under the umbrella of the SS, will have caused lasting pain to countless families from Eastern Europe who lost their children for ever. The Office for Repatriation of Ethnic Germans (VoMi); the Reich Security Office (RSHA), the Reich Commission for the Consolidation of the German Race (RKFDV) played important administrative roles. NSV, the already mentioned Nazi People's Welfare Association, supplied the 'Brown Sisters'; RuSHA, the Office for Race and Resettlement's phoney racial 'scientists', decided children's suitability for Germanization on the basis of measurements of sixty-two parts of their bodies; and then, of course, there was the SS model 'charitable society', the *Lebensborn*. Finally, a comparatively rare occurrence, as German legislature preferred to pretend ignorance of the party's outrageous acts, the Ministry of the Interior lent the criminal undertaking legal status by conferring on the *Lebensborn* society the right of civil registry and of guardianship, thereby enabling them both to issue official birth certificates with (invented) places and dates of birth and (false) names, and – the ultimate control – of acting as the stolen children's legal guardian.

The procedure, carried out in stages, was identical in all countries where children were abducted, but it was in Poland that the largest number (estimated at 200,000) was taken. In the Warthegau, the programme was applied as soon as all Poles had been ejected. The children – always the majority of them boys – were largely taken from institutions, and from ethnic German parents who refused to sign a document of allegiance; in the 'General Government', where it began somewhat later, most of the children were taken directly from their families.

It was the SS and the 'Brown Sisters' who made the first decision and it was very simply arrived at: on secretly designated, always varying days, children were picked up off the streets, in playgrounds, in schools and homes. Unless the child (including babies) was pretty, healthy and well built, and had blonde or light-brown hair and blue eyes, it was eliminated from the selection. If chosen in this first stage, parents were told that children would be returned home after physical and IQ examinations which would decide their future schooling. Children were then taken by train to one of five children's homes in the Warthegau (this now 'German' territory being well out of reach of parents), which had been specially installed for Germanization. Children who in the course of testing there came to be considered below the required IQ for Germanization, would either, if young, be returned home, or, if older and fit, sent to Germany to work. (If, although of the right colouring and build, they were found to be physically unfit or racially 'tainted', they would end up in what to all intents and purposes was a children's concentration camp in Lodz (renamed Litzmanstadt), about which little documentation exists except some harrowing photographs, but where it is said most of them died.) For those 'qualified' by about six weeks of tests, new birth certificates with German names were issued – frequently, no one knows why, close translations of their Polish names – and their parents were notified that they were being sent to Germany for their health; subsequent inquiries were not answered. While small children were then placed in *Lebensborn* homes in Germany until they were considered ready to be placed in families, older ones were sent in small groups to so-called *Heimschulen* there – state boarding schools physically run by *Lebensborn* but staffed and supervised by the SS – where, with intensive language courses added for them, they otherwise shared the physical and ideological education of native Germans.

According to testimony obtained in the Allies' Nuremberg trial of *Lebensborn* in 1947, which, incidentally, acquitted its staff of all guilt – a decision that was, four years later, reversed by a German court in Munich – all German documentation for this programme was ordered to be destroyed in April 1945. In telling the story of the process of Germanization, from the point of view of the children involved, I am therefore relying on nearly identical descriptions given to me by five boys aged between ten and twelve whom I worked with during a six-week assignment to a 'special children's centre' in the late spring of 1946.

Here psychiatrists and other staff, experienced in child trauma, worked both on helping them to overcome the pain of separation, and on trying to reawaken memories in the youngest, in most of whom they had been deeply buried or entirely eliminated. Children of twelve or above who had been brought in for forced labour (they were usually fourteen to sixteen by the end of the war), had all remained perfectly aware of their identities, and while all were versed if not fluent in German, they retained their native languages. But interestingly enough, and proof of just *how* effective the Germanizing process was, this did not apply even to those who had been ten when taken, although it was considerably easier to bring back memories in them than in the youngest ones. For them, the most effective reminders, we found, were songs. Even though songs are deeply part of German family culture, and singing was a vital part of Nazi youth education, the sound of Polish nursery songs and children's prayers in many cases won out and brought back images of home.

The ten- to twelve-year-olds I mention had apparently all been taken away from their families in Poland in late 1942. They all remembered it had been in the weeks before Christmas and that they had stayed, some thought 'for a month or two', in two children's homes, in Brockau (Bruczkow) and Kalisch (Kalisz) – they only remembered the German names.

Their main memory was of having 'good food' but being cold, especially at night, when – manifestly new to these Polish country children – the bedroom windows were always open; in Kalisz, they remembered four beds to a room, except for two dormitories with ten beds each, 'for bigger boys'. The 'Brown Sisters' took care of them. Were they nice to them, I asked. 'Except when they were horrid,' one of them said; he remembered getting a beating with a switch on his bare bottom because he and a friend had sung a Polish ditty after lights out. During those first weeks, they had German, history and geography lessons for several hours every day, but, except for mealtimes, when 'quite soon', they said, they had to speak German or be silent, outside the schoolrooms they could speak Polish. There were 'lots of doctors in white coats but also in uniforms' and they had 'lots' of medical examinations.

Was that frightening?

'No, it was silly,' one of them said. 'We had to be all bare and they kept measuring every bit of us.'

What was it they measured?

'Oh, everything, they just went on and on.' (The decisive characteristics for being placed in the top racial categories, aside from the colour of hair and eyes, were the shape of nose and lips, hairline, toes and fingernails, and the condition of genitalia. What counted too were reactions to neurological tests and personal habits: persistent uncleanliness and bedwetting and farting, nailbiting and masturbation – which older boys were told on arrival was forbidden – were, if repeatedly observed, automatic disqualifications from top classification.)

Did they hurt them in any way?

'Hurt? No, they didn't hurt me; why should they hurt me?' – there was quite a lot of defensiveness in these Germanized children and many of their memories, particularly of the years in the manifestly pleasant *Lebensborn* homes and schools in Germany and Austria which followed this first initiation, were joyful. 'We did lots of climbing and obstacle courses and we learned to march; we sang around campfires; yes, it was strict but the [German] boys were nice . . .'

Had they been homesick?

They looked at each other, almost puzzled . . . it was so long ago.

'When we were small perhaps,' the oldest one finally said of that long time, four years before, when he had been eight, and then he shrugged, 'Then no more.' But . . . yes, he added later, he had remembered some Polish and he remembered his mother, though hardly his father. 'It'll be funny to have a mother,' he said, and laughed, a sort of half-laugh.

In the summer of 1946, after having had the experience of accompanying two children's repatriation transports back to Poland, I was assigned to the special children's centre in Bavaria. When I arrived there – I recount it with sorrow – I was brought face to face with Johann and Marie. I had not known they were there, and UNRRA had forgotten my involvement with them. Had they remembered and consulted the centre's staff on the advisability of my going there – this centre really was a special place, with devoted specialist UNRRA staff, assisted by both German and Polish-speaking experts in child therapy – it is doubtful whether I would have been sent there at that point. The children's appearance – their faces sallow, with shadows under their eyes – Johann's very hostile reaction to me and Marie's awful apathy shook me to the core. Marie was crunched up in a chair, her eyes closed, the lids transparent, her thumb in her mouth, while Johann, racing up as soon as he saw me, and shouting hoarsely, 'Du, Du, Du' (You, you, you), hit out at me with feet and fists. If I had not learned that they were due to leave for Poland three days later, I would have requested an immediate transfer in order to protect them from having to see me. The staff tried to console me by saying that, sadly, they were only too familiar with this reaction by children separated from their German home. Like some other very distressed children before them, they had been kept at the centre beyond their scheduled departure date, in the hope they could be helped to get through this second loss in their young lives, before they had to confront the emotional expectations of their natural parents. Nothing had helped, however; Johann had become increasingly defiant, with other moments of the real violence he had displayed towards me, and Marie, who, bedwetting and taking food only by bottle, did not speak and had reverted to babyhood. The decision now to send them home, with the parents pre-informed of their condition and one of the centre's German-speaking therapists accompanying them – for of course they spoke no

Polish – was a kind of last resort which had worked in a few previous cases, counting on the parents' tenderness to give them relief. Reluctantly, that night, following the direction of the resident psychiatrist, who thought it couldn't harm and, even if as a shock, might help, I gave Marie her bottle, holding her in my lap. There was no shock; she lay there, her eyes shut, her body apparently boneless, the only movement the sucking of her lips and the swallowing of her small thin throat. I held her until she was asleep. It helped me, but not, I fear, her. What are we doing, I asked myself. What in God's name were we doing?

The question which so often occupied us was what was the 'right' solution of this human conundrum? To return the children to parents who longed for them but in an impoverished and largely destroyed Eastern Europe, to an ideology unacceptable to many of us? Or to leave them with their loving German second families, in Germany, our immediate past enemy which had obtained them by a crime of truly biblical proportions? What *was* in the best interest of the children? The question became even more disturbing when we learned late that summer of 1946 that the issuing of a fanatically anti-Soviet order was being considered in Washington (and agreement sought for it in Britain) for the resettlement overseas – in America, Australia and Canada – of all children of Russian origin from the reconquered German empire, including those from the contested Ukrainian and Baltic border regions, instead of returning them to their homes and a life under the Soviets.

By the autumn of 1946, many UNRRA workers had already been concerned for months about the so far unofficial 'advice' from above not to allow Soviet liaison officers into DP camps nor to expose unaccompanied children to them. While their addresses were posted for those DPs who might want to visit them, they were in fact not allowed in as their presence would have been too inflammatory. But some of us, individually, feeling not only that the Soviets had as much right to their children as anyone else, but also that we needed their help to locate parents, had ignored this advice at least with regard to the youngest unaccompanied children. Various changes in rulings we received over the preceeding twelve months – about the age at which minors should be allowed to make their own decisions whether or not to return home and what facilities should be granted to either communist or anti-communist Polish liaison officers for contact with children – convinced us that neither our governments, the British Control Commission, nor USFET (US Forces European Theatre) who were the highest authority in the US Zone of Germany, really knew what to do about these difficult matters.

When the – to us – appalling news of the planned new order about Russian children reached us, I knew, for example, of seven children under ten in special child centres in my region alone, whose Ukrainian parents were waiting for them and who, with therapy and language lessons, were being prepared for going home; there were, of course, many others both in the US and British Zones of occupation. How could anyone think of ordering that children who had twice suffered the trauma of losing parents, homes and language, should, like so many packages, be transported overseas and dropped into yet another new and entirely strange environment?

Several of us who felt passionate about the impending order embarked, with the help and approval of the UNRRA director for the US Zone, John Whiting, on a campaign to defeat this plan. Working out of his office in Frankfurt for three weeks, we circulated a protest and sought signatures from all UNRRA field workers, made hundreds of phone calls to teams as well as to congressmen and MPs in Washington and London, and bombarded the State Department, the Foreign Office and USFET with letters. While many UNRRA team workers signed the protest, replies from official Washington and London were sparse, saying only that our opinion was noted and that no definite decision had yet been made.

I had by this time had a number of arguments with UNRRA HQ, both about various aspects of the unaccompanied children problem and about the screening of DPs. When, during a short posting to a screening team, I had discovered the continuing existence of a Ruthenian collaborationist organization called *Samochova* (Self-Defence) which had worked for the Nazis, and the continuing presence of a number of other individuals who had manifestly horribly collaborated with them, I had suggested to HQ that the screening, largely carried out by unsophisticated GIs, which allowed such people to maintain their DP status, instead of being arrested as war criminals, was deeply flawed and needed to be fundamentally revised. In the 'cold war' atmosphere of the time, no changes were made and, pretty tired of it all, I had advised HQ that I would resign before the end of the year. The new controversy about the Russian children, which finally began to look insoluble, reinforced that decision and I left UNRRA in October to undertake a lecture tour to schools and colleges in America.

Mysteriously, at neither the National Archives in Washington, the UNRRA archives in New York nor the Public Records Office in Kew, is there any sign of our copious and certainly official correspondence with Washington and London, all of it co-signed by the highest UNRRA official in the US Zone, John Whiting. And although a ruling about sending the Russian-born children overseas is frequently referred to in documents until UNRRA ceased to exist on 1 July 1947 (and many such children were in fact sent abroad), there is no trace of a document actually recording such a ruling.

The closest we have come to it is in a report dated 19 March 1947, by Eileen Blackey, Chief Child Search and Repatriation Consultant at UNRRA HQ. On pages 10 and 11 of this paper, under the heading of 'Problems Concerning Nationality Status', she reports on the continuing difficulties about a clear directive affecting Ukrainian and Baltic children.

Children who are from that part of the Ukraine (and the Baltics) which by [the Yalta] agreement has now become part of Russia, are not being referred to the Soviet liaison officers for clearance and repatriation . . . USFET . . . without consulting Soviet liaison officers on these children . . . are themselves accepting responsibility for releasing them for emigration.

Miss Blackey, who was known to be deeply opposed to these proposals and had long lobbied the State Department that UNRRA and not impersonal bureaucrats should be authorized to make final decisions about these children, and evidently thought she had succeeded, writes:

The cable, which our Washington Office had reported as being prepared by the State Department for USFET, has [still] not reached them. This is an extremely important cable since it [is to] recommend to USFET that they not release any policy [on nationality and resettlement of children abroad] . . . unless it conforms to the recommendations [against this practice] made by UNRRA . . .

If a directive is actually formulated and in operation prior to July 1st, the chances of it remaining effective [after UNRRA leaves] are quite good. If nothing is in effect by that time, the disposition of the problem may have . . . catastrophic results.

About 40,000 Polish children out of the reported missing 200,000 were returned home, and, entirely through individual UNRRA team initiative, two transports of just over 100 young Russians slipped through in December 1946. Otherwise, there is no record of how many children of contested nationality there were, how many of them were sent overseas or otherwise resettled, or indeed, how many of the stolen children were never discovered and, ignorant of their origins, have remained in Germany. I don't know whether, in the final analysis, that was or was not the best solution for the children – I do not think anyone knows. But what we should never forget is that their birth parents have never even been able to mourn them.

4

Generation without a Past

February 2000

In 1947, living in Paris trying to write a book, I met at a cocktail party given by a friend working at *Vogue*, Don Honeyman, a fine young American photographer who had been sent to Paris a few months earlier from New York to help reopen the Paris studios. In January 1948 we married; in April 1949, then living in Neuilly, we had Christopher (now a well-known mediator-arbitrator in America and husband of environmentalist Elaine, the two of them the parents of our grandchildren Ian, now twenty-one, and Catie, eighteen) and soon afterwards, following an invitation to Don from British *Vogue*, moved to London and to a beautiful house in Pembroke Studios in Kensington. Don was recalled to New York *Vogue* in 1952, so we tried living in New York City and then in Westchester. I loved it, but Don hated the world of New York fashion. I wrote my first book, *The Medallion*, in America, but when six years later Don received an invitation from British *Vogue*, we decided that London was the place where we wanted to live for good and bring up our family. Our daughter Mandy, now a film-maker, was born in July 1960 and shortly afterwards we moved back into our Kensington studio where we would live for the next thirty-one years. We sent Christopher to King's, Canterbury, as a boarder, but the first six years of Mandy's life I spent at home, trying – unsuccessfully – to write further novels. It was only in 1966 that I became a professional journalist, and was extraordinarily lucky in the support I immediately received.

I had only written two features in 1966, one for the *Woman's Mirror* on children in care and one for the *People* on underqualified lay magistrates dispensing questionable justice in Domestic (now Family) Courts, when I was asked to go and see John Anstey, editor of what was then generally considered the best of the weekend colour supplements, the *Daily Telegraph Magazine*. There are dozens of people, now literary and journalistic household names, who benefited from John's gift for discovering and supporting writers, all of whom, under his difficult but extraordinary patronage, learned to write better than they ever dreamed they would. Many of them, certainly including me, have to thank his genius for enabling them to expand the subjects first commissioned and developed with his help, into books which reached a wide public. Though many of the pieces I was to write for him over the next twelve years were to be republished in other countries, I wrote exclusively for him until I received an irresistible contributor's contract offer from the *Sunday Times* in 1977 which he could not match. Sadly, John, who with Joanna his wife, an English beauty, had remained our good friends, died of cancer much too young in 1988. (In 1993, Joanna, one of only two friends I asked to take on the onerous task of reading the immensely long draft of my book on Albert Speer, provided me with an infinitely valuable detailed critique.) My professional luck continued over the years and now into the twenty-first century, allowing me to work all along for equally generous editors, such as Harry Evans and Magnus Linklater on the *Sunday Times*, Richard Williams on *The Times*, Liz Jobey on the *Independent on Sunday Review*, and finally Peter Stothard, again on *The Times*. There were of course others (such as David Robson, then on the *Sunday Times Magazine*, who worked with me for weeks in 1988, editing the longest feature of many I wrote on the case of John Demjanjuk, the alleged 'Ivan the Terrible' of Treblinka), but the six I mention here backed me and worked with me, in several instances for years, on extremely difficult stories. Without courageous editors such as these, editors who are willing to take real risks on writers who need a lot of financial and editorial support – my journalistic writing is always lengthy, and my suggested subjects have more often than not needed considerable financial investment ('*When*,' I remember John Anstey once asking me despairingly when I explained three pieces I wanted to research in South America, 'when are you going to propose a piece that you can do in Balham?') – without such editorial commitment, now becoming a rarity, journalism such as I have chosen to do cannot exist.

As chance would have it, the very first thing I had written for publication was about someone who would much later on, in the context of this and other books, play a special and crucial role in my life. It was in 1937 when, not yet fifteen and a first-year dramatic student at the Reinhardt Seminar in Vienna, Helene Thimig, one of the finest actresses of the German-speaking stage and Max Reinhardt's wife, came to spend a day at the school, working with a number of much-envied second-year students. That night when I returned home in a state of adolescent euphoria about her, one of my mother's guests at a dinner party, the editor of a Vienna weekly I think called *Die Welt am Montag*, asked me to write down for him what I felt about Helene Thimig. I said I couldn't do that, it would sound like currying favour. He said he'd publish it without my name. In fact, to my fury breaking his promise, he published it under my initials, but nobody at the school seemed to notice – maybe nobody read the paper – and, as I would find out nine years later in California when I spent Christmas and New Year with her in the house in Pacific Palisades she and Reinhardt had made into an Austrian jewel – she herself never saw it until Reinhardt's secretary drew her attention to it in Hollywood in 1939.

I had met Helene Thimig again early in the summer of 1946 on a train to Salzburg. I was in UNRRA uniform, on my first leave in more than a year, and coming from Rome to the Salzburg Festival. She was on her way from America to reopen the festival which Reinhardt, with Richard Strauss and Hugo von Hofmannsthal, had founded in 1920 – and to direct and star in Reinhardt's famous production of Hofmannsthal's *Jedermann* (adapted from the English morality play *Everyman*). A beautiful woman, blonde, fine-boned, intensely reserved with strangers, with a face almost Gothic in its purity, Helene was then fifty-seven and I was twenty-three. The deep friendship that began in the dining car of that train and, though with occasional hiccups, essentially lasted until she died in 1974, was incomprehensible not only to others, but for quite some time to me too. Over these twenty-eight years, when we saw plays and films together across Europe, in England or in America and talked endlessly about art not in the usual meaning of the word, but in the sense of the art of life, of being human; when she 'gave me away' (in 1948) at my marriage at the church of my early childhood in Vienna, with the Vienna Boys' Choir singing the Ave Maria; when I stayed with her many times in Vienna, at her country house near Salzburg, and she stayed with us in London – at all these times I often puzzled (and this was not false modesty but realism) what she, so elegant, so accomplished and so famous, saw or found in me. But I decided quite soon that what probably drew us to each other across that wide gap of age, experience and sophistication was the capacity, indeed the lust we shared for laughter. As I write this, I can still see us walking on the mountain trails around Salzburg, or in the Cologne, Düsseldorf and Hamburg streets when, as I frequently did in the 1950s, I accompanied her on German tours, and we burst into laughter so uncontrollable that we could no longer walk, and had to stand still, leaning against walls for support. It must have been an incomprehensible spectacle for passers-by – to many of whom (Germans and Austrians being passionate theatregoers) she was the epitome of the distinguished dramatic actress.

What I didn't know then but learned to understand later – the particular reason why I write about her here – was that through her, for whom language, which she spoke with a distinction and finesse never equalled for me by anyone I have known, was the focus of existence, I regained not only my affection but my appreciation for the German tongue which, in my anger and contempt for the Nazis, I had rejected for years. I have often felt that it was partly this new feeling for German speech, inspired by someone who was spiritually so totally incapable of shallowness or bigotry, that I slowly developed a different, a less emotional and less narrow attitude towards Germany and Germans.

Helene, a member of Austria's greatest theatrical family – the equivalent of the Redgraves in Britain or the Barrymores in America – had committed herself very near the beginning of her brilliant career, at twenty-four, to life with a man who, true enough, was the giant then of European theatre, but a man of forty and a Jew. After huge successes in America as a visiting producer during the early 1930s, he was totally spurned after arriving as a refugee in 1938, and Helene herself, who then spoke no English, would hardly ever be able to act there except in virtual walk-ons in Hollywood films. I am certain that during the twenty-five years they would spend together, the last five before Reinhardt's death in 1943 in profound unhappiness and homesickness in America where she had followed him into exile, it would never have occurred to her to think of him in terms of someone 'different' from her because of his religion, but only as the great artist he was, her teacher and mentor from the moment she met him to the moment he died.

It so happened I was with her in the autumn of 1946 when (the first though not the only time it happened after her return to her country and profession after the war) she received an anonymous note in her dressing-room at the Akademietheater in Vienna, calling her a *Rassenschänderin*, an untranslatable term the Nazis applied to women who slept with – or indeed married – Jews. Already in her costume and make-up for Eugene O'Neill's *Mourning Becomes Electra*, she held the note in her lap, her hands white with tension, her face momentarily stiff with pain. 'I don't understand people like that,' she then said, her voice tight, not with anger but with bewilderment. Except for telling me later that she had had a number of similar notes when she first started her liaison with Reinhardt thirty-three years earlier (though not yet living with him), she never talked, indeed appeared almost deliberately to avoid talking about the subject of anti-semitism, about which debates were already so painfully rife in Germany (if certainly less in Austria). This was always strange, because except for sex, which to her, as the most private and possibly rather puzzling act, was taboo as a subject of conversation, she was not only ready but eager to discuss anything under the sun. I asked her once, several years later, why she so manifestly recoiled from discussing this issue, which essentially meant that she tended to shun all conversations about Germany and Austria's 'recent past' as it was called (an attitude rather welcomed by Austrians at the time). To my dismay, my question provoked that same expression of suffering in her face I had seen that night in 1946 in her dressing-room and it is the first and only time I heard her stammer. 'I c-c-can't . . . I can't stand it,' she said. I was never sure whether it was the conflict between the moral vulgarity of anti-semitism and her long love for Germany where, between 1911 and 1936, she had acted the whole repertoire of classic leads, or whether, on a personal and emotional level, she associated it after all with the professional catastrophe it had caused for Reinhardt.

There was one more time, entirely perplexing for me, when I would see this profoundly unhappy expression in her face. It was when I gave her a copy of the *Daily Telegraph Magazine* of 8 October 1971 with my first account (which I would later develop into the book *Into That Darkness*) of my conversations in Düsseldorf prison with Franz Stangl, former commandant of Sobibor and Treblinka (see page 93). I had known that she would never read it if I sent it to her, just as she had not read any of the articles I wrote about Germany and the Germans over the years. But I had spent half a year working on this; it was important to me and, a stubbornness I was to regret, I was determined to get her to read it. So, early that December I flew to Vienna and, taking the magazine to her flat, told her I would sit next door until she had read it. I heard her turn the pages, and then there was silence. This is when I found her, the magazine in her lap, her always thin and bony face again parchment white. After a long continuing silence, she looked up at me. 'Why you?' she asked, with that same pressed voice I had heard twice before. 'Why just you?' I never found an answer, for I never understood the question and, seeing her so distraught, could not subject her to a discussion of it.

There have been some periods over the last fifty years when the majority of Germans, from different generations, did not want, or no longer wanted, to think of or be reminded of Hitler. This applied, immediately after the war, both to the generation then between fourteen and forty, the essence of Hitler's dreams, who had fought the war for him, and their parent generation, most of whom had shared the dream and put him into power. This resistance – or denial – flared up again sharply in the 1960s when German courts began the NS trials, which were to continue over more than two decades, and many of which, reported meticulously by the media, went on for many months and even years. Forced to confront yet again the terrible crimes which had been committed in their name, the majority of Germans wanted nothing more than that all trials, all writings, films and plays about that period would stop. And up to a point one could sympathize with their feelings. For while, true enough, owing partly to the dearth of qualified teachers in the 1940s and early 1950s, it would be years before the history of the Third Reich and its crimes was properly taught in German schools and colleges, it seems to me that much of the world has never recognized the extent to which by contrast German writers, film-makers and the media concentrated on the subject from very early on – from the early 1950s – soon producing a veritable stream of books, films, commentaries and debates of considerable quality, all focusing on the moral degeneracy of the Nazis. And I believe that it was this intense preoccupation with their country's past of leading writers, artists, thinkers, the judiciary and, yes, also of politicians in those early years, and their ability to maintain their convictions against the pressures of large sections of the public, which, even more than the Marshall Plan and the resultant *Wirtschaftswunder*, has been the source of Germany's remarkable moral recovery.

13 March 1967

Most Germans cannot understand why they are not understood. They see themselves leading an inoffensive and constructive life. They love their children, are kind to each other, are generous to strangers, have supported for twenty-two years democratic rule and look upon themselves as essential partners in a new Europe. They are willing to admire and adopt many ideas from abroad and they feel a genuine and deep sense of aggrievement for being continuously criticized and distrusted.

There has also emerged in West Germany in the past twenty years a group of outstanding men and women, many of them active now in public life – in literature, the press, radio, television and the law; a few in education, the churches and government. They are attempting to exert prodigious, even unparalleled efforts, quite disproportionate to their number, to counteract the nefarious influences of Germany's recent past, and to deal with her present ills of which they are entirely and despairingly aware. They are, alas, spread tragically thin and much of the time unable to affect the overwhelming majority of the adult population.

For this majority it is impossible to realize that the reason for the world's inability to understand them is the fact that, as a nation, as family units and as individuals, they are living a profoundly dangerous and misleading double life.

A life on the one hand permeated with the monstrous events in their nation's recent past – events that despite the time elapsed and the rich and solid continuity of their present life are continuously so near the surface of their minds that at the slightest opportunity or provocation, excuses, justifications, accusations or regrets pour forth.

A life on the other hand where, rationalizing and minimizing that which simply cannot be borne, they pretend vehemently to everyone, and above all to their own children whom they thereby infect with this self-delusion, that the past did not really happen – because they themselves as individuals 'weren't there', or 'didn't know', both quite frequently true.

Basically however – and they prove it by this continuous preoccupation – they all know right from wrong. Basically they know that they were a party, if only passively, to the terrible wrong. Under the extraordinary illusion of self-sufficiency that Hitler was able to inspire in them, they could ignore occasional misgivings. Because of the war they could justify putting off decisions of morality.

The ultimate question of resistance or revolt could not occur to any but a few not-to-be-forgotten isolated Christian martyrs among them, for on the whole the Germans have in the past entirely lacked that inborn civic sense which in turn breeds the civic courage natural to people in older democratic states. By this same deficiency, the free acceptance of co-responsibility for their own history has simply been beyond their capacity.

In 1945 we might have helped them come to terms with it. We didn't. The problem proved too vast. The Allies too were soon split in purpose, understanding and ideas. At a time when the Germans were undeniably in a state of moral shock at the discovery of their own iniquities, and singularly susceptible to positive influence, through bewilderment rather than malign intentions we created and nurtured in them a deep dependence on 'abroad' and they ended up relinquishing rather than learning any semblance of self-determination. Denazification was a farce and the swiftly arising political expediencies of the moment prompted the reinstatement of individuals deeply involved with National Socialism to essential functions in government, justice, education and industry. Soon their economy was artificially stimulated and supported – indeed supported to such a degree that these ridiculous riches became their prerogative. The state of moral schizophrenia, already in the making, was now intensified by inducing a vanquished nation to feel itself a victor. This condition in Germany has been continuously enhanced by extraneous political developments and needs and has made it impossible for the few who understand the deep need for clarification, to assert their own integrity.

It is very late now. Contrary to popular belief abroad, the Germans are consumed by impotent guilt. They are a country not only geographically divided, but divided from their own history and divided, what is more, into sharply defined age groups, each with an entirely separate and yet primarily evasive perspective of their past and present. The nation's guilt – entirely unresolved – has become the nation's trauma.

This is not the past. This is now. This is not just their business. It is ours too in this new world of interdependence. For the result in Germany is that any clarity of national purpose is nearly impossible, as very few men of an age to govern or administer in highest places are either above suspicion by others, or, just as destructive, the fear of guilt in themselves. This state of mind necessarily affects every decision they make and causes the country to live in a state of explosive malaise.

Because we don't appear to understand, because we appear to misjudge and to suspect them – and it is of course true that we do – in impotent frustration they threaten us with dire consequences: the consequences of their own confusions. These *are* potentially disastrous. Not only because Germany, whether one likes it or not, is the natural 'centrum' of Europe and because of its geographical position almost impossible to neutralize. Not only because, for mysterious reasons of nature, they have been endowed with unique funds of energy which cannot be suppressed but must be put to use. But, most important of all, because the deeply authoritarian nature of their national character cannot but radically affect their national life. It makes it as nearly impossible for their still-dominant generation of 45- to 55-year-olds to liberalize their young as it may be for the young – who have had no opportunity to develop the instinct towards revolt and self-determination – to liberate themselves. A captive German youth may turn out to be Europe's gravest danger.

They don't want to be a danger. They don't think they are. They are the young: uncompromised, uninvolved. None of the things Germany is accused of, they feel, apply to them. West Germany has 60 million people. Thirty million of them are under thirty-five. In other countries a man of twenty-seven or thirty is an adult – in Germany the term 'youth' must apply even to those of thirty-five and over. For the only valid point of division is who was part – and who was not part – of the Hitler era.

But – these young are not nationalists. They are not selfish, overbearing or arrogant. Nor are they bigoted. They are not proud of being German; not given to dangerous ideologies, and of all things, not admiring the military mind.

They are a charming youth: honest, kind, clean, polite – even friendly, to adults.

One *wants* to look at them in the same way as at any other youth.

One *wants* to speak of them in terms of the future.

The dilemma is that by their own reactions one finds oneself forced back into the past.

In the rest of the Western world the young are challenging the values of the past – above all, the glorification of compromise as a principal virtue. This repudiation of the past has created a common bond. The German young know that this identity exists 'outside'. They long, and they demand to be part of it. But they are not. For compromise is the pivot of German life. And the past is the one thing their parents cannot afford to reject – rejection would presuppose acknowledgement.

In a world where youth is gaining increasing freedoms and far earlier maturity, the parent generation in Germany firmly maintain their traditional hold, and young Germans remain children while their contemporaries abroad begin to affect the course of nations. The German parents *need* their children as a living proof of their own intrinsic honour, a vindication of their values – an extension of themselves. They cannot free them.

I met young West Germans in their schools, apprentice homes and clubs; students in universities and technical schools; young workers in their hostels. I saw young trade unionists, representatives of young political groups, and, in their homes or at gatherings set up for me, met the 'oldest young', those between twenty-seven and thirty-five who are in professions, trades, and often have young families.

Of all the young Germans, this last group is the most important: they are mature, highly articulate, and have very few illusions. In 1945 many of them – although very young – witnessed the end of the Nazi time. They have forgotten nothing. They challenged their parents, accepted the division of Germany as a logical consequence of Germany's actions, despised the famous *Wirtschaftswunder*'s material benefits and now question all the values that are being imposed upon those younger than themselves. They are the only age-group to show signs of progress, change – of having freed themselves and acquired responsibility in the process. They are also unfortunately over-extended and already showing signs of cynical fatigue.

It would be imprudent to underrate the effect of Germany's high standard of living on the young. They lack nothing, and this unprecedented plenty has given rise to a new set of problems: complacency, a kind of lethargy, and already an only-thinly-veiled contempt and condescension for people living in less opulent societies.

'The parents and the state vie with each other to see who can offer the young the greatest ease, more comfort, greater luxuries,' a TV producer, aged thirty, said in Cologne. 'They say of course, that they want their children to have what they didn't have themselves, but that's really too simple. I think subconsciously they compensate for other things: for the fact that this is a divided country; for the fact that we aren't supposed to have nuclear weapons perhaps. In the final analysis, I suppose, for the fact that the children are Germans.'

'Our youth are given everything material on a silver platter,' a twenty-eight-year-old doctor said in Hamburg, 'soi-disant to give them greater "security". What it really is, is that they are given it as a kind of bribery: "We'll give you all this and you'll be proud of being German. You won't think of all the things you can't be proud of".'

In the classrooms, I asked the eighteen- to nineteen-year-olds to bring their chairs up to where I sat on a table facing them.

They are pupils and live at home, but it is not the parents alone who limit and control their horizon. It is that whole generation, including all their teachers and their government. It is the system. Mass media has shown them that there is another way of life, different reactions in other youths of other nations, and they admire and imitate them: in their dress, their bearing and their way of speaking peppered with American expressions. But it's makeshift, make-believe. They talk freedom but don't know how to free themselves, how to be and stay free. You cannot be with them for more than a few moments without the subject of the detested *Obrigkeit* – authority or hierarchy – coming up.

'Everything we do in school has its effect on the marks we get,' a boy in Wiesbaden said. This same sort of remark was repeated over and over.

'It's essential to have the "right" attitude, the "right" opinions.'

'The right opinions are the "safe" opinions. Not on the left – that is heresy, treason. Not *too* much on the right, that would be risky.'

'When we write our German compositions we must be very careful. In a so-called "free essay" it wouldn't do to express any ideas the teacher mightn't like. And that could be almost anything that is outside the "established". They wouldn't argue it with us, they'd just give us a "four" (the lowest mark).'

'We are afraid of them, and they are afraid of the headmaster who is afraid of the inspectors who are afraid of the State Ministry.'

'All you have to do is collect enough "fours" and you fail the class; you lose a year out of your life.'

'We tell our parents when we think the teachers give us low marks because they've taken a personal dislike to us,' a seventeen-year-old girl said in Cologne, 'but they say "Be diplomatic, be pleasant, pretend" – so we say what we think the teachers want to hear.' She shrugged her shoulders. 'It's easier. And anyway, our parents want us to. They want us to succeed.'

'Yes, we have student government, but it means nothing. There is nothing we can really do about anything, so all the student representatives do is to arrange shows and competitions – it's a farce.'

'Yes, we have school newspapers – but they have a teacher-adviser, and he has the right to censor and cancel anything.'

At a meeting with the *Junge Union* in Frankfurt – a very active youth group of the Christian Democratic Union – Jürgen, aged eighteen, said: 'Yes, I try to propose changes. Many of us on the Student Councils try – but it's not possible, the student body won't go along with us. Each is afraid to raise his hand and finally we are afraid too. There is no corporate feeling in any of our schools, and no way of instilling it. We don't live together, we don't do sports together, we don't even compete intellectually – each man for himself, that's what it is. There is a terrible social passivity – it stems out of the teachers' attitude and our fear of them – and our parents' attitude and our love and respect for them.'

There can be no question of the attitude of the young towards those events of the past they are familiar with. The little they know about the excesses of the Hitler regime, they deplore and condemn.

'Awful what they did to the Jews,' they say. But they connect the whole Nazi time only with the atrocities against the Jews – it means nothing to them otherwise. Only few of them connect their own incapacity for battling with authority, with the unprecedented success of the totalitarian idea in Germany. They do however ache to know more – not of the horrors, but how it all came about, how such a system could maintain itself. This, seen from the vantage point of their own lifetime, the way they feel about themselves, each other, the world and, above all, their own parents is incomprehensible to them.

'Practically everything that happens in Germany today has its roots in the Hitler time,' a twenty-three-year-old Munich student said. 'There isn't one single part of our life, cultural, scientific or political of course, that isn't affected by it. Twenty-five years is nothing in relation to the depth of this influence and it endures. We see and feel the consequences of this past every day. We can't visualize it, and how it came about. And we can't reconcile to it, or for that matter fight the effects, because our parents' rejection of their part in it makes it entirely unreal to us. We must either brand them as liars, or construct our lives upon a void.'

And so they limit the scope of that time in their own minds to what they can understand and accept, blame it on a few who are now dead, and merely condemn and reject the obvious. No one they trust, or respect, will tell them more. And although the subject is treated continuously in papers, television and in books, they will not *read* about it. The printed word, or TV is 'propaganda'. They want to *talk*. For conversation between generations, however, it is taboo, covered by a grim, stubborn, deeply defensive silence from parents and teachers alike. Now they no longer know who or how to ask.

In a youth club in Stuttgart, a sixteen-year-old boy, Uwe, spoke of his life at home: 'We talk about everything,' he said, 'school, my career, sex – you know, everything. Except about that . . . that past. There are things I want to know about it. But how can I ask my father? *How make him tell me?* There is such a thing as loyalty, you know.'

A girl in Düsseldorf: 'How can we even mention these things to our parents? How can we let them think that we connect them even remotely with these terrible events, in our minds? It would . . . it would dirty our family, our love.'

A boy in Berlin: 'I have had very difficult moments with my parents. I have asked them many questions. They are liberal by comparison with most – we get on awfully well. They support me in anything I want to do. But even they can't answer. Not about the past – it's taboo, taboo.'

Only the oldest young group in Germany, the twenty-five to thirty-fives or thereabouts, have faced and frequently come to terms with this problem.

'But don't forget, this was fifteen years ago,' a thirty-two-year-old designer said in Munich. 'Our reactions were more direct then; we had been exposed to some of the effects ourselves; our parents' wounds and guilt were more recent, the whole situation more fluid, the population on the whole not as stagnant.'

'I left home as soon as I could' . . . 'Got out' . . . 'Left them to it' . . . 'Hardly see them' . . . 'Impossible to be in the same room' . . . 'No common ground on anything that's important.' For many of this group the closeness of the family situation sadly no longer exists – it had to be sacrificed to truth. 'But at least we feel comparatively clean – we know, we accept and we can begin from there,' a thirty-three-year-old industrial psychologist in Berlin said.

It is not the generation gap that is at the basis of the problem of the German young. There cannot really be a gap where there is no battle. It goes much deeper, derives on the contrary from the fundamental closeness, indeed the love, in German family life, and the deeply disturbing contrast between this established parental authority and supposed integrity, and the impenetrable protective wall of silence the parents have erected between themselves and their children about Germany's recent history.

Perhaps the effects would be less constant if there had been in Germany a real divorce between past and present, if in fact at least the official life of the country had been able to return to normal. But it hasn't, and it can't. Because – contrary to the rest of Europe – the Germans are continuing to live the consequences of the war. The existence of two Germanys and the constant discussions pertaining to it serve as a continuous reminder of the past. It is interpreted by most Germans as a situation imposed upon Germany by 'abroad' and accepted by leaders they despise for their compliance. Thus, the past and the present are inevitably combined, impossible to ignore or to forget, and German politicians are forced on to the defensive by the very system that they are trying so hard to establish.

In Hamburg, a state prosecutor working on Nazi criminal trials came along to a youth club. Here too, as everywhere else, the subject of the past soon cropped up. It usually begins with 'The Trials', goes on to 'The Jews' and then to 'Compensations paid by us'.

'Those trials *must* stop,' one boy said. 'There's no doubt about that. Anyway, they are only held to kowtow to the *Ausland*.'

'The people who are being tried were just soldiers, they did what they were ordered to do.'

A small blonde next to me was snuggling up to her boyfriend. 'I don't believe any of it,' she said, half to him, half to me. 'I don't know anyone who'd behave like that, do you?'

Prosecutor Kurt Tegge then told them about a man in Hamburg who, only a few weeks before, had come to him of his own free will and confessed that he had volunteered for service with the infamous SS Division 1005.

'He told me he shot children,' Tegge said simply. 'He didn't even know any more precisely how many, but he thought 114 anyway. He'd make them kneel down near a pit and then he'd stand behind one after the other and shoot them in the neck.' This man had identified eighteen other SS men in Hamburg who had also volunteered. There was dead silence in the room when Tegge had finished.

'Did you hear that?' the little blonde whispered to her boyfriend. 'Eighteen men like that living now in Hamburg volunteered to shoot children? It gives me goose-pimples.'

I was certain that this had been the first time she – possibly any of them – had connected this horror-tale past with today, themselves, their city and their homes.

The Jews come into every conversation, obsessively – it is impossible to stop them. The attitude is often sympathetic, always careful, not entirely unreasonable and profoundly reflective of confusion and smouldering resentment.

'I am sick and tired of hearing about the Jews,' a boy would say. 'It is unhealthy for us. Unhealthy for them, too, I should think. Sometimes I think if I hear that damn word Jew once more, I shall explode.' Or 'Did you know that in Germany you cannot describe someone as a "Jew" any more? You have to say "This man of Jewish faith". How silly can we get?'

A girl: 'I think it is natural that we treat them differently. After all, we know what was done to them by Germans. I don't know any Jews, but I'd feel ashamed to even make them talk to me.'

While as yet very limited, the increasing awareness of this subject is doubtlessly conducive to ever-increasing anti-semitism.

Nobody is more aware of the lack of factual knowledge than the responsible press and radio. There are constant discussions, editorials and directives on this subject. The magazine *Deutsche Jugend* said, 'Just because the parents have (unhappily) achieved a solidarity with their children, we cannot agree to a cheap and misleading piecemeal presentation of the so-called heroes and even the crimes of the Nazi time. We must painfully expose to our youth the fundamental facts and fallacies of this past and by these means – through our youth – battle with the parent generation for the truth. We maintain that *Mein Kampf* hidden away is far more dangerous than read.'

A discussion between young department heads of the West German Broadcasting Company in Cologne all aged between twenty-eight and thirty-eight: 'We must return to conventional unemotional journalism – like on the BBC. Stop these eternal dramatizations of the events of the past – stop filling the airwaves with polemics.'

Opinions are sharply divided on this question. 'If we do so much in this sense,' a director of drama said, 'how do you explain that our youth is so abysmally ignorant?'

'They are ignorant because they reject dramatics. Give them fact, fact and facts again and they'll listen. Expose them to discussion groups, controversy – let them think and then decide for themselves.'

But press and TV are part of the élite, tragically divided from their audience by their own excellence. The right to think and decide for themselves is precisely what the vast majority of adults will not accord to young Germans. At the youth club Dahlem in Berlin a nineteen-year-old girl told me: 'We had managed to set up a debate here with representatives of the SED (Socialist Unity Party of East Germany) – we were very excited about it. Then the club administration said we couldn't have them – too dangerous I suppose.'

At another youth club it was impossible to get the *Clubleiter* – the youthworker, a man of forty-two, to leave me alone with the group.

'Can we talk about anything? Anything at all?' they asked, but within minutes of the beginning of discussion (and this had happened in other places too) the youthworker interrupted. 'No, no,' he said, 'say what you think, really think, not what you think she wants to hear.' A few moments later, again, 'No, no, you must think clearly – that isn't what you mean at all. You are going to give her a wrong impression . . .' The disturbing thing was that they took it, and were silenced.

In the South German Broadcasting Company in Munich I was given the opportunity to meet young people of all ages who had taken part in a weekly broadcast for the young. Here – and also later in Cologne – I encountered young Germans sympathizing with the National Democratic Party. If this deserves some comment it is only because the NDP is now the only protest party in West Germany and could – if cleverly handled – attract a great many of the young who need a platform for their opposition. However, it is worth noting that among what must have been about 3,500 young people whom I spoke with at considerable length, there were just five who appeared sympathetic to these old and dangerous ideas. These five were of different ages but similar backgrounds.

'Our programme is orientated towards the lower classes – opinion polls prove them to be uncommitted,' one of them said. They speak in obviously emotional slogans. And most of their woefully familiar battle cries are vehemently opposed by other young.

NDP: 'Germany must be reunited; powers alien to our part of the world must cease to interfere in the affairs of Europe.'

Others: 'You are talking of America. How can you speak of them as "alien"? Who do you think kept us afloat after the war? Who in fact made us rich? And reunite Germany? How? You are only appealing to sentiment – your people don't know any more than anyone else how it could be done.'

NDP: 'Foreign workers are filthy, lecherous and taking the jobs of Germans.'

Others (shoulders shrugging): 'Yes, they are dirty and rude. But if they weren't here, who would do menial jobs? Germans won't do them.'

NDP: 'We are paying for the whole development of Israel out of a misplaced sense of guilt. And we pay billions elsewhere in compensation. How long must this go on?'

On this one point, although defended by an idealistic few, most young Germans appear to agree. This matter is as important to them as it is misunderstood. As they *will not* learn facts they are ideal material for rumours, and the thought of all this money going out already rankles deeply. The fact is that the West German government has spent about ten times as much on compensation and pensions to *German* victims of the war as they have to 'victims of Nazi persecution'. And the payments abroad are ending now, while the others, in the public mind all lumped together, will of course continue indefinitely. Development aid to Israel will be provided on a loan basis, one of fifty similar trade agreements with underdeveloped nations.

While many young Germans have gone to Israel on 'friendship trips' organized by every kind of German youth organization, this has not proved a very successful endeavour, and many young Germans complain bitterly at the lack of 'friendliness' from young Israelis.

'What more can we do?' some Munich students said. 'We go there, we want to make friends – it's they who refuse to see us.'

Perhaps this is the clearest proof of all of their deplorable incomprehension of the past: their own twenty-two years is all they can consider – their own uninvolvement – and they find it quite incomprehensible that to the young Israelis this may not be long enough.

On the whole the lunatic fringe among the German young is infinitesimal and, as can be seen, the positive as yet far outweighs the negative in their attitudes. But this is because they are young – and the instincts of the young are almost always towards the 'good'. Unfortunately as they grow older in this same environment, subject to the same influences, this cannot but change.

It is too much to ask of a youth to grow up without a sense of national dignity. But no one can confer this dignity upon the German young except German adults. And dignity can only come out of truth.

If – soon – the German youth cannot find dignity, they will look for pride. Dignity grows and lives in freedom. Pride can arise out of oppression. An enormous and belated effort of courage is required of the adults of West Germany: they must free their children, against themselves.

This is a German story – let it be ended by a young German . . . 'We need to be free to stop bowing and curtsying. We need to arrest this eternal German process whereby we always feel inferior to someone in an iron hierarchy, both within the family and without. But if this were possible . . . if from somewhere, out of the air, we could take the capacity for revolt, do you know what it would mean? It would mean saying to our parents: "It can be done. *You* didn't do it". It would mean saying to those we love: "We accuse you."'

20 March 1967

The intellectual élite in Germany today is minute. It is here that the country is most heavily paying the price for its own past. The physical and moral decimation of the adult population has tragically reduced the number of genuinely superior men and women who are also morally qualified for leadership. This tiny group, with awesome determination and energy, is attempting to exert its influence in nearly every field of endeavour. There is no doubt at all that among them there is a far greater awareness of the dangers in Germany than there is outside Germany's borders; no doubt either that this group is less willing to make moral compromises or concessions than many a well-meaning muddled thinker abroad.

Because 'élite' in the particular situation of Germany cannot be restricted entirely to the exceptionally brilliant, it includes now also a number of men and women who ordinarily would be leading very anonymous lives. Primarily civil servants, they have become part of this opinion-developing group only because they themselves were presented with such stark and compelling facts that they were driven into action.

These are the lawyers – the judges, prosecutors and the defence attorneys too, who are concerned with the most extreme and most controversial of the attempts towards achieving some sort of clarification of the past, the trials for the National Socialist crimes of violence. *These are not war crimes trials. They are trials for civil murder.* Here, against a background of basic and violent emotions, and representing the bitterly unwilling conscience of their countrymen, *German* courts, *German* lawyers are attempting to solve an unprecedented moral problem, of unprecedented legal dimensions.

A total of 61,761 people, with very few exceptions almost all former members of the SS or SD, have so far been investigated, the vast majority within the past ten years, since Germany regained her sovereignty. At a cost of approximately £10 million, 150 major trials have taken place in the eleven states (*Länder*) of West Germany since 1958, and in all of them the defendants were accused of specific individual acts of murder, or of being accessory to murder. For ten years now, approximately 250 prosecutors and judges and 300 police officers have worked full time on the investigations into Nazi crimes.

Very few originally came into this work by choice. In almost all of them it has caused tremendous intellectual, moral and personal quandaries, and yet most of them are committed to the necessity for the trials and – though often unhappily – to the necessity of their own part in them.

Perhaps it is an irony of fate, or of general human psychology, that the *Ausland* – all the other nations – who, according to the Germans, concentrate so exclusively on Germany's past, are quite unaware of the mammoth effort that is being made here. The instinct to forget that which is too awful to remember is not limited to Germany.

In nine cities of West Germany and in East Berlin I spent many hours talking with lawyers who work on these Nazi trials. There was not a single one of them who did not say: 'These are *murderers*. And murder cannot go unpunished.'

'It's not true,' many other Germans said to me. 'It only happened because of the war. Wars create special circumstances. It isn't fair to try people twenty or twenty-five years later for so-called war crimes. Thirty million blameless young have grown up – been born – since then. Retributive justice isn't just, it isn't even legal. Statutes of limitations exist in all countries.'

All the misunderstandings, all the confusion that is rampant in Germany about these trials, is in these sentences.

The circumstances of the war may have assisted the Nazis in carrying out their plans. But cataloguing the whole of European society – by no means only the Jews – into inferior racial groups was plainly stated in their pseudo-philosophical writings long before the war, and if one had but taken it more seriously, the plan for genocide and enslavement was implicit here.

The Allies until 1951, and since then the Germans, have persistently held trials for war crimes and Nazi crimes side by side. And yet these are two completely separate categories of crime: a war crime is a deed committed exclusively in connection with the war and could logically be subject to military courts martial. But Nazi crimes of violence are civil crimes, committed exclusively under the order of the SS, a uniformed *police* body *without military status*, against civilian population who were totally uninvolved in actions of war. 'To confuse these trials with trials for war crimes is madness,' says Staatsanwalt Richard Dietz, a slight sandy-haired young prosecutor with a narrow sensitive face. 'The result has been that the German people combine these two categories in their minds. It provides an easy way out . . . they say, well, the Russian civilians were killed because they were helping partisans, and the Jews wouldn't have been killed either if it hadn't been for the war. But it isn't true. They killed out of principle: the *Untermenschen* – the subhumans – were there to be used, or killed. They *said* so. It's murderers we are after. It's our duty to prosecute murderers.'

I attended sessions of several trials. Most large West German cities have now built new courts. They are always very modern, very light, very warm.

Perhaps the greatest shock comes because the proceedings, on the face of it, are so terribly ordinary.

The seats for the public are often filled with boys and girls – school classes brought by young teachers. The children munch sweets and chocolates. They chat and giggle.

Ten feet away, on three benches, sit the accused. Well dressed, ruddy faced, they too talk and laugh together. Defence counsel in black robes walk up and down the tiers, stop here and there, say a word, a smile, touch a shoulder.

These are the men. They are all so pink, so healthy, well preserved . . . it's like Madame Tussaud's come to life. One tries to look at them – they look like any other men. But one cannot meet their eyes – one looks away.

The prosecutors across the room are quieter. There are four of them – two on duty, two in reserve.

The court files in, the chatting ceases, we all stand up. Three judges (one presiding, two juniors), six jurors (among them two women) and alternate jurors who sit behind. Every provision is made to avoid a mistrial.

The German legal system is very different from ours. The judge has done his own investigations (after the prosecutor finished his) and has examined the accused in private. Now he conducts the trial, interrogates defendants and witnesses, and finally he will deliberate on judgement and sentence with the jury. This judge is a tall, slim man, about fifty-five, with greying hair. During the Third Reich he had abandoned law for an administrative post in the army. Now this is his third Nazi trial. He's had years of it. Earlier on, when he had talked to me, I thought I had detected a deep weariness and unease. But now his voice is quiet, almost without expression.

The first defendant is called to the stand – a table and a chair in the centre of the room, a microphone on the table. He walks the few steps to this seat very quickly. He is a man of fifty-two, married, three children. Profession: grocer. He sits with his back to us.

The judge: 'Herr R, let me just read to you what this part of the accusation says, and then we'll see what you have to say about it.' He reads, without expression: 'Johann R is accused, as SS chief of guards of the forced labour camp of T in June 1943, in the course of the liquidation of the city's ghetto, to have caught about sixty children under ten years of age who had tried to hide . . . to have stood them up alongside a pit, to have killed them individually through repeated blows on their heads with a hammer, whereupon the bodies fell into the pit, while their parents were forced to watch.'

The children behind me had stopped their fidgeting. Some were sitting very still; others had craned forward to hear better; a few had blushed; a few gone pale. The young teacher had been sitting, her chin supported by her hand. For a moment she leaned back and covered her eyes.

Judge: 'Well now, Herr R, you've heard the accusation. What do you have to say?'

R (portentous and fluent): 'I want to do everything to help the court, of course, but all this was so long ago.'

Judge: 'One could hardly forget such a scene – unless of course it happened so often . . .' He left the sentence hanging in the air.

'It is of course entirely untrue,' R said very quickly. 'Entirely a lie.'

Judge: 'Four witnesses are here to confirm what has just been read to you. They saw it happen. They will swear that they saw you do this.'

R (straightening up): 'Whatever was done, whatever we did, all of us, any of us, we did under orders.'

Judge: 'Did you know that no one is obliged to obey a criminal order? Did you know that this was part of the Army code and applied all through the time of the Third Reich?'

R: 'An order is an order.'

Judge: 'But these were children, small children.' He stopped for a moment, a visible effort at control. 'Tell me, Herr R did you consider Russians, Poles, Jews human, or not?'

The accused doesn't answer. The judge repeats the question, no answer. A defence counsel steps up to his client, bends down and whispers to him, he shakes his head. Defence counsel walks up to the bench and speaks quietly to the court. The judge shrugs.

'You can go and sit down for the moment,' he says stonily. 'You will be recalled later.'

Oberstaatsanwalt Kurt Tegge, forty-nine, of Hamburg, is a man of quick light movements. He has humour and spirit. He is chief of a large department conducting Nazi investigations and has worked on the trials for six years.

'No, I don't know how long I'll stay with it,' he says. 'It'll be a matter of conscience, but also simply how long I can stand it.' He tells me of nervous breakdowns among colleagues . . . of how a man's robustness is taken into account when he is considered for these assignments.

In a few months three Hamburg courts will hear trials of sixteen members of the Einsatzkommando 1005, the most secret of all the 'Special Commands' which were active all over Eastern Europe and the Balkans. 'It would really be impossible to guess how many murders the 1005 was responsible for,' Tegge says. 'Millions anyway.' In the case he will prosecute, three men are accused of the specific individual murder of 500 Russians and Poles who, having been forced to dig up and rebury murdered Jews, were themselves killed.

'The high SS officers who headed the sections of the 1005 were almost all originally trained in the euthanasia programme,' he said. 'That was in the very beginning – in 1938–9. We know now how it worked: they would be ordered to kill all patients in certain institutions and hospitals for the insane, incurably ill or severely retarded. They would be told that "this is a difficult job, but, for the sake of Germany, and the patients themselves, it has to be done". If it turned out that they were sickened by this assignment – and many were – they would be asked on another occasion to try again, and then once more. By the third time, they had either overcome their objections and revulsion and would then be considered capable of "hard" assignments – or else they had shown themselves incapable of this sort of work and were transferred to other duties. It is certain that this was quite deliberately used as the training ground for the SS. It was considered that if these men turned out to be capable of killing sick German children and old people, they'd be capable of anything. We've had numerous euthanasia trials in West Germany and there are more to come.'

The question of duress comes up in every trial. 'There is not one single case where a member of the SS or anyone else who refused to take part in the killings, was himself hurt in any way, and quite a few did refuse. We have their names,' Oberstaatsanwalt Tegge said. 'That doesn't mean that they weren't under pressure, or that it didn't harm their careers. Their records were marked as too soft, but all that usually happened was that they'd be transferred to different duties, often back in Germany. No, the men who did the killing, although conditioned for it by training, basically were "gifted" for it and did *not* feel "under duress". The insistence on secrecy, however, was absolute. If they talked about what they had seen or done, the chances were that they'd be shot immediately. That is why so many German people may have *guessed* something of what was happening, but so few really *knew*.'

In Hamburg there are another seventy cases under investigation. Three prosecutors and four police officers are working on the Warsaw Ghetto case alone.

In Düsseldorf I spent many hours with Oberstaatsanwalt Alfred Spiess who has recently been assigned by the new Minister of Justice of North Rhine-Westphalia to the task of co-ordinating and expediting prosecution of Nazi criminals in this state.

'A people cannot separate themselves from their history. You cannot say yes to Beethoven as part of you, and no to Hitler. The men who did this are living among us. If we don't call them to account for these crimes, we condone, again passively, what they have done.'

Alfred Spiess was prosecuting attorney in the Treblinka trial, held in Düsseldorf in 1964. (And four years later in the eight months' trial of Franz Stangl, commandant of Treblinka.) After pre-trial investigations lasting four years, ten men stood before the state court for eleven months, and 153 witnesses, men and women, were brought from eight countries to give evidence.

Today 'Treblinka' in the west of Poland is a large, empty tract of land, with straggling grass, and flowers, and a few pine trees. That indeed is what it must have looked like in July 1942 when the famous 'technicians' of the SS, looking for a site for an extermination camp, found it.

It is richer land today though, richer by (the most conservative count) 700,000 bodies which were buried there. 'Buried in circumstances and rites of a depravity such as the world cannot have known before,' Herr Spiess says. Treblinka – one of four extermination camps – was an industrial installation for the killing of men, women and children, the counting and freighting of their effects, and the efficient disposal of their bodies.

The camp was administered by 35 SS and 120 Ukrainian volunteer personnel, and had a constant prisoner-worker population of 1,000.

Treblinka existed for exactly one year and one week. 700,000. They came, handed in their belongings, had their hair cut off, stripped to the skin, stood in line to wait their turn, and then they went. The camp's commandant, Franz Stangl, told me that it took two to three hours to process 5,000 people. No one was there longer than that minimal time between early morning and noon. There was never any need for housing nor for food.

Who were the men who ran these places? What did they look like? What produced them? And what happened to them afterwards? Are they alive? If so, how are they living with themselves?

The courts of West Germany today try to show us. The defendant, under the West German system, gets endless opportunities to explain his reasons, feelings, possible outside influences.

We now meet monsters like Kurt Franz, who commanded Treblinka for its final weeks in the autumn of 1943 after Stangl had been transferred to Trieste. Men still handsome, healthy, in the prime of life and manhood, unvanquished men, unbent and unrepentant, men who for twenty years, until finally found and arrested, lived peaceful unhampered lives, married, sired children, earned their living, entertained their friends and neighbours. Kurt Franz is tall, light blond, of muscular graceful build, with a clean pink complexion and a roundish face. The prisoners called him Lalka, Polish for doll. 'I was good to my prisoners. They liked me,' he said.

Stangl, whose place he had taken, had kept back from the unendingly arriving transports famous architects, landscape designers, gardeners, sculptors. Treblinka was rebuilt. The barracks, the German quarters, watchtowers and gates of Camp I were all reconstructed in the style of the Middle Ages. Lawns and flower beds, and paths covered with fine white gravel; an adjoining zoological garden, nightingales in cages, squirrels; rustic benches, fountains and artistic sculpture.

Franz, on 3 September 1965, was convicted of murder in 35 cases involving 139 people – meaning that he himself, with his own hands, murdered 139 people – and of being accessory to the murder of 700,000. He was sentenced to life imprisonment, as were three others in this trial. All of these men, and six others who received lesser sentences, had lived under their own names in their own communities until arrested a few years before the trial. There are thousands like them all over West Germany.

'We can't allow it,' Oberstaatsanwalt Spiess said. 'I admit it, I can hardly stand the thought of such men living among us, going around free, being with children . . . among our children, *these* men.'

Spiess, like many of his colleagues, within a few months was caught up in the work . . . it became a mission. When the Treblinka trial was over he had a nervous breakdown. Even now, a year later, the tension is still there. He speaks in staccato sentences in a voice that shakes as he tells of his wife who 'is entirely in favour of these proceedings and my part in them'; of his seventeen-year-old daughter ('she has read widely about it and has been to the trial, with her school and alone') and his charming thirteen-year-old boy ('he wants to know about all this, and I tell him. They *must* know').

They must know. This, I suppose, is the very crux of the problem. The trials are reported almost verbatim by the German press and by radio and TV. Of the 1,460 newspapers and 30 magazines published in West Germany, an approximate 85 to 90 per cent are said to be in favour of continued trials.

However, the average German's almost automatic reflex upon seeing or hearing the term *NS Prozess* is to turn the page, or the knob. This is not all. The desperate rejection of history prompts other, more direct reactions: twenty-five miles from Stuttgart, just above the river Neckar, lies the small spa of Ludwigsburg, a particularly pretty baroque eighteenth-century town of 59,000 inhabitants. The town produces musical instruments and china and in the summer plays host to countless tourists. Since the autumn of 1958 they have accommodated a group of different guests, the 'Central Agency for Prosecution of Nazi Criminals'. This is a federal law agency, the first in German legal history. It was set up by a conference of the Ministers of Justice of the eleven West German *Länder*, not actually to prosecute, but to do research into large-scale Nazi crimes.

The director is Bavarian Oberstaatsanwalt Adelbert Rückerl, a big, thoughtful, slow-speaking man.

'We are responsible here for all preliminary investigations of the *Komplex*, the totality of each crime. We separate what can and cannot be brought to trial and once identities and probable degree of responsibility are established, the cases are referred for committal proceedings to the courts of the individual states where the defendants now reside. Pre-investigation of the *Komplex* takes about three years, committal proceedings in the *Länder* another four or so. There are now 110 people on our staff here; 28 are prosecutors, 22 judges, the rest lay assistants and secretaries.

'Unfortunately,' he says, 'we live in a certain isolation here. I try to meet people from the town – I think I know now one or two . . . of course, I've been here five years.'

The agency is housed in the former women's prison, a bleak building surrounded by a high wall. Inside it has been reconstructed, all very white and functional, with fluorescent lighting, blond office furniture, excessive central heating – it is all intensely impersonal and tidy.

Every one of the 110 employees, down to the most junior secretary, once they agree to take the job, has had to leave their town, their home, their families, many coming from as far as 700 miles away. They live in rented rooms or small hotels. Hardly any of them – even of the highest echelon – have brought their wives and families.

Two of the young prosecutors, thirty-six-year-old Richard Dietz and Hans Büschgens, thirty-three, sat with me around a small bare table in one of the glaringly bright offices.

Hans Büschgens is from North Rhine-Westphalia. Son of a labourer, he is married and has two young children. 'The people here have the gall to say we are "career-mad", or even worse, because we come to work here. I see my family once every six to eight weeks, if I'm lucky. We live in mingy little rooms and have our meals in indifferent pubs. Our heads are full of horror and death. We have no personal axe to grind – at our age there's no question of personal guilt. We now lead a completely abnormal life, only because we feel it has to be done. How can anyone believe that we would choose to live like this out of anything but conviction? We even try to start arguments with the townspeople. I argue with my landlady. After a year, she's just beginning to get an inkling of what I'm talking about – not because she's stupid, she's not. But because she doesn't want to hear, to know. You see, they say that the people we investigate "didn't know what they were doing", and "anyway, they were just obeying orders".

'They knew,' Dietz said bitterly. 'They knew. Now the people here say – they actually say it to us – that they are "sick and tired of hearing these lies about our soldiers". Perhaps it should be publicized more, not less, that 132 SS men in Byelorussia managed to kill 138,000 men, women and children in seven months by shooting each in the back of the neck as they knelt awaiting the shot, and carefully kept book while doing so. Can anyone really believe that it is possible for a man to do this without knowing what he is doing? That's what I'm working on, living with, now. Those are the men we try to bring to trial.'

Richard Dietz, like many of the young lawyers working on Nazi crimes, was a boy when the war ended. From a strictly Catholic farming family, he had been in the Hitler Youth like all other German boys. There are millions of young Germans like him. The drama lies in the intimate confrontation of these average men with extraordinary circumstances and events very few other people in their country really know – or want to know – about. None of the young prosecutors I met likes being in this job. But their resentment at what they are forced to discover exceeds their resentment at having to do the job at all.

The older ones too, after all, are just ordinary men who share the doubts, the guilt feelings, indeed the whole background of this Germany. They are not crusaders; at the same time they are not out for revenge. The conclusions they have reached are conclusions of despair. Dr Rückerl and I sat together late one night. He looked drawn and tired. He had shown me everything in the building, unspeakable letters and reports phrased in unspeakable bureaucratic terms treating the death of human beings not even as cattle, but as inanimate objects – not by numbers, but by weight; the files containing hundreds of thousands of documents and microfilms.

'The day will never come,' he said, 'when we can say "it's done now, it's finished". There is no end to it except a biological one, when at last they will all be dead. And *then* it will only be finished if, in the meantime, we have succeeded in teaching those who come after us. The only guarantee of it never happening again lies in knowledge. We try. All of us here go out and lecture in our free time wherever we are allowed, to the young, and so do prosecutors in other places.'

Again and again, all over Germany, the point was made to me that the German people on the whole had never accepted, hardly knew, that genocide was perpetrated on other people beside the Jews. The Jews too tend towards this misinterpretation of events. 'They killed 6 million Jews – we know,' says Herr Rückerl. 'But they also killed 5 million Russian civilians, 2 million Poles – including a large part of their finest intelligentsia – and a million other people: gypsies, German free-thinkers, and German insane or incurably sick . . . 8 million of what they chose to call "inferior stock". But these dreadful numbers – 14 million – they are not even the point, it's the basic insanity of categorizing humanity that matters. How can we make our people understand? And unless they understand this at least, how can we have any hope for the future?'

Certainly the citizens of Ludwigsburg do not understand. The mayor of the town said last year on German TV: 'I'm not saying the Central Agency is a burden to us, but certainly it doesn't help our reputation to have them here, because surely not only in this country, but abroad as well, there is a certain smell about them, and naturally this clings to our city.'

The Ludwigsburg attorneys don't think there are many large-scale crimes they now don't know about, but neither do they, or any of the other lawyers, think that everyone connected with them can be brought to trial.

There are two categories of people above all who – although guilty beyond a shadow of doubt – are free and will remain so. This causes tremendous bitterness, and confusion.

The first of these are the so-called *Schreibtischtäter* – the 'desk-murderers', the people who sat at their desk, quite often hundreds of miles away, and with one signature, or even one telephone call, condemned thousands to death. But legally this is an unprecedented problem; there is no legal way of indicting a man for murder because he signed a piece of paper. No one has as yet found a solution to this although there have been cases made against some of the most famous or infamous 'desk-murderers', first by the Allies in the first fervour and fury after the war, then in Eastern Europe where various special decrees have 'widened' the law, in Israel in the case against Eichmann, and lately two or three test cases in Germany too. One may be forgiven for feeling that at least in some nominal manner these people *must* be held to account for what they did. 'At the very least,' said the new Minister of Justice of North Rhine-Westphalia, Dr Josef Neuberger, 'separate them from public life, don't let them hold any kind of office.'

The second group of people who are at liberty while, by all counts they should be in gaol, are a considerable number of major Nazi criminals who, convicted by the Allies in the 1940s, were released in the course of Allied amnesties in the early 1950s and cannot be retried even on new evidence because a treaty signed in 1954 prohibits the Germans from repealing any decision or judgement rendered by the Allies.

It is unlikely that this situation can now change, at least until the formal peace treaty is signed between Germany and the Western Allies. In the meantime the schism is very wide and bewildering.

I saw the arrival of one witness at a trial now taking place. He arrived at the court building in a large shiny chauffeur-driven Mercedes. He wore a cashmere coat, his face and his whole person shone with prosperity and well-being, the chauffeur stood at near attention when opening the car door, a bowing attendant awaited him at the entrance doors.

'This,' I was told, 'is a man who was sentenced to death by the Americans in 1947; the sentence was commuted to life imprisonment after review. In 1951, under the provision of the general amnesty, with many others just as bad, he was released. Today, he is a millionaire industrialist.

'Of course,' my informant added, 'he is an excellent experienced administrator. During the Third Reich at a Ministry in Berlin he administered a "death department" – that's what we call it. You had to be pretty good at your job to do that.' He shrugged his shoulders. 'And *that*,' he said, 'is what we have to admit as witnesses here. *That* is what is running around free as the air while we . . . and quite rightly so, for they committed murder . . . try their former underlings for individual deeds.'

What then is one left with, after this exposure to this particular aspect of the German scene, an aspect which is so basic to their whole situation that it has contributed to every government crisis, and is a major policy of the disturbing new party, the National Democratic Party (NPD).

It takes time and effort, first of all, to regain one's own calm and composure. One has realized terribly quickly that twenty-five years, although the age of a new generation of man, is very little in the context of memory for those of us who, even though young in the war, had reached the age of reason. It was a time of terribly strong emotions for all of us, whether there or here, and these emotions can be submerged but not forgotten. In the rest of the world as well as in Germany the Second World War generation is still in control, and will be for some time to come. The men who are being tried in Germany are that same age, the same level of adulthood, the same human level of responsibility as are the judges, the jurors, the lawyers who try them, as are furthermore the teachers, the priests, the heads of government of all nations – *and* half the population of the world. They are therefore not old men of the past.

Unless for all time we were to accept that weakness, ignorance and being many rather than few is to constitute justification of crime in law, it would seem that the prosecution of these men in Germany is a foregone conclusion.

One would like to put it in these simplified terms. But alas, it is not possible – for the questions raised are many, and one must perforce join the Germans in their perplexities. Is it justifiable to hold these men responsible within present legal concepts for what they did twenty-five years ago under the laws of that period under deliberately created circumstances unequalled anywhere else in the history of the world? Also, are they not changed after this long time? Rehumanized? Rehabilitated?

How long is it to go on? For ever?

Is it not true that brutality and violence exist everywhere, that the killings of the Polish officers at Katyn, and of the Kulaks in the Ukraine, the excesses in Kenya and Vietnam are comparable to the Nazi murders?

Perhaps we should aim towards the establishment of a World Court where perpetrators of such acts – of and against whatever nation – could be prosecuted in the name of humanity and decency. When, as a world society, we get to the point when all nations will *accept* the authority of such a super-national body, we shall already be a long way toward the time when we would hardly *need* it.

However, there *are* degrees. In Germany, the only country where uniquely methodical mass murders have become part of a nation's psyche, the dilemma of justice now is deep indeed.

It is here that we have learned that there are subjective limitations to law. The Nazi trials are being held because the best in Germany feel that the integrity of society depends on the integrity of its laws. Unhappily here we have also learned that the law depends for its integrity on the integrity of society.

Understandably perhaps, West German society has so far been unable to accept the wilful murder of millions as individual crimes in law. We see ourselves faced therefore with the curious fact that the application of law – and this may be not only in Germany – is only acceptable to society to the extent to which the crimes it is concerned with are 'acceptable'. It is true that 'murder' in millions has a different sound and feel to it from the murder of 'one'. It is only when such acts are personalized, when one can hear, no, almost see, the details, that the sudden and terrible realization comes of the incredible and immeasurable value of one single human life. It is then and only then that whoever one is, of whatever age or nationality, one accepts with awe, humility and shame that 14 million were not 14 times six zeros, but warm and living human bodies, small and large, old and young who laughed, and cried, who loved and hoped and would have lived.

The fact is though that the criminals here, while vile and weak and a stain on the name of humanity as well as their own country, have basically become unimportant. Not only that: there is no penalty in law commensurate with these crimes. In the final analysis, any punishment handed out belittles the crime. What is important – no, imperative – is that their actions should at last be accepted by all the people of Germany for what they were: crimes of individual men, against individual human beings. The general recognition of these men's responsibility for their individual actions could lead to the essential acceptance in Germany – and perhaps elsewhere too – that any man can, but also must, bear the responsibility for himself and his own actions. The rejection of these persons by their own society could result in a redemption of sorts. If this could be made to happen, even at this late date, the integrity of those in Germany who insisted on the necessity for these trials would be vindicated, their tenacity rewarded. And the further prosecution of these individuals would at last become superfluous.

One would therefore hope that the Germans could see their way to make one huge – perhaps federal – effort to complete the trials by

1970 when the extended statute of limitations now runs out. But this effort should be supported at every level of government, by every educational and communication media, without mental reservations, without fear or favour, without consideration of yeas or nays from foreign countries: one final public recognition of the truth – a catharsis they have never had and desperately need. This then might indeed become for them an end and a beginning.

5

Colloquy with a Conscience

February 2000

The decision in December 1970 to spend time with Franz Stangl had not been easily made and John Anstey's support for this open-ended project not easily obtained. He was tired of concentration camp memories, as in fact I was too. Furthermore, the long ramblings of Rudolf Höss, commandant of the huge labour camp at Auschwitz (not of the subcamp Birkenau where the gassings took place and which had its own commandant), with pathologically inflated numbers of the dead drawn out of him in his prison euphoria by his Polish interrogators, had been published in America not long before. (These mad figures which, however wild and however often rectified later, became part of the record, would contribute to the persistent historical error – immensely helpful to revisionists who claim the gas chambers never existed – of establishing Auschwitz in the world's mind as the 'largest extermination camp').

It was only after weeks of talks, during which I finally convinced Anstey of the fundamental difference, still not understood by the public anywhere, between concentration and extermination camps and between the men who worked in these so very different installations, that he saw the potential in my proposal.

By the time I had gone to Düsseldorf in December 1970 for the last weeks of Stangl's eight-month trial, I had attended dozens of West German NS trials over the previous four years, some for weeks at a time. Though I was often on assignment, I went to others at my own expense, partly because I needed to know, and later because I was by then looking for one man.

The process of observing men and women accused of the most awful acts, and listening to their accusers describing dreadful suffering, was emotionally numbing. But what depressed me more, was not only that in many cases the results were inconclusive, but that what we heard finally taught us so little. The results were not inconclusive because anyone doubted the witnesses' testimony. It was always essential to retain an open mind, but doubts were hardly possible: the experiences the witnesses described were the most harrowing one could imagine any human beings having endured and were therefore seared into their minds and bodies. And, contrary to the almost invariably elderly and physically fragile witnesses two decades and more later, in the 1990s, whose memories some of us would consider dubious, these witnesses were recalling relatively recent events – just twenty-three years previously at most.

The reason why many of the trials were finally inconclusive was because, in these places of daily systematic assembly-line killing of thousands of naked people who were not registered when they arrived and left no trace when a few hours later they had gone, evidence of individual acts of murder by the accused, which German law stipulated as a condition of conviction, was extremely difficult to establish and many men got off who were doubtlessly guilty. But what I found finally more frustrating was that what we heard added so little to the knowledge we already had. I do not mean knowledge of the events in the camps, but about the nature of the men in Berlin who had unleashed these horrors (none of whom, except for the bureaucrat Eichmann, was ever tried), and the personalities and inner lives of those who, in those isolated installations from hell in the midst of the deep forests of occupied Poland, executed their orders. All of them appeared similarly primitive, and of similarly limited intelligence, none of them adding even in the slightest degree to our understanding – not of the processes by which such crimes could have come about, but of how they, individual men or women, could have carried them out.

When, sometime in 1968, I realized that this was the reason for my frustration, I decided to try to find one perpetrator if possible less primitive and with at least a semblance of moral awareness, who, if approached not as a monster but as a human being, might be able to explain his own catastrophic moral failure. During my comparatively long attendance at individual trials I had made a number of friends among prosecutors, lawyers and judges, and it was Alfred Spiess, chief prosecutor in the 1964 Treblinka trial and, in 1970, at the long trial of Franz Stangl, who telephoned me in London that October and told me that he thought Stangl, who was testifying at that point, might be the man I was looking for. I went to Düsseldorf the next day and, as Spiess thought, found Stangl more complex, more open, serious and even sad than any of the others I had observed: the only man with such a horrific record who appeared to manifest a semblance of conscience. When I went back in December for the last two weeks of his trial, at the end of which Stangl was sentenced to life imprisonment for co-responsibility in the murder of 900,000 people in Treblinka,* I met his wife who had come from Brazil to be with him for the verdict and told her what I wanted to do. The morning I was flying back to London, 23 December 1970, she told me he had agreed to talk with me if I could obtain the necessary permissions. It took another three months to get a book I was still working on (*The Case of Mary Bell*, Methuen, 1972) ready for publication and to persuade the relevant German judicial and prison authorities, and John Anstey, to support the project.

Of the many friendships that had developed for me during the 1950s in West Germany, the most valuable, particularly for the work with Stangl, was that with Klaus and Ruth-Alice von Bismarck and their eight children. I think if anyone has specifically, though never intentionally, influenced my attitude towards Germany, it was this in many ways ideal German post-Hitler family group, which in the course of time would come to include nieces and nephews and then the younger ones' husbands, wives and children, many of whom I would stay with for weeks and even months in the course of my work.

Klaus and Ruth-Alice, like all of the Bismarck family – Klaus was a great-nephew of the Iron Chancellor and Ruth-Alice a member of another distinguished landowning family, the von Wedemeyers – were

* The first official figure issued by the Poles was 400,000, the second, 700,000. At the Nuremberg Trial, the cited figure was 900,000. And in 1971, the stationmaster of Treblinka, who had registered the transports car by car as they arrived, calculated the figure as 1,100,000.

Prussians and devout Christians.* After 1945, when their part of the country was ceded to Poland, they became refugees in West Germany. After sixteen years of increasingly high positions for Klaus in social, youth and labour work (in all of which Ruth-Alice actively participated – she would eventually become President of the Society for Evangelical-Jewish ecumenism) and finally as member of the synod of the German Protestant Church, in 1961 he became Director-General (*Intendant*) of WDR (West German Radio and Television). In 1977, at sixty-five, he crowned an extraordinary career of public service by becoming president of the Goethe Society.

I had stayed with the Bismarcks repeatedly over the years in their large house in Cologne, so moving into the familiar guest-room two days before beginning the work with Stangl in Düsseldorf prison was like coming home. None of us knew how long it would take, nor how I or indeed they and their children, seven boys and one girl then aged between ten and twenty-five, would react to the experience.

Superfically, the days very quickly took on a routine: we all, including their *Hausdame* (housekeeper) of many years, had breakfast together in the kitchen at 7 a.m. Three quarters of an hour later, the children had left for school, Klaus for his office and I for the station to take my train to Düsseldorf, a trip of 40 minutes. By 9 a.m., with plastic beakers of coffee from the station buffet on the table, I was sitting in the cell-like room on the second floor of the prison where my conversations with Stangl took place, in the morning from nine to twelve, in the afternoon from one-thirty to five. Most days I spent a little time after we finished with the prison director Eberhard Mies and his wife, who were deeply interested in my project and had been very helpful in getting me access to Stangl. By 6.30 I was back in Cologne. Supper was at seven in the dining-room, after which – a family custom throughout the Bismarck children's lives with which I was familiar from previous visits – all of us repaired to Klaus's study (*die Höhle*) to discuss what everybody had been doing during the day and, quite often,

* Ruth-Alice's sister, Maria von Wedemeyer, who died in 1977, was pastor Dietrich Bonhoeffer's fiancée. In 1993, forty-eight years after Bonhoeffer was hanged in Flossenburg concentration camp less than one month before the end of the Third Reich, Ruth-Alice published their wonderful 'Loveletters from Cell 92' (Harper Collins, 1994).

to listen to music or readings from books, the Bible and, frequently, newspapers or magazines.

Although the purpose of these evening gatherings – to uphold a mutual openness within the family – was never forgotten, it did become somewhat submerged by the interest of both parents and all but the two youngest children in what I was trying to do with Stangl. For me, the extent of their curiosity, and the reactions and questions, particularly of the young, were more valuable than I could ever have expected. Years later I would remember this when Albert Speer tried to explain to me how he approached the writing of *Inside the Third Reich* and why what was eventually printed was different in many places from the draft he had written in Spandau prison.

'I wanted to talk to young people,' he said (not to his own children but) '. . . with . . . people who had nothing to do with me, who felt no need to protect me and who, I thought, would not hesitate to attack or contradict me.' And when he did, he realized, he said, 'what it was young people wanted to know . . . that there were still things I hadn't sufficiently considered, and thus (that there were) many answers missing in my "Spandau draft"'.

This is akin to what happened to me on those evenings in Klaus Bismarck's *Höhle*: I had talked for years to innumerable people, older and young, about their feelings about the Third Reich, but this was different. With Stangl and Treblinka we were at the abyss.* And these young people, some of them nearer childhood than adulthood, understanding this, asked questions and made arguments which in their simple profundity helped me every night towards taking a step further with Stangl the next day. How, they asked, could someone even nominally Christian become so deeply involved in horrifying events of this kind? How could it be that his wife, a practising Catholic, did not stop him? The Bismarck parents told me that the children took these questions to school, involved their friends and teachers, and that our conversations in the *Höhle* over those weeks have remained with them all for the rest of their lives.

As I describe in the pages which follow, I told Stangl at the start of

* *Am Abgrund* as I would later title the German edition of *Into That Darkness*, a title unfortunately changed at its most recent publication there.

these encounters what I was aiming for and that none of it was meant to or would help him in his forthcoming appeal against the life sentence, and he accepted this. By the time I met him, he had been in prison, first in Brazil awaiting his extradition, then in Germany, for over four years. The difference between him and others, as I had hoped, was that although he was still 'blocking' any acknowledgement of personal guilt, it became obvious very soon that he had been capable of using this long solitary confinement to ponder the circumstances which had brought him to where he was, and to do a considerable amount of reading. In the pages which follow (and of course in *Into That Darkness*) I have tried to provide a description of what this confrontation with his own guilt which I then forced upon him did to Stangl, and what being there was like for me.

During this agonized process, Stangl had many moments of despair, particularly as he came to realize that even if by some miracle his, then pending, appeal was granted, his life was over because he knew that his wife, now not only fully aware of what he had done but of the world's contempt for him, could never live with him again. Nevertheless, the whole experience was a huge relief to him. At the end of it – I had no doubt about it and his wife would years later in Brazil show me a letter in which he had said so explicitly – he wanted to die, and I was neither surprised nor sorry when he did indeed die of a heart attack, nineteen hours after I left him.

For me, being with this man showed me as no other could have done the very essence of the process of corruption. It was an experience I might not have given myself had I known what it would do to me. I have often been asked why I did do it, what drew me to this awful task. All I could ever say was that, no, it wasn't an 'obsession with evil' as has been suggested in connection with that and other books, or some religious fervour to help a sinner towards redemption; and it certainly wasn't, as some have suspected, ambition for fame or riches. I think my reason for doing the things I do, is and always has been quite simply – or perhaps not so simply – a need, a drive to know. The price one pays (and, selfishly, expects the people one loves to pay) for giving in to this inner need, in shock, in tension and in a very particular kind of fatigue, can be high.

Perhaps something that happened when I was about half-way

through the conversations with Stangl, can illustrate these tensions. It happened on an evening after I had stayed late talking to the prison director and the Düsseldorf station platform was virtually empty as I waited for my train. I heard the sound of crying . . . of many children crying, it seemed to me . . . for a long time before a freight train, slowing down during its passage through the station, went past us. And as it rolled through – the cries by now, I thought, desperate – I saw parts of pale small faces pressing against the narrow openings in each car. I'm not given to fainting, but I blacked out. The railway worker who helped me up told me the freight train carried cattle. It was calves, calves crying just like children. I can still hear them now, as I write.

In the weeks I worked with Stangl, I barely slept; in the years afterwards, when I prepared and wrote *Into That Darkness*, a nightmare of harm coming to my young daughter – the kind of harm Stangl so graphically described to me – pursued me virtually every night. 'If one exposes oneself to the devil,' a kind bishop at the Vatican warned me a year or so later, 'he can invade one. Be careful, my child,' he said, and made the sign of the cross on my forehead.

October 1971

After an eight months' trial, considered by the Germans the most important Nazi-crime (NS) trial to be held in Germany since Nuremberg, Franz Stangl, *Kommandant* of the extermination camp Treblinka in Poland from August 1942 to August 1943 (and Sobibor for the preceding four months), was sentenced on 22 December 1970 to life imprisonment for co-responsibility for the murder of 900,000 men, women and children in Treblinka during the year of his command. While the evidence presented in the course of the trial did not prove Stangl himself to have committed specific acts of murder, it did prove to the satisfaction of the judges that by virtue of his attitude and the orders he gave, enforced and/or approved in his role of camp commander, he was an active participant in the murder of the prisoners.

'Franz Stangl,' said Chief Prosecutor Alfred Spiess, 'is the highest ranking official of a deathcamp we have been able to try. The only other one of similar importance was Höss, the commandant of Auschwitz, who was tried and executed by the Poles immediately after the end of the war. The few others there were of this rank either committed suicide before coming to trial or – like Mengele – escaped.'

Stangl, too, had originally escaped: held in Austria after the war by the Americans, who did not at the time identify him with the extermination camps, he was turned over to the Austrians in 1947 to be tried for his part in the euthanasia *Aktion* in 1941. He escaped from remand prison in May 1948. Passing through the 'Vatican Escape Route', he went first to Syria and later, in 1951, after he had been joined in Damascus by his family, to Brazil where he lived quite openly under his own name until 'Nazi-hunter' Simon Wiesenthal found him in 1967.

'I looked for him for years,' said Herr Wiesenthal, director of the Jewish Archives of Nazi Crimes in Vienna. 'I was sure he would have changed his name – that's where I lost time. Even when I heard that he had been seen in São Paulo I looked for him under an assumed name. When I finally got him I addressed myself to Robert Kennedy. He was a great man. He said, "There is no statute of limitations to a moral obligation." And he let the Brazilians know that America would not be pleased if there was any delay in the agreement to Stangl's extradition. His intervention at that time affected the subsequent attitude of all South American governments: they found out where America stood.'

Herr Wiesenthal says that he has (so far) tracked down 1,100 Nazis in hiding, among them Adolf Eichmann for the Israelis. But he feels that finding Stangl was at least as important. 'The Stangl case,' he says, 'provided West Germany with its most significant criminal case of the century. If I had done nothing else in my life but to get this evil man, I would not have lived in vain.'

It was very difficult to associate the quiet courteous man I found in the Düsseldorf prison with this description.

Franz Stangl, tall, with receding grey hair, a deeply lined face and red-rimmed eyes, was sixty-three years old when we began our conversations in April 1971. During the three-year pre-trial preparations (at which time this prison also accommodated several of his former subordinates, among them the notoriously brutal Kurt Franz who briefly commanded and then liquidated Treblinka after Stangl was relieved), he was kept in the strictest isolation in his six- by twelve-foot cell. But even after the other Treblinka men, their sentences confirmed, were moved to another prison, it emerged that several young prisoners had muttered threats against Stangl's life and he remained in isolation for his own protection. Just before Easter his increasing state of depression decided the prison authorities, who run an enlightened institution, to allow him a daily hour of exercise in the prison yard and gradually some contact with selected prisoners. 'But even now, he hardly talks to anyone,' said the guards. 'He is a loner.'

Despite his sedentary life – most of his day in his light, modern cell was spent reading and listening to the radio – Stangl was muscular, straightbacked and disciplined.

'No, thank you very much,' he said, when I offered him chocolate biscuits the first day we talked. 'I don't want to taste anything I may not be able to have in the future.' He spoke the soft German of his native Austria in the semi-formal way it is taught in Austrian provincial schools. His voice was as quiet as his bearing. Only his broad red workman's hands were in slight discord with the overall impression he gave (in no way diminished by his obvious apprehensions about our meeting) of an imposing and dominant personality, very different from the 'small man' I had expected to find.

He and the prison governor, Herr Eberhard Mies, a former lawyer, shook hands and bowed when they met on the occasion of my first visit. They discussed the facilities available for the prisoners: chess, discussion groups, and soon technical college courses. 'I have signed up for the chess club,' Stangl informed the governor conversationally. 'I think I'll attend some classes too when they start.' (Two weeks later he joined a twice-weekly course in literature.)

Prison staff in West Germany are well trained (the courses include 200 hours of lectures in psychology). In this huge remand prison in a bleak suburb of Düsseldorf they appear to be an articulate and compassionate group of men who, intensely interested in what these conversations would produce, spoke freely about the complicated conflicts Stangl's presence in the prison brought to their minds. Many of them question – as do most people in Germany – the continuation of these Nazi-crime trials so many years after the events. At the same time almost all of them agree unhappily that as long as any of these men are alive, it is immoral to do nothing. A young prison officer who was not yet born in the early 1940s spoke thoughtfully about the problem that moved him most. 'He seems to us like a *man*,' he said, 'you know what I mean: an intelligent human being. Not a brute like Franz. Perhaps now, at long last, someone is going to have the courage to explain to my generation how any individual with mind and heart and brain could – not even "do" what was done – it isn't our function to say whether a man is "guilty as charged" or not – but even see it being done, and consent to remain alive.'

But all the staff liked the prisoner. 'If they were only all like Stangl [some of them – a subtle and indicative difference – said "like *Herr* Stangl"] our life would be a bed of roses.'

Later I told Stangl that the guards seemed well-disposed towards him. 'I see no reason to complicate their lives,' he said. 'If I conduct myself properly towards them, they will behave properly towards me. It is all a matter of accommodating oneself to one's situation.'

The need to 'accommodate' himself to a situation appears to have followed Franz Stangl from the cradle. He was born in Altmunster, a small town in Austria, on 26 March 1908. His only sister was then ten, his mother still young and pretty but his father already an ageing man. 'He was a nightwatchman by the time I was born. But all he could ever think about were his days as a *Dragoner* (one of the Imperial élite regiments). His *Dragoner* uniform, always carefully brushed and pressed, hung in the wardrobe. I was so sick of it, I got to hate uniforms,' Stangl said. 'I knew since I was very small, I don't remember exactly when, that my father hadn't really wanted me. I heard them talk. He thought I wasn't really his. He thought my mother . . . you know . . .'

'*Even so, was he kind to you?*'

He laughed without mirth, 'He was a *Dragoner*. Our lives were run on regimental lines. I was scared to death of him. I remember one day – I was about four or five and I'd just been given new slippers. It was a cold winter morning. The people next door to us were moving. The moving van had come – a horsedrawn carriage then, of course. The driver had gone into the house to help get the furniture and there was this wonderful carriage and nobody about. I ran out through the snow, new slippers and all. I climbed up and I sat in the driver's seat, high above the ground, everything as far as I could see quiet and white and still. Only far in the distance there was a black spot in the whiteness of the new snow. I watched it but I couldn't recognize what it was until suddenly I realized it was my father coming home. I got down as fast as I could and raced back through the deep snow into the kitchen and hid behind my mother. But he got there almost as fast as I. "Where is the boy?" he asked and I had to come out. He put me over his knees and "leathered" me. He had cut his finger some days before and wore a bandage. He thrashed me so hard, the cut opened and blood poured out. I heard my mother scream, "Stop it, you are splashing blood all over the clean walls."'

When Stangl was eight – two years after the beginning of the First World War – his father died of malnutrition. A year later his mother married a widower who also had two children.

'*Did he treat you like his own son?*'

'He was all right.' He paused. 'Well, of course, I wasn't his son, was I?' He paused again. 'I remember, sometimes I felt jealous of his own boy who was just my age.'

'*Did you have many friends?*'

'No. But when I was fourteen I taught myself to play the zither and I joined the zither club.' He began to cry quietly, wiping his eyes with the back of his hand. 'Excuse me.'

He left school at fifteen and became an apprentice weaver. 'I finished my apprenticeship in three years,' he said. 'When I was eighteen and a half I became the youngest master weaver in Austria.' He was still proud of this achievement now. 'I worked in the mill and two years later I had fifteen workers under me. I earned 200 schillings a month. I gave four-fifths of it to my parents.'

'*Is that all you kept for yourself? At twenty, was that enough?*'

He smiled. 'I was making twice that by giving zither lessons at night.'

'*Did you have more friends by then?*'

'No. But I had the zither. On Sundays I built myself a sailboat.' Again he began to cry and continued for a long time. 'Excuse me . . .'

'*What is it that makes you cry when you remember this?*'

'It was my happiest time.' He shook his head again and again.

By 1931, at twenty-three, five years after becoming a master weaver, he had come to realize that he was at a dead end.

'Without "higher" education I couldn't get further promotion. But to go on doing all my life what I was doing then? Around me I saw men of thirty-five who had started at the same age as I and who were now old men. The work was too unhealthy. The dust got into your lungs – the noise . . . I had often looked at young policemen in the streets: they looked so healthy, so secure, you know what I mean. And so clean and spruce in their uniforms . . .'

'But you hated uniforms?'

He looked surprised. 'That – that was different.'

He applied to join the police and went for an interview. 'It was quite difficult, quite an exam you know.'

Several months later, when he had already more or less given up hope, he was notified that he was to report within days to the *Kaplanhof* – the police training barracks in Linz (capital of Upper Austria).

'I went to see the *Direktor* of the mill and explained why I'd made that decision. He said, "Why didn't you come and talk to me about it rather than do it secretly? I intended to send you to school, in Vienna." ' He cried again.

'Couldn't you have changed your plans when he told you that?'

He shook his head. 'He didn't ask me.'

The Austrian police training was tough. 'They called it the Vienna School,' he said. 'They were a sadistic lot. They drilled the feeling into us that everyone was against us: that all men were rotten.'

He stayed at the school for a year, then became a 'rookie'. Working first as a traffic policeman and then on the flying squad (riot squad), he graduated in 1933.

In July 1934, after the assassination of Dollfuss ('Of course the Nazis killed him,' he said), he found a Nazi arms cache in a forest, a feat which three months later earned him a decoration – the Austrian Eagle with green-white ribbon – and a posting to the CID school. 'That was the beginning,' he said now, grimly. This medal, and the reason for it, was to become a sword of Damocles for him a few years later, and the training at the CID school the first step 'on the road to catastrophe'.

In the autumn of 1936 he was transferred to the political division of the CID in the town of Wels, at that time a hotbed of Nazi activities. 'I was just getting married. Wels was a very nice place to live in, and the assignment was considered a great plum for a man not yet 30,' Stangl said.

'*What were your duties in your new assignment?*'

'Well, you know what Austria was like then. We had to ferret out anti-government activities by anyone: Social Democrats, Communists and Nazis.'

'*But perhaps seeing it was Wels, and the way many of you felt privately about the Nazis, perhaps you acted a little less severely, did you, against the Nazis than the others? A little differently in your manners?*'

'Among the eighteen men in that department there were certainly some who favoured the Nazis,' he answered. 'But in general, you know, the Austrian police was very professional. Our job was to uphold the law of the land. And on the whole that's what we did, never mind who was involved.'

'*But surely for an intelligent man in the midst of the political turmoil of Austria at that time, it was impossible not to form his own ideas. What did you yourself feel about the Nazis then?*'

Stangl had a curious habit, which was to become very familiar in the days to come, of changing from the semi-formal German he usually speaks, to the popular vernacular of his childhood whenever he had to deal with questions he found difficult to answer. In this perilous first attempt at self-examination, the 'cosy' language and mannerisms of his childhood were his instinctive refuge from danger: danger from within now, not without.

'You know, outside of course of doing my job properly, I wasn't really very interested,' he said. 'You see, I had just got married. I had for the first time a home of my own. All I wanted was just to close the door of my house and be alone with my wife. I was mad about her. I really wasn't political you see. I know it sounds now as if I should – or must have been. But I wasn't. I was just a police officer doing a job.'

'*But a job you liked?*'

'Oh yes, I liked it. But there was nothing heinous or even very dramatic about it then. It was just a job one tried to do as correctly – as kindly if you like – as possible.' He paused. 'Of course, it all changed on 13 March 1938.'

'Had you known in advance that the Germans were coming that day?'

'Oh no. I suppose there were people among our lot who knew, but I didn't. You have no idea though how organized they were, nor how frightened we became at once.' In his account of these times Stangl manifested a prodigious memory. By noon of the third day of our meetings he had mentioned fifty-four names, mostly of people who had only briefly crossed his path. 'What affected us quite a lot though,' he continued, 'was Cardinal Innitzer's call to Catholics to co-operate. But I felt above all fear. You remember that medal I'd been given – the Eagle? Well, five people had received that at that time. The Nazis took over on the 13th: on the 14th they arrested two of the five who had the Eagle, a few days later a third. That left only my friend Ludwig Werner and myself. Meanwhile in Linz they had shot two of the chiefs of our department. People we'd seen just a few days before, no trial, nothing – just shot them. Another one, a friend of mine, was arrested too. I remember one of the other men in my section – his name was Hermann Treidl – he said to me, "You'd better let your Eagle fly out of the window." Werner and I were becoming frantic. We had all been given a questionnaire to fill out. One of the questions – the most important we thought – was whether we had been illegal party members. Werner said we had to *do* something – we couldn't just sit and wait for them to take us. First we flushed our filecards (about Nazis) which had notes in our handwriting on them, down the lavatory. And then Werner remembered a man – a lawyer – a Nazi, who he, another colleague and I had helped a bit not long before . . .'

'What do you mean "helped"?'

'It's the sort of thing one was able to do at times before '38: just quietly warn someone who was under suspicion, to watch his step.'

'Nazis?'

'Not necessarily. Anybody nice – decent you know.' It was essential to let him develop his story in his own way. I intended to challenge evasiveness only on the most crucial points. This was not one of them.

'Werner thought we could ask this lawyer – Dr Bruno Wille was his name – to say that he knew we had been illegal members.'

'Did it work?'

'Yes. Werner went to see him and he said he'd arrange for our names to appear on the illegal party lists of the previous two years. So we said on the questionnaire that we'd been party members since 1936.'

'*And that wasn't true?*'

He shook his head. 'No. I went home that day, you know terrifically relieved. I was so grateful to Werner for finding that solution – you have no idea. Anyway, the moment I got home I told my wife: I thought she'd be as relieved as I . . .' suddenly he cried again, but differently this time, the deep sobs of a man reliving a pain long supressed.

'*What happened?*'

'She hated them you see,' he finally went on. 'We are Catholics, of course – she is very devout, always was. She was so terribly angry. "You betrayed me with these swine," she said, and I suddenly realized that she didn't believe me. She thought I really had been an illegal Nazi. Oh my God . . .' He cried again for many minutes.

'*Did you end up by convincing her?*'

'A long time – it took a long time.' It was clear he is still not sure he ever convinced her.

'*What was your first specific contact with the Jewish situation in Austria after the* Anschluss*?*'

'At that time they said that what they wanted was to force the Jews to emigrate – you know, just leave.'

'*That's what you thought the policy was?*'

'It *was* the policy. They had set up a special section of the Gestapo, for "Jewish Action" – Section IIB2, where they established a register of Jews and their property.' (In Berlin, the main office of this department was called IVB4.)

'*What did you have to do with that?*'

'In principle nothing. I was in the political section, 2C. But you see I think they knew how I felt. You know: that I wasn't *really* with them. Because after the "Kristallnacht" (November 1938) the gauleiter – Eigruber – called me in and he advised me to keep my mouth shut and help IIB2 whenever I was asked.'

'*Didn't that sound sufficiently ominous to you to indicate that this was the moment to get out?*'

'But you see, it wasn't ominous then, and it wasn't a question of "getting out": if it had only been as simple as that. By this time every day we heard of this one and that one being arrested, sent to a KZ (concentration camp) – shot. It wasn't a matter of choosing to stay or not stay in our profession. What it had already become, so quickly, was a question of survival.'

In time the political branch of the police was incorporated into the Gestapo. Shortly after this, in January 1939, the Gestapo offices of the police in Wels were moved to Gestapo HQ in the provincial capital, Linz. 'Our chief was now a German,' Stangl said. 'A terrible reactionary from Munich, Georg Prohaska. Soon after we were transferred some man came from Berlin and "In the name of the Führer" read out our new ranks. Me, they appointed *Kriminalassistent* in the name of the Führer. But I wasn't having it: that was a reduction in rank, not a promotion.'

'*Was this ever rectified?*'

'Oh yes, a few weeks later. They acknowledged they'd made a mistake and confirmed my status of *Beamter auf Lebenszeit* as they called it. And they promoted me to *Kriminaloberassistent*, the equivalent of what my next promotion would have been in Austria. But Prohaska had found out that I wasn't somebody who'd allow himself to be pushed around and he hated me from that moment on and made my life a misery. Not long afterwards I was ordered to sign a paper certifying that I was prepared to give up my religion.'

'*What exactly did it say on the paper?*'

'It said that I certified I was a *Gottgläubiger* [believer in God] but affirmed my agreement to break my affiliation to the Church.'

'*How did you feel about signing that?*'

'Well, of course I've always been a Catholic . . .' he stopped.

'*But?*' *He didn't answer.* '*Were you a regular churchgoer?*'

'My wife and children always go.'

'*Yes, but you?*'

'No,' he finally said. 'I always went at Christmas of course, and Easter . . .'

'*So signing this document wasn't really all that difficult, was it?*'

'I didn't like to.'

'*But it was a compromise you felt you had to make to keep your job?*'

'Not just my job, much more than that – as I told you before. By then I had heard that I had originally been on a list of officials to be shot after the *Anschluss*.

'I hate . . . I hate the Germans,' he suddenly said with passion, 'for what they pulled me into. I should have killed myself in 1938.' There was nothing maudlin about the way this was said: he was merely stating a fact. 'That's when it started for me. I must acknowledge my guilt.'

This, on the second day of our talks, was the only time he was to use this phrase in this direct way until almost the end. In his mind the later events in his life (which we were now approaching) were inseparable from these beginnings. When he volunteered an acknowledgement of guilt for his comparatively harmless failings at this stage of his life, it was because he *wanted* to say 'I am guilty' but could not pronounce it when he spoke of the murder of 900,000 people. Thus he sought to find an acceptable substitute for which he could afford to admit guilt. For, except for a monster, no man who *actually participated* can concede guilt for such a monstrosity and – as the young prison officer had said – 'consent to remain alive'.

In November 1940, Stangl, by now again promoted, was ordered to report for instructions to Berlin.

'The order was signed by Himmler,' he said, even now a tone of awe in his voice. 'It said I was transferred to the General Foundation for Institutional Care (Allgemeine Stiftung für Anstaltspflege) and that I was to report to *Kriminalrath* Werner at the *Reichskriminalpolizeiamt* Berlin, Werd'scher Markt 5.

'*Kriminalrath* Werner told me,' he continued, 'that it had been decided to confide to me the very difficult and demanding job of police superintendent of a special "Institute" which was administered by this foundation, the HQ of which was Tiergartenstrasse 4 in Berlin.'

'*Did you know then what Tiergartenstrasse 4 was?*'

'I had no idea. It had been vaguely mentioned now and then as T4, but I didn't know what its specific function was.'

(Tiergartenstrasse 4 was the hub of what was for years the most secret operation in the Third Reich: it was here that a very special group of men, all officially members of the *Führerkanzlei* (Führer's Chancellery) laid the plans first for the 'mercy-killings' of the mentally handicapped in Germany and Austria, and later the 'Final Solution': the extermination of the Jews (and gypsies). These were the planners: the so-called *Schreibtischtäter* (desk-murderers): Bouhler, Brack, Blankenburg, the deplorable psychiatrist Professor Heyde, and a host of others, all now dead, mostly by suicide.)

When Stangl began to speak of this I noticed for the first time an alarming change come over his face: it thickened and became slack and suffused. The veins stood out and the lines in his cheeks and on his forehead – immediately wet with sweat – deepened. This was to happen repeatedly when he had to speak about a new and terrible phase in his life.

'*Kriminalrath* Werner said that both Russia and America had for some considerable time had a law which permitted them to carry out euthanasia (mercy killings) – on people who were hopelessly insane or monstrously deformed. He said this law – already in existence everywhere else in the world – was going to be passed in Germany in the near future. But that, to protect the sensibilities of the population, *they* were going to do it very slowly, and only after a great deal of psychological preparation. But that in the meantime the difficult task had begun under the cloak of absolute secrecy. He explained that the only patients affected by this *Aktion* were those who after the most careful examination – a series of four tests carried out by at least two physicians – were considered absolutely incurable so that, he assured me, a totally painless death represented a real release from what, more often than not, was an intolerable life.'

'*What was your first reaction – your first thoughts when he said these things?*'

'I . . . I was speechless. And then I finally said I didn't really feel I was suited for this assignment. He was, you know, very friendly, very sympathetic when I said that. He said he understood well that that should be my first reaction but that I had to remember that my being asked to take this job showed proof of their exceptional trust in me. It was a most difficult task, they fully recognized it, but that I myself would have nothing whatever to do with the actual operation – this was carried out entirely by doctors and nurses. I was merely to be responsible for law and order.'

'*Did he specify what he meant by "law and order"?*'

'Yes. I would be responsible for maintaining the maximum security provisions. But the way he put it, almost my main responsibility would be to ascertain that the protective regulations regarding the eligibility of patients would be adhered to, to the letter.'

'But the way you are telling about it, here, obviously you were not ordered to do something. You were given a choice. Your own immediate reaction – quite properly – was horror. What made you agree to go?'

'Several times during this talk he mentioned – sort of by the way – that he had heard I wasn't altogether happy in Linz. And then, he said, there was a disciplinary action pending against me. That would, of course, be suspended if I accepted a transfer. He said I could also choose either to go to an institute in Saxonia, or one in Austria. But that, if I chose to refuse the assignment, no doubt my present chief in Linz – Prohaska – would find something else for me to do.'

'And that decided you, did it?'

'The combination of things did – the way he had presented it: it was already being done by law in America and in Russia; the fact that doctors and nurses were involved; the careful examination of the patients; the concern for the feelings of the population. And then, it is true, for months I had felt myself to be in the greatest danger in Linz from Prohaska. After all I already knew since 13 March that it was simpler to be dead in Germany than anywhere else.'

'So what happened?'

'I reported to Tiergartenstrasse 4, I think to SS Oberführer Brack, who explained what my specific police duties would be. I said I'd try to do it, and that I would like to stay in Austria where I would be nearer my family.'

'Were you to wear uniform?'

'Yes, the green police uniform.' (This continued until Christmas 1942, when he became assimilated into the SS and was given the grey SS field uniform.) 'He gave me the name of a village not too far from Linz and a telephone number: I remember, it was Alkoven 913. I was to return to Linz, pack and tell nobody where I was going. I was to go to an inn on the outskirts of Linz – the Gasthaus Drei Kronen it was, on the Landstrasse – and phone that number. And I'd be given instructions.'

He followed the instructions and was driven to Schloss Hartheim. 'Almost the first person I saw – it was such a relief – was a friend: a colleague from the police, Franz Reichleitner.' This friend took him to meet the doctors and Hauptmann (Captain) Wirth.

Wirth was to become Stangl's next *bête noire*.

'He was a gross and florid man,' Stangl said, 'And my heart sank when I met him. He stayed several days that time, and came back often. Whenever he was there he addressed us daily at lunch. And when he spoke about the necessity of this euthanasia operation, he wasn't speaking in humane or scientific terms, the way Dr Werner at T4 had described it to me. He laughed. He spoke of "doing away with useless mouths", and that "sentimental slobber" about such people made him "puke".'

'*What about the other people there? What were they like?*'

'There were two chief medical officers: Dr Lohnauer and Dr Renno. And fourteen nurses: seven men and seven women. Dr Lohnauer was a rather aloof sort of man, but very correct. Dr Renno was very nice.'

'*In the weeks and months to come, did they ever talk to you about what was being done there?*'

'Often, very often, especially Dr Renno. You know . . .' he suddenly said, sadly, 'you have no idea what the patients were like who were brought there. I had never known there *were* such people. Oh my God – the children . . .'

'*But didn't it ever occur to you to think "what if* my *mother or* my *child were in this position"?*'

'Ah,' he answered at once, 'but they told us immediately that there were four groups who were exempt: the senile: those who had served in the armed forces: those who had been decorated with the *Mutterkreuz* (a maternity decoration for women) *and* relatives of Euthanasia Aktion staff. Of course, they had to do that.'

'*Quite aside from that then, did you have any moral scruples?*'

'For a long time. After the first two or three days I told Reichleitner that I didn't think I could stand it. By then I'd heard that the police official who had had the job before me had been relieved upon his request because he had stomach trouble. I too couldn't eat – you know, one just couldn't.'

'*Then it was possible to ask to be relieved?*'

'Yes. But Franz Reichleitner said "What do you think will happen if you do the same? Just remember Ludwig Werner." He knew of course about Werner's being sent to the KZ. [Six months after the take-over of Austria he had been sent to a concentration camp.] No, I had very little doubt of what would happen to me if I returned to Linz and Prohaska.'

'Do you think the patients at Schloss Hartheim knew what was happening to them?'

'No,' he said with assurance. 'It was run as a hospital. After they arrived they were again examined you know.'

'Did you get to the point where you convinced yourself you were involved in something that was right?'

'One day,' he answered, 'I had to make a duty visit to an institution for severely handicapped children run by nuns.'

'Why?' I interrupted. 'What did you have to do there?'

'It was part of my function to see that the families of patients – afterwards – received their things: clothes and all that, and identity papers, certificates, you know. I was responsible for everything being correctly done.'

'What do you mean "correctly done". How were the families notified?'

'Well, they were told the patient had died of a heart attack or something like that. And they received a little urn with the ashes. But for our records, as I told you, we always had to have those four attestations – otherwise it . . . it couldn't be carried out. Well, in this case the mother of a child who had been brought from that particular institution had written to say she hadn't received a candle she had sent the child as a present shortly before it died. That's why I had to go there: to find the candle. The mother superior, who I had to see, was up in a ward with the priest when I arrived, and they took me up to see her. We talked for a moment and then she pointed at a child – well, it looked like a small child – lying in a basket. "Do you know how old he is?" she asked me. I said no, how old was he? "Sixteen," she said. "He looks like five, doesn't he? He'll never change, ever. But they rejected him." (The nun was referring to the medical commission who decided on individual "eligibility" for mercy killings.) "How could they not accept him?" And the priest stood next to her, nodding fervently. "Just look at him," she went on. "No good to himself or anyone else. How could they refuse to deliver him from this miserable life?" 'This really shook me,' said Stangl. 'Here was a Catholic nun, a mother superior, *and* a priest. And they thought it was right. Who was I then to doubt what was being done?'

The exact number of those killed has never been established, but varies between 60,000 and 80,000. But after many Germans publicly protested against the killing of German and Austrian patients, on 21 August 1941 (by which time approximately 50,000 had been killed), Hitler ordered the *Aktion* stopped.

A few months later, after a brief tour of duty at another institute, Bernburg, near Hanover, Stangl was told to report back to T4 in Berlin to get new orders. 'My briefing there was very short: I was told that I could either return to Linz and put myself at the disposal of Prohaska, or alternatively I could be assigned to go east, to Lublin.'

'*What did they tell you you'd be doing in Lublin?*'

'Something was murmured about the difficult situation of the army in Russia, and anti-partisan action, but this was never elaborated on. Anyway, for me it wasn't a difficult decision: I'd rather fight partisans any day than Prohaska in Linz. I was told to proceed to Lublin and to report to SS Polizeiführer (Higher SS and Police Chief) Brigadeführer (Major-General) Globocnik.'

(Odilo Globocnik, who directed the *Einsatz Reinhard* – the extermination of the Jews in Poland – committed suicide on 6 June 1945, when about to be arrested by a British patrol in Carinthia.)

We began on this part of Franz Stangl's story on the morning of the fourth day. Everything he had told me up to now, sitting across from me at the small round table in the otherwise empty room with barred windows in the Düsseldorf prison had led up to this moment. If his description of his childhood and youth had frequently been interrupted by deep emotion and tears, then the prospect this morning of having to begin the account of his work in the Nazi death camps would – I was sure – be even more daunting to his spirits.

As he walked towards me down the long corridor from his cell I noticed immediately a subtle change in his bearing: where before there had always been a mixture of eagerness and slight diffidence in his morning greeting, there was now a curious kind of bland composure and when he bowed smilingly, from the waist, an overdone *bonhomie.*

When, without being urged or requestioned, he began instantly where we had left off the evening before, he sounded brisk and confident. And spoke in the manner of an objective observer who can describe macabre and terrifying events with feeling and yet fluency and detachment.

'I reported to SS HQ Lublin as soon as I arrived. It was very strange. The SS HQ was in the Julius Schreck Kaserne; it was a kind of palace surrounded by a large park. When I gave my name I was taken through the building into the park. They said the general would meet me there. It was a beautiful spring day, the grass was very green, the trees in bud and there were flowers everywhere. I came upon Globocnik sitting by himself on a bench with his back to the building. He greeted me warmly. "Sit down," he said patting the space next to him; "tell me all about yourself." After I had told him about my family and career he said that no doubt I knew that the army had just had some major setbacks in the East. The SS was going to have to help: it had been decided, he told me, to open a number of supply camps from which the front troops could be re-equipped. He said that he intended confiding to me the construction of a camp called Sobibor. He called an aide – who must have lurked somewhere near by – and told him to bring the plans.'

'To the bench?'

'Yes.' He shook his head. 'It really was very odd. The plans arrived and he spread them out on the bench between us and on the ground in front of us. They showed a design for a camp: barracks, railway tracks, fences, gates. Some of the buildings – bunkers they were – were crossed out with red ink. "Don't worry about those," he said. "Concentrate on getting the rest done first. It has been started but they've got Poles working there. It's going so slowly I think they must be asleep. What the place needs is someone to organize it properly and I think you are the man to do it." And then he said he'd arrange for me to leave for Sobibor the next day – that was all.'

'Did he ever hint at what the real purpose of Sobibor was? Did he mention the Jews?'

'Not with one word. I had no idea whatever. The next day a car with driver picked me up at my quarters and we drove first to Cholm where he had said I was to make myself known to a construction engineer, Baurath Moser, who was in charge of the materials I would need for Sobibor.'

'*Did* he *tell you anything about Sobibor's ultimate purpose?*'

'No. We only discussed materials and he invited me to go on a drive with him to see the camps he supplied in the district Cholm. We saw two small work camps using Jewish labour: men and women. But there was nothing sinister about it. They seemed quite happy. We didn't get to the site of the new Sobibor camp on this occasion.

'I went to Cholm for the night, and back to Lublin in the morning. Three days later I was told to go to Sobibor with six men.'

'*What did Sobibor camp look like when you got there?*'

'It was just the Sobibor railway station: the station house and across from it a forester's hut and a barn – that was all. Just those three wooden buildings.'

'*And who was there when you arrived?*'

'There was an SS *Unterführer* and a few subalterns – they all left the next day. After that all the men who were there had been in the ... you know, the euthanasia *Aktion*. The one I was specially glad to have with me was Michel; he'd been the head nurse at Schloss Hartheim.'

'*Weren't you a bit surprised? What was a nurse doing on this supply camp site?*'

'Well, I didn't really think about it. I knew of course that, as the *Aktion* was over, the staff had become available – something had to be done with them. Also, it was very nice for me to have a friend there.' It was quite clear to me that the whole story of his beginnings in Poland (and some of the euthanasia phase) was in part fabrication, rationalization and partly an evasion: but having pressed him on it repeatedly, on several occasions, I hoped that if I didn't press him on it any further at this point, he would find it possible a little later along in his story, to revert to telling me the truth about the rest of it, however difficult. As it turned out I was right.

He next told me about the Polish workers and that he found them to be 'a lackadaisical lot'. Within two or three days he obtained a

Jewish 'work commando' of twenty-five men, and some Ukrainian guards from a nearby training camp.

'There really was nothing there, no amenities for anybody. Those first weeks we all bunked in together.'

'*What do you mean "all together"? The German staff, the Ukrainian guards and the Jews?*'

'At first we just used one hut, while we were working on the others: we slept on the floor in the kitchen, and the others in the loft.'

'*When did you first find out what the camp was really for?*'

'Two things happened: when I'd been there about three days I think, Michel came running one day and said he'd found a funny building back in the woods. "I think there is something fishy going on here," he said. "Come and see what it reminds you of."'

'*What did he mean "in the woods"?*'

'It was about ten – even fifteen minutes' – walk away from the railway station where we were building the main camp. It was a new brick building with three rooms of three by four metres. The moment I saw it I knew what Michel meant: it looked exactly like the gas chamber at Schloss Hartheim.'

'*But, who had built this? How could you possibly not have noticed it before? Or not seen it on the plans?*'

'The Poles had built it – they didn't know what it was. Neither Michel nor I had had any time yet to go for walks in the woods. We were very busy. Yes, it was on the plans, but so were lots of other buildings ...' The sentence trailed off.

'*All right, you hadn't known: but* now *you knew. What did you do?*'

His face had gone red. I didn't know whether it was because he had been caught out in a lie, or because of what he was about to say next: it was much more usual for him to blush in advance than in retrospect.

'The second thing I mentioned happened almost simultaneously: a transport officer – a sergeant – arrived from Lublin and said, to me [he sounded angry even now] that Globocnik was dissatisfied with the progress of the camp and had said to tell me that "if these Jews don't work properly, just kill them off and we'll get others."'

'*What did that indicate to you?*'

'I went the very next day to Lublin to see Globocnik. He received me at once. I said to him, "How can this sergeant be permitted to give *me* such a message? And anyway I am a police officer. How can I be expected to do anything like that?" Globocnik was very friendly. He said I had misunderstood; I was just overwrought. "We'd better get you some leave," he said. "You just go back for the moment and get on with the building. You are doing fine." And then he said, "Perhaps we can arrange to have your family come out for a bit." So I went back. What else could I do?'

'*Did you ask Globocnik about the gas chamber?*'

'There was no opportunity,' he said firmly. 'I went back to Sobibor and talked it over with Michel. We decided that somehow we had to get out. But the very next day Wirth came. He told me to assemble the (German) personnel and he made a speech – just as awful, just as vulgar as his speeches had been at Hartheim. He said that any Jews who didn't work properly here would be "eliminated". "If any of you don't like that," he said to us, "you can leave. But under the earth," he added in his heavy wit, "not over it." And then he left. I went back to Lublin the next morning. *Sturmbannführer* (Major) Höfle, Globocnik's aide, kept me waiting in the office all day, and again the next morning. Then he finally told me that the general would not be available for me. [Hans Höfle, deputy director of the *Einsatz Reinhard*, hanged himself while awaiting trial in the Vienna remand prison in August 1962.] I went back to Sobibor. Four days later a courier came from Lublin with a formal letter from Globocnik informing me that Wirth had been appointed Inspector of Camps and that I was to report to him at Belzec forthwith.'

Wirth had by then commanded both Chelmno, where the old-fashioned method of gas vans was found to be impractical for the huge task at hand, and Belzec, where the first large-scale gas exterminations in gas chambers were begun as early as March 1942.

'I can't tell you what it was like,' Stangl said: he spoke slowly now, in his more formal German, his face strained and grim. He passed his hand over his eyes and rubbed his forehead. 'I went there by car. As one arrived one first reached Belzec railway station, on the left side of the road. The camp was on the same side but up a hill. The *Kommandantur* was 200 metres away, on the other side of the road. It was a one-storey building. The smell . . .' he said. 'Oh God, the smell. It was everywhere. Wirth wasn't in his office, they said he was up in the camp. I asked whether I should go up there, and they said, "I wouldn't if I were you – he's mad with fury, it isn't healthy to go near him." I asked what was the matter. The man I was talking to said that one of the pits had overflowed. They had put too many corpses in it, and putrefaction had progressed so fast that the liquid underneath had pushed the bodies on top up and over, and the corpses had rolled down the hill. I saw some of them – oh God, it was awful. A bit later Wirth came down. And that's when he told me. He said that was what Sobibor was for. And that he was putting me officially in charge. I said I couldn't do it. I simply wasn't up to it. There wasn't any argument, or discussion. He just said my reply would be reported to HQ and for me to go back to Sobibor. In fact I went to Lublin, tried again to see Globocnik, again without success: he wouldn't see me. When I got back to Sobibor, Michel and I talked and talked about it. We agreed that what they were doing was a crime. We considered deserting – we discussed it for a long time. But how? Where could we go? What about our families?' He stopped. He stopped now, just as he and Michel must have stopped talking about it then, because as long as there was nothing they could or dared to do, there was nothing else to say.

'*But you knew that day that what was being done was wrong?*'

'Yes, I knew, Michel knew. But we also knew what had happened in the past to other people who had said no. The only way out we could see was to keep trying in various and devious ways to get a transfer. The direct way was impossible. As Wirth had said, that led "under the earth". Wirth came back the next day. He ignored me; he stayed several days and organized everything. Half the workers were detailed to finish the gas chambers.'

It appears that Wirth tested their potential efficiency by, as Stangl said, 'pushing our twenty-five worker Jews in one afternoon and gassing them'.

'*What were* you *doing?*'

'I continued the construction of the camp. Michel had been put in charge of carrying out the gassings.'

'*So now the exterminations had really started: it was happening right in front of you. How did you feel?*'

'At Sobibor one could avoid seeing almost any of it – it all happened so far away from the camp buildings. All I could think of was that I wanted out. I planned and planned. I heard there was a new police unit at Mogilev. I went back to Lublin and filled out an application blank for transfer. I asked Höfle to help me get Globocnik's signature. He said he would do what he could, but I never heard of it again. Two months later – in June – my wife wrote that she had been requested to supply details about the children's ages: they were going to be granted a visit to Poland.'

'*Did you want them to come there?*'

'I wanted to see them, of course. But don't you see what this signified? Globocnik had said to me, months before, that I needed "leave". But they weren't going to let me go home, like other people. I was in danger, it was quite obvious. And they were making damn sure I knew about it.'

Stangl's wife and two daughters, six and four, arrived very shortly after that and they all went to stay with the construction engineer in Cholm, twenty miles from the camp.

'*Were you officially on leave then or did you have to go to Sobibor during this time?*'

'While we were in Cholm I was on leave.'

'*Did your wife ask you what you were doing in Sobibor? What sort of camp it was?*'

'Very little then: she was used to my not being able to speak to her of service matters. And we were so glad just to be together. The funny thing was, though, that I heard nothing from Lublin, or from Wirth. I didn't have any official instructions how long my leave was to be, how long the family would be allowed to stay or anything. After about three weeks I went to see Höfle and asked him. He said, "Why make waves? If nobody's said anything to you why not just keep them here for a while. Find a place to stay near by, and don't worry."'

'*What did you think that meant?*'

'I was so glad to have them there, you know, it was such a relief, I just decided not to think, just to enjoy it. I found rooms for us on an estate just a few kilometres from Sobibor camp, near the village.

'*How far exactly was that from the camp?*'

'Five kilometres.'

Sobibor survivors testified at the trial that Stangl used to ride into the camp and attend 'selections' dressed in a white riding habit.

'How could you go to the camp in this get-up?'

'The roads were very bad,' he replied. 'Riding was really the best mode of transport.'

I tried once more. *'Yes, but to attend the unloading of these people who were about to die, in a white riding habit . . . ?'*

'It was hot,' he said.

'The people in whose house you and your family were staying – they must have known or guessed what was going on at Sobibor. However secret an operation it was, there must have been rumours. Did your wife still not know?'

'I don't think they would have dared to talk about it even if they had heard rumours. But my wife *did* find out, though not from them: one of the young officers, an *Unterscharführer* Ludwig, came by once while I was out. He had been drinking and he told her about Sobibor. When I got back she was waiting for me. She was terribly upset. She said "Ludwig has been here. He told me. My God, what are you doing in that place?" I said "Now child, this is a service matter and you know I can't discuss it. All I can tell you, and you must believe me: whatever is wrong – I have nothing to do with it."'

'Did she believe this, without further questions or arguments?'

He shrugged his shoulders. 'She spoke of it sometimes. But what else could I say to her? It did make me feel though that I wanted her away from there. I wanted them to go home. The school term was about to start for the older of the girls anyway . . .' The sentence trailed off.

'It was too difficult having them there now that she knew. Wasn't that it?'

He shrugged his shoulders again and buried his face in his hands. 'Just about then I had a message that I was to come to Warsaw to see Globocnik – by this time he had two offices, in Warsaw and Lublin. Now it seemed even more urgent to me to get the family home. I got hold of Michel and said that I entrusted my family to him: for him to get them out as quickly as possible. Then I said goodbye to my wife and children and went to Warsaw.'

'When did they leave?'

'Later I found that Michel got them out in four days. But I didn't know that at the time. And I didn't know what awaited me in Warsaw.

I thought that this was probably it – that I was finally for it. But when I got to Globocnik's office he was nearly as friendly as he'd been that first time we met. I couldn't understand it. He said, almost as soon as I came in, "I have a job for you: it is strictly a police assignment" [*einen rein polizeilichen Auftrag*]. I knew right away there was something wrong with it, but I didn't know what. He said, "You are going to Treblinka. We've already sent 100,000 Jews up there and nothing has arrived here in money or materials. I want you to find out what's happening to the stuff. Where is it disappearing to?"'

'But this time you knew where you were being sent: you knew all about Treblinka and that it was the biggest extermination camp. Here was your chance: here you were, face to face with him at last. Why didn't you say right there and then that you couldn't go on with this work?'

'Don't you see? He had me just where he wanted me: I had no idea where my family was. Had Michel got them out? Or had they perhaps stopped them? Were they holding them as hostages? And even if they were out: the alternative was still the same: Prohaska was still in Linz. Can you imagine what would have happened to me if I had returned there under these circumstances? No, he had me flat: I was a prisoner.'

'But even so – even admitting there was danger – wasn't anything preferable by now to going on with this work in Poland?'

'Yes, that's what we know now, what we can say now. But then?'

'Well, in point of fact, we know now, don't we, that they did not automatically kill men who asked to be relieved from this type of job. You knew this yourself, didn't you, at the time?'

'I knew it *could* happen that they didn't shoot someone. But I also knew that more often they *did* shoot them, or send them to concentration camps. How could I know which would apply to me?'

This argument of course runs through all of Stangl's story: it is the most essential question at which, over and over, I found myself stopped. Heroes and martyrs are born – not made – and I don't know at which point one human being can make the moral decision for another that he should have had the courage to die.

Stangl left for Treblinka immediately. As he began to speak of what he found there, his voice became slurred and his face underwent the metamorphosis I had noticed first when he had begun to speak of his work in the euthanasia programme and again since whenever a really intolerable subject arose. 'I drove there, with an SS driver. We could smell it kilometres away. The road ran alongside the railway tracks. As we got nearer Treblinka but still perhaps fifteen, twenty minutes' drive away, we began to see corpses next to the rails, first just two or three, then more and as we drove into what was Treblinka station there were hundreds of them – just lying there – they'd obviously been there for days, in the heat. In the station was a train full of Jews, some dead, some still alive . . . it looked as if it had been there for days.'

'*But all this was nothing new to you? You had seen these transports constantly, in Sobibor?*'

'Nothing like *this*. And in Sobibor – I told you – unless one was actually working in the forest, one could live without actually seeing anybody dying or dead. Treblinka that day was the most awful thing I saw all during the Third Reich,' once again he buried his face in his hands. 'It was Dante's *Inferno*,' he said through his fingers. 'Dante come to life. When I got out of the car on the *Sortierungsplatz* I stepped knee-deep into money: I didn't know which way to turn, where to go. I waded in paper notes, currency, precious stones, jewellery and clothes. They were everywhere, strewn all over the square. The smell was indescribable: the hundreds, no, the thousands of bodies everywhere, putrefying, decomposing. Across the square in the woods, just a few hundred yards away on the other side of the barbed-wire fence, there were tents and open fires with groups of Ukrainian guards and girls – whores from Warsaw I found out later – weaving drunk, dancing, singing, playing music . . . Dr Eberl, the *Kommandant*, showed me around the camp – there was shooting everywhere . . . I asked him what was happening to the valuables, why weren't they being sent to HQ. He said – in the face of all the stuff we were wading through – he said: "The transports are ransacked before they ever leave Warsaw." I went straight back to Warsaw and told Globocnik that it was impossible: no order such as he had given me could be carried out in that place. "It's the end of the world," I said to him and told him about the thousands of rotting corpses. He said, "It's supposed to be the end of the world for them." He told me to stay in Warsaw that night, that he would call in Wirth for a meeting . . . I had heard that the new police chief of Warsaw was a man from my wife's home town in Austria. I went to see him as soon as I left Globocnik, and I begged him to help.'

'*Did you tell him about Treblinka?*'

'No, no, you don't understand: it would have been madness; the secrecy regulations were absolute.'

(This was of course ridiculous when, as he put it, 'whores from Warsaw' had congregated around the camp. But there is ample evidence in the records of these rigorous though futile security regulations.)

'But he said anyway he'd help. He'd try to get me into an anti-partisan unit. He wrote everything down – I really thought this time it would work. But it didn't. I never heard from him again either. Of course any transfer needed Globocnik's signature – without that it couldn't be done. And I know now it was stupid of me ever to hope: Globocnik could never have let me go . . .

'Wirth came the next day. We went back to Treblinka. He went into a long meeting with Eberl as soon as we arrived. I went to the mess for some coffee and talked to some of the officers. They said they had great fun: shooting was "sport"; there was more money and stuff around than one could dream of, and all there for the taking: all one had to do was go and help oneself. In the evenings, they said, Eberl had naked Jewesses dance for them, on the tables. Disgusting – it was all disgusting . . . That night at dinner, Wirth announced that Eberl and four of his staff had been recalled for an important mission and that he, Wirth, would be staying for a while. Eberl and the others left the next morning. Wirth stayed for two weeks or so and reorganized the camp. He tidied it up, I will say that for him. He rang Warsaw and stopped all transports until the place could be cleaned up.'

'*What were* you *doing during this time?*'

'Well, of course, I had my specific orders: to find out about the valuables and the money. I'd got a funny feeling that something fishy had been going on there between Wirth and Eberl . . .' He now spoke with the animation and interest characteristic of the dedicated police officer. 'It seemed to me the chaos – the complete breakdown in security – might almost have been deliberate so as to make control impossible and then bypass HQ in Poland and send things straight to the Führer Chancellery in Berlin.' He sounded secretive about this even now and went on, in this same secretive manner, to mention names of people, such as Blankenburg (Section Chief of the Führer Chancellery) whom he said he had always suspected of illegal dealings in Jewish property.

'But wasn't there a "common interest" involved here?'

'Oh, you have no idea of the rivalries and intrigues between different departments, sections, ministries and individuals. There were enormous – fantastic – sums involved: everybody wanted a piece of it and everybody wanted control.'

Stangl had moved into Eberl's quarters in the *Kommandantenbarracke* and Wirth had the guest-room next to him. One evening Wirth told him that Kurt Franz, whose reputation for ruthlessness had preceded him, was going to arrive shortly to 'get this heap moving'.

'I went back to see Globocnik,' he said, 'and told him that I believed Eberl and Wirth to have conspired about routeing the Treblinka valuables to Berlin instead of the HQ in Poland. Globocnik said "Ah, the villains" as if this had finally cleared up something that had puzzled him all along. I told him that I was prepared to see that all material as of now would be safely delivered to his office.'

(The prosecution later contended that this offer was not motivated by Stangl's desire to limit his function in the camp, but rather, having heard that Kurt Franz was about to arrive, by a wish to protect his superior position in the hierarchy. There is no doubt – Stangl confirmed this to me during our second series of conversations four weeks after the first – that as of this day Globocnik considered and treated him as 'one of his men' on whose loyalty he relied completely.)

'But this means that you actually volunteered your collaboration, doesn't it?'

'All I was doing,' he replied sharply, his face once again undergoing that now familiar change, 'was to confirm to him that I would be carrying out this *assignment* as a police officer under his command.'

'But you and Michel, months before, had acknowledged to yourselves that what was being committed here was a crime. *How could you, in all conscience, propose – as you were doing now – even to take part in this crime?'*

'It was a matter of survival – always of survival. What I had to do, while I continued my efforts to get out, was to limit my own activities to what I – in my own conscience – could answer for. At police training school they taught us that the definition of a crime must meet four requirements: there has to be a subject, an object, an action and intent. If any of these four elements are missing, then we are not dealing with a punishable offence.'

'*I cannot see how you can possibly apply this concept here.*'

'That's what I am trying to explain to you: the only way I could live was to compartmentalize my thinking.' (Here he came as close as he ever did to acknowledge in words his 'creation' of an *alter ego* for himself.) 'By doing this I could apply it to my own situation: if the "subject" was the (Nazi) government, the "object" the Jews, and the "action" the gassings, then I could tell myself that for me the fourth element, "intent" [he called it "free will"], was missing.'

'*Except as far as administering the valuables was concerned?*'

'Yes. But having established the possibility of illegal trafficking, this had become a legitimate police activity.'

'*But these valuables which you were proposing – or agreeing – to administer wouldn't have been* there *but for the gassings. How could you isolate one from the other? Even in your own thinking?*'

'I could, because my specific assignment from the start had been the responsibility for these effects.'

'*What if you had been specifically assigned to carry out the actual gassings?*'

'I wasn't,' he said drily, and added in a reasonable, explanatory tone, 'that was done by two Russians – Ivan and Nicolov – under the command of a sub . . .'

In this exploration of how a 'machinery' like this can be created, exploiting the weaknesses and fears of such men, Stangl's own account of his daily life at Treblinka and the deliberate manipulation and repression of his own moral scruples is particularly illuminating. Throughout the three days of this part of his story, he manifested an intense desire to seek and tell the truth. This need, strangely enough, was emphasized rather than belied by the extraordinary callousness of many of his explanations and anecdotes. He was telling the truth as he saw it, thirty years ago and still now. But in so doing he voluntarily but unwittingly told us more than the truth: he showed us the two men he had become in order to survive.

'I got up at dawn,' he began. 'The men used to be livid because I made my first round at 5 a.m. It kept them on their toes. I first checked the guards – the British were supposed to have dropped parachutists in the region and I had had to secure the camp against the outside. We had put up a second fence of steel antitank obstacles. And then I went up to the *Totenlager*.'

'*What were you doing at the* Totenlager *at 5 a.m.?*'

'It was a *round*: I went everywhere. At seven I went into breakfast. After a while I had them build our own bakery. One of the worker-Jews was a wonderful Viennese baker. He made delicious cakes, very good bread. After that we gave our army issue bread to the *Arbeitsjuden* of course.'

'*Of course? Did everybody?*'

'I don't know. I did. Why not – they could use it. I tried other ways to get them food too: you know the Poles had ration books which allowed them an egg a week, so much fat, so much meat. Well, it occurred to me that if everybody in Poland had the right to ration tickets – if that was the law – then our *Arbeitsjuden* were in Poland too and also had the right to ration tickets. So I told Maetzig, my bookkeeper, to go to the town council and request 1,000 ration books for our thousand worker-Jews.'

'*What happened?*'

He laughed. 'Well, in the surprise of the moment they gave him 1,000 rations for that week. But afterwards the Poles – the town council – complained to somebody at HQ and I was hauled over the coals for it. Still, it was a good try and we did get something out of it: they had 1,000 eggs that week.'

'*Getting back to your daily routine, what did you do after breakfast?*'

'At about eight I'd go to my office.'

'*What time did the transports arrive?*'

'Usually about that time.'

'*Didn't you attend their arrival?*'

'Not necessarily. Sometimes I went.'

'*How many people would arrive on a transport?*'

'Usually about 5,000. Sometimes more.'

'*Did you ever talk to any of the people who arrived?*'

'Talk? No. But I remember one occasion – they were standing there just after they'd arrived, and one Jew came up to me and said he wanted to make a complaint. So I said yes, certainly, what was it. He said that one of the Lithuanian guards (who were only used for transport duties) had promised to give him water if he gave him his watch. But he had taken the watch and not given him any water. Well, that wasn't right, was it? Anyway, I didn't permit pilfering. I asked the Lithuanians then and there who it was who had taken the watch, but nobody came forward. Franz – you know, Kurt Franz – whispered to me that the man involved could be one of the Lithuanian officers – they had so-called officers – and that I couldn't embarrass an officer in front of his men. "Well," I said. "I am not interested what sort of uniform a man wears. I am only interested in what is inside a man." Don't think *that* didn't get to Warsaw in a hurry. But, what's right is right, isn't it? I made them all line up and turn out their pockets.'

'*In front of the prisoners?*'

'Yes, what else? Once a complaint is made it has to be investigated. Of course, we didn't find the watch – whoever it was had got rid of it.'

'*What happened to the complainant?*'

'Who?'

'*The man who had lodged the complaint about the watch?*'

'I don't know,' he said vaguely. 'Of course, as I said, usually I'd be working in my office: there was a great deal of paperwork – till about eleven. Then I made my next round, starting on top at the *Totenlager*. By that time they were well ahead with the work up there.' [*Da hat der Betrieb schon gelaufen.*]

What he meant was that by this time the 5,000 people who had arrived that morning were dead: the 'work' he referred to was the disposal of the bodies, which took most of the rest of the day. I knew this but I wanted to get him to speak more directly about the *people* and asked where the people were who had come on the transport. But his answer was still evasive: he still avoided referring to them as 'people'.

'Oh, by that time of the morning everything was pretty much finished in the lower camp. A transport was normally dealt with in two or three hours. At twelve I had lunch and after that about half an hour's rest. Then another round and more work in the office.'

'*What did you do in the evenings?*'

'After supper people sat around and talked. When I first came they

1. Vienna, February 1938, one month before the 'Anschluss': I'm wearing my first evening dress for a dance at the Reinhardt Drama School in Schönbrunn.

2. Winter 1940: with our seventeen children (and the head nurse, Mme Baudrier) in the courtyard of the Château de Villandry. The children's coats were made from French naval uniforms.

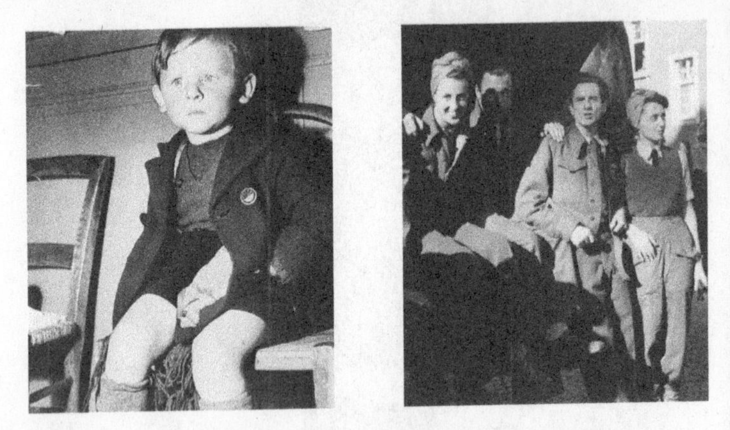

3. Paris, May 1940: a little boy lost, at the 'Auxiliaire Social' reception centre, in Paris; two weeks later he was among the group of orphaned, lost or abandoned children I took to Villandry (*above left*).
4. UNRRA HQ, Karlsruhe, Germany, June 1945: Jan (Transport Officer), Dido (nurse), Ole (Principal Welfare Officer) and me just before leaving for our first team assignment in Bavaria (*above right*).
5. UNRRA Team 539 warehouse at Vilshofen, Bavaria: clothes distribution for 'unaccompanied children' (*below*).

6. Schloss Moos, Bavaria, the attic in winter 1945 with my 'adopted' family: with Baron Fritz Waldbott and Isabella (*top*). 7. Baroness Waldbott, the former Archduchess Alicia, who grew up at the palace of Schönbrunn (*below left*). 8. Maria (Mädi), now Countess Törring (*below right*).

9. Paris, *c.* 1949: my friend Liliane Crespelle, who, like so many other Resistance fighters could so easily have been executed only a few years earlier, with Anne and Nicolas in their summery garden in Neuilly.

10. Munich, Germany, photo *c.* 1985: Klaus von Bismarck, a remarkable man with a remarkable family, who were my hosts and moral support during the weeks of work in Düsseldorf prison with Franz Stangl, Commandant of Treblinka.

11. Salzburg, Austria, summer 1948: Helene Thimig, Max Reinhardt's widow and one of the century's greatest German-speaking actresses, as Faith in *Jedermann* at the Salzburg Festival, one of the two roles in the production she had played ever since Reinhardt founded the Festival in 1920.

12. Franz Stangl, *c.* 1940 (*above*).

13. Düsseldorf, Germany, April 1971: to the fury of prisoners in the cells behind him, Stangl, having taken two hours dressing, poses in the staircase of the prison (*right*).

14. The next day, in conversation in the cell-like lawyers' conference room where, between 2 April and 27 June, we talked for three weeks. Strangl died one day later, just after noon on 28 June.

15. Nuremberg: Leni Riefenstahl, Hitler's favourite film-maker, next to the mammoth eagle which figured prominently in her famous film of the 1936 Nuremberg Rally. A controversial personality ever since 1945, she produced in the 1970s great photographs of the African Nuba, and continued with underwater photography until 2000 (when she was 97).

16. Traudl Junge, the last survivor of Hitler's intimate circle, in her Munich apartment. She was his youngest secretary after 1942, and took down Hitler's last testament, hours before his suicide in the Berlin Bunker.

17. Munich, 1979: Hans Jürgen Syberberg is probably the most original film-maker post-war Germany produced. His monumental seven-hour film *Hitler, A Film from Germany* was too controversial to find a German distributor until it was premièred in Britain and awarded Best Film of the Year by the British Film Institute in 1977.

used to drink for hours in the mess. But I put a stop to that. Afterwards they drank in their rooms.'

'*What did you do? Did you have any friends there, anyone you felt you had something in common with?*'

'Nobody. Nobody with whom I could really talk. I knew none of them.'

'*Even after a while? A month?*'

He shrugged his shoulders 'What's a month? I never found anybody there – like Michel – with whom I felt I could speak freely of what I felt about this *Schweinerei*. I usually went to my room and went to bed.'

'*Did you read?*'

'Oh no. I couldn't have read there. I was too unquiet . . . The electricity went off at ten – after that everything was quiet. Except of course when the transports were so big that the work had to continue in the night.'

'*Well now, this was your routine. But how did you feel? Was there anything you enjoyed – you felt "good" about?*'

'It was interesting to me to find out who was cheating. As I told you, I didn't care who it was: my professional ethos was that if something wrong was going on, it had to be found out. That was my profession: I enjoyed it. It fulfilled me. And yes, I was ambitious about that: I won't deny that.'

'*Would it be true to say that you got used to the liquidations?*'

He thought a moment. 'To tell the truth,' he then said slowly and thoughtfully, 'one did become used to it.'

'*In days? Weeks? Months?*'

'Months. It was months before I could look one of them in the eye. I repressed it all by trying to create a special place: gardens, new barracks, new kitchens, new everything – barbers, tailors, shoemakers, carpenters. There were hundreds of ways to take one's mind off it: I used them all.'

'*Even so, if you felt that strongly, there had to be times, perhaps at night in the dark, when you couldn't avoid thinking about it?*'

'In the end the only way to deal with it was to drink. I took a large glass of brandy to bed with me each night and I drank.'

'*I think you are evading my question.*'

'No, I don't mean to: of course thoughts came. But I forced them away. I made myself concentrate on work, work and again work.'

'Would it be true to say that you finally felt they weren't really human beings?'

'When I was on a trip once, years later in Brazil,' he said, his face deeply concentrated, and obviously reliving this experience, 'my train stopped next to a slaughterhouse. The cattle in the pens, hearing the noise of the train, trotted up to the fence and stared at the train. They were very close to my window, one crowding the other, looking at me through that fence. I thought then "look at this; this reminds me of Poland; that's just how the people looked, trustingly, just before they went into the tins . . ."'

'You said "tins",' I interrupted. 'What do you mean?'

But he went on without hearing – or answering me. '. . . I couldn't eat tinned meat after that. Those big eyes . . . which looked at me . . . not knowing that in no time at all they'd be dead.' He paused. His face was drawn. At this moment he looked old and worn and real – it was his moment of truth.

'So you didn't feel they were human beings?'

'Cargo,' he said tonelessly, 'they were cargo.' He raised and dropped a hand in a gesture of despair. Both our voices had dropped. It was one of the few times in those weeks of talks that he made no effort to cloak his despair, and his hopeless grief allowed an instant of sympathy.

'When do you think you began to think of them as cargo? The way you spoke earlier, of the day you first came to Treblinka – the horror you felt seeing the bodies everywhere – they weren't "cargo" to you then, were they?'

'I think it started the day I first saw the *Totenlager* in Treblinka. I remember Wirth standing there, next to these pits full of blue black corpses. It had nothing to do with humanity – it couldn't have: it was a mass – a mass of rotting flesh. Wirth said, "What shall we do with this garbage." I think unconsciously that started me thinking of them as cargo.'

'There were so many children – did they ever make you think of your children, of how you would feel in the position of those parents?'

'No,' he said slowly. 'I can't say I ever thought that way,' he paused.

'You see,' he then continued, still speaking with this extreme seriousness and obvious intent of finding a new truth in himself, 'I rarely saw them as individuals. It was always a huge mass. I sometimes stood on the "wall" and saw them in the "tube". But – how can I explain it – they were naked, packed together, running, being driven with whips like . . .' The sentence trailed off.

'*Could you not have changed that? In your position could you not have stopped the nakedness, the whips, the horror of the cattle pens?*'

'No, no, no. This was the system. Wirth had invented it. It worked. And because it worked, it was irreversible.'

'*What was the worst place in the camp for you?*'

'The *Auskleidebarracke* [the undressing barrack],' he said at once. 'I avoided it from my innermost being: I couldn't confront them; I couldn't lie to them; I refrained at any price talking to those who were about to die: I couldn't stand it.'

'*But were there never moments when this wall you built around yourself was breached? When the sight of a beautiful child perhaps, or a girl, brought you up against the knowledge that these were human beings?*'

It became clear that as soon as the people were in the *Auskleidebarracke* – that is as soon as they were naked – they were no longer human beings for him. What he described as 'avoiding at any price' was witnessing the transition. And when he cited instants and instances of human relations with prisoners, it was never with any of those who were about to die.

'There was a beautiful red-blonde girl,' he said. 'She usually worked in the clinic, but when one of the maids in our living quarters was ill, she replaced her for a time. It was just around the time when I had put up new barracks with single rooms for quite a few of the *Arbeitsjuden*. This girl – I knew one of the Kapos (Jewish guards) was her boyfriend . . . one always knew about things like that . . .'

'*What nationality was she?*'

'Polish I think. But she spoke German well. She was – you know, a well-educated girl. Well, she came to my office that day to dust or something. I suppose I thought to myself what a pretty girl she is, and now she can have some privacy with her boyfriend. So I asked her – just to say something nice you know – "Have you chosen a room yet for yourself?" I remember, she stopped dusting and stood very still looking at me. And then she said, very quietly you know, "Why do you ask?"'

His tone of voice even now reflected the astonishment he felt twenty-nine years before when this young girl responded to him not as a subject to her master, but a free human being to a man she rejected. Not only that: she responded as a member of a superior social class to a social inferior and the wording and tone of his reply confirm that he was immediately aware of this.

'I said "Why shouldn't I ask? I can ask, can't I?" and again she just stood there, very straight, not moving, just looking right at me. And then she said, "Can I go?" and I said, "Yes, of course." She went. I felt so ashamed. I realized she thought I'd asked because – well you know, because I wanted her myself. I so admired her for facing up to me, for saying "Can I go?" I felt ashamed for days because of the way she had misunderstood.'

'Do you know what happened to her?' I asked this question each time he spoke of any of the prisoners in individual terms. But each time the answer was precisely the same, in the same tone of aloofness, with the same politely interested expression in his face.

'I don't know . . .'

In this case I persisted. 'But here was a girl who enormously impressed you. Didn't you ever want to find out what happened to her?'

He looked uncomfortable. 'I heard something about her having been transferred to the *Totenlager*.' (The life expectancy of prisoners working in that part of the camp rarely exceeded a couple of months.)

'How did that happen?'

'I am not really sure. You see when our usual maid returned, this girl had gone back to her work at the clinic. The doctor – I can't remember his name – had a run-in with Kurt Franz. I was away at the time and it was never very clear what had happened. But the doctor killed himself – he took poison. And the girl was there when this happened and Franz sent her up to the *Totenlager*.'

'Couldn't you have ordered her to be brought back?'

He shook his head. 'No.'

(According to the records, this doctor, a famous Warsaw consultant, had become treasurer for the committee who were preparing the forthcoming Treblinka revolt, and killed himself when Kurt Franz surprised him in possession of a bag of gold.)

'But,' Stangl went on a moment later, 'with the *Arbeitsjuden* I did have contact – you know, quite friendly relations. You asked me a while ago, whether there was anything I enjoyed. Outside of my specific assignment that's what I enjoyed: human relations. Especially with people like Singer and Blau. They were both Viennese: I always tried to give as many jobs as possible to Vienna Jews. It made for a lot of talk at the time I know. But after all, I was Austrian . . . Singer I had made the chief of the *Totenjuden*. I saw a lot of him, I think he was a dentist in Vienna. Or perhaps an engineer,' he mused. 'He was killed later during the revolt – it started in the upper camp you know. Blau was the one I talked to most: him and his wife. No, I don't know what his was. Business, I think. I'd made him the cook in the lower camp. He knew I'd help wherever I could. There was one day when he knocked at the door of my office about mid-morning and stood at attention and asked permission to speak to me. He looked very worried. I said, "Of course Blau, come on in. What's your problem?" (*Was haben Sie denn auf dem Herzen?*) He said it was his eighty-year-old father. He'd arrived on that morning's transport. Was there anything I could do? I said, "Really Blau, you must understand, it's impossible. A man of eighty . . ." He said quickly that yes, he understood, of course. But could he ask me for permission to take his father to the *Lazarett* [where the old and sick were shot] rather than the gas chambers? And could he take his father first to the kitchen and give him a meal? I said, "You go and do what you think best, Blau. Officially I don't know anything, but unofficially you can tell the Kapo I said it was all right." In the afternoon, when I came back to my office, he was waiting for me. He had tears in his eyes. He stood at attention and said, "*Herr Hauptsturmführer*, I want to thank you. I gave my father a meal. And I've just taken him to the *Lazarett* – it's all over. Thank you very much." I said, "Well Blau, there's no need to thank me, but of course if you *want* to thank me, you may."'

'*What happened to Blau and his wife?*'

The same vagueness. 'I don't know.'

'*In the midst of all this horror that surrounded you and which you were so aware of that you drank yourself to sleep each night, what kept you going? What was there for you to hold on to?*'

'I don't know. Perhaps my wife. My love for my wife.'

'*How often did you see her?*'

'After that first time in Poland they let me go on leave quite regularly – every three or four months.'

'*Did you feel close to your wife – when so much had to be hidden between you?*'

'The little time we had together we usually talked about the children and ordinary everyday things. But it is true, things changed between us after that time when Ludwig told her about Sobibor. There was tension. And I knew she was terribly worried about me. Even I only learned to understand the full extent of what had been done and *how* all the secrecy had been managed, much later, by listening to the testimony at my trial. Believe me, I was horrified, astounded by many things I heard there. It was . . . it gave me quite a different perspective.' He shrugged his shoulders in a gesture of helplessness.

'*At the trial it was said over and over that you had the reputation of being superb at your job. The prisoners called you a* "Burgherr" *(Lord-of-the-Manor), a Napoleon. And in fact you received an official commendation as the "Best camp commander in Poland", didn't you? Would it not have been possible for you, in order to register* some *protest, if only to yourself, to do your work a little less superbly?*'

It was one of the few times during those weeks that he showed anger at a question. 'Everything I did out of my own free will,' he answered sharply. 'I had to do as best I could. That is how I am.'

'*But would it not have been possible to show* some *evidence of your inner conflict?*'

'But that would have been the end. That is precisely why I was so alone.'

'*Supposing for a moment it* would *have been the end, as you say. There were people in Germany who stood up for their principles: not many, it is true, but some. Yours was a very special position. There can't have been more than a dozen men like you in all of the Third Reich. Don't you think, if you had found that extraordinary courage, it would have had an effect on the people who served under you?*'

He shook his head. 'If I had sacrificed myself,' he said slowly. 'If I had made public what I felt and had died . . . it would have made no difference. Not an iota. It would all have gone on just the same, as if it and I had never happened.'

'I believe that. But even so, don't you think somewhere, underneath, it would have affected the atmosphere in the camp, would have given some others courage?'

'Not even that. It would have caused a tiny ripple, for a fraction of an instant – that's all.'

'What did you think at the time was the reason for the exterminations?'

His answer came at once: 'They wanted the Jews' money.'

'You can't be serious?'

He was bewildered by my reaction of disbelief. 'But of course. Have you any idea of the fantastic sums that were involved? That's how the steel in Sweden was bought.'

'But . . . they weren't all rich; 900,000 Jews were killed in Treblinka – more than 3 million in Poland altogether. There were hundreds of thousands of them, from the ghettos, who had nothing . . .'

'Nobody had nothing. Everybody had *something*. That racial business was just secondary. Otherwise, how could they have had all those "honorary Aryans"? They used to say General Milch was a Jew, you know.'

'If the racial business was so secondary, why all that hate propaganda?'

'To condition those who actually had to carry out these policies: to make it possible for them to do what they did.'

'Well, you were part of this: did you hate?'

'Never. I wouldn't let anybody dictate to me who to hate. Anyway, the only people I could ever hate would be those who were out to destroy me – like Prohaska.'

'What is the difference to you between hate – and contempt, which results in considering people as cargo?'

'It has nothing to do with hate. They were so weak; they allowed everything to happen – to be done to them. They were people with whom there was no common ground, no possibility of communication – that is how contempt is born. I could never understand how they could just give in as they did. Quite recently I read a book about lemmings, who every five or six years just wander into the sea and die: that made me think of Treblinka.'

'*If you didn't feel an overriding sense of loyalty to the party or their ideas, just what did you believe in during that time in Poland?*'

'Survival,' he said at once. 'In the midst of all that death – life. And what sustained me most was my fundamental faith in the existence of just retribution.'

'*But you knew your own position. You were so afraid of a few men like Globocnik, Wirth, Prohaska. How is it that you were not as afraid of this "just retribution" you were certain existed and which, when it came, was bound to include you?*'

'It was all part of the way I construed it for myself: I am responsible only to myself and my God. Only *I* know what I did of my own free will. And for that I can answer to my God. What I did without or against my free will, for that I need not answer . . . Yes, I knew that the day would come when the Nazis would go under and that I'd probably go under with them. If it did happen it just couldn't be helped.'

The long-prepared heroic Treblinka revolt took place on 2 August 1943. According to official records 500 escaped but only 52 survived the war. Some 40 of them are alive today [1971].

'*When the war was over, what did you want to do?*'

'All I could think of was Knut Hamsun's novel, *Growth of the Soil* (*Segen der Erde*). That was what I wanted: to start from the beginning; cleanly, quietly, only with my family who I loved around me.'

In 1945 the Americans – unaware of Stangl's connection with the *Einsatz Reinhard* – interned him in Austria as an SS officer. In the summer of 1947 he was handed over to the Austrian authorities for trial for his participation in the euthanasia programme. He escaped from remand prison in Linz on 30 May 1948.

'Originally we had intended to ask for help from the Duque di Corsini, for whom my wife had worked as a nanny. But then I heard that there was a Bishop Hulgar at the Vatican who was helping Catholic SS officers, so I went to Rome.' (Stangl had the name wrong: Dr Alois Hudal, the bishop in question, was rector of Rome's Pontifical Teutonic College; he died in 1963.)

'*Was there someone who helped Protestant SS officers too?*'

'Oh yes, he sat in Rome too. Probst Heinemann.'

'Did you have money?'

'Very little. Just some my wife had saved. But it got me to Rome.'

'What did Bishop Hudal do for you?'

'Well, first he got me quarters in Rome where I was to stay till my papers came through. And he gave me a bit more money. Then, after a couple of weeks he called me in and gave me my new passport – a Red Cross passport.'

'One thing: you said you always knew that one day you would have to answer questions about that time in Poland. If you knew, why didn't you just face up to it? Why run away?'

'I am an old policeman. I know from experience that the first moments are never the right ones. But you know, in Brazil I never hid. I lived and worked there from the beginning under my own name. I registered at the Austrian Consulate. First, because my papers read that way – as Paul Franz Stangl. But later I had to get a copy of my birth certificate through them, from Austria, and my name was then altered to the correct sequence. Anybody could have found me.'

'Did people – friends you made in São Paulo know about your past?'

'It never came up.'

'But in all these years, have you never talked it out with someone? Your wife? Your priest? A special friend?'

'My wife and I talked sometimes about some of it: but not like this. I never talked to anyone like this.'

'Did your children know?'

His face went scarlet: it was the second time he showed anger at a question. 'My children believe in me.'

'The young all over the world question their parents' attitudes. Are you saying that your children knew what you had been involved in but never asked any questions?'

'They . . . they . . . my children believe in me,' he said again. 'My family is with me.'

'When did you first realize that people were looking for you?'

'In 1964 when my son-in-law showed me a Viennese newspaper where it said that Wiesenthal was after me.'

'So you weren't really surprised when it happened, were you? When you were caught?'

'I wasn't surprised anyway. I had always expected it.'

The awful distortion in his thinking had shown up time after time while we talked. And here now it was again, as we ended our conversations.

'*Do you think that that time in Poland taught you anything?*'

'Yes. That everything human has its origin in human weakness.'

'*In retrospect, do you think there was any conceivable sense in this horror?*'

'Yes, I am sure there was. Perhaps the Jews were meant to have this enormous jolt to pull them together; to create a people; to identify themselves with each other.'

'*When you say "meant to" – are you speaking of God?*'

'Yes.'

'*What is God?*'

'God is everything higher which I cannot understand but only believe.'

'*Was God in Treblinka?*'

'Yes. Otherwise how could it have happened?'

The last day I spent with Stangl was Sunday, 27 June. He'd felt unwell most of that week, but when I came back to the prison after a half-hour lunch-break on Sunday he looked elated. 'I can't tell you how wonderful I suddenly feel,' he said. 'I ate my soup and then I lay down. And I rested so deeply, somehow like never before. Oh, I feel wonderful,' he repeated.

He then told me a lot about his life in Brazil. He was fascinated by the subject of stupidity in high places. As he warmed to the subject, he went back to relating it to his own experiences and, as often before during these conversations, his personality changed brusquely and startlingly, his voice became harsher, louder, his accent more parochial and his face coarse.

'In Brazil,' he said, 'at VW (Volkswagen), the stupidity of some of the people had to be seen to be believed. It sometimes drove me wild.' He gestured with his hands. 'There were idiots among them – morons. I often opened my mouth too wide and let them have it. "My God," I'd say to them, "Euthanasia passed *you* by, didn't it?" and I'd tell my wife when I got home, "These morons were overlooked by the Euthanasia."'

Towards the end of that afternoon we returned to religion and to what he had said about God in Treblinka.

'But isn't God good?' I asked.

'No,' he said slowly. 'I wouldn't say that. He is good *and* bad. But then, laws are made by men; and faith in God too depends on men – so that doesn't prove much of anything, does it? The only thing is, there *are* things which are inexplicable by science, so there must be something beyond man. Tell me, though, if a man has a goal he calls God, what can he do to achieve it? Do you know?'

'Don't you think it differs for each man? In your case, could it be to seek truth?'

'Truth?'

'Well, to face up to yourself? Perhaps as a start, just about what you have been trying to do in these past weeks?'

His response was automatic, and automatically unyielding. 'My conscience is clear about what I did, myself,' he said, in the same stiffly spoken words he had used countless times in the past weeks, and at his trial. He paused and the room remained silent. 'I have never intentionally hurt anyone, myself,' he said, with a different, less incisive emphasis, and waited again, for a long time. He gripped the table with both hands as if he was holding on to it. 'But I was there,' he said then in a curiously dry and tired tone of resignation. 'So yes, in reality I share the guilt.'

'You always give a little, progress a little, then you take back – retreat; you've done it often in the past weeks, you know.'

'Because my guilt . . . my guilt . . . only now in these talks, now that I have talked about it all for the first time . . .' Once again, as so often when he tried to come to grips with the impossibly difficult question of his guilt, the sentence trailed off. 'My guilt,' he started again, 'is that I am still here. That is my guilt.'

'Still here?'

'I should have died. That was my guilt.'

'You say that now, But then? . . .'

'That *is* true. I did have another twenty years – twenty good years. But believe me, now I would have preferred to die rather than this . . .' He looked around the little prison room. 'I have no more hope,' he said then in a factual way, 'and anyway, it is enough now. I want to carry through these talks we are having and then – let it be finished. Let there be an end.'

Franz Stangl died nineteen hours later, of heart failure. On a piece of paper tacked to his wall he had jotted down a name he had been trying to remember, for our talk the next day. On his table were orderly files of correspondence, photographs, legal documents, and notes in his precise and tight handwriting. The prison library book he was reading at the time of his death was *Laws and Honour* by Josef Pidulski.

6

Men Who Whitewash Hitler

November 1979

There is a degree of indecency in entertaining a dialogue with individuals such as Richard Verrall and those of his persuasion. None the less, it is necessary. We may despise them, but only at our peril do we mock or underrate them, for the best – or worst – of them lack neither intelligence nor resources. According to the farmer and part-time publisher Robin Beauclerc (one of the original backers of the National Front), whose busy printing press produced not only Verrall's obnoxious pamphlet *Did Six Million Really Die?*, but also A. R. Butz's book *The Hoax of the Twentieth Century*, almost a million copies of the pamphlet have been distributed in forty countries. I have seen them myself, as well as the Butz book, in schools, universities and libraries in Western Europe as well as the United States. Notoriously, both have arrived in Australia.

People who consider themselves generally well informed say: 'But why go on with this ridiculous argument? If there is anything we know, surely, good God, we know about the horrible camps and the six million?' It is not only the Second World War generation: an intelligent young person, glancing at the material on my desk, also said: 'But *why* does the *New Statesman* give him space? *Why* take him seriously? Why spend precious time and space on refuting obvious lies?'

Time and space are indeed precious, and neither writers nor editors should squander them. There are two weighty reasons why one must pursue these debates with the Verralls, the Irvings, the Butzes and their like.

The first is that they are by no means motivated by an ethical or intellectual preoccupation with the historical truth, but rather by precise political aims for the future. As all political philosophies have needed their precursors, and parties their prophets, so they require a model, a hero, and it is of course Hitler whom they need to serve in that role. But, because people in general are good rather than evil, it must be a Hitler shown to have been not only powerful, but moral.

It does not matter that he created a police state – justification can be cobbled up for something which others have also done. It does not matter that he appropriated neighbouring lands and peoples. Ideological and demographic justifications can be devised. And it does not matter that he provoked and fought a bitter war, which cost the lives of millions. Wars have always been fought, they have always cost too many lives, and have always been 'justified'. None of these things, not even the ruthlessness with which he first pursued these aims, detracts from Hitler's fitness to be the hero they seek and need.

There is one thing only for which there was no reason of war; no precedent; no justification. One thing of pure evil, and this they cannot afford to accept: the murderous gas chambers in occupied Poland, the attempt to exterminate the Jews.

Time and again in their diatribes – here again in Verrall's letters – regardless of the mountains of evidence, regardless of the living witnesses, they harp on their obsessional claim: there *was* no systematic genocide; there *were* no gas chambers. And of course they return to their polemic about the 6 million figure, with which they perform degrading mental acrobatics.

The second reason why we must come to grips with both the substance and detail of the neo-Nazi claims is that sometimes mistakes have been made, have been given immense publicity, and become part of genocide lore. At the risk of offence, we must correct and explain these mistakes, in order that they cannot be exploited again.

The likes of Verrall and Butz have shown a considerable talent for mixing truth with lies, by repetitive injecting of some truth into all lies, and lies into the truth. They make astute use of human errors (and of latent prejudice). So, they have succeeded to some extent in exploiting a terrible and astonishing fact, which is that after thirty-five years and billions of words, confusion still abounds on the subject of Hitler's murder of the Jews.

This has never shown up more plainly than in the case of the American television film *Holocaust*. As a member of a BBC panel of the night of its showing. I voiced misgivings about its factual errors, and tried to explain why these would be particularly difficult for the Germans to accept. Via satellite, the Hollywood producer was more than impatient with my remarks. 'Who are you?' he asked. 'What do *you* know compared to the experts who advised us?' The film was a kind of watershed, however. Perhaps because it was highly sentimentalized, it provided an emotional link for millions of people, with events which many of them had rejected because they were impossible to visualize.

The current argument with Mr Verrall, for example, deals with one main element in this confusion. He makes much of what he calls the 'admission' by the Institute for Contemporary History in Munich that 'no such things (as gas chambers) existed in . . . Belsen, Buchenwald and Dachau . . . etc., etc.'.

This so-called 'admission' stems from a letter which the historian Martin Broszat, now director of the institute, addressed in 1962 to the weekly *Die Zeit*. Professor Broszat remembers the letter well – 'How could I forget it? Neo-Nazi and far-right publications have used it out of context ever since . . .'

The letter was written in yet another attempt – many have been made, by many people – to set the record straight. What Broszat was trying to do, he explains

> was to hammer home, once more, the persistently ignored or denied difference between concentration and extermination camps; the fundamental distinction between the methodical mass murder of millions of Jews in the *extermination* camps in occupied Poland on the one hand, and on the other the individual disposals of *concentration*-camp inmates in Germany – not necessarily, or even primarily Jews – who were no longer useful as workers.

Most of the concentration camps in Germany-proper had no gas chambers. Dachau had one which was never used. 'Mauthausen, Natzweiler, had one. Sachsenhausen, too, I think', says Broszat. 'They used them towards the end, to replace the shootings and injections of small groups of prisoners, which had become so demoralizing for the staff.'

How is it then that the myth of gassing in the camps in Germany has been so universally accepted, thereby providing the neo-Nazis with their most treasured ammunition (the opportunity to refute what was never the case)? The explanation is both simple and infinitely complex.

German concentration camps, set up at first as SS-controlled detention centres for political, criminal and religious dissidents, and for sexual deviants and Jews, were neither then nor later *primarily* used for the imprisonment of Jews.

After 1940, as the need arose for an immense workforce for the war industries, the small penal camps, until then used only for Germans, Austrians and Czechs (including Jews from those countries) grew into huge installations with many hundreds of thousands of Russians, Poles and 'undesirables' from occupied Western Europe making up a vast slave-labour population.

Harshness of treatment varied between categories of prisoners. The German criminals were usually at the top of the camp hierarchy. 'Politicals' were in the middle, followed by religious and sexual deviants; with the Poles, the Russians and the Jews – in that order – at the bottom.

Millions of people died in these concentration-plus-labour camps: some – the most publicized – by torture, brutality or hideous medical experiments. But far more of them died from sickness and disease.

These were the camps that all Germans knew about and dreaded. *These* were the corpses found by the horrified Allied armies as they entered Germany. *These* made the photos and films we have principally seen. These emaciated skeletons, some still somehow upright, some lying on bunks in stupor, still others piled in naked, tumbled heaps ready for burning – these are the images that haunt us.

These people died by the million, but they were not 'exterminated' in the sense that the Nazis made uniquely their own. These camps had gas-oven crematoria, to dispose of the bodies. The chimneys belched out the smell of burning flesh, and the guards, in threat or mockery, told the prisoners: 'The only way you'll get out of here is through the chimneys.'

'Gassing' had been a part of the vocabulary in central Europe, and particularly in Germany proper, since the Nazis' destruction by gas of 80,000 physically and mentally handicapped people (children and adults) between 1939 and 1941. Thus, when sick or disabled prisoners in the German camps disappeared, when the chimneys smoked, and prisoner-workers reported that those missing had 'gone into the gas' – this was among men and women living in constant, deadly fear – it was not hard for 'gassing' to become a general term, used without much distinction.

The Allied troops who entered the camps had no idea what 'gassing' really was. All they knew was what they saw or heard about: the skeletons, some gas chambers, and hundreds of thousands of agonized tales and memories. As a welfare officer with UNRRA in 1945–6, I saw many of those sights, heard many of those tales, and tried to visualize those fearsome memories.

And then there was Auschwitz, and later Majdanek: the two, the *only* two, where the Nazis combined enormous labour installations and nearby facilities for extermination. Auschwitz, because so many people survived it, has added most to our knowledge, but also most to our confusion as between the two types of camps. What exactly was Auschwitz, which has become for many people the symbol-word for the whole Nazi horror?

It was, above all, by 1943, the largest slave-labour camp the Nazis had, with a population of 100,000 workers who were treated worse than animals, and whose expectation of life varied between ten days – if they were Jews or Russians – and a few weeks or months. Until the spring of 1942 it was just a small work camp, with only the most rudimentary gassing installation. Then, I. G. Farben began to build a synthetic fuel and rubber factory – the *Bunawerke* – on the adjacent marches, and ever-larger numbers of slave-labourers were dragged in, to build and then to operate it.

It was under the cover of constructing the *Bunawerke* that the Nazis made the slaves build the gas chambers at Birkenau, in a wooded area three miles from the main camp, called Camp II. It was here that, mainly in 1943, the 'selected' – mostly Jews, and some Russians – were brought from the railway sidings several miles away, and from the main camp. Also from Camp I, uniquely, came thousands of sick and feeble – the Muselmanner, not primarily Jews at all – not, for some mysterious reason, to die at once, but to be kept in utter squalor, virtually without rations, until they finally slipped away.

By the autumn of 1944, just over 700,000 Jews (including 400,000 Hungarians) had died in the gas chambers *at Birkenau* (Camp II), and

20,000 Russians had been killed, but not gassed (that method was reserved for Jews). And by the time of liberation, 146,200 more Jews and several hundred thousand others had died of overwork and disease in Camp I. The final figure for Auschwitz is now 1,100,00 dead.

Richard Verrall, busy with his vile numbers game, asserts that the confessions of Rudolf Höss, commandant of Auschwitz, were obtained 'under torture' in Poland, were 'nonsense' and are thus 'proof positive' of a hoax.

Whatever may be said about Höss, his role and his later manic pretensions, what really counts is that his statements to the American psychiatrist Dr G. M. Gilbert at Nuremberg were made *before* he was handed over to Poland, and that he said at Nuremberg almost exactly what he said in Poland – including two sets of estimates for the dead at Auschwitz. The second figure he cited each time, a total of about 1.3 million dead, comes very close to Gerald Reitlinger's most careful estimate in his book *The Final Solution*: 700,000 Jews gassed in Camp II, and 500,000 prisoners (including 146,000 Jews) dead from exhaustion and disease in Camp I.

But this is in a sense beside the point, because Verrall and Butz, while trying to discredit Höss, cite him whenever they hope to make a point. As they totally deny the existence of the other extermination camps in occupied Poland, Auschwitz is something of a beam in their eye. But it is important for those of us interested in the truth to recall that Auschwitz, despite its emblematic name, was *not* primarily an extermination camp for Jews, and is not the central case through which to study extermination policy.

The first mass murders occurred while Auschwitz was still a penal labour camp: they followed the 'Commissar Order' of March and July 1941, which commanded the liquidation of Soviet political commissars, gypsies, racial inferiors, 'asocials' and Jews. These killings – and none of the neo-Nazis has much to say about them – were presented as paramilitary operations. The hundreds of thousands of naked men, women and children who were shot on the edge of mass graves were described, even to their murderers, the *Einsatzgruppen*, as 'partisans' and 'bandits'.

But the *Einsatzgruppen* actions showed the Nazis that this pseudo-military method could not work for the great masses of Jews yet to be dealt with. As we know from many soldiers' letters found over the last years, and hundreds of statements by German witnesses in the *Einsatzgruppen* trials in West Germany, the killings put an intolerable strain on personnel – despite liberal supplies of alcohol and sex – and provoked protests from the *Wehrmacht*.

However, the Nazis had a tested solution at hand. Of the 80,000 unwanted people killed in the 'euthanasia *Aktion*' some (but only small children) had been killed by injections in special hospital wards. Most had died in gas chambers in the euthanasia institutes. Over 400 men and women – police, medical and administrative staff, under the direct authority of the Führer-Chancellery, in Department T-4 – had done these murders.

Here was a technique, and a staff to operate it. The 'specialists' who had been prepared to kill helpless Germans and Austrians could safely be entrusted with the slaughter of millions of Jews and thousands of gypsies: eradicating, as Hitler put it, 'the bacilli on the body politic of the German race'.

Mr Verrall complains that among the vast documentation surviving 'there is not a single order . . . etc. for a "gas chamber"'. Typically, neo-Nazi diatribes claim that there is no record of the vast transportation arrangements which would have been required to carry out an extermination programme.

Few of those who read this rubbish have an opportunity to examine the record themselves. But anyone who has actually worked in the archives is familiar with the hundreds of railway signals which survive, describing with horrible monotony the destination and contents of the trains to Sobibor and Treblinka.

And all researchers are only too familiar with the countless documents, 'orders, invoices, plans', and indeed 'blueprints' concerning precisely the construction of gas chambers.

One of the documents (NO 365), the earliest I know of concerning gassing camps (and significantly linking them to T-4), is dated 25 October 1941, and states that 'Victor Brack (Chief of Section II of T-4) is ready to collaborate in the installation of the necessary buildings and gassing machinery . . .' The longish letter, which concerns camps to be erected in Riga and Minsk, is quite explicit in the use to which the equipment is to be put.

Thus between December 1941 and April 1942, ninety-six of Brack's T-4 men were posted to Occupied Poland and the *Aktion Reinhard*. They were assigned to the four specialized extermination camps, which were Chelmno, Belzec, Sobibor and Treblinka. These had been built under the command of the SS chief in Lublin, Odilo Globocnik.

These were not concentration or labour camps. The facilities provided housing for just a few German Waffen-SS, less than 100 Baltic or Ukrainian SS overseers, and a constantly changing group of between 300 and 1,000 'work-Jews' (*Arbeitsjuden*). Although millions arrived, no one else lived long enough to eat, wash or sleep. These were meticulously planned killing-plants. The official Polish estimates (which probably err on the conservative side) are that 2 million Jews and 52,000 gypsies, at least one third of them children, were killed in these four installations between December 1941 and October 1943. Of all those who reached them, eighty-two survived.

I am able to bear some witness to these events. My knowledge comes from research I did for my book *Into That Darkness*, the story of Franz Stangl, commandant of Treblinka. I talked with Stangl for weeks in prison; I talked to others who worked under him, and to their families. I talked to people who, otherwise uninvolved, witnessed these events in Poland. And I talked to a few of those very few who survived.

Butz claims in his *Hoax* that those (hundreds) who admitted taking part in extermination were doing so as plea-bargaining, in order to get lighter sentences. But those I talked to had been tried. Many had served their sentences, and none of them had anything to gain – except shame – by what they told me. Stangl himself wanted only to talk, and then to die. And Stangl is dead. But if Verrall, Butz & Co. were really interested in the truth, Stangl's wife, and many other witnesses, are still able to testify.

The *Aktion Reinhard* camps existed for one purpose only, totally unconnected with any requirement of war, and they were totally eradicated when their purpose was served. The buildings were pulled down, and trees were planted in the earth which had become so rich. Thirty-five years later they have grown tall. A letter from Globocnik to Himmler survives, dated Trieste, 5 January 1944, and carefully phrased:

For reasons of surveillance a small farm has been built on the site of each of the [former] camps, to be occupied by a farmer to whom an annuity must be assured in order to encourage him to maintain the farm . . .

In his own letter of commendation to Globocnik, dated 30 November 1943, Himmler used his pet name for Globocnik:

Dear Globus,
I confirm your letter of 4.11.43 and your report on the completion of the Aktion Reinhardt [sic] . . . I want to express to you my gratitude and appreciation for the great and unique services you have rendered the whole of the German people by carrying through the Aktion Reinhardt.

Heil Hitler!
Cordially yours, H. H.

Here, then, is the truth for those who desire knowledge. Within one terrible universe of oppression and death – known to us through words like Belsen, Mauthausen, Dachau – there was another universe, of methodically crazy slaughter of an unprecedented kind – the place-names being Chelmno, Belzec, Sobibor and Treblinka. Auschwitz, the most-cited, was a complex, transitional example. There are reasons why the worst names are least cited: one, complex in its roots, is that the Third Reich tried to present its (marginally) less hideous face towards the West, and the Western armies never reached the territory of the death camps. And well-run extermination camps leave few survivors to tell their stories.

The situation therefore presents some possibilities for confusion to pseudo-historians and neo-Nazi apologists. And they are assisted further by the fact that events of such magnitude lend themselves to dramatic 'use', are therefore used, and not infrequently misused. In turn the Verralls and Butzes can allege that all such misuses are part of a 'Zionist' conspiracy.

It is vital for them to believe that anyone who is involved with this question must be Jewish, and thus unreliable. This to begin with, is nonsense: (a) many of the leading authorities on the Third Reich are not Jewish, and (b) many of those who are, are as objective as anyone can be. (In their anti-semitic outpourings, these individuals never refer to 'Jews', but almost invariably to 'Zionists'. They know that thirty-five years after Hitler many people will not accept the attack on 'Jews' but may be persuaded by the more 'political' label 'Zionist'. Of course, many Jews are not Zionists.)

But it *is* true that, along with many authentic works, there have been books or films which were only partly true, or even were partly faked. And unfortunately, even reputable historians are not infallible. For instance Martin Gilbert (biographer of Churchill) offers in *Final Journey* what is in many ways an admirably presented résumé of what happened to the European Jews.

But by quoting supposed 'eyewitnesses' who in fact are repeating hearsay, Gilbert perpetuates errors which – because they are so easily disproved – provide revisionists' opportunities. For instance, from his chapter 'The Treblinka Deathcamp': none of the 'Nazis in the camp . . . lived in the camp together with their families' as he says; SS Hauptsturmführer von Eupen was never commandant of Treblinka, but of the nearby training-camp Trawniki; the 'cries of the victims and the weeping of the children' could *not* be heard in the neighbouring villages, for with good reason the murderers ensured there were no villages within miles; and the Germans did *not* bring 'the most famous musicians in the world from the Warsaw ghetto' to 'play when the transports arrived'. There *were* such orchestras, for instance at Auschwitz, which played when the slave-labourers marched to and from work. But there was no need for such a thing at any pure extermination camp.

David Irving's *Hitler's War* falls into a special category. It had some interesting historical material, but sold (admirably) both here and overseas because of its bold and spurious claim that Hitler himself was largely unaware of the 'Final Solution'. Such books do better than, for example, Helen Fein's scholarly socio-history *Accounting for Genocide*, which is surely essential for any serious researcher. But this is an area in which anything but the truth can have terrible long-term consequences.

'Personal' accounts, such as the recently published *Dora*, can be valuable (I later quoted passages from it in *Albert Speer, His Battle with Truth*). Jean Michel *was* a labourer at the terrible slave-camp in the Harz Mountains where the V-2 rockets were built, and the story of *Dora* is appalling. The problem with books like this is that they are inevitably 'ghosted' by professional wordsmiths – the French are especially adept – whose main function is to supply a commercial product.

Books which are partially true, such as Jean-François Steiner's *Treblinka* or Martin Gray's *For Those I Loved*, are in some degrees worse. Steiner's book on the surface seems right: he is a man of talent, conviction and manifestly good will; it is hard to know how he could go so wrong. But what he finally produced was a hotchpotch of truth and falsehood, libelling both the dead and the living. He agreed to withdraw the original French book and it was reissued with all names changed as 'faction'. Incredibly it has remained in serious bibliographies.

Gray's *For Those I Loved* was edited by Max Gallo, who denied later that he functioned as its ghost writer. During the research for a *Sunday Times* inquiry into Gray's work, however, M. Gallo informed me coolly that he had 'needed' a long chapter on Treblinka because the book required something strong for pulling in readers. When I myself told Gray, the 'author', that he had manifestly never been to, nor escaped from Treblinka, he finally asked, despairingly: 'But does it matter? Wasn't the only important thing that Treblinka *did* happen, that it *should* be written about, and that some Jews should be shown to have been heroes?'

It happened, and indeed many Jews were heroes. But untruth always matters, and not just because it is unnecessary to lie when so much terrible truth is available. Every falsification, every error, every slick rewrite job is an advantage to the neo-Nazis.

One other thing assists the revisionists: many Jews, including survivors from the Warsaw Ghetto and Treblinka, are unwilling to bear witness and expose people like Gray for what they are. Understandably, they do not wish to bring back their fearsome experiences into the lives they have rebuilt. Tragically, they fear renewed anti-semitism.

To return to Britain, now sadly enough a kind of neo-Nazi centre: who are the 'growing number of academic and public figures' whom Richard Verrall cites (*New Statesman* letters, 21 September 1977) as moving towards his position? I think David Irving's silly claim has been adequately dealt with in the *Sunday Times*, and although he repeatedly changed his stance later, at least originally, he did not deny that the murders occurred.

Robert Faurisson, an associate professor of literature at Lyons, author of some light literary guides (*As t'on lu Rimbaud etc.*) is certainly a study: I had a long telephone conversation with him recently in which he sought an urgent meeting with me, on the grounds that the 'artistry' of my work *Into That Darkness* had produced 'final proof that the gas chambers never existed'. The mechanism of double-think is admittedly fascinating.

A principal authority for Verrall is Paul Rassinier, whose work has been well described by Raul Hilberg as 'a mixture of error, fantasy and fabrication'. Rassinier, now dead, *was* a historian and *was* for a while imprisoned at Buchenwald. But neither of those facts place him necessarily on the side of the angels: when he sued a writer for defamation who said that he had made common cause with neo-Nazis, the allegation was found proved.

And the 'respected German historian Helmut Diwald' is in fact just that. His field, however, is the period from Charlemagne to Wallenstein (the Thirty Years War), and when his *Geschichte der Deutschen* (*History of the Germans*) appeared early this year, his chapter on the Third Reich was almost universally found to be defective and incomplete. The publishers withdrew the book, issuing jointly with Diwald an apology and a promise that a new edition would deal 'unequivocally . . . with the persecution and murder of the Jews in the Third Reich'.

Finally, A. R. Butz, who is an associate professor of engineering at Northwestern University, Illinois. His *Hoax of the Twentieth Century* makes, as Hugh Trevor-Roper observed, 'a great parade of scholarship (but) . . . most of the book is irrelevant, and the central issue is evaded'. Northwestern's admirable response was to initiate, in the year Butz's tirade reached the US, first a course and then a summer school on their own campus, dealing with the facts of the genocide of the Jews. Always, the proper reply to these dishonourable men begins with knowledge.

7
The Hitler Wave

May 1978

Twenty books on the Hitler era have been published in the past three years, twelve of them by Germans, and I know of eight more now in preparation. Five major works, four of them – a fact of some significance – originating in English, have appeared just during the past twelve months. Every major magazine in Germany has been running long serializations on Hitler, or other Third Reich figures; every newspaper in the country devotes vast space to reviews and discussions of Hitlerian topics; every television channel screens at least two peak-time programmes a month with a Hitler or the Second World War theme, and Hitler films are big business. Hans Jürgen Syberberg's extraordinary *Confessions of Winifred Wagner*, in which, under his gently relentless questioning 'Winni', Richard Wagner's eighty-year-old daughter-in-law, one of Hitler's intimates, confirms her continued devotion to 'Wolf', has been seen by most intelligent Germans, and is already considered a classic of its kind. And historian Hans Joachim Fest's two-and-a-half-hour documentary *Hitler, A Career*, produced entirely with film clips from Nazi archives, has been playing to full houses all over Germany and has been seen by over a million people, 70 per cent of them under thirty-five, since last summer.

The media – not just in Germany – pounces on everything to do with the Nazi era, and the showbiz of it extends to a rock musical, *The Führer* (in English!), Hitler records, Hitler souvenirs, God help us, Bormann's teeth, an alleged Hitler son.

What is it all about? Thirst for knowledge, neo-Nazism rampant, rebirth of anti-semitism? Is Hitler 'the Hero of the Seventies', as the *Frankfurter Allgemeine Zeitung* has asked? Or is this nothing but the result of publishers, film-makers and television executives anxious to make a mint? The answers are important to the equanimity of Europe, but they appear to depend on complex factors, none of which can be treated in isolation. My attempt to come to terms with them has centred on a series of interviews with young Germans, and with intellectuals who are able to recall the events of Nazism.

In the United States and Britain, although among some of the older generations the distrust of the Germans seems incurable, the Hitler wave, motivated either commercially, purely intellectually, or frankly ideologically, comes from without. In Germany, where with few exceptions it stems primarily from the immense need of most thinking people to understand and come to terms with the past, it comes from within.

There is a deep conflict between moralists and pragmatists: the moralists feel that the *Vergangenheitsbewältigung* – the psychological acceptance and management of the Hitler past – is imperative to Germany's health as a nation. Without it, they say, what exists now and lies ahead is moral and spiritual stagnation. The pragmatists, most of whom agree that ideally the Hitler generation of Germans should have accepted – and admitted to their children – their share of guilt, feel that after thirty-two years it is pointless to continue that battle. The only rational solution is to relegate Hitler and his Third Reich to the past, and to what they regard as strictly historical, rather than psychoanalytical, research.

Neo-Nazism as a political force is negligible in Germany: it consists of a minute lunatic fringe (0.4 per cent in the last federal – none in any recent municipal – elections), a few silly kids playing cops and robbers under two Nazi fanatics called Hoffmann and Röder, and a couple of right-radical papers with a readership of about 200,000 sixty- to eighty-year olds. There is probably less effective neo-Nazism in Germany than, for example, in Britain with her severe labour and immigrant problems.

'There is also virtually no overt anti-semitism,' says Michel Friedman, a twenty-three-year-old Jewish law student in Frankfurt, 'the principal reason being that there are virtually no Jews: 35,000 in all of Western Germany (the equivalent of, perhaps, ten blocks in New York City), a few young children, 2,000 students between fifteen and thirty, and the rest old.' This, as we shall see, is only true up to a point: the Jews' ineradicable link with Hitler is unfinished business for the

Germans and remains the country's most fundamental problem. The terrorists and all of the Hitler-revisionist elements, in and outside Germany, are involved with the Hitler past; above all, they *use* it. And virtually all of them direct their efforts at the youth of Germany, and the young in other countries.

The terrorists – the plans of whose leaders require a Europe, and particularly a Germany, in chaos – are young, stuffed with unexperienced ideologies and desperate ideals (many of them have come out of the Christian youth movements), deeply disillusioned with their parent-generation, and deeply resentful of the role of the 'ugly German'.

'They do see the present-day German establishment as the heirs to Hitler,' says the psychoanalyst Dr Margarete Mitscherlich, who, at the Sigmund Freud Institute in Frankfurt, works with many young people. 'To put it in extreme terms, to them Schleyer (head of the German employers' union, kidnapped and killed by the Red Army Faction) was a symbol of Himmler, and our police are the equivalent of the SS. When they fight against them, they basically feel they are doing what their parents should have done.' This is not just a psychiatrist's opinion. A Lutheran pastor used a very similar explanation for the act of some young officers in Munich who recently, while drunk, burned a Jew in effigy. 'It is appalling,' he said. 'But rather than expressing anti-semitism of their own, it could represent a protest against their parents who they feel to be cowards for not owning up to what they did or felt thirty years ago. The relationships of many of our young with their parents (and *our* young, he said, contrary to those in other countries, are *all* the post-war generations, up to forty-five) are so complicated by the undigested Hitler past, that what these young officers did could also be interpreted as a gesture of solidarity with their parents, who, now that they are getting old, they no longer wish to deny.'

The title of South African writer Jillian Becker's recent book about the terrorists, *Hitler's Children*, has caused an outcry in some of the German press. 'But,' said the film director Hans Jürgen Syberberg – who has made *four* films about Hitlerian themes – 'how can people deny the connection? I don't sympathize with the terrorists' aims or means in any way, but I do feel sympathy with their cause, which, whatever way you put it, is Germany's past.'

Even this extent of sympathy for the terrorists is rare. The vast majority of people, including the young, are unqualifiedly opposed to them, whatever the terrorists' reasons, and want them stopped – by any means. To my astonishment, in a high-school class of thirty-six sixteen-year-olds in a strictly working-class district of Hamburg, more than half spoke up for the reintroduction of the death penalty, and this, I was told everywhere, was representative of the population.

'Here are the dangers,' says Dr Mitscherlich: 'Many older people, as you see, are calling for a return to law and order, which they associate, not unnaturally, with their happy youth under Hitler. There is nothing much to be done about this: it is a problem that will only be solved biologically, with time. But the thinking young German who joins the call for authoritarian violence, is abandoning a battle he has waged quite deliberately, quite consciously since Hitler, against the innate authority-hunger which he knows is part of his nature. And that battle, he abandons to his and our peril.'

Margarete Mitscherlich's husband, Alexander Mitscherlich, is professor in social psychology at Frankfurt University, director of the Freud Institute, and, as head of the German medical commission at the Nuremberg 'Doctors' trials' spent seven months observing and talking to all the accused. 'One of our great dangers at present,' he says, 'are the film-makers and writers – a virtual flood of them – who claim to present Hitler from a "historical perspective" – by no means only in Germany, but just as much, if not even more, abroad! "Historical perspective" sounds good, but given that Hitler's principal characteristic was his fundamental immorality, it is of course impossible, and even immoral, to view him objectively!'

'After three decades,' said his wife, 'it is right to look for new explanations; but they must be sought in the social and intellectual phenomena that led up to Hitler: to the fact that he is the only dictator in history who was *voted* into power . . .' J. P. Stern, Professor at Large at Cornell, and head of the German Department at University College, London, says in his book *Hitler, The Führer and The People* (which will doubtlessly cause new furore when it appears in Germany this year) that Hitler was not the creator, but the creature of his time. He merely echoed the self-destructive, ego-centred tradition of German thinkers and writers (however great) of the late nineteenth and twentieth centuries: Franz Werfel, Thomas Mann, Freud, Jung, Jaspers,

Kafka. The devotion of so many Germans for Hitler, says Professor Stern, thus had its origin in German society's traditional conformity, concentration on self and passivity towards individual liberty.

'The explanation can *not* be sought,' said Dr Mitscherlich, 'in a pseudo-objective consideration of Hitler's person and deeds: that approach is dangerously persuasive for our young – as we can see from Joachim Fest's film.'

Hitler, A Career, the documentary with Joachim Fest's text and Josef Goebbels's films, with its deliberate attempt to portray Hitler as Germans saw him from 1918 to 1945, has unleashed a storm of controversy. In a poll conducted recently by *Der Spiegel*, 60 per cent of all young Germans between sixteen and twenty-four said they expected to see, or had already seen it. I took three groups to the film and talked with each for hours afterwards. Hundreds of thousands of words – analysis and criticism – have been written about it in the German papers, but none of them, I thought, was as significant as the reactions of the young – slowly changing and evolving – when they were given a chance to think together.

Florian, aged sixteen, said he really thought it was pretty good, pretty much what he had expected. 'If I saw a film announced, say, of Frank Sinatra's "Career", I wouldn't expect a moral essay,' he said, 'I'd just expect to see a portrait of his life.' 'There was an awful lot I hadn't known,' said eighteen-year-old Herbert. 'All that pomp, those fantastic rallies – it was really theatre, wasn't it? Art. Beautiful.' 'For the first time,' said Norbert, aged seventeen, 'I could understand my grandparents.' 'Yes,' said Karl Heinz, 'it was exactly the way my parents' fifty- and sixty-year-old friends talked about it.'

'It really got to me,' Dorothea said – she was sixteen. 'That model they showed of Speer's post-war Berlin. So impressive.' 'Yes,' said Gaby, 'and when they said it was planned that every year deputations of slaves from the East were to march through the streets, I could just see it happen – fantastic . . .'

'But when they showed the beginning of the war,' said Traude, aged eighteen – by now they had been talking for two hours, with very little help aside from an occasional nudge from me – 'and the commentator said that the Germans were just helping the German minorities in Danzig. That wasn't true, was it? Wasn't there something about

German convicts dressed up as Poles being used to fake an attack, and then all being killed by "defending" Germans? Is that not how they started the war?'*

It was remarkable to watch how, once they began to question what they had seen and felt, both their knowledge, and moral sense emerged: 'He says Hitler was incorruptible,' said Norbert (the 'he' always refers to Fest, the writer), 'that Hitler only accepted money from industrialists if given without strings. But surely that wasn't so? In those circumstances, conditions wouldn't have had to be spelled out: they would have been implicit. And of course there had to be strings. But if the speaker actually *says* Hitler was incorruptible – that's sort of impressive, isn't it?'

'Nor did he mention *Mein Kampf*,' said Traude. 'And the concentration camps just once, for five seconds . . .' 'Yes,' said Florian, 'and what *about* the Jews? They came in three times: first when he talks about Hitler at eighteen, in Vienna, when they show film of bearded dirty-looking men with funny braids, and a couple of pretty girls and say how shocked Hitler was by the racial defilement of Austrian girls . . .' 'Yes,' said Gaby, 'and I thought, my God, they *do* look pretty awful. Just think: that's what it made *me* feel . . .' 'The second time the Jews were mentioned was when he said Jews began to leave, and showed photos of Einstein, Thomas Mann – *was* he a Jew? – Reinhardt and some actors. And then, do you remember, he had the gall to say, "They left, and left the country to provincialism." My God, as if they left by choice!'

'And then,' said Herbert, 'there was that bit where they showed people being shot in a pit – the only time, incidentally, they showed people being killed except by Allied bombs – and they said it was in Russia and they were partisans and Jews, thereby linking the Jews with partisans: as if they'd killed Jews because they were partisans. And then he said, do you remember, "90,000 Russians were killed here," and not more than two minutes later, "91,000 Germans were taken prisoner by the Soviets; only 5,000 returned." Herbert was angry

* She was almost right: the SS faked several incidents, and left bodies of a dozen German convicts dressed in Polish uniforms, first fatally injected then shot several times, as evidence of 'Polish' attacks. (See Nuremberg Affidavit, Naujock, 2,751-PS.)

now. "Outrageous," he said, 'that this should not be a Nazi, but Fest's, commentary.'

'I found myself feeling sorry for Hitler,' said Rudolf, a young teacher and our host. 'The way he suddenly became an old man towards the end; the trembling hand; the last lonely birthday celebrated with nothing except a parade of a couple of dozen of Hitler Youths in the garden of the *Reichskanzlei* in Berlin. And then the way they kept emphasizing that his main purpose was to save the world from Marxism. With our whole country now an armed camp against Marxists, how can the film avoid making people feel, "Well, if he had succeeded, we wouldn't be having all these troubles now"?' 'And what about the ending?' asked Monika, also a teacher, and Rudolf's wife. 'Fifty nations fought against Germany. Germany stood alone. I couldn't believe my ears. I know he didn't mean it the way it sounded, but that's not the point. We were right back in 1918.' 'There is no indication whatever,' said Thomas – aged 15 – 'of an indictment.'

'That's what my father said,' said university student, Manfred. 'He said, all the time he was watching he kept thinking, "The essence is missing," and when I asked him, "What is the essence?" he said, "A judgement."'

'I consider it a deeply dangerous film', said Siegfried Lenz, one of Germany's great post-war writers, all of whose books (*The German Lesson*, *The Example*, etc.) have as their basic theme the Hitler past. 'It is impermissible to amputate morality out of a treatment of the Nazi history, whether the medium be a film, a book or articles.'

Joachim Fest's Hitler biography, all 1,200 pages of it, is highly readable and covers thoroughly all of Hitler's terror, leaving no doubt whatever where the author stands. It has sold 500,000 copies in Germany. He is co-publisher of one of Germany's best papers, the *Frankfurter Allgemeine Zeitung*, and writes many of their political commentaries. He is young, energetic, intelligent, nervy and, despite his rise to fame, engagingly modest. He gave me an excellent three-hour lunch in Frankfurt, and, passionately defending his film throughout, made me feel that I wished I could agree with him.

'I think the most tragic mistake that was made in 1945,' he said, 'was to identify Hitler exclusively with the extermination of the Jews – basically effacing the knowledge about all the other millions he killed, and his plans for the future. The result has not only been a catastrophic distortion of the Hitler period, but also that the majority of Germans, and others too, are sick of the subject. To me, Hitler's immorality, the political monstrosity of his regime are incontestable: it doesn't *need* reiterating. What I felt was needed – and for which the medium of film is superbly suitable – was a redressing of the balance by conveying unemotional, rational and factual new understanding of how it came about.'

This is precisely what another distinguished journalist, Karl Heinz Janssen, contests. 'Young people,' he said, 'should *not* be exposed to this film unprepared – the appallingly dangerous thing is that of course they are.' Professor Eberhard Jäckel, a historian at Stuttgart, says: 'We may have made mistakes; but what we did achieve (since 1945) is that there is virtually no one in Germany who does not (in his bones) associate Hitler with immorality.' 'The awful thing is,' said Janssen, 'that Fest's film, with its phenomenal appeal, could undo this achievement. Because the film not only makes Hitler appear attractive, but above all, an object of sympathy.'

Fest, who acted from the best of motives, can in no way be compared with those who produce the other categories of what the Mitscherlichs called 'pseudo-objective (or totally *subjective*) presentations of Hitler's person and deeds'. And this applies, above all, to the blatantly neo-Nazi publications which can be found all over Germany (as well as Britain and the United States), such as the invidious pamphlet *Did Six Million Really Die?* by a British journalist writing under the pseudonym Richard Harwood, and *The Hoax of the Twentieth Century*, an expansion of the odious theme, by A. R. Butz, an electrical engineer from Illinois. These writers propose that (a) the Jews weren't exterminated at all – the 6 million claim, they say, is nothing but a politically inspired conspiracy by world Zionism, and (b) if some Jews did die – a few 100,000 at best – then they died as others did, because of the war. (Of all countries in the world, only in South Africa is an attempt being made to outlaw these publications!)

But Dr Mitscherlich's words apply in equal measure to less obviously emotive books, by no means concentrating on this one subject: for example, to name but two, the 'totally revised and expanded' 1976 German edition of *Hitler's Tabletalk* by Henry Picker, the only book available in the German language supposedly based on Hitler's own words (*Mein Kampf* being illegal in Germany), and *Hitler's War* by the British writer David Irving.

In the first German version of *Tabletalk*, Dr Picker, a lawyer and self-taught historian, and Bormann's temporary adjutant at Hitler's HQ when he was thirty, produced notes of Hitler's conversations for four of the fifteen months they were recorded. The note-taker for most of that time was another Bormann adjutant, Heinrich Heim, and it was his version that provided the much fuller foreign and later German editions.

After the war, having managed to secure his own and a few other chroniclers' notes, Picker made literally hundreds of changes and 'improvements' and eventually, for his 1976 edition, added 150 pages of his own commentaries to the Hitler material. Albert Speer, formerly Hitler's architect and minister of armaments, told me that Picker had so totally changed Hitler's language in places that, except for those who knew him well and can, of course, recognize many quotes, he ends up 'sounding like just anybody, rather than Hitler'. In Spandau prison, where he first read the book in 1960, Speer noted that

> These Tabletalks don't provide a true picture of Hitler. Picker not only filtered and stylized the wording . . . but above all [Hitler] was normally . . . far more primitive than Picker allows him to appear, far coarser and rougher, but also . . . (partly because of Hitler's informal Austrian phraseology, all of which Picker removed) . . . far more persuasive.

'For those of us who *have* to read *Tabletalk*', said an eighteen-year-old history student in Munich, 'it is very misleading. You see, most of us have too little preknowledge to question those who are presented to us as authorities in their field. I happen to have grown up with a historian-father. This book is a hapless pretence (*eine plumpe Vorspiegelung*) at objectivity. How *dare* these men who were Hitler's sycophants, profiting from his favour, now pretend to be capable of objectivity, while the young of our country, who, with the fewest exceptions such, as luck will have it, myself, have no one to turn to for true objectivity, as their captive audience?'

David Irving's claim, in his sensationalist opus *Hitler's War*, that

Hitler neither ordered nor was aware of the extermination of the Jews (yet again, we can see, *using* this most sensitive subject, to mislead), was allowed to stand in the US and British editions, but was removed from the German edition by the publishers Ullstein. 'No house for which I am responsible,' wrote Ullstein's managing director, Wolf Jobst Siedler, on 7 May 1974 to Irving

> will publish material that I cannot justify politically or historically . . . I do not think my cuts have . . . harmed your book but . . . should you . . . be of a different opinion, then we must part . . .

Irving, who had been paid an advance of DM90,000, elected not to take up the suggestion.

While his thesis about Hitler's ignorance, produced with the help of misinterpreted German documents, therefore didn't appear in the German edition, the German press, not surprisingly, reported fully the storm of protest that arose when the book was published in Britain last summer. Almost all adults I talked to in Germany seemed to know all about it. 'Unfortunately,' says Albert Speer, 'it has already provided longed-for ammunition for those here in Germany who are busy building up the new "war-blame lie".'

But in the final analysis, Irving's basically absurd thesis is not the only harmful thing about this book. 'The real problem,' said Manfred, a thirty-year-old economist in Mainz, 'is that he wrote his book, so to speak, from Hitler's point of view. But how can our young people deal with such a perspective without being misled, when all they know are the bare bones of the history of the Third Reich?'

None of these manipulated versions of history matters for the old: all of them are profoundly dangerous for the young – now two thirds of Germany's population. The ignorance of young Germans about their recent history is a continuous talking point in Germany.

My first meeting with young Germans, on the morning I arrived, was unplanned. My hosts, Monika and Rudolf Petzenhauser, are both teachers, and Rudolf, a thirty-nine-year-old historian and Germanist, was, it so happened – as he does every year – taking his graduating class to see Dachau, Hitler's first concentration camp, near Munich. His colleague and friend, Father Böckle, Catholic priest, teacher of religion, and, incidentally, a native of Dachau village, who was ten when the camp existed, also took a class: thirty-four fourteen-year-old boys.

Organized visits to the camp began immediately after its liberation in 1945. During those first years of revulsion and remorse, Dachau, conveniently located near a major city, and believed by the vast majority of people to have been, like all the camps (they thought), an extermination camp for Jews, became a kind of symbol, a place of pilgrimage. In fact, comparatively few Jews were held at Dachau, or at many other of the concentration camps within Germany's borders. It was primarily a bitterly harsh punitive camp for political prisoners, and while many died of overwork and starvation, and the bodies (just like in the *extermination* camps, all located in occupied Poland) were burned in the camp crematorium, no one was 'exterminated' there.

Rudolf, partly for my benefit, had decided not to 'guide' his group, but to wait for questions. Walking around the huge compound, through the curiously sterile-seeming crematorium, the oven doors somehow obscenely open, and the tiny gas chamber, never used, where hundreds of visitors, God knows why, had scribbled their names on the walls, the questions were slow in coming. The students seemed vaguely troubled, but incapable of putting their discomfort into words, without help.

'Well, it's . . . it's a *museum* really, isn't it?' said eighteen-year-old Gaby who, particularly interested in contemporary history, was on her second visit. 'It isn't *real*. You'll see,' she added in an aside, to me, 'at our age, unless they *are* guided, it's just history to them; it's like the Inquisition, you know: quite interesting.' And up to a point this was true. As an UNRRA child welfare officer, I had seen Dachau immediately after liberation, and there was no relationship between this hygienized reconstruction, and the reeking reality of that time. What there is now – and how can it be otherwise? – is not real. In the one reconstructed barrack, the bunks, tables and chairs smell agreeably of pine. 'I don't see that it's so different from our youth hostels,' one seventeen-year-old finally said, somewhat defensively. 'Look, here on the notice it says they had to keep their blue-checked sheets symmetrically tidy. Well, so what? So do we on our skiing holidays. And our sheets are blue-checked too.' It was a telling demonstration of the need to identify their perplexity, not least over their own detachment, and the virtual impossibility of imparting real understanding of the complex facts except by careful preparation and guidance. History is not learnt easily.

The next day, during a discussion in the Petzenhausers' living room following a visit to Fest's film, this same group indicated that part of the difficulty at Dachau had been, not only that they knew that we – Rudolf and I – had expected them to be appalled (and they are very authority-conscious), but that they themselves had expected to be horrified. 'I was shocked at myself for not being shocked,' said that same seventeen-year-old boy. 'I felt there had to be something wrong with me that I didn't feel sick to my stomach.'

This is already a key: perhaps it is true that young Germans – as is so widely claimed – know even fewer facts about Hitler and his Third Reich than other young. But they are inescapably 'involved'. 'Unless children are systematically conditioned by an amoral environment such as happened during the Third Reich,' said Albert Speer, 'their instinct tells them what is right and wrong. Given full access to all facts in an atmosphere of freedom, I believe they have unfailing moral judgement.'

This is precisely what I found: the young Germans are a profoundly moral generation, and the indifference the younger among them so often – so defensively – proclaim ('We don't care about Hitler; we weren't even born then; what has it to do with us?') is less than skin-deep, even for the youngest.

In the Dachau museum, Father Böckle – as we see *has* to be done – *was* guiding his younger boys around the beautifully mounted life-size photographic exhibits. Wide-eyed, they listened as he told them that on occasions, when the prisoners would be taken through the town on their way to work, he had actually *seen* them when he was ten, and yes, they did look just like what they were seeing in these photographs.

They stared. 'Like this, you mean?' a boy pointed unbelievingly at a scarecrow figure in a convict uniform. They became extraordinarily excited: they pulled the priest from exhibit to exhibit and the questions virtually tumbled over each other. 'What sort of work did they have to do? How long were they imprisoned? How could you tell Jews apart from other people? What really was a communist? A Quaker? A freemason?'

'What was the crystal night?' asked a small thin boy standing in front of a picture showing men in uniform with swastika armbands breaking up shop windows. 'Why, *why*, would they smash up shops owned by Jews? That's terribly unfair: it costs money to repair windows.'

They stood for a long time looking at a huge photograph of burning books while one boy read aloud the long caption. Einstein, Heine, Thomas Mann left them cold. But when they heard the name of Erich Kästner, they jumped. 'Why would they burn books of someone who wrote *Emil and the Detectives*?' ('Felix Salten?' asked a thirteen-year-old girl in Hamburg ten days later when the book burnings came up. 'What was wrong with *Bambi*?').

Ten years later, a class of sixteen-year-olds in Hamburg who, like most other people, had never associated 'Hitler with anything' except the lost war and the murder of the Jews, were aghast to hear of his euthanasia programme, in the course of which around 80,000 physically and mentally handicapped German and Austrian hospital patients, about a third, I told them, children, were gassed. Some of them, as a matter of fact, I said, were killed in one of the special 'children's sections' in a hospital in their own city, Hamburg.

'You mean *Germans*?' a boy said in a tone of utter disbelief. '*Children? German children*?' said another. 'Here? In Hamburg?' They came back to it, time and again. Jews were unreal to them: in that class of thirty-six children (and in nine of the eleven young groups with whom I met) no one had ever met a Jew. And figures like the murder of 6 million Jews, or 11 million Russian civilians – or for that matter 50 million dead altogether by 1945 – are as impossible to absorb or visualize as is, in fact, the word 'extermination'. But the thought that sick *children* had been deliberately killed, in a *hospital*, in their own city, Hamburg . . . that struck a chord. One young teacher, Christa, said later, 'This was worth weeks of lessons; they'll never forget it.' But another teacher, elsewhere, disapproved of children being given such information . . . which may be as good an explanation as any why no German children are given it. 'You shouldn't have told them things like that,' she said. 'They won't sleep tonight.'

Her reaction was significant. But I found it even more important, that a shy and obviously inarticulate boy, who, throughout the two hours I had spent with that Hamburg class, had not said a word, *did* say something in the end, long after we had left the subject of 'mercy killing'.

'I've been thinking about what you said, that they killed all those people,' he said, 'Jews and Russians and Poles, and people who were handicapped and mentally ill. I've been thinking,' he repeated, the class deathly still. 'It is wrong,' he said in his ponderous way. 'Every human being is of value.'

At Dachau that day, walking his group past the 'whipping post' in the square, the priest told the boys about the punishments the SS meted out every day. 'They didn't say anything for quite a while,' he told me, 'and then one of them said, "If one sees that . . . that thing, one has to feel ashamed of being German." And another said, "But were they human beings at all if they did such things?"' And then finally a third, after a long pause, 'But not *all* SS were bad like those who were here,' and then he added after a moment, 'My grandpa was in the SS.' I think that shook Father Böckle; he couldn't think of an answer for this boy. Who can?

When I saw *Hitler, A Career* I remembered something from my own childhood I had pushed away. I knew, at eleven, what Hitler was. I had listened to clever people; and I knew that dreadful things were going to happen in our lives. After feeling enticed by Hitler speaking in Vienna, I never told anyone about my hour at the Nuremberg rally. It had become, and remains, a thing of shame. But sitting in the Fest film, I knew what these young people were feeling, for I had felt it, and I knew and know the danger.

If today's elders have produced the 'economic miracle' – the envy of all Europe – their back-breaking work was not because, but instead of repentance: the power of the gun was replaced by the power of the D-mark, and they could, after all, offer their children the promised glorious future.

Perhaps it is time, in Germany and elsewhere, to exercise much sharper self-censorship: to avoid, for the sake of the young – theirs and no less our own – what is inflammatory, tendentious and merely titillating for its own sake. Perhaps we need to make clearer than we have done, to those who have not learned the lesson: that we will not accept the slightest falsification of that particular period in history – whether for personal or political gain – and that we will fight such attempts wherever they occur.

But perhaps, above all, it is time that we say loud and clear to the young Germans that we do not consider the children responsible for the parents' sins; that we do not believe in inherited guilt; that we do not accept the transferred image of the 'ugly German'.

8

Fakes and Hoaxes: The Hitler Diaries

February 2000

I want to write here about a kind of passion, the curious and, in some cases I think, sad passion about Hitler and his Third Reich which has ruled and continues to rule the lives of a considerable number of people who write or inspire books.

Those who create these situations, or writings, are bitter and more often than not in some way or another dysfunctional men, out to use – or misuse – this terrible part of history, partly, no doubt, for material gain and improved career prospects, but sometimes quite as much because of their need to be retrospectively involved and to assuage their anger, dissatisfaction or pain.

The question of the reliability of survivor testimony, recently much discussed in David Irving's libel action in the British High Court against Deborah Lipstadt and Penguin, is of course a thorny matter and there can be no doubt that men and women, emerging from the hell of the Nazi camps, at times altered their experiences, sometimes consciously and sometimes no doubt unconsciously dramatizing or minimizing their own roles. To understand, or, more, to sit in judgement on these people, however, demands rather more than, as Mr Irving repeatedly urged the court to judge his actions, sitting at a desk in a Mayfair flat examining documents: it requires the capacity, not for sentimentality, but for empathy with the suffering of survivors. Anyone who is incapable of such empathy – perhaps because of their own prejudices, or perhaps quite simply because their nature does not permit it – has, I feel, neither the ability nor the right to comment on their apparent flaws. I have sat listening to hundreds of these eyewitness accounts and have read as many survivor memoirs as I could bear to. More than that, however, I have spent weeks and months not 'interviewing' in the usual sense of the term but *talking* with some of them. If there is anything I have learned, it is that these people cannot be looked at as a group, a category, but only as individuals, with very individual experiences and very individual and personal needs.

With this I do not mean to convey approval or even acceptance of the many exaggerations or untruths I have heard: I am unhappy when it happens; I reject what I hear and no longer quite trust such a person. But I always know that I have not lived through what they suffered; I have not seen what they saw, nor have I done what in many cases they had to do in order to stay alive. The most telling example for me of this was, strangely enough, something that happened to perhaps the most remarkable survivor I worked with when preparing *Into That Darkness*, Richard Glazar, a Czech who survived Treblinka.

Richard, twenty-two when he arrived at Treblinka, was not only one of the most intelligent but also one of the most honest men I met. He settled in Switzerland after the war and it was sitting in his living room in a village near Bern late one night in 1972 that – I think because we had talked for many hours and he was tired – he told me something truly quite terrible. It was about the month of March in 1943 when the transports to Treblinka had dried up. They had killed most of the Jews they were going to kill there, and for the so-called 'work-Jews' (*Arbeitsjuden*), strong young men like Richard (and a few girls, too), it meant that once they had finished packing up and sending off to Germany all the things collected from the victims, 'clothes, watches, spectacles, shoes, walking sticks, cooking pots, linen, not to speak of food', there would be no work for them. 'Everything went and one day there was nothing left,' he said. 'You can't imagine what we felt when there was nothing there. You see, the *things* were our justification for being alive. If there were no *things* to administer, why would they let us stay alive?' he said. One day towards the end of March, when they had reached the lowest ebb in their morale, Kurt Franz, the deputy commandant, walked into their barracks, a wide grin on his face. '"As of tomorrow," he said, "transports will be rolling in again." And do you know what we did?' Richard asked. 'We shouted, "Hurrah, hurrah." It seems impossible now. Every time I think of it, I die a small death; but it's the truth. That is what we did; that is where we had got to . . .'

It was one of the most terrible truths anyone had ever told me. But if you read the latest editions of *Into That Darkness* you will find that this sentence has been changed, because by the time when first André Deutsch, in 1991, and then Pimlico in 1995, issued these new editions, Richard had gone through enormous difficulties, in Israel and elsewhere, because of having spoken this truth. And of course, when he asked me to modify the sentence, I did. Sadly, Richard and his wife are dead now: I think he would forgive me setting it right again, for the good purpose of showing what the cost of the truth can be, and how it can be perverted sometimes even by good intentions.

But there are quite different examples of untrue testimonies, some dishonourable lies, others simply pathological. There has never been any doubt that the already mentioned Martin Gray, who was sixteen years old in the Warsaw Ghetto, was motivated by the vision of a bestseller when he came to write his memoirs *For Those I Loved* in 1972. He had made a remarkable career after the war, becoming rich very young by dealing in fake antiques from Germany and settling in a castle in the south of France with a beautiful model wife and two enchanting children. The book was suggested to him by a French publisher after his family died in an atrocious forest fire: his published intention was to donate the proceeds to a charity combating forest fires.

It could have been a really interesting book, but after he was told by his editor that the Polish part of the story needed more drama, it was decided to add on an invented chapter describing his imprisonment and escape from Treblinka. He spent months in a Jewish archive in Paris, and got additional information from Jean-François Steiner's book, *Treblinka*. (Steiner's parents had died there, but when his account was attacked by real Treblinka survivors about its accuracy, as already said, he quickly and honourably withdrew it and republished it as fiction, or 'faction'.)

Gray repeated many of its original mistakes and, representing himself as a heroic escapee, added many others. After a lecture he delivered in London for the publication of the book here, I told him that what he had written was not true. He telephoned me the next morning to offer me the job of consultant on a planned film of his book, which I refused.

The much more recent literary scandal of Binjamin Wilkomirski's

Fragments, supposedly a Latvian Jewish child's memoirs which was translated into twelve languages and received many prizes, is a different matter, not a deliberate lie but, I believe, an example of pathological sadness. Wilkomirski, a Swiss musician and clarinet-maker and a gentile, whose real name seems to be Bruno Grosjean, apparently suffered from depression and conceived a Jewish identity – and the idea to write these false memoirs – while in psychiatric treatment. Had he, or had his many publishers, presented this slim book as a parable, he might well have won the same prizes, for, impossible as a document, it is deeply touching as a work of the imagination. Several people I know, including Elena Lappin for *Granta*, have spent long days with him and found him dreadfully sad: this is not a man who wanted money, but a human being who, out of a need I suspect of sharing the suffering, attempted to adopt the identity of the suffering child. He hurt no one as much as himself.

The most famous falsification was, of course, the 1983 'Hitler diaries' scandal, the effects of which keep reverberating in the literature. It so happens that I was closely involved with it from the start. In December 1982, David Irving had approached the *Sunday Times* with the information that he had been shown by a reporter from *Stern* magazine in Hamburg, Gerd Heidemann, who had a large collection of Nazi memorabilia, Hitler diaries (or perhaps 'a' Hitler diary), of which there were allegedly twenty-seven and which, on first perusal, he said, looked interesting. He proposed to the paper to use his expertise to research their origin and authenticity. But this came only five years after the *Sunday Times* publication of our highly critical analysis of the methods he had used to write his controversial book *Hitler's War*. So his offer was declined and I was sent to Hamburg instead.

As is now well known, the whole *Stern* scoop – sixty-two diaries in Hitler's handwriting – was found to be a fake, on the face of it conceived by a small-time crook, Konrad Kujau, and paid for with *Stern*'s money, DM11 million. Gerd Heidemann, who I would go and see in January 1983, was apparently the 'patsy' through whom these riches were disbursed.

During my first meetings with Heidemann, he let me read one of the 'diaries' but, more significantly to me at the time, showed me around his huge and doubtlessly at least partially genuine collection of Third Reich memorabilia. My first opinion was that although the text of the only diary I had seen seemed rather simplistic, that was not necessarily proof of forgery: diaries written by complex personalities quite often *are* deceptively banal. Already at this stage he told me in great detail about his searches for Nazi material, but not that *Stern* already had many of the alleged diaries. In his impressive archive he had, for example, the entire library of 100,000 negatives of photographs taken by Hitler's photographer Heinrich Hoffmann – which he had bought (with *Stern* money, of course) from Hoffmann's son. He also had a letter from former SS General Karl Wolff, the highest-ranking SS officer then still alive, who doubtless would have held important historical documents, appointing Heidemann as his literary heir and executor (which Wolff would later confirm to me). He had a considerable number of what looked like extraordinary items, such as the original of the infamous 'Commissar Order', which he said he had had authenticated by – among others – SS Generals Wolff and Mohnke; and he had a huge collection of quite pretty paintings and sculptures, all signed by Hitler, (some quite authentic, as a highly reputable Munich dealer from whom he had bought them would later confirm to me; others faked by Kujau, whose house, as I would later find, was full of little landscapes he signed 'Hitler'). Dozens of these paintings, I was appalled to see, and a large portrait of Hitler, hung on three walls surrounding the Heidemann marital bed (a fact which appeared to please his rather silly wife more than it did him).

I thought then, and think now, that Heidemann was not a crook, but rather what Germans call a *Fantast*. That too, of course, can lead to crime. But I do not believe he was part of any conspiracy. If he really had found Hitler diaries, it was obvious – and he himself had insisted on it from the start – that the volumes would be subjected to minute examination. If their authenticity had been confirmed, they would have been worth a fortune and would have brought him extraordinary fame and riches. If on the other hand they turned out to be fakes, then equally obviously he would at the very least be a laughing stock and probably unemployed. In retrospect, of course, Heidemann's great problem was that he *wanted* them to be real – not so much for the fame or the money, but simply for the satisfaction of having found them. Obsession overshadows and indeed obliterates rational thought and morality. Heidemann's obsession with Hitler dominated his life and determined all his actions.

As I say, my first reaction, conceived in the context of the astonishing nature of his collection, was that this strange man *might* have found a diary or diaries: that they *could* be authentic but that no one should think of publishing them without thorough research into their origin. Rupert Murdoch's successful negotiations with *Stern* for the British rights to the diaries meanwhile created a problem in London. Many *Sunday Times* journalists were furious that publishing such material was even being contemplated. But to some of us, their potential historical importance – if they could be shown to be authentic – seemed to override such objections. And we thought we would have just enough time – three weeks – to check them out before publication – synchronized with *Stern* in Germany – began. An investigative team including Brian MacArthur, Paul Eddy and Anthony Terry was quickly formed – seven of us in all to liaise with *Stern* while making our own verifications.

Rupert Murdoch called a meeting of the team to explore the situation, but first I had a private meeting with him in his office at Gray's Inn Road. I asked what he would do, given that he had just committed a very large sum to *Stern*, if, for example, as one of the team charged with the investigation of the diaries, I came to the conclusion they were suspect. At the first proof or reasonable suspicion that they were forgeries, he said, he would cancel publication, never mind the money, and he instructed his secretary to connect me to him wherever he was if I telephoned during the investigation. When he repeated this assurance at the subsequent meeting with the whole of the 'Diary' investigation team, all of whom, without exception, were highly sceptical both of the volumes and of the idea of their being published in the *Sunday Times*, there was a real sense of reassurance. 'Investigative journalism' is not, or never should be, a one-person task. Because it is a kind of detective work, it needs several minds who exchange information, challenge each other's findings, and support or reject conclusions. Usually it also needs a great deal of time and more often than not a great deal of money. True enough, we had only three weeks. But I think we all felt that for the seven of us, with all the power of News International behind us, it should be enough.

As it happened, we didn't have three weeks: on hearing that *Der Spiegel*, their chief rival in Germany, was on to the story, *Stern* panicked and insisted on publishing immediately. It was decided that we would have to accept *Stern*'s assurances that complete authentification had already been carried out, and Hugh Trevor-Roper, who had already visited Heidemann and had also seen his collection, was hastily commissioned to prepare the first announcement in *The Times*. He quickly delivered the piece, but overnight became suspicious of one letter Heidemann had shown him. He tried to warn the editors of *The Times* and the *Sunday Times* to be cautious, a warning he was never given credit for, but was too late to delay publication.

Within two weeks, the German Federal Archives who, contrary to *Stern*'s assurances to Times Newspapers, had never seen a diary or known of their alleged existence, forensically established the forgery. What Heidemann *had* shown them, were pages from one of several 'special' volumes Kujau had sold to him – supposedly Hitler's thoughts on the flight to Scotland (in 1941) of his deputy, Rudolf Hess. The Federal Archives had authenticated the pre-1945 paper and the historical content. But they had no idea that these were supposed to be from a Hitler diary, and were not asked to check the handwriting. Intriguingly enough, also among these 'special volumes' (I have seen two of them) were twelve pages Hitler allegedly wrote on 28 January 1942 with his proposals for the 'Final Solution' which was not mass murder but the resettlement of the Jews, males and females thousands of miles apart, in Siberia (one of several possibilities, we now know from recent research, considered at the time).

By the time of the débâcle, when we returned to London, however, I had some evidence of the existence of at least one real Hitler diary, very different in appearance and content from the ones so crazily purchased by *Stern*. And I began to suspect that the real initiators of this *coup*, far more troubling than the crooked clown Konrad Kujau, or the naïve Gerd Heidemann, could be people of far more sinister calibre and motivations.

A few weeks later, when everything had calmed down, I convinced the *Sunday Times* to let me investigate the background. Pained at having fallen for *Stern*'s assurances of authenticity, my suspicion of a very different and more serious explanation no doubt gave the editors hope for a surprise solution that would reduce their embarrassment. And so I finally spent seven months criss-crossing the world, seeing almost everybody who had anything to do with it. One of the most interesting things about this odyssey, much more interesting than that some people had lied – above all, of course, Konrad Kujau who is hardly capable of speaking a true word – is how many people manifestly spoke the truth. Here for the first time is the story I finally wrote, now considerably expanded to show the truths I found.

December 1983

The two men are kept firmly apart in Hamburg's remand prison. But their cells are close enough for Gerd Heidemann to be able to hear Konrad Kujau making fun of him. 'Then you can hear Heidemann respond with rage,' says one official. 'I don't know which is more disconcerting.' There is, indeed, an extraordinary contrast between the two characters at the heart of the great Hitler diaries hoax.

Heidemann greets visitors with a frozen smile. He tries to be like his meticulous old self but the tension in his face and body defeat him. He talks ceaselessly, repeating the litany he has kept up since his world fell apart: yes, he was stupid; no, he was *not* a crook. He is a man on the brink of a nervous collapse, or worse.

Kujau does not just stand up when the visitor enters, he *jumps* up. He looks much older than forty-five, but he bubbles with energy and joy. He is the prison clown, and he has prison officials in stitches, deliberately drawing them into the conversation when they sit in on interviews. His emotions can vary wildly. At the mention of his East German family, he is suddenly furious: 'They have nothing to do with it,' he shouts. Then, in seconds, the smile is back, the hostility is replaced by heavy charm.

He enjoys reciting lists of the reference material he claims to have used in forging the diaries. 'I'm really grateful to *Die Bild-Zeitung* [a mass market German newspaper]', he says. 'Their long stories on Hitler and Eva Braun provided a rich harvest.' He laughs so much that his whole body shakes, so delighted is he at the thought that the right-wing *Bild-Zeitung* should have supplied some of the raw material he used to hoodwink the leftish *Stern*.

He is adamant that the diaries are all his own work. 'I know more about Hitler than anyone else in Germany,' he says. 'Nobody knows as much about him as I. All these historians, all they ever do is repeat each other's mistakes. It took me no time at all. Do you know how long it took? Two and a half hours for one diary.'

He proceeds to write eight lines in Hitler's handwriting, to dictation, signing the page six times. 'That's how he wrote in 1905, that's 1908,' and so on, he explains, as he painstakingly completes each signature.

He is well primed on other notorious forgers – 'but I've outdone them all'. He can't resist adding in a whisper, that when he gets out of gaol he will produce a really *big* surprise: Hitler's daughter.

For a man facing a long prison sentence, it is an astonishing performance. But it is possible to crack the clown's pose.

Ask him, for example, how it was that his one-time Stuttgart lawyer had some of Kujau's diaries in his safe three or four years *before* Kujau claims he started to write them. He waffles. Ask him about the man he calls his 'patron', who offered diaries for sale in America, years before they are supposed to have existed. He erupts into anger.

Above all, test him with specific factual points taken from the diaries he is so proud of composing. He cannot answer; he hums and haws and does his best to change the subject.

Heidemann lies too, but the compulsion is different. Although he will not admit it, the diaries and his belief that he had a direct line to Martin Bormann were only some of the strands of the web of fantasies in which he was trapped. Heidemann also believed that he knew the whereabouts of twelve hidden Nazi treasure caches; he still clings to that belief because it is his only hope for the future.

Though certain of a long prison sentence, he refuses to give anyone – even his despairing lawyer – evidence which, if true, could free him. The prosecution believes that Heidemann stole at least £500,000, and possibly more, from the money given him by *Stern* to buy the diaries. He claims that four men advanced him money for a share in the hidden Nazi treasure. 'If he gave us the chance to prove that claim he could be out of prison within days,' says the Hamburg prosecutor.

The prosecution thinks that Heidemann's story is nonsense because he stays silent. 'I have given a promise,' he says, repeating almost word for word a fateful pledge of silence he gave eighteen months ago to Kujau when he promised never to reveal him as the source of the diaries. 'If the only way for me to get out of prison is break my promise, then I will go to prison.'

So, to a large extent, the official version of the Hitler diaries hoax is flawed by the silence of one of the two key participants, and the testimony of the other, who is almost incapable of telling the truth.

Pick any chapter in Konrad Kujau's life story, and it will be riddled with deception. Take, for example, his account of his childhood.

He was born in 1938, the third of five children, in the small town of Löbau, about forty miles from Dresden in what became communist East Germany. He claims to have been at school until he was eighteen, gaining the equivalent of A levels, and then to have gone to the Dresden Academy of Art, which he had to leave after only two terms because 'my father did not belong to the working classes'. He was then 'allotted' a job in the clubhouse of the Free German Youth in Löbau where he was an 'organization manager'. After three weeks of this, however, he decided to escape to the West in order to avoid conscription into the People's Army.

Doris, his sister, who still lives in Löbau, tells a different story. True, she says, 'he was always the brightest of us all and got good marks at school'. But according to her, he left at sixteen, and there was no question of A levels. 'We were very poor,' she says. 'All of us grew up in children's homes.' Neither did Connie, as Kujau was always called, go to any academy. Instead he became a locksmith's apprentice for a year, a worker in a textile plant for one month, a labourer for two months, a painter for three weeks. At the youth centre he was merely a waiter.

Then, take his dramatic escape from East Germany. With the practised art of a good confidence trickster, he describes it in loving detail: 'I left Löbau and East Germany by train, at 2.29 a.m., on 7 June 1957.' True, he did. But it was not army service he was fleeing so much as a warrant for his arrest, on suspicion of having stolen a microphone from the youth club.

His description of his life in Stuttgart, in West Germany, is also an intriguing mix of truth and fantasy. In 1963, Kujau and his girlfriend, Edith Lieblang, set up an industrial cleaning company. 'I had savings of about DM100,000 (£33,000) when we started,' he says. Edith, now his common-law wife, remains unfailingly loyal. But even she cannot hide her disbelief: '*Connie?* Savings of DM100,000?' Her incredulous tone says it all.

Kujau describes the company's success: 'We had the biggest customers . . . I assigned myself a salary of DM8,000 a month but banked it all; I didn't need it. Frau Lieblang was earning DM1,500 and we lived together. We had an annual turnover of DM1.8 million and by the time we sold out in 1977, we got DM800,000 for it.'

This recital leaves Edith practically speechless. Finally she says: 'He's mad. He's simply going mad. No, he's having them on, he's making fun of them; don't they know it? By the time we sold we had hardly any customers left, nor employees. It was worth virtually nothing when we gave up, and that's what we got – virtually nothing.'

But then, as she well knows, talking about big money is 'his vice'. He cannot bear to speak or even think in hundreds: it is always thousands or equally non-existent hundreds of thousands. Exaggerations and boasts pour out of him, like water from a burst pipe.

After his escape to the West, Kujau's family in Löbau had heard little from him in years. But the prodigal son returned with Edith in 1970 laden with gifts and stories of his own success.

Kujau courted anyone with contacts in the Löbau community – the priest, a television repairman, a housepainter. For Kujau had developed a deep interest in military relics, particularly from the Third Reich, and his return to East Germany after thirteen years was not motivated entirely by family sentiment.

He had guessed, rightly, that although it is illegal in East Germany to possess relics from the Nazi era, people had held on to their wartime and other old mementoes. He also reckoned that they could be tempted to part with them for hard Western currency. So via family and friends in Löbau (and, later, via carefully worded newspaper advertisements) he spread the word that he was interested in buying 'militaria'. He was, he says, 'swamped' with offers. Since the West German deutschmark was worth five East German marks on the black market, he was able to buy for hundreds what he could sell in the West for thousands.

Some of the relics were smuggled into West Germany by Kujau and Edith on their return from what, after 1970, became annual visits to Löbau, Dresden and East Berlin. The rest were hidden in pianos, manufactured in Löbau and exported to the west.

Anything Kujau ascribed to Hitler is doubtful in origin or an outright fake. The important point, however, is that the racket enabled Kujau to become a substantial dealer in Third Reich memorabilia. That gave him an entrée to the shadowy world of those in West Germany and elsewhere who remain obsessed with the Nazi era.

When the war ended, Kujau was aged seven, Heidemann fourteen. Both were much too young to have played any active part in the Third Reich or to have understood how it was to last for a thousand years. Both, however, were to become obsessed by it.

When Heidemann, already successful as a reporter for *Stern* magazine, was forty-two, he bought a yacht, the *Carin II*, once owned by the head of the Luftwaffe, Hermann Göring. He found it rotting in a boatyard and purchased it in the hope of doing it up and reselling it at a big profit. Instead, the boat became the venue for informal reunions of former Nazis, with Heidemann as host. He was fascinated by the extraordinary memories of men such as General Wilhelm Mohnke, the last defender of Hitler's bunker, and General Wolff, head of the SS in Italy. 'Suddenly I realized that what they were talking about was much more exciting, more intriguing than any thriller,' Heidemann says. 'This extraordinary man, Hitler, rose to those heights from nowhere at all. I became so curious about him – it was finally all I could think of.'

Kujau had come under the same spell in a different way. His father, a shoemaker by trade, had become an ardent Nazi party worker in 1933. Even as a boy, Kujau loved anything to do with martial splendour. When he was fourteen, he painted a huge swastika on his grandmother's kitchen wall.

This childhood interest became an obsession when he began dealing in smuggled Nazi relics after 1970. Like Heidemann, he was intrigued with the Nazi veterans he met. They included the odious Hoffmann Group, a neo-Nazi 'youth training' organization since outlawed; Hitler's driver Erich Kempka; and most important to his future activities, members of HIAG, the 'mutual aid society' of the Waffen-SS.

In time he also established his own group of collectors, who met at his showroom in Stuttgart. They included several senior police officers of the state of Baden-Württemberg, a post office official, a steel industrialist from Burlafingen-Ulm and Fritz Stiefel, a self-made Stuttgart businessman, aged fifty-three.

Under Kujau's influence, and despite his wife's objections, Stiefel developed a passion for collecting Hitler relics, mostly supplied by Kujau, to whom he paid hundreds of thousands of Deutsch marks. He kept them – and his unique collection of porcelain made by concentration camp inmates – in a beautifully-lit room in his house, behind a steel door.

Much of his collection, certainly as far as it originated with Kujau, is likely to be fake. What fooled Stiefel, as well as the other collectors, was not so much Kujau's handiwork, as the elaborate stories he invented to prove their authenticity.

His buyers knew him not as Kujau but as Konrad Fischer. He claimed that his 'very high-up' relations in East Germany included a museum director and a general in the secret police, who, he said, were supplying him with relics. Later, when he began to sell forged Hitler documents, he added another dimension.

He said these came from a plane which had crashed in Börnersdorf in April 1945, in what is now East Germany, while ferrying some of Hitler's most precious archives from besieged Berlin. The story was particularly seductive because there *were* important Fischers in East Germany. And, as it turns out, the story about the plane crash *was* based on truth too.

So, when Kujau telephoned Fritz Stiefel in June 1979 to tell him he had just come back from his latest trip to East Germany with something quite extraordinary – a handwritten Hitler diary – Stiefel was not in the least sceptical. The next day, in Kujau's shop, he was shown a slim volume, bound in dark blue embossed cardboard and inscribed 'Year book of the party'. It covered the first six months of 1935. Kujau would not vouch for its authenticity; indeed, he said, he could not read the diary because it was written in old German script.

Stiefel therefore called in August Priesack, a self-styled professor whose expertise derived from having been a junior archivist at the Brown House, the Nazi party HQ in Munich.

Priesack hurried from Munich to Stuttgart and declared the book '101 per cent' authentic. He told Stiefel that, as this volume covered six months, there should be a total of twenty-seven diaries in all.

On 21 September 1979, Priesack lured to Stiefel's house one of West Germany's most eminent Third Reich historians, Professor Eberhard Jäckel of Stuttgart University. Jäckel was then in the last stages of preparing a massive work on Hitler's writings between 1905 and 1924. Priesack promised: 'I'm going to open Hitler's treasure chest for you.'

Jäckel was shown dozens of Hitler documents for his book, *and* the Hitler diary. He was told that they all came from the crashed plane.

Successfully distracted, he only leafed through the diary. Not unlike myself years later, he thought the content insignificant but considered it *could* be authentic: 'Stranger things have happened,' he rightly said.

Kujau admits he was 'amazed'. Priesack, he says, was almost beside himself with excitement and told Stiefel he *had* to buy whatever diaries Kujau could obtain. Professor Jäckel, giving Kujau a lift back to his shop in Stuttgart, said that if there were more diaries, he would like to edit them.

But Kujau, in his confession, says there were no more diaries at that stage: he had only written one.

That is a lie.

I established that unbound versions of Hitler diaries from Kujau were for sale in the United States early in 1976. Both his one-time lawyer in Stuttgart, Peter Stöckicht, and his 'patron', a German-born US citizen now living in Florida, Wolfgang Schulze, confirmed to me that they saw and handled them, and thought them authentic. Indeed, Schulze says that some of the diaries were sold, though he refuses to say to whom.

Piecing together the evidence from Stöckicht and Schulze, the best guess is that by September 1979 Kujau had seven or nine diaries for sale to private collectors. He probably would have continued with this lucrative racket, which was essentially safe: collectors, knowing public disdain for their passion, would be unlikely to protest even if they discovered the diaries were false. Events, however, were about to take a new turn.

On 21 October 1979, a month after Jäckel had seen the 1935 diary, Fritz Stiefel had a party at his house in Stuttgart. It was for the birthday of Senta Baur, the wife of one of the more distinguished members of the old Hitler circle. Hans Baur, who held the rank of lieutenant-general in the SS, was Hitler's personal pilot from 1933 until the end. It was he who dispatched the aircraft which had crashed at Börnersdorf in April 1945. He would have been intrigued, therefore, to see the diary which supposedly came from that plane. But his wife was ill, and the Baurs could not make it.

Among Stiefel's guests were Kujau and Edith Lieblang – and a couple named Tiefenthäler.

Jakob Tiefenthäler was a member of the SS and a close friend of General Baur. He knew generals Mohnke and Wolff and has extensive contacts through his membership of HIAG. Astonishingly, he works as chief of audio-visual instruction for the United States army in Southern Germany.

The birthday party at Stiefel's house was extremely merry, 'We drank a lot of wine,' Tiefenthäler told me, 'and ended up all of us, on very familiar terms.' Kujau told Tiefenthäler about his impressive relations in East Germany, and about the plane crash at Börnersdorf. The next morning, at 10 a.m., Tiefenthäler was solemnly taken behind the steel door of Stiefel's special room and shown one of the Hitler diaries.

A few days after the party, Tiefenthäler passed on that sensational news to Heidemann at *Stern*. They had first spoken six months before when – introduced by General Mohnke – Tiefenthäler had told Heidemann he represented an Australian syndicate interested in buying Göring's yacht. At the same time he mentioned that a Stuttgart collector, whose name he could not yet divulge, might also be interested in the yacht. Now, in late October, he told Heidemann that the collector's name was Fritz Stiefel. He urged the reporter to go and see him: 'You'll faint when you meet him. He even has a Hitler diary.'

Heidemann duly went to Stiefel's house in November 1979. He was dumbfounded by what he saw: not only the diary, but Stiefel's extraordinary collection of supposed Hitler paintings, drawings and documents.

Heidemann's attempts to discover the name of the supplier of this collection were to be frustrated for over a year. At his request, both Stiefel and Tiefenthäler asked Kujau if they could reveal his identity, but Kujau was understandably appalled. His business depended on shy collectors; a journalist from *Stern* might ruin it. 'No, no, no,' he told Stiefel. 'Do *not* pass on my name.'

Enter one of the more sinister characters in this saga. I will call him X. Like Kujau, he comes from what is now East Germany: like Kujau, he has settled in the state of Baden-Württemberg, just fifty-seven miles from Stuttgart. Like Kujau, he is a dealer in military relics, though his General Gun Store in Karlsruhe specializes in weapons. Like Kujau, he inhabits the shadowy Nazi world. But his links are more solid because of his own past.

Under his left arm he bears the tattoo of the SS. He was, he says, a member of the élite *Leibstandarte*, Hitler's personal guard. He performs a role for HIAG which puts him in a position to know every surviving SS bigshot.

Gerd Heidemann had known X for ten years when he first heard of the diaries. Also a police informer, they had met when X helped Heidemann on a story about stolen paintings. Their relationship developed after Heidemann bought Göring's yacht: X became a regular visitor, spending weekends and holidays aboard, and attending some of the 'old men's' conversations. He and Heidemann became close. Yet, it was not until after X knew that Heidemann was on the trail of the Hitler diaries that he revealed that he, too, had extraordinary secrets.

The exact sequence of events is important. In early 1980, after visiting Stiefel's house, Heidemann told X about the diary he had seen. X immediately cast a bait. He responded to Heidemann's confidence by revealing that he had maps showing the exact whereabouts of twelve hidden Nazi treasures – the loot buried in the last weeks of the Third Reich on the orders of Göring and Bormann. Most of it lay in East Germany. X invited Heidemann to act as his front man in the negotiations with the East German authorities; his share of the 'finder's fee' would make him a multimillionaire overnight. Heidemann accepted the offer. The two men were now partners.

For the next few months of 1980 Heidemann, researching for *Stern*, was preoccupied with other Nazi-related stories. The previous year he had been on a tour of South America with General Wolff, looking for escaped Nazis, including Martin Bormann. They had not found him. But Heidemann had found and interviewed Klaus Barbie, the 'Butcher of Lyons' (who died in prison after being deported and tried in France), and he was planning a book about the Nazis' escape route after the war.

In the autumn, however, he returned to his search for the diaries. Still no nearer discovering the identity of Stiefel's mysterious supplier, he concentrated instead on checking out the plane-crash story. Through records in Berlin he discovered where the plane had gone down, and in November he went there – to Börnersdorf – to photograph the graves of the crew and passengers.

In December 1980 he asked his friend and partner X if he knew of any military dealer in Stuttgart called Fischer who could be Stiefel's supplier. X shook his head. But within days of that conversation, Kujau, after a year of studiously avoiding Heidemann, suddenly gave both Stiefel and Tiefenthäler permission to reveal his whereabouts to the *Stern* reporter.

That may have been coincidence: perhaps Kujau's caution about *Stern* was finally overcome by his greed. Or, X *did* know Kujau, and persuaded him that Heidemann would be easy to fool.

In any event, in January 1981, Heidemann finally met Kujau and said that *Stern* was willing to pay DM2 million for the twenty-seven diaries. A month later, the diaries began to emerge 'from East Germany'.

X now revealed that he had a second, even more extraordinary, secret. He knew that the covers of some of the diaries bore a label with the supposed signature of Martin Bormann – who, if alive, would be the most wanted Nazi on earth. In early 1982, X told Heidemann that Bormann *was* alive in Spain, and that he, X, was in constant contact with him. He said he would show Bormann pages of the diaries for authentication. He duly reported back that Bormann had declared them to be real; indeed, Bormann had enlarged one of the pages, framed it, and hung it in the library of his house in Madrid.

Having now hooked his fish, X began the process of reeling him in.

He told a thoroughly bedazzled Heidemann: 'Martin wants to meet you.'

By the middle of 1982 Gerd Heidemann was almost totally brainwashed: he believed that he had been chosen by Martin Bormann to set up in Spain a pro-Nazi Institute for Contemporary History, to rival the official and celebrated one in Munich, and a museum of National Socialist relics. He also believed that he was to be the first and only journalist in the world to interview Bormann. Subsequently, he would become his literary executor: the keeper of the Nazi grail.

But, as always, Martin Bormann was proving elusive. From March onwards countless meetings were set up by X. On his instructions, Heidemann bought aeroplane tickets to just about everywhere: to Zurich where X said, 'Martin' lived next door to a synagogue; to Spain, where 'Martin' owned houses in Madrid and Alicante; to Mexico, *en route* to 'somewhere in South America' where 'Martin' ran a German colony.

Each time X called it off at the last moment. 'Martin is not well,' he said. Or, 'We hear somebody may have got wind of our plans.' When even Heidemann began to doubt 'Martin's' existence, X gave him – in the utmost confidence, of course – Bormann's Spanish cover name, 'Martin di Calde Villa', and his Madrid telephone number. (I tried it: it was 'out of order'!)

Then towards the end of 1982, something happened that not only convinced Heidemann that Bormann *was* alive, but also removed doubts for him, and *Stern*, that the Hitler diaries were authentic.

In Hamburg, a special suite of offices had been established, in an annexe of *Stern*'s main building, for the tiny group of people working on 'Green Arches', the magazine's cover name for the Hitler diaries project. They were Dr Thomas Walde, head of *Stern*'s contemporary history section, Leo Pesch, a young journalist with a history degree, and two secretaries.

The diaries were arriving at the rate of about three a month. Heidemann would collect them from Konrad Kujau in Stuttgart, make three photocopies and then begin the considerable task of transcribing them from the old German script.

Walde and Pesch would in their words, 'leaf through them'. But in the main they concentrated on the special volume devoted to Hitler's deputy Rudolf Hess which Heidemann had collected in November 1981. *Stern*'s plan at that time was to launch the Hitler enterprise – and 'test the water' – by publishing a series of articles, built around the twenty pages of Hitler's supposed revelations about Hess's flight to Scotland. In that endeavour Walde and Pesch were checking every word of the volume against published sources.

In late December 1982, however, they came across a name in the Hess volume they could not find anywhere: Hauptsturmführer (SS Captain) Anton Laackman. He had been appointed, supposedly, by Hitler to watch over Hess. 'We searched through everything we could lay our hands on,' says Walde. 'Not a thing.'

There are a number of archives in West Germany, Britain, the United States and, of course, East Germany, rich in Nazi material. But the main source for information on members of the SS is the American-administered Berlin Document Centre, which was closed to journalists. So Walde and Pesch asked friends at the West German Federal Archives in Koblenz to check the document centre for any record of Captain Laackman.

Three weeks later they duly received, via Koblenz, thirty photocopied pages of Laackman's military record. That was impressive enough; what was even more convincing was what Heidemann now came up with.

He had decided to initiate his own check on Laackman. Since Laackman was described in the Hess volume as a member of Bormann's staff, and since X claimed to be in 'constant touch' with Bormann, Heidemann challenged him to ask 'Martin' what he knew about the obscure captain. Shortly after *Stern*'s photocopies arrived from Berlin, X provided three pages of Laackman's SS record which had not been part of the Document Centre file. They were not photocopies, but *originals*, and they were undoubtedly authentic.

X's story was that he had been to see Bormann, on Heidemann's behalf, in Spain. Bormann had produced his own file on Laackman, which had included the captain's genealogical tree – the necessary proof of his good Aryan stock – and such things as a record of a misdemeanour Laackman had committed in 1938. X told Heidemann that he had stolen three of the documents from Bormann's desk in

Madrid. He had not dared take more, and he had only taken the three because he realized Heidemann harboured doubts about Bormann's existence.

It was a winning piece of deception. The only true part of X's story was that the documents were stolen – but not by him, nor from any desk of Martin Bormann.

I believe that X played a pivotal role – perhaps the central role – in the diary fraud. I believe that he provided the knowledge that enabled Kujau to forge so many diaries. I believe he entrapped Heidemann in a web of clever lies about Martin Bormann. And, I believe, he was therefore able to get some of the DM9.4 million (£2.5m) which *Stern* paid for the diaries.

That judgement is shared by a senior West German police officer who knows him well. For fifteen years he was one of those who used X as an informer for various government agencies: the federal criminal police, the BKA; the state criminal police, the LKA; and the West German secret service, the BND. X worked with these agencies on arms and drugs deals, and stolen paintings and furs. He was a 'highly effective' source.

The officer says that X was also part of the directorate of HIAG, which is why he is convinced that the money X got from *Stern* via Heidemann went into HIAG's funds: 'They [the members] continue to be totally ideologically orientated,' he said. 'They take the term "mutual aid society" literally. They work for a living as long as they can, but any monies above and beyond their own basic needs go to HIAG.'

Despite this, he says, the organization is running short of money. Many members of the SS lost their pensions after the war and thousands of them, now old men, are in need. Hence fund-raising operations.

If X did not orchestrate the hoax, he certainly went to a great deal of trouble to help it succeed. That fact is best demonstrated by the true story of how he really obtained the Laackman papers.

Rainer Hess worked as a photocopier and messenger in one of West Germany's state archives where Second World War records are kept. He had easy access to hundreds of thousands of files. In late 1982, or early 1983, he began methodically removing files or individual documents from the archives at X's request.

Rainer (as we will call him in order to avoid confusion) collects military relics in a small way, and had been a customer of X's Gun Store for five years. In addition, they shared an interest in, of all things, American Red Indians. Rainer made Indian jewellery as a hobby, and X belonged to an *Indianer* club where the members dressed up as braves and squaws. The appeal of Red Indians to men like X is their racial purity – a subject which Hitler's favourite author, Karl May, wrote about incessantly. Kujau, the forger, was a member of an *Indianer* club in Stuttgart.

At the moment when Laackman's name was beginning to raise doubts at *Stern*'s offices in Hamburg, Rainer suddenly discovered that he and X apparently shared a third interest: underwater exploration. Rainer's passion is aqualung diving and his photograph had just appeared in the press. In January 1983, X invited him to go for a drink in a bar where he regularly entertained. There, X began to spin his web around Rainer Hess, in the same way, two years before, he had spun it around Gerd Heidemann.

He told Rainer that he knew from his contacts the whereabouts of 'buried treasures' from the Nazi era. To prove his connection with top Nazis, he showed him what Rainer describes as 'a long roll of paper' with dozens of names and addresses, most of them abroad. He said that these were all people who had gone underground after the war. Rainer already knew that X had himself been in the SS, and was active in HIAG. Now he revealed to him that his responsibility was to ensure that all these people 'from the old times' were provided with money to live on.

'If you knew what I know,' X hinted. He produced photographs which showed Hermann Göring, head of the Luftwaffe, standing in an extraordinary room, the walls of which were lined in amber. This, he explained, was the historic Amber Room, one of the greatest art treasures in the world, which the Nazis looted from near Leningrad, dismantled and removed piece by piece to Königsberg. By the end of the war it had disappeared. X said that the Russians, who desperately wanted the room back, estimated its value at over 100 million roubles and would pay a 'finder's fee' of 20 per cent. He knew where it had been hidden. Salvaging it would require discretion, intelligence and divers.

X then revealed to the awestruck Rainer that the Amber Room was hidden in a disused and flooded coal mine on the outskirts of Goslar near Hanover. He said he had a plan which showed the location of three chambers, protected by an air pocket. In one the chests of amber were stored. In the other two were Göring's archives, worth yet another fortune to historians. He warned that in the flooded shaft the divers would probably find skeletons of four concentration camp prisoners who had carried the loot into the mine and were then shot.

Having thoroughly hooked Rainer, just as he had hooked Heidemann, X extracted his price. He said he would happily share the 'finder's fee' because money was not his real interest. He and others, he said, were engaged in the creation of a museum and an Institute for Contemporary History and what they wanted were authentic documents and relics from the Nazi era. As a quid pro quo for taking part in the treasure hunt, would Rainer supply him, from time to time, with 'interesting documents' from the archive where he worked?

Two weeks later, X instructed Rainer to get him anything the archive had on SS Captain Anton Laackman. Rainer complied. He delivered to him three sheets of original documents from Laackman's file.

But how did the forger, Konrad Kujau, know about the obscure and long-dead Captain Laackman?

Kujau says that Heidemann discovered by accident he was forging the diaries in the summer of 1981, by which time *Stern* had bought nine. Heidemann, he says, 'went pale' but then told him it did not matter: the diaries were merely an accompaniment to his plan to present Martin Bormann to the world. Instead of exposing the hoax he joined it, even providing Kujau with occasional ideas for future diaries. For the special Hess volume he supplied the name Laackman. 'He came along with these papers he'd had from X and told me, here was a real good one – a man nobody had written about, a name nobody knew,' Kujau says. 'How better to prove our diaries authentic?'

But all this is nonsense: Kujau had completed and delivered the Hess volume in November 1981, fourteen months *before* X gave the Laackman papers to Heidemann.

The true explanation is prosaic. Although *Stern*'s researchers could not find Captain Laackman's name in any book, two indefatigable investigators for the Hamburg State prosecutor have done so. It appears on page 221 of the National Socialist Party's yearbook for 1941, which lists the hierarchy of the Nazi party. Laackman's entry was copied into the Hess volume virtually word for word. The investigators found the yearbook, with the page marked, in Kujau's house.

That does not mean, however, that it was Kujau who selected Laackman's name. While there is no doubt that he wrote the words in the diaries, copying the entries from passages in books, it is unlikely that he was capable of organizing the necessary and considerable research, and selecting the content. For though the diaries are often trivial and banal, when read as a whole they show consistent lines of political insight, above all attempts throughout to show that Hitler was not a fanatical anti-semite and was not involved with the decisions to commit genocide.

At the time when Kujau was allegedly engaged in this complex research, however, he was living a deeply sedentary life. Each weekday morning he would leave the house where he lived with Edith to join his thirty-four-year-old assistant, Maria Modritsch. She told me they would spend the day either at his showroom, writing nothing more than a few invoices, or at her flat. In either event, she is adamant that he never spent time reading or writing. When he got home in the evenings, according to Edith, he drank heavily and invariably fell asleep in front of the television. It was only at midnight – after Edith had gone to bed, and after he had telephoned Maria to say good-night (he told me) – that he retired to his workroom on the second floor to work on the diaries for, at the most four hours.

That schedule allowed him time to *write* the diaries, which he was producing at the rate of about three a month. But when did he select the thousands of words from the hundreds of books and magazines he used to present this benevolent Hitler?

That question leads to a major mystery. When the police raided Kujau's house last May, they found a library of books on the Third Reich, 427 in all, most of them marked with slips of paper which indicated the passages he copied.

Kujau certainly provided some improvised book marks: he cut the paper up on the ironing board and Edith complained to him that the sharp knife he used was liable to damage the board's cover. But regular visitors to his house and showroom – including his son – insist that he did not have a library of 427 books, or hundreds of magazines.

So, where were the books kept, and who selected the passages for Kujau to copy? And how did they wind up in Kujau's house for the police to find? There is an easy solution to this mystery *if* X was, as I believe, the central organizer of the conspiracy.

'It bears his stamp,' says the police officer who knows him well. 'He knows 80 per cent more about Nazi things than anybody I know of. He is constantly in touch with people who can inform him about things no one else still alive can possibly know about. For the diaries he will have acted as – or supplied – a *spiritus rector.*'

The money came from a special account set up by *Stern*'s parent company, Grüner & Jahr, on which Heidemann could draw virtually at will. He would pack the cash into a Samsonite suitcase and disappear, to return a day later with one or more diaries. No receipts were asked for or expected, and *Stern* only had Heidemann's word for how much he was paying to 'the South German collector'.

According to Heidemann, the price, for what was originally said to be twenty-seven diaries was DM85,000 per volume. But the price, as well as the number of diaries, escalated dramatically. By the end, *Stern* had bought sixty-two diaries, including the Hess volume, for an average of DM150,000 per book. Of this Kujau says Heidemann gave him only DM40,000 for each book, or about DM2,400,000 in all. He says that Heidemann kept the rest.

The temptation for Heidemann to dip into the suitcase must have been enormous. Until 1981, he had been more or less continually broke. The cost of repairing and maintaining the Göring yacht – his main link with the old Nazis with whom he had become obsessed – stretched his *Stern* salary, about £20,000 a year after taxes, to the limit. He and his family were forced to live modestly and he was in the habit of borrowing small sums of money from his colleagues, even secretaries, at work.

In 1981, after *Stern*'s money began to flow, there was a dramatic improvement in the Heidemanns' lifestyle. They moved to a luxurious flat overlooking the River Elbe in Hamburg, and rented the identical flat above to serve as Heidemann's office. A few months later he took over yet another flat, in the centre of Hamburg, to store his ever-growing archives. He also bought two houses in Spain.

This can be explained partly by the fact that Heidemann's income also increased dramatically. *Stern* eventually paid him DM1.5 million in advances and bonuses for his Hitler 'scoop'. But the police say that, even allowing for that, Heidemann spent over DM2.5 million more than he earned between February 1981 and April 1983, and he has not provided convincing proof of where this money comes from.

From very early on, Heidemann could not tell fact from fantasy, nor could he differentiate between the various strands of the web of fantasies in which he had been trapped. For him, the diaries were merely one element of a stupendous enterprise. Bormann, the hidden Nazi treasure, the Nazi museum, and the Institute for Contemporary History in Spain, as a rival to the famous one in Munich, were all vital parts of the package that he believed he could deliver.

He therefore regarded as legitimate expenditure any money – *Stern*'s or his own – that he spent in chasing that dream. As *Stern* knew, at the same time as he was buying diaries he was also buying paintings, decorations, uniforms and documents for his archives. And, as *Stern* also knew, he paid thousands of pounds to old Nazis for their help in authenticating the diaries, or their silence about their existence.

What *Stern* did *not* know was that Heidemann's 'direct line' to Martin Bormann via X was also very expensive.

A carpet dealer in Baden-Württemberg told me that five years before I did this research (i.e. in 1978) X attempted to settle a DM5,000 debt with an offer of 'Hitler diaries'. And two weeks ago, when I saw him last, he still insisted that he was in constant communication with the elusive Martin Bormann: 'I'll take you to him,' he told me, and there wasn't a hint of a smile on his face. And in April this year he unwittingly made a confession.

Rainer Hess, the diver, had come to fear X and regret removing documents from the archives where he worked. He decided to confess to his employers and has since provided them and the police with a list of everything he took. Before doing so, however, he was advised to secretly tape-record conversations with X. And on 27 April (I have heard the tape) X boasted to him that *he* was responsible for giving

Hitler's diaries to the world. There were, he said, more than the sixty-two that had been sold to *Stern*. The rest were being held back 'for the moment', he said. This, as I will show, is meaningful in the context of the story I discovered.

X now admits to having received DM185,000, or around £46,000 for his 'expenses' from Heidemann. Heidemann told me it was nearer £50,000. The Hamburg police, after raiding X's house and shop in November, have evidence that it was £100,000 and possibly a good deal more.

Certainly, well over DM4 million of *Stern*'s money remains unaccounted for. *Stern* is convinced that Heidemann has it, hidden away in Argentina or the Philippines. But despite suing him and a determined search for the missing millions all over the world, they cannot prove it.

And the fact is that Heidemann, released from prison after two years, divorced, shunned by virtually all his friends, and for a long time unemployable, lived with a woman friend in her small flat, their extremely modest lifestyle – which I observed – paid for by her secretarial salary. Much later, I understand, he was able to get some small freelance commissions, under a different name. All one can say is that if he had had any hidden fortune, it would have required more self-control than he was known to have to have resisted travelling towards the money.

February 2000

The story I ended up with, which I have no doubt is true, was that it all started with four men, all in the past knee-deep in the Nazi mire. X was certainly one of them, as was SS General Mohnke, who is dead. But, as my research was finally cut short, I was unable to complete my search for the two others. What is interesting, significant and very different here from the hoax story so widely publicized in May 1983, is that my subsequent research showed that the project, as planned by these four men, involved at least two real Hitler writings, one of which was what Jakob Tiefenthäler described first to me and then also to the *Sunday Times* editor Paul Eddy, who joined me briefly to check his story, as a diary 'covered in finest leather': he and a number of 'trustworthy others' he said, had handled and read it and had no doubt of its authenticity. The other, really more important to this story, was the *Denkschrift* (Notes) Professor Jäckel had seen in Fritz Stiefel's house which, 'bound in dark blue embossed cardboard' and titled on the cover 'Year Book of the Party', covered, in Hitler's handwriting, the first six months of 1935. The 'Notebook' and possibly others like it had at some point been in the hands of one or more of this group and became the models for their project.

Years later, after Hitler's second senior secretary Christa Schröder had died, an intelligent and admirably objective editor friend of hers, Anton Joachimsthaler, published in 1985 with her authorization her notes and recollections *Er War Mein Chef*, a book which deserved a far greater public than it ever had. From it, I finally understood that the purloining of the 'Yearbook' and probably that of at least one other, had quite probably happened in the last week of April 1945, when Hitler had sent Julius Schaub, his most trusted personal aide, to the Chancellery, to his Munich flat and then to the Berghof to burn all letters, documents or anything else private or bearing his signature. Christa Schröder describes the scene on page 213 of *Er War Mein Chef*. She herself, she says, seeing the half-burned papers, succumbed to temptation (less for reasons of nostalgia than, she says frankly, with realistic estimation of their potential value), and took a 'bundle' of Hitler's architectural sketches (Speer had a hundred of them which Hitler had given him – or indeed made for him – over the years), and a letter to Hitler from his niece Geli Raubal, with whom he had been in love and who had killed herself when he forbade her to marry. But Schröder also describes a *Denkschrift* she saw and says she wished she had had the courage to take it. Although it was manifestly not the one the four men eventually had in their possession, her description of it tallies precisely with the format of the sixty-two 'diaries'. It was 'something like an old-fashioned account book,' she said, 'size A4 with hard covers and a white label on which was typed: "Concept for the Construction of the Greater German Reich" (*Idee und Aufbau des Grossdeutschen Reiches*).'

This is particularly significant in view of the veritable chorus of claims both from Hitler contemporaries and present-day historians that 'Hitler NEVER wrote'. It is, of course, an established fact that in his last two years he was increasingly handicapped by Parkinson's disease. It is true, too, that while his war was going well and he began dreaming of retirement, he often told his senior secretaries, Johanna Wolf and Christa Schröder, that he would need them then to work on his memoirs. In these posthumously published memoirs, Frau Schröder mentions taking dictation from Hitler many times, but says nothing about the many 'notes' (*aide-mémoires*) he wrote, many of them in bed after retiring, which were copied and shredded the next day. The only one who has talked to me about this night-time writing (and reading) was Rochus Misch, chief of Hitler's personal telephone switchboard and one of the most truthful witnesses I spoke to, who, while frequently on night duty at his board just outside Hitler's private rooms, remembered him writing and reading for hours every night 'often till 4 or 5 am when I saw his light at last go out'.

'How did he know that that was what Hitler was doing behind his closed door?' I asked.

Quite often, there were urgent messages for him in the night, Misch said, and the order was that if his light was on, they had to be delivered. Linge, Hitler's ever-present valet, who had to stay awake till Hitler went to sleep, would take them in and Misch many times saw papers and books on his bed and a pen in his hand when the door opened and closed.

Thirty-eight years later, the fact that the faked diaries were all written in 'old-fashioned account books' – the puzzled Hamburg police agreed with me that no one could possibly have had this idea without a model – was almost the first thing that raised doubts about their authenticity. 'Can you imagine Hitler using such cheap notebooks to write his diaries in?' colleagues asked me. It just so happened that I could, even before I realized how it had probably come about, when I read Christa Schröder's book years later. Hitler was many dreadful things, but he was not materialistic.

I met and talked repeatedly and at length with two of the four men I believed responsible for the hoax (X and Mohnke) and, although surly and angry, and even though what they said gave them away, they couldn't resist *talking* – as is the case for so many people living in a social semi-darkness. Certainly they told me enough to confirm my suspicions, and also to make me feel sure I could eventually find the two others. But by this stage I was exhausted, needed a rest, and unfortunately a newly appointed editor of the *Sunday Times*, worried (with some justification) about the considerable monies already expended on this project, and uncomfortable with conspiracy theories (as I usually am, too) cut short the research just before I might have got to them.

What I did find out before I was ordered back to London to write the still incomplete story, was that Kujau, well known for his talent at forging handwriting and sketching, had been hired by the four-man group for a tidy fee many years before the scandal erupted, to create six diaries from what Hitler had written both in the 'book bound in finest leather', the 'account book or books' no doubt obtained under the circumstances described by Christa Schröder, as well as in his published speeches and in his 'Tabletalk' – his monologues at table, recorded on Martin Bormann's orders. Each of the six 'diaries', written by Kujau in similar old-fashioned 'account books', dealt with a period of two years from 1933, using Hitler's own written or spoken opinions and descriptions of events, but adding new material in each book which these four men created and supplied for him with the sole intention of demonstrating Hitler's statesmanlike qualities. Above all – like all neo-Nazis and revisionists – their compilations were intended to emphasize Hitler's comparatively benign intentions and innocence in the murder of the Jews.

These original six specimens, benefiting from the supervision of these relatively educated men (they had allegedly all been officers in Hitler's regiment, the *Leibstandarte*, or elsewhere in the armed forces), were no doubt of a very different quality from those Kujau subsequently put together from Nazi books and documents in the public domain, bits of reports he found in newspaper archives, and titbits of *Bierstube* gossip with people from Hitler's circle, such as his former chauffeur Erich Kempka with whom he had made friends.

The original plan had been to produce only the six whitewashing 'diaries', for distribution (not for sale) to public institutions – universities, historians and the media. It was Kujau who very early on, in

1976 began, via middlemen in the memorabilia market, to offer 'diary' pages, copied from the six books, for sale in the United States. One of these middlemen, Wolfgang Schulze, who I visited in Florida in the course of my research (and whom I quote earlier) said that the offers had had 'lucrative results'. Kujau, now knowing that even pages of such diaries could sell for large sums, became ever greedier and, again on the sly, bought stacks of old-fashioned account books and began to produce diaries by the dozen. We know – because he later told me all this himself – that by the time he met Gerd Heidemann in January 1981, he already had twenty-seven diaries ready, for which, Heidemann told him at once, *Stern* would be willing to pay DM2 million. After a long search I found the wholesale stationery firm from which the four men – and later Kujau – had obtained pre-1945 account books which were no longer on the market, and I saw the signature of X, as the buyer. ('Sure I bought them,' Kujau told me later, incapable as ever of resisting showing off. 'I got the suppliers' name out of him.')

One of the reasons Heidemann suspected nothing, aside from his obsession with Nazi matters and his astonishing naïvety about them, was that he had in his collection a number of genuine Hitler writings he had been given or sold by his Nazi friends – letters, memos and documents. He was no more a handwriting expert than any of us, and the writing and even some of the phraseology in Kujau's 'diaries' looked identical. Heidemann had seen the same 'dark-blue embossed "Year Book of the Party"', which Fritz Stiefel held in his Nazi memorabilia sanctuary, and which had also been shown to Professor Jäckel, but none of the six books Kujau had produced first. Like the models they were based on – the 'diary in finest leather' and whichever others of the original Hitler (account) books which had been used – the six first books had all disappeared into a hiding place well before the world's media and the police arrived on the scene. Rumour had it that they were in the safe of a holiday villa in Italy. I might have been able to explore this if I had been able to continue my research. But time ran out, and the actual whereabouts of these two awful sacred relics of Hitler's time remain unknown.

However, anyone who knows the literature about Hitler and the Third Reich and who took the trouble to read the sixty-two volumes of the fake diaries – copies of which I still have in boxes in my London study – would have to conclude that, however pedestrian they were, there were some elements in them Konrad Kujau could not have created. Kujau was a talented handwriting forger with a trick memory. He undoubtedly penned the 'diaries' as he also drew some of the sketches included in or accompanying them. Sketching and reciting from memory was one of the party tricks with which he was wont to entertain visitors and police in prison. What was totally beyond the capabilities of this uneducated rogue was the coherent psycho-political line which here and there slips into them. But, he was clever enough to make some use of the 'six books', created by him under the guidance of the four men, placing small parts from them – a line here, a paragraph there – in timely spots, thereby suddenly confronting the reader of the other sixty-two fakes with intelligence where a few lines earlier there had been none. And he thereby succeeded, even in the welter of chit-chat and copied historical material he used, in infusing some of the ridiculously primitive writings with the line his employers had established: an innocent Hitler betrayed by others. If one reads carefully, one finds here a Hitler who is a reasonable and lonely man, forced into a war he did not want. He doesn't like Slavs and he doesn't like Jews, though he regards neither of them with any particular violence. This outrageous fictional character, created not by invention but by insertion of some existing material – no doubt the informed quality which deceived Heidemann – is far more abusive about his henchmen and generals (who were to be blamed for the 'failures' of his regime) than about those whom he ordered to be enslaved and murdered.

Ending seven exhausting months without being able to expose the men who were really behind the whole affair made the investigation into the origin of the Hitler diary scandal the least satisfying journalistic task I had ever undertaken. Used eventually as the subject of a comic film in Germany, and an equally entertaining well-written satire in Britain, the event remains, alas, mainly remembered as the creation of a clever little crook and a manifestation of media greed, allowing some quite wicked people to spend the remainder of their days smiling.

The real danger the 'Hitler diary' phenomenon has uncovered is that the only acceptable Nazi past may now be a prettified one, like the film *Holocaust* or the belief that the forging of 'Hitler diaries' or of anything else connected with that period, is a petty crime, or indeed no crime at all but a joke, and the characters connected with it comical figures. The real Hitler and his legacy is something the world cannot bear to face. He is still the nightmare, an unresolved horror in our lives. Anything written about him will be read. But the idea that this man should himself speak to us, using our common language, describing commonplace events, has been for a long time unacceptable. For if it was accepted, it would allow him to become part of a human dimension from which, by virtually universal consent, he has to be excluded so that we can protect ourselves from the acknowledgement that he happened, and that he was, for years, loved by millions.*

* Extraordinarily enough, the presentation of a human Hitler in David Edgar's play *Albert Speer*, based on my book and premiered at the Royal National Theatre in London on 25 May 2000, has been accepted by critics and audiences alike.

9

The Great Globocnik Hunt

February 2000

My second venture into the area of obsessed liars, though very different in origin, in the personality involved, and the solution we were able to establish after eight months of research, was equally puzzling.

It was during my search for US documentation about the 'Hitler diaries' in 1983, that a respected historian at the Hoover Institute in California put me in touch with a man he called 'Peter Stahl', who he said was a collector of 'militaria' and 'memorabilia'. He was exceptionally well informed on the Third Reich and had been helpful in the past to him and a number of other American historians in locating source material. And indeed, both in 1983 and on later occasions I would find Stahl, rather like David Irving, to have an almost encyclopedic store of information about Third Reich documentation and to be only too willing to share it. But although I realized almost at once that Stahl's interest in the Nazis was obsessive, nothing he had ever said to me (unlike others) indicated right-radical extremism, anti-semitism or personal political ambitions. Shortly before Christmas 1987, five years after our first contact, he phoned to say he was sending me the first page of an extraordinary four-page document he had found. He made me promise that, as knowledge of this find could be dangerous to him, I would keep the fact of his having these papers entirely secret; it was understood he would only send three additional pages he had if I expressed interest in investigating what the first four revealed. My reaction was that this sounded very melodramatic and that anyway, as I was horribly busy, he shouldn't send me anything until after Christmas.

When the four pages arrived by courier on 28 December, the information in them was, to put it mildly, startling. The fact that the

Eastern and Western Allies had competed for useful Nazis at the end of the war was well known. This applied not only to physicists and rocket engineers such as Wernher von Braun, but also to one-time Nazi Intelligence chiefs, several of whom, like Reinhard Gehlen, had been used by the United States, and some by Moscow. The most prominent and dangerous – to the West – was Heinrich Müller, head of the Gestapo, who had disappeared from Berlin without trace in April 1945, with an undoubted fund of knowledge on spies not only in Germany but all over the world, and who had long been believed to be in Moscow.

The first page of the document which arrived through my door in Kensington appeared to indicate that it was the British and Americans who in 1945 had spirited Müller and another Nazi criminal out of Europe and settled them overseas. It was the second name that shook me even more than Müller's: Odilo Globocnik, Himmler's special favourite and SS police chief of Lublin, was head of the *Aktion Reinhard* – the organization in charge of the four death-camps in occupied Poland where most of Europe's Jews had been gassed. All the information I had gathered from Stangl and others who had worked under the umbrella of the *Aktion Reinhard*, and from my research in the archives for *Into That Darkness*, indicated that Globocnik was a monstrously cruel and venal man who, on any count, had to be considered one of the very worst of the Nazi criminals.

In the course of a long telephone conversation in early January, Stahl told me that he himself was primarily interested in Müller and that it had been among archival material on Müller which he had requested under the FOI (Freedom of Information) Act from Fort Meade (where CIC records were kept) that he had come upon these four pages which, he felt sure, were top secret and which had got by mistake into the 400 comparatively harmless Müller papers he had been sent. He had been in touch about them with various government people he knew, he said, but they seemed oddly uninterested in his information. Of course, it was essential to check the document's authenticity, but he had few illusions about American and British behaviour after the war and his feeling was that if this was true – that is, if careful investigation first of the origin of the documents, then, with the help of eyewitnesses and of retired CIC officers who had been involved, proved it to be true – then this surely had to be made public. If the Western Allies in their cold war mania had been induced to save, of all people, the man whose terrible crimes, he said, I myself had described in my book and whose supposed death by suicide in Carinthia in May 1945 when the British caught him had been recorded in every history of the time, the discovery that he had been brought to America and was perhaps still alive there, would and should cause unprecedented indignation.

What did he, Stahl, hope to get out of this, I asked. The truth, he said, nothing else – his name, as he had said before, was to be kept entirely out of it. A week later he sent me three more pages – and three months later a further three would arrive.

As I say in the following account, my first priority, before involving any newspaper, was to establish the authenticity of the papers as a CIC document, a task which I proposed to Dr Robert Wolfe, who, as the head of the military section of the National Archives in Washington, was a highly respected archivist.

By the end of April 1988, several US agencies – the FBI, Fort Meade and others – had said they were unable to fault the CIC pages, but others, appearing to justify Peter Stahl's contentions, seemed strangely reluctant to give Dr Wolfe the information he sought and to which he was certainly entitled. So a decision had to be made to undertake further research, and with Stahl's agreement I approached *The Times*.

I had worked for the two previous years with Richard Williams, then their brilliant features editor, on the story of John Demjanjuk, accused in America and Israel of having been the dreadful Treblinka guard 'Ivan the Terrible' (see page 309) and I knew that if anyone would be able to take on as difficult and controversial a story as this and convince the editor both of its importance and of the need for absolute discretion, he could. Charles Wilson, then editor of *The Times*, was to become as curious about it as we were, but Williams' involvement was exceptional.

The first thing Richard did, an enormous gift to me after the exhausting loneliness of the work on the 'Hitler diaries', was to agree that my husband, Don Honeyman, who is not only a fine photographer but exceptionally talented in research, could go with me wherever I would have to go.

Richard was to support us in many different ways throughout the investigation, but, equally important, he understood from the very beginning that the story was a two-headed monster, both heads being of decided public interest. What we had to seek was collaborative authentication: if we found it, we would have evidence of an act of truly appalling governmental cynicism, worse than any that had so far come to light, for which both the Americans and the British would need to be held to account. On the other hand, if we found reason to indicate Stahl's document was faked – and none of us could think of a motivation for faking it – then the forger needed to be found and punished.

July 1992

The date on the four-page document was 30 November 1948, and it carried the signatures of two officers of the US Counter-Intelligence Corps, stationed in occupied Berlin. It arrived in London by courier, from a man in California, and it revealed potentially the biggest of all the scandals involving the Allies' post-war protection of top Nazis.

The document was headed 'Soviet Investigations: Project Übersee/3'. Some passages had been painstakingly obliterated; since the 'SECRET' stamps had been crossed through, it could be assumed that the blocking-out of individual sentences and paragraphs had been made during an official declassification process. But what was left was still dynamite.

The author of the report, Special Agent Severin F. Wallach, described measures taken by British and American intelligence agencies to protect from Soviet detection two former SS generals: Heinrich Müller, head of the Gestapo from 1935 to 1945, and Odilo Globocnik, whose last posting before the Nazis' defeat was on the Adriatic seaboard, with responsibility for anti-partisan warfare in the three-frontier area around Trieste.

Rumours that 'Gestapo' Müller had evaded death in Berlin have circulated for years. Sightings have been reported in South America, Cairo, Damascus, Moscow and East Berlin. Certainly a man with his experience had to be of considerable interest to the Intelligence services of many countries. It was not surprising to find his name on such a document. But the idea that the Allies might have saved Globocnik was nothing short of staggering.

Born in Trieste of Austrian parents in 1904, Globocnik was an early 'illegal' Nazi and favourite of Himmler, and was named the first Gauleiter of Vienna in 1938. In 1941, Himmler entrusted him with a new post, SS and police leader of Lublin in occupied Poland, and a very special assignment – to carry out the *Aktion Reinhard*, the strategy for the extermination of the Jews. He built, staffed and operated the four extermination camps of Chelmno, Belzec, Sobibor and Treblinka. By late 1943, when these killing centres, plus the labour-cum-extermination camp of Majdanek, also in his charge, were closed down as the Russians approached, Globocnik had been directly responsible for the murder of at least 3 million men, women and children.

'Dear Globus,' Himmler wrote in November 1943, addressing him by his schoolboy nickname, 'I acknowledge receipt of your letter of 4.11.43, and your report on the completion of the *Aktion Reinhard* .... For the great and unique service you have rendered to all of the German people in carrying out the *Aktion Reinhard*, please accept my gratitude ...'

Globocnik was captured by British troops in Carinthia in May 1945 and apparently committed suicide a few hours later, in the court of Paternion Castle, the HQ of the British Fourth Hussars, who had arrived from Italy a week before. But the events of those days were often murky and difficult to confirm. Was it conceivable, as Wallach's report stated, that the Allies could have been willing to save this man and to establish him with a new identity, first in Canada then in the United States?

Our source for the documents had not the slightest doubt of their authenticity. Peter Stahl is a collector and dealer in 'militaria' and Third Reich memorabilia who lives in California. There are said to be 3,000 such people in America, and many others in Europe. Some of them, like the late Marquess of Bath, who reputedly had the largest collection in England, or Billy Price, the Texan millionaire who in 1983 privately published a handsome volume of 723 drawings and paintings by Adolf Hitler, and many other less rich and less ambitious collectors, are basically ordinary people, albeit with a quirk. Some, however, including Peter Stahl, are not ordinary. For them, collecting and dealing in these items is more than a hobby: it is a passion which dominates their lives.

Between January 1988 and May, when a three-page 'Annex', which Stahl said had been mislaid while he moved house, arrived, his story of the provenance of the documents remained the same. He had found them in 1983, in a large file on 'Gestapo' Müller which he – or a 'not-to-be-named friend in the intelligence community' – had requested under the Freedom of Information Act from Fort Meade, the US Army Intelligence Repository in Virginia.

The presence of this 'sanitized' English-language CIC report in the middle of 'hundreds' of German pages on Müller was, Stahl was sure, a pure accident, and the fact that such ultra-sensitive material should have been released at all simply confirmed his characteristically scathing opinion that 'the clerks at Fort Meade are idiots'.

If he had found the document in 1983, I asked, why wait several years to do anything about it? And why now pass it to me, rather than his American connections? Stahl responded that he had mentioned the possibility of Globocnik's survival to historians and US government officials several times, and their unanimous disparagement convinced him he would only make a fool of himself if he showed anyone the document. And then I remembered that in 1983 he had asked me, too, whether I was certain Globocnik had died. I had referred him to Gerald Reitlinger's book, *The Final Solution*, which described a British soldier photographing the corpse in order 'to have a picture of the worst man in the world'.

But the previous year, he said, he read my articles about the trial of John Demjanjuk, and had reread my book *Into That Darkness*, in which Globocnik figures. He decided then that 'they' (the British and US governments) could not be allowed to get away with this. If 'they' had really saved this monstrous man, and were perhaps keeping him alive to this day on the proceeds of his awful activities in Poland, then it had to be exposed, come what may.

Peter Stahl agreed that the document had to be authenticated before one could think of publishing such an accusation, and volunteered to help the experts we would turn to. His address and phone number were not to be disclosed. If the experts wanted to talk to him, they would have to tell me and he would phone them.

Dr Robert Wolfe at the National Archives in Washington, a world authority on documentation on the Third Reich and its aftermath was the first person I turned to. When he saw the document, he was horrified: if authentic, it recorded the most outrageous act his country – and Britain – would have committed after the war.

True, the language seemed extravagant in places, but many CIC agents in the field (including Wallach) were men of foreign extraction whose English was stilted. And the patchiness of the 'sanitizing' could be due to the inexperience or apathy of the clerks who prepared documents for release under the Freedom of Information Act. In view of the then-recent disclosures of the CIC's misdeeds in the case of Klaus Barbie it seemed only too possible that the document was genuine.

And when Dr Wolfe took it to the director of the Fort Meade Repository, Colonel Walsh, his reaction was that, except for a declassification stamp which was missing (not a unique occurrence), it looked authentic. Colonel Walsh would assign an assistant to look for either the original, or any other documents that might substantiate it.

In the meantime, in the Public Records Office at Kew, we had found a detailed account of Globocnik's capture and suicide in Carinthia, in the mountains of central Austria, on 31 May 1945. The War Diary of the 4th Queen's Own Hussars described how an SS sergeant being held prisoner by the British at their headquarters in Paternion, up the Drau valley from Villach, had told his captors that Globocnik and five of his staff were hiding in a mountain hut, and guided a thirty-strong expedition in a successful dawn raid. The captives – who included an unexpected prize, the local *Gauleiter* – denied any knowledge of the SS or Globocnik. They were brought down to the Hussars' headquarters in Paternion Castle, and were locked up. One man who claimed to be a merchant from Klagenfurt, however, was kept in the courtyard of the castle. The diary says:

1130: Man who was suspected of being GLOVOCNIK [*sic*] was trapped into acknowledging his name by a slight movement of his head when

Major RAMSAY shouted his name across the courtyard. He was ordered into arrest and poisoned himself with Prussic acid while walking 150 yds between the castle yard and the prison . . .

1200: Three subjects on viewing the body of GLOVOCNIK confessed their [SS] identities.

So this was the account prepared within days of the incident – surely that was definitive? And yet, wasn't calling out a name a rather primitive way of 'trapping' a war-crimes suspect? Might not anyone hearing a sudden shout respond with 'a slight movement of the head'? There were no independent witnesses who knew him, only members of his own staff. Could there have been a misidentification – or perhaps a conspiracy by his own men?

Dr Wolfe had soon found in the National Archives another report by Special Agent Severin Wallach, concerning the 20 July plot on Hitler's life: it confirmed that Wallach had indeed been working in Berlin at the time when the report found by Stahl was written. But given the urgency Dr Wolfe had impressed upon Fort Meade, their search appeared frustratingly half-hearted.

At the end of April, Wolfe decided that restraint was ineffective, and wrote an official letter, requesting all information held on Müller or Globocnik. Colonel Walsh was on holiday, but a few days later Dr Wolfe had a phone call from an assistant to say that they had no information at all on Müller – the head of Nazi Germany's secret police. That was incredible enough, but it was followed by a letter extending this absence of knowledge to Globocnik: they claimed to have nothing at all on the man in charge of the murder of the Jews in Poland.

One person who appeared entirely unsurprised by these developments was Peter Stahl, who had said from the start that such an embarrassing document would have been removed or destroyed after the revelations of the Barbie case. Meanwhile his files had arrived at his house, and he sent a three-page document titled 'The Development and Usage of Former Senior SS Officers'.

This was an even more disturbing document, allegedly written by Wallach's superior, Andrew Venters, whose signature was also immediately authenticated from known documents. It included a simplistic account of the political situation and the 'valuable contribution' Müller had made to Western intelligence, plus a suggestion that Hitler had survived the war and a mention of the 'vast sums' Martin Bormann had transferred abroad. And it attributed to 'the British' an outrageous suggestion that 'in the event it should prove necessary . . . to take military action against the Zionists . . . former SS men such as Globocnik . . . [could] be set up in Syria in the event they are needed as specialists in . . . coping with dissident elements.' I did know, in fact, of other high-ranking SS who had been offered refuge in Syria as potential military and intelligence advisers. None the less the style, even more than the content, of this second document seemed outrageously polemical, and my immediate reaction was to dismiss it as grotesque, and to cancel plans to visit Carinthia to verify the story of Globocnik's suicide. But American experts familiar with CIC reports assured me that such reporting methods were sometimes resorted to, to shock reluctant 'brass' into action. It seemed that finding out what really happened in Paternion in May 1945 was now doubly essential: if I could be sure that Globocnik had died there, the document was a fake, whatever the mystery in Washington. But if I could not confirm his death, Dr Wolfe would carry his search beyond Fort Meade.

We – my husband Don and I – set out for Carinthia in the early summer of 1988. Over the next three weeks, interviews first in northern Italy – Globocnik's last stamping ground before retreating to the Carinthian Alps – then around Paternion, the picturesque village where he allegedly died, produced striking contradictions and improbabilities in the eyewitness reports. In Italy we talked to Dr Pier Arrigo Carnier, whose book *Lo Stermino Mancato*, containing a detailed account of Globocnik's retreat and death, based entirely on eyewitness reports – above all by former SS Major Ernst Lerch, Globocnik's favoured aide in Lublin and in Trieste – had just been republished. Dr Carnier described a violent argument between Globocnik and a British field security officer, Captain Josep, during which a furious Globocnik was threatened with immediate deportation to Yugoslavia. It was after this ruthless interrogation, Carnier was told by Lerch and others, that Globocnik committed suicide.

But it wasn't true. There was no such interrogation, and although there was a field security officer named Josep, he didn't arrive in Paternion until days later. Why had the story been planted?

Frau Brabeck, the sprightly eighty-two-year-old widow of Paternion Castle's former estate manager, was able to provide a minute description of a 'massive' man in a navy-blue suit and white shirt, nervously chain-smoking while 'to all appearances totally unguarded' as he paced about the courtyard. 'That's a candidate for suicide,' she had told her sister-in-law. Was it possible that a suspected war criminal had been left unguarded in an open courtyard?

Herbert Dunkl, now a local businessman, but a boy in 1945, told us that he and two young friends had rushed up to the castle when they heard that one of those captured was the gauleiter of Carinthia, Friedrich Rainer, whom they admired. They had seen a group of prisoners walking towards them from the gaolhouse, and witnessed a man on the gauleiter's right collapse on the path, after which the British chased them away. But the War Diary stated that the suicide occurred on the way *to* the prison, and this was confirmed to us later by Ernst Lerch, Globocnik's principal aide in Poland, during a four-hour interview in Klagenfurt. He said it took place in full view of a window in his cell, and he had watched Globocnik die. However, back in Paternion next day, a check at the prison showed no windows from which one could see the path from the castle.

Another prisoner, formerly a propaganda chief in the region, had told his daughter that the suicide took place at night, not at 11.30 a.m., and that they were woken up to identify the body. He remembered being shocked when the prisoners were forced to watch the body being thrown into a hole in 'a pig-field', after which 'tanks' drove over it to remove the traces. But the record shows (and the British officers present confirmed it to us later) that none of this was true, either: the burial took place that evening, when the prisoners had already been dispersed to interrogation centres. Frau Maria Tschernutter had watched the hasty burial that spring night in 1945 with her young farmer husband, from their attic across the road. She still lives on the same farm and, after considerable urging, she pointed out the burial corner: 200 metres from a garbage dump on the other side of the road. Just to add to the confusion, the War Diary at Kew on the last page of its report on the incident, listed Globocnik as one of the eight prisoners removed by the provost officer, Captain Willett, that day.

We had tried to find the photograph of Globocnik's body mentioned by Gerald Reitlinger. Research at Kew and other archives not only turned up no trace of it, but threw doubt on the whole story – as, clearly, while the Allies already knew a lot about the concentration camps, such as Belsen, Buchenwald, Auschwitz and Dachau, the extermination camps in Poland remained unknown for months. As late as July 1945, on a list of wanted war criminals at Kew which includes the name of every concentration camp commander, not one of the staff of the Polish murder camps was mentioned. Globocnik *was* on a British 'wanted' list in May 1945, but not for his role in Poland. For the British troops who captured him, his SS activities in Trieste were quite enough to make him a prime target.

Copies of one photograph did finally turn up, both in the Klagenfurt court records, and also in the papers kept by relatives of Friedrich Rainer, the former gauleiter of the area, who were eager to help. It showed six prisoners and several British soldiers, standing next to an object on the ground, so blurred as to be barely recognizable as a human body, but identified in the caption as the corpse of Globocnik.

How was one to distinguish between memory and myth? Between truth and lies? And given that 'CIC report', which even after months of investigation no one had been able to discredit, how could one be *sure* the blur in the photograph was the dead Odilo Globocnik?

Of all the people we saw in Austria, Globocnik's forty-two-year-old son Peter was probably the most impressive. He was born in January 1946 in Wolfsburg – where, prior to the birth, his mother, once the leader of Carinthia's Federation of German Girls, was interned with thousands of other ranking Nazis.

Incredibly, it turns out that Lore Globocnik was half-Jewish. She had married Globocnik in October 1944. Peter never knew his father, and his mother – who died in 1974 – would hardly talk about him. As he grew up he devoured any information he could find, but there was no one he could really ask about his father: the only Carinthian known to have been with him in Poland and to have remained at liberty, Ernst Lerch, had always refused to see him.

How did he feel about it all?

'I don't know what to feel,' he replied, sounding forlorn. 'I've listened to three old men, the only people who knew him, but they were his friends. I've read all the proof for and all the claims against the Holocaust. If I believe the "pros" . . . then, well, I have to believe that my father . . .' He stopped. 'But if I believe the "contras", then I'd be siding with people whose ideological and political motivation I abhor.'

Had he heard of money and valuables brought out by his father when his group retreated to Austria? His mother, he said, had their house repaired after the British, who had requisitioned it in May 1945, moved out. But he had never seen any indication of real money, and his mother had always worked. There was some furniture, he said, and showed us a large inlaid desk and an antique cupboard. 'That's all that came here,' he said, 'but there's lots more which was left at the Hotel Enzian on the Weissensee, where they stayed for a while before hiding in the mountains.' (Lerch had told Dr Carnier of a convoy of trucks coming from Italy, and to me he would not deny that they contained gold, money and other valuables.)

Had he considered the possibility that his father might have survived?

'Of course. There were always rumours. And so many did survive. Still . . . if he made a new life, perhaps even had a new family, wouldn't he have wanted to know about me?'

Peter Globocnik was the last major witness we saw in Austria. And, significantly, he demonstrated deep distrust of his father's closest aide, Ernst Lerch, who had told us what we knew was a lie – that he had actually seen Globocnik commit suicide, from a vantage point which didn't exist.

The West German office for investigation into Nazi crimes at Ludwigsburg found a transcript of the interrogation of his mother in the course of an investigation in 1964 into a 'suggestion that Globocnik may still be alive'. It seemed curious that Lore had rejected three requests over the years to authorize the exhumation and examination of the body.

The conflicting evidence certainly left open the possibility of a substitution in May 1945. And Fort Meade's apparent reluctance to co-operate fully with Dr Wolfe led to his decision at the end of June to hand over the investigation to a young historian at the Justice Department's Office for Special Investigations (OSI) – who had investigated America's involvement with Barbie and Mengele. This was the only US government agency with the motivation, the clout and indeed the obligation to find the answers we sought.

But Peter Stahl was an increasing worry. Now he was going back on a months-old promise to send us two more pages of the report as soon as he could extricate them from his mass of documents. He had described them from memory as 'a kind of US army transfer order', indicating that on such and such a date 'subjects' would be transferred from Berlin's Tempelhof airport to Rhein-Main airport in Frankfurt, from there to an intermediate point, and then transhipped overseas. Globocnik, whose new name and Yugoslav passport number were cited on the first page, would go to Canada, and Müller to Miami. On the second sheet – just handwritten notes, he said – was the number of an account which had been opened for one of them – Globocnik, he thought – at the Chase National Bank.

He had now found these pages, he told us the day we returned from Austria. With the OSI getting into the act, though, he thought he would hold on to them as his 'hole card', a sort of insurance policy. But I had to see these papers, and two days later we left for California.

We had meant to surprise Peter Stahl, but he found out we were coming and his little box of a house in Merced, a Californian desert town, was immaculate but also empty of life: no books or papers and – I was to find – no food or drink. Even in the bathroom there was nothing but an old cake of soap and a crumpled hand towel. Disconcertingly, the house felt like a place that had been hastily 'sanitized'. During most of our two days there a beautiful silver bitch, part wolf and part German shepherd, lay at either Stahl's feet or the feet of a young man he had introduced as his son Greg. Several decrepit German shepherd dogs wandered in and out constantly. 'I won't put down any animals,' Stahl said. It was a curious introduction to this curious man.

He was in his late fifties, tall, with cropped grey hair and a firm handshake. He talked in a torrent of words, with an educated but tight American voice, often dropping in German words in a heavy accent.

He gave the impression of being a tense, guarded man, but with an overriding need to impress.

He and 'Greg' were living there under a cover name and with an unlisted phone, he said. Two years earlier he had given away to the FBI and the California authorities a couple of wrongdoers – one an arsonist who had burnt down the house of a Jew, the other a man who wanted him to help smuggle plastic handguns into the United States. Both, he said, were now after him.

It was unfortunate, he said almost gleefully, that I hadn't let him know that I was coming. As soon as he had learned that the OSI were involved, he had sent the papers we wanted along with his other valuable things to relatives in Illinois for safe-keeping. He was afraid of the US army's reaction – he was absolutely sure they wouldn't stand still to be 'investigated by this agency they loathe and despise'. And as the OSI was 'the leakiest body in Washington', he was sure the army would soon have his name and come banging on his door, demanding that he hand over everything he had. But I had to have those papers. I suggested that he come with me to Illinois to pick them up, and he agreed.

The next morning he told me he had been telephoning much of the night, trying to find the relatives, who had apparently gone off on a two-week trip, visiting various members of the family. We would just have to wait, he said.

How about the rest of the Müller file, I asked. It would help in the archives search – was it also in Illinois? No, he said. As I had said I was only interested in Globocnik, he'd sold it to a client in the Washington area. But he had protected us – he had blacked out all mentions of Globocnik. No, he hadn't kept a copy.

Dr Wolfe had been stonewalled by Fort Meade; now I felt I had been filibustered by Stahl. I had no doubt that he was lying. But why? Was the whole thing a hoax, a fake? But Stahl wanted neither money (though he was obviously hard up) nor credit. What would be the point of such a dangerous game? He had been offered several opportunities to drop the whole matter, with no hard feelings. But he insisted that the documents were genuine, and that the only important thing was to get them published, to pin the blame on the governments who had protected such a monster.

That weekend, we discussed the situation with four top OSI officials in Washington. There was complete agreement that a document so potentially damaging to the British and US governments had to be thoroughly examined. There were details which worried them: the classification, the tone, the 'sanitizing'. But, as Dr Wolfe had also found, any of these could have various explanations.

The OSI was ready now to undertake an official investigation. Their remit included access to the Fort Meade archives, forensic examination by the FBI, and psycho-linguistic analysis of the documents. I had presented them with all the findings. They would in turn keep me informed as far as they could – withholding only details which they could not properly release. The important thing now was to get Stahl's last two pages: a name and passport number could be checked in minutes. In order to motivate Stahl, I told him that the OSI, though they – like us – had serious doubts about the documents, did not suspect him personally of any wrongdoing.

Two days later, when I was back in London, Stahl telephoned. After the good news about the OSI's positive attitude towards him, he had spent a night working through the cartons of documents we had seen stacked high in his garage. He had found something momentous: the identity of the man who had given him the papers. Suddenly it was no longer direct from Fort Meade that he had got them, but via a well-known writer on secret service matters, John Costello, who in 1983 had wanted from him information on intelligence matters in wartime Britain which might exist in a Gestapo microfilm Stahl owned. As Costello also had a mass of documents, he asked what Stahl would like in return. Stahl said anything on Heinrich Müller would be useful.

This writer, Stahl now told me, meeting him in a Reno, Nevada, hotel in May, had brought with him the 'Müller file', mostly in German, in which he later discovered the CIC documents. He didn't think Costello – who didn't speak German, wasn't very interested in the Third Reich, and probably had never heard of Globocnik – had even looked carefully at the file. Their negotiations broke down over money, and they had barely communicated since. (Costello subsequently denied to me giving Stahl any such papers, though he confirmed the meeting in Reno and remembered sending him quite different documents. He died a few years later.)

Costello's name was now added to the list of those whose requests for material from Fort Meade would be looked at by the OSI. Meanwhile Stahl kept the transatlantic phone lines busy with more news: aware of my frustration during our visit, he had not dared to tell me that the 'Müller file' had been paginated – up to 427 – and that, fearful of leading the army back to him, he had whited out both the pagination and the declassification stamps on the papers he sent me. He was 'really sorry' about this, but the good news was that he had sent another copy of the original Xeroxed documents including the two final pages, to a safe place 'in the Bay Area'. Now that he'd remembered who gave them to him, there was no further danger, and he would get them to me.

Our main contact at the OSI also had news: their three-man team had found, within a couple of days at Fort Meade, that there was indeed a Heinrich Müller file, but rather than showing him in the service of the West, these 40-odd pages (not 400-odd) indicated that he was suspected of working for the Russians. Added to the file, however, they found a note of recent date, obviously inserted by Fort Meade staff, that Dr Robert Wolfe had requested a Heinrich Müller file and had been informed that there was nothing on record. And the very next day an OSI investigator found three frames of microfilm relating to Globocnik. They had no visible relation to Stahl's document – but they showed again that the archive's initial denial was either a mistake, or an incomprehensible lie.

The FBI's report was inconclusive: the many-times copied document did not lend itself to forensic examination, but the typewriters and typefaces were of the correct period. The OSI now had some information about the putative signatories of the documents, though they were both dead. Severin Wallach and Andrew Venters, his operations officer who countersigned the first report and was the author of the 'Annex', had worked as a team in Berlin at the relevant time. And it was quite normal for a special agent to prepare a report while the operations officer wrote an 'Annex' – an explanation or extension of the report.

The OSI also had a list of those who had requested material on Müller in the last five years, which was the limit of Fort Meade's register. The writer whom Stahl had mentioned had requested material on other subjects in that time, but nothing on Müller. They were beginning to build a picture of Peter Stahl. If the document was forged, they thought perhaps he had been used – a victim rather than a perpetrator.

Did they now think it was a forgery, I asked. 'I have a gut feeling that it is,' my OSI contact said, 'but we have no proof. We cannot specifically fault it.'

On the other hand, we had located Major Ken Hedley, who as a lieutenant in the 4th Hussars had commanded the party which captured Globocnik, and was now living in Ireland. He in turn would lead us to two other officers, Brigadier Guy Wheeler and Ted Birkett, who was the junior intelligence officer on that raid.

In May 1945 the 4th Hussars, who had crossed over into Carinthia after the last hard fighting in Italy, were euphoric that the war in Europe had ended. 'It was a beautiful spring, the place was full of delightful popsies, and we were *alive*,' was Ken Hedley's memory of that May in Paternion, where they had taken over the castle as their billet. There were warnings of possible 'Werewolf' activities, of SS hiding out in the nearby mountains, and a list of wanted men headed by Gauleiter Friedrich Rainer and SS General Odilo Globocnik.

'I was driving my jeep up a mountain road when I suddenly saw a *Wehrmacht* major in full uniform standing in the road,' Hedley told me. 'I had my pistol out quick as a flash but, "No, no," he said, "you don't need that – we are on your side now." Turned out to be a thoroughly decent fellow, major in the Brandenburgers – very good chaps.'

The Brandenburgers – an *Abwehr* special regiment, similar to the Commandos – had already reported to British Intelligence at Spittal, had heard they were looking for the gauleiter and SS people, and volunteered their help in order to 'buy their ticket home'. And they delivered: the little gaolhouse in the castle grounds was soon occupied by a string of SS men picked up in the mountains.

On the evening of 30 May the Hussars, having discovered 'a rich liquor cache', were throwing a party at the castle. The festivities were well under way when the lock-up sergeant – 'I think he'd seen too many American films,' Hedley said – marched in and whispered to Hedley that one of the prisoners wanted to make a statement. Hedley went along, with two fellow officers – one of them Major Alex Ramsay, of Special Forces, who spoke seven languages – as witnesses.

'The young sergeant was from an SS mountain unit,' Hedley said, 'and he told us he'd been taking food up to a very special group hiding out in a mountain hut. General Globocnik was there with his staff, he said, and he could lead us up.'

Twenty-five-year-old SS *Unterscharführer* Siegfried Kummerer's record, we found out later, was not quite as innocuous as he told his captors. A member of Carinthia's illegal Hitler Youth in the 1930s, when Globocnik was one of the top men in the movement there, he served after the *Anschluss* as a guard at Dachau and Mauthausen. After a brief period of combat in an SS mountain division in Finland, he was transferred for 'special training' to Lublin – Globocnik's command – and then, yet again under Globocnik, to Italy. Why would such a man betray his own commander?

A speedily organized group – three Hussar officers, the two intelligence officers, and the Brandenburger major, plus twenty-four soldiers – started up the mountain at 2.30 a.m.

Ernst Lerch had told us that the fugitives stood guard at night – he had the first watch, Major Michalsen (who, in Poland, had been in charge of the Jewish transports) the second, and Major Höfle (Globocnik's executive officer) the third.

'Guards?' said Ken Hedley. 'Nonsense. It was as quiet as a grave when we got up there.'

They surrounded the house before dawn, and were ready to burst in when one man came out in shirtsleeves, stretching. 'My sergeant,' said Major Hedley, 'brawny chap, gave him a good kick in the behind to move him out of the doorway and he said – would you believe it? – "You can't behave like this to me – I'm the gauleiter." Well, that was a nice surprise.'

Wheeler recalled another man coming out – he remembered him as 'small, fat, insignificant'. This was supposedly Globocnik, who was in fact inches taller than Rainer.

During a perfunctory interrogation, all the fugitives denied having anything to do with the SS. The Brandenburgers – apparently unsupervised – searched the hut and found two poison containers, one of them empty. The man Wheeler had seen coming out – whom Birkett clearly remembered as wearing 'lederhosen, a *Jäger* [hunting] jacket and particularly nice mountain boots, which I coveted' – said he was a merchant from Klagenfurt, named König, and gave references there.

Hedley, eager to get his prize locked up, went down first with Rainer. 'I rather liked him,' he said. 'We talked most of the way down. He seemed a nice man.' The rest were brought down later, and were put in the lock-up, except for the 'merchant', who, after walking down with Birkett, was kept in the castle courtyard. Birkett, who spoke fluent German, talked to him for some time 'about Austria, the future, things like that. He seemed perfectly happy – an intelligent, quietly spoken man. We were preparing to let him go.'

But Kummerer, standing near by, stopped them. 'No, no, you mustn't,' he whispered urgently to Hedley. 'That's Globocnik, you want him. Don't let him go.'

So they decided to set a little trap: Ramsay would go up to a little balcony and shout Globocnik's name, while Hedley and Birkett watched for his reaction. And sure enough, when Ramsay shouted the name in 'parade-ground tones', the prisoner – 'though he didn't falter in his stride, I'll give him that,' said Hedley – fractionally moved his head.

'I told him: "You've given yourself away – you moved your head; you're Globocnik," Hedley said. 'And I told the sergeant to lock him up with the others, and went up to have a bath.' Birkett and the Company Sergeant Sowler walked the prisoner out through an archway and up the path. Almost at the lock-up, Birkett was just behind him when he saw him 'hit his mouth with his right hand. He immediately collapsed on the ground.'

Lerch had told us that he watched from his cell window, and saw him bite on the pill, fall down, turn blue and die immediately. This, Birkett and Hedley said, was nonsense: he was not in sight of any cell window, he didn't turn blue, and he didn't die immediately. There was time to call Hedley from his bath, and the doctor arrived and gave two injections. 'He said it was useless,' Birkett told us. 'He'd be dead in a moment. There was a tremendous hullabaloo. Ramsay came running, and said we'd get a rocket for letting him kill himself. I said Why? Good riddance, saves a lot of trouble.'

When I showed Birkett the photograph with the blurred image of the body which I had found in Klagenfurt, he recognized the British soldiers but found the corpse quite unfamiliar. 'Funny,' he said, 'he's wearing a suit. I could have sworn it was lederhosen.' He shook his head, perplexed. 'Couldn't have been a switch, could there?'

The other prisoners were called out and given a body-search after they had identified the dead man. 'Two of them – Höfle and Lerch – handed me poison capsules,' Birkett said.

Ramsay, who always had a camera, took photographs of the British and the prisoners, with the body in the foreground, and Birkett remembered him straddling the corpse to get a close-up of the face. Ken Hedley had several of these photographs, but none in which the face of the corpse was identifiable. Birkett had once had a full set of enlargements, but they had disappeared. Neither Hedley, Wheeler nor Birkett could recognize Globocnik on several photographs we showed them.

So the possibility of a mistake still existed: a loud shout of the name; a fractional movement of a head; a man dying, watched from a non-existent vantage point by his closest aide; and the identification made only by his staff – all men profoundly implicated in the crimes in Poland, all men who knew about trucks full of money and valuables which they had brought into Carinthia during their escape from northern Italy and which had since disappeared.

A statement by Dr M. C. Leigh of the Royal Army Medical Corps, sent to Vienna by the Foreign Office, and here retranslated from German, was carefully phrased. 'Dr Leigh says that he is not in a position to confirm Major Hedley's statement that Globocnik's identity was incontestably established. All he can say is that the man Major Hedley described as Globocnik died in his presence.' Dr Leigh is now dead.

Could the British have been fooled?

Peter Stahl was being totally unhelpful. The last pages were refused, then promised again, but did not arrive. The OSI were stymied: they could not authenticate the document, but except for that 'gut feeling' they couldn't declare it a fake either.

Finally Stahl did send a 'Müller file' and new copies of the original papers, this time with pagination restored – or added – but still without the declassification stamps. These bore no resemblance to the file he had described: in fact they were photocopies of records from the Berlin Document Centre. He said it was his lawyer's fault: he didn't read German, and sent the wrong papers.

In Washington, several former CIC officers had been contacted and, while some were understandably reticent and all were appalled at the prospect of further scandalous disclosures, none seemed to consider that it was impossible. Severin Wallach, Viennese by birth and a lawyer by profession, was described as a brilliant and solitary man, convinced of the Soviet threat. He had run thirty to sixty agents at any one time, and conceived a number of projects which he 'kept very close to his chest'. And Venters, the alleged author of the 'Annex', was apparently prone to high-flown language.

However, a former CIC officer whom I visited in Germany, who had worked closely with both men for years, finally provided an authoritative 'bottom line'. 'It is extraordinary,' he said. 'Whoever produced this had to have been in – or closely advised by someone from – Region VIII. The format is right, the methodology is correct and, given the personalities of the two people who allegedly wrote this, even the tone and the breadth of the concept fits.'

But there were two fundamental flaws, he said. First, it would have been impossible to run such a project from Soviet-infested Berlin – it would have had to be done from Frankfurt, at the US Zone HQ. Secondly, he said the author's knowledge of Wallach and Venters was superficial. Venters was a sophisticated man. Such 'Annexes' were indeed sometimes written to set up a framework of support for projects. Familiar as Venters was with the army hierarchy, he might have 'lectured', but not in this simplistic manner, which would insult the intelligence of his superiors. Worse, in psychological terms, was the mistake about Severin Wallach: true, he was politically to the right. 'But my God,' said this officer, 'he was a Jew – almost all his family had been killed by the Nazis. Not in a million years would Severin Wallach have lifted a finger to save Globocnik, or Müller either.'

And just two days later, in Austria, we finally had the proof we had sought for seven months. With the help of a former SOE officer, I located Major Ramsay's widow in Vienna. She knew all about the raid, and had one photo from those her husband took in Paternion on

31 May 1945. It had been taken at almost the same time as the fuzzy photo, and showed – sharply – the corpse on the ground, and behind it three other prisoners: Höfle, Michalsen and Helletsberger. But here the face of the body on the ground – in dark suit and white shirt – was unmistakably that of Odilo Globocnik. And he was unmistakably dead.

February 2000

After Richard Williams's switch from *The Times* to the new *Independent on Sunday*, this feature was finally published in the *Independent on Sunday Review*, where I worked on it with Liz Jobey. I had developed misgivings about Peter Stahl within a few months of first hearing from him. If, none the less, we persisted in our research, it was first because, from the start, so much of the information we gathered in Austria was incompatible with the long-established record of Globocnik's death, and secondly because neither we nor Richard Williams could think of a rational explanation for anyone faking those documents or for sending them to me. It is true, however, that from the moment we met Stahl in his weird house in the Californian desert, alarm bells rang strongly in my mind even though the OSI, during our secret Sunday meeting in their Washington HQ with the director and three of his aides, assured us that if the document turned out to be forged, they saw Stahl as a victim rather than a perpetrator. He was too intelligent, they said, to try to play such tricks.

Peter Stahl's final pages never came and were, in any case, immaterial, as we found the photograph we had sought for so long. The puzzle, however, remains: I have no doubt that these documents were fabricated and all the authorities I dealt with in America finally thought so too.

In the matter of that faked CIA document, at least four US agencies – the OSI, the FBI, Fort Meade and the CIA – became involved. Why did so many people of high rank lie about Globocnik, about Müller and, of course, about Stahl too? Disturbingly, we are left with the question, how can it be that the American authorities take such a light view of the forgery of government documents, and indeed of the forger?

10

Private Lives

February 2000

Of all journalistic work, the writing of profiles is the most demanding, for however much the writer dislikes it, he (or she) is forced into indiscretions and the revelation of distressing truths. There are consequences: the warm letters of Franz Stangl's wife, who was not in the least upset about my profile of Stangl, ceased after she read what I wrote about *her* two years afterwards in my book about *him*, and, as one of her Brazilian grandsons would tell me years later, after she had died (when he telephoned to ask me to send him a copy of *Into that Darkness*), she forbade her daughters to show their children the book. And in my book on Albert Speer I describe a letter he wrote to me more than two years after my profile of him had been published both in Britain and in Germany – two years during which we had exchanged numerous letters about a book we planned to do together and he had telephoned me perhaps thirty, forty times.* It was written, I understood later, under the effect of a late-life liaison he had formed with a young woman who, well-meaningly no doubt, assured him that he had never done anything he need reproach himself for.

He had been terribly hurt, he wrote in this long agonized letter, that I had accused him of 'knowledge' – the question about the genocide of the Jews which was 'absolutely central to his life'. He had thought (quite rightly, I told him later) that I, differently from others, had not come with the intention to 'catch me out and pass judgement'. Saying finally that I was not to worry about his reaction and that he was looking forward to our collaboration on the new book we planned to do together, he wrote, 'You have a difficult profession I know, which

* See *Albert Speer, His Battle With Truth*, Macmillan, pp. 709–11.

forces you to enter and disclose the private lives of others. It can't be helped.'

Speer, on whom, inevitably, I was hard, was a generous man, but there are relationships between writers and the subjects of their profiles which cannot survive publication. Because, as Speer quite rightly said, if profiles are to serve their purpose of showing the reader what he did not know before, intrusion into their private lives and often hidden or repressed motivations is inevitable.

As I write these lines in early February 2000, we are witnessing the passionate rejection by many EU member states of the coalition in Austria of the long-established liberal-conservative 'People's Party' and the extreme but democratically elected right-wing 'Freedom Party' under its 'leader' Jörg Haider. This reaction is highly significant, for it shows how strong the memories remain of another charismatic and intelligent Austrian politician sixty-seven years ago and how alive are the fears of the potential growth of the extreme right in twenty-first-century Europe.

None the less, the extent of it was ill considered and counter-productive. For while a firm expression of disapproval of Haider and his various unacceptable opinions was certainly justified, it seemed entirely inappropriate to have turned this into a with-no-end-in-view political ostracization by the EU of Austria and a general denunciation of all Austrians as Nazis. It is, of course, perfectly true that, crassly contrary to Germany, Austria, until very recently, did little to take issue with her own Nazi past, and this failure to think and teach their young, can not be excused or justified by the fact that, ridiculously enough, the Allies declared Austria in 1945 to have been Hitler's first victim. Reality should have taught them better. But the country's government conduct since 1945, both from the point of view of the liberal laws which were passed and their open-door policy (closely resembling that of Germany) toward refugees – which incidentally included entry permits and financial support for tens of thousands of Russian Jews – has shown no vestige of Nazi ideas. However, it is no doubt true that there remains more anti-semitism in Austria than in Germany, the reasons for which have never yet been properly evaluated. Also, there can be little doubt of Haider's right-wing opinions and his frequently expressed admiration for some of Hitler's social measures. But large numbers of intelligent Austrians know all this as well and better than France and Belgium, their principal EU critics, and deplore his statements when they are deplorable. Haider has since given up or been persuaded to give up the party's leadership and, a family man with inherited wealth, has retreated to his fiefdom in Carinthia, where he is the elected governor. And since the election a year ago, the Freedom Party, closely watched by the suspicious Vienna media, have so far appeared to be socially and politically on the side of the angels.

It is, of course, quite right that the EU should be concerned about the moral and political rectitude of member states. Where this concern, however, can become dangerous is when it interferes with the expressed will of the electorate. One can imagine scenarios where this could become necessary, but perhaps very special arrangements need to be in place in the EU's constitution to deal with such eventualities; open-ended economic sanctions against a country because of the results of a free election of a party (not an individual) seems hardly the way, and reaction to foreign interference could easily lead to a defiance vote.

This happened, also in Austria, when Kurt Waldheim – hysterically attacked, particularly in America, for alleged war crimes (which were later disproved) while serving in the (German) army during the war – was elected president of Austria by a huge majority. It was lucky that, as I would find when I talked with him in 1986, he was a harmless and fundamentally decent man (see page 247).

Of the seven people whose profiles are published in this book, and in fact of all the many profiles I have written on subjects other than Germany or the Nazis, Waldheim is the only one whose home and family I didn't see – I talked with him over tea in the sitting room of his suite in the Hofburg (the former Imperial Palace) in Vienna. Other writers may not consider the intrusion into subjects' private lives necessary, but for me the three essentials for the writing of profiles, or biographies, are: an understanding of a person's childhood, of their emotional past and present lives; the influence on them of the people with whom they live and among whom they work; and finally, of course, the circumstances which determined whatever it is that makes them into subjects for a profile.

Aside from Stangl and Speer, you will read five profiles in this book – Waldheim, François Genoud, a punctiliously honest Swiss who remained an ideological Nazi until his death in 1996 and who, with his wife, had become good friends of ours as from 1976; Dr Hans Münch, an Auschwitz SS doctor, who with great courage refused to take part in selection of inmates for gassing and who, though now eighty-eight and slowly sinking into forgetfulness, was fully *compos mentis* when I talked to him in 1982; Hans Jürgen Syberberg, perhaps the most imaginative cinematic mind post-war Germany has produced and who, with his beautiful Viennese wife Helga and their intelligent daughter Amelie, my husband (who photographed them) and I saw a lot of in the late 1970s and early 1980s; and Leni Riefenstahl, one of the twentieth-century's finest film-makers and photographers, whom I had known for some years and who had been helpful to me during my Speer research. Of all of them, only she, understandably enough, took umbrage at what I wrote and angrily broke off relations with me after the publication of the profile.

Although Hans Jürgen Syberberg has a considerable cult following abroad, he has not made a film in years and to have lost him as an active force in German cinema is a tragedy for anyone who loves films. His is an immense, even unique talent. He is, however, very German in a traditional sense, and – there can be no doubt about it from the reams of hate-filled writings about him – the rejection of him, both by German critics and by the German public, is entirely because while post-Hitler Germans, who are really very different from their effusively romantic ancestors, are only too ready to accept straightforward documentaries about their 'recent past' (as they call it), they now dismiss and despise romanticized-imaginative and moralistic interpretations.

II

The Three Sins of Syberberg

May 1978

When the British Film Institute recently awarded its Best Film of the Year prize to the German director Hans Jürgen Syberberg the news passed unnoticed in Germany, where reviewers have virtually boycotted his three latest films. These films shared themes related to that of his award winning *Hitler, a Film from Germany*, a mammoth seven-hour production.

'They kill my films by silence,' says Syberberg in his quiet voice. 'No film can exist without reviews.' In Britain one review called his Hitler film 'the *War and Peace* of cinema art', and critic Alan Brien described it as 'like a slow-motion Catherine wheel that casts off an endless flow of burning questions'.

Because of what he calls the 'destructive attitude' of the German press, Syberberg wrote an open letter to leading newspapers last year announcing his decision to withdraw the film from Germany. That letter remained unpublished. In another open letter Wolf Donner, the director of the Berlin Film Festival, invited him to show the film there this year, but Syberberg refused because, in his opinion, the invitation was so maliciously worded. 'Syberberg revels,' wrote Donner, 'in posing as the persecuted Jesus of Germany's *Kultur*.'

What is the cause of this extraordinary enmity, whereby a film hailed in Britain as 'the Hitler film we have waited for for thirty years' risks being shown in Britain, France, Italy and the United States, but not in its own country?* And who is this film-maker, until now little known

* WDR (West German television), one of the backers of the Hitler epic, which has screened all of Syberberg's films in the past, intends to show it on four successive evenings when permitted to do so by contractual arrangements that preclude television showings until after theatre release.

in Britain? What is so special, or different, about Syberberg's films that they provoke these reactions?

Syberberg *is* exceptionally sensitive to criticism and does believe he is isolated in a sea of hate. He writes long letters constantly and makes calls to editors and in 1976 wrote a book denouncing the critics. But could any personality problem explain such a conspiracy of silence.

It would be an oversimplification too, to blame it on a rejection by the critics of the Hitler theme. The Germans do not reject indictments of Hitler – innumerable books, films and plays on the subject receive fair hearings every year.

'I am an outsider,' says Syberberg. 'An irritant; an intellectual aesthete, which is a dirty word here. I am the antithesis of what life and values in Germany have become: I believe Hitler came out of us, was one of us; I am not interested in money, except for my work; and I love Germany. Those are my three sins.'

Syberberg made 185 short films for Bavarian Television in two years after leaving university in Munich in 1962. Between 1965 and 1970 he made six full-length films, five of them documentaries.

'But those were not on "dangerous subjects",' says Eckart Schmidt, a young freelance reviewer in Munich who, at risk to his own career ('You wouldn't believe it, if I told you how he has been threatened,' says his wife), continues to support Syberberg. 'He got prize after prize, and the critics heaped praise on his head for his novel investigative approach to documentary filming. But in 1970, with *San Domingo*, in which he took issue with communes, rockers and even the emerging terrorist movement, he began to touch the raw nerve of our German taboos, and came a cropper with the critics. Each of his subsequent films has been increasingly offensive to our special German sensibilities.'

Three films harmed him most in Germany and, paradoxically, made his reputation abroad. They were: *Ludwig – Requiem for a Virgin King* (1972), *Karl May* (1974), and the documentary *Confessions of Winifred Wagner* (1975) – all three exceptionally long films on difficult German themes. In Syberberg's *Ludwig*, Hitler appears to the king in a nightmare during the victory celebration in 1871 ('The foundation of the German Reich,' says Syberberg) dancing a rumba with the king's valet, who is wearing an SA uniform. All of this takes place in the Venus Grotto from *Tannhäuser*. And in the nightmare Hitler, the king and the valet are joined by the adventure-story writer Karl May – favourite author of millions of Germans, and of Hitler – who speaks familiarly to Ludwig, as a Wagner lover, about the Germany of the future.

'Here I had them all together,' says Syberberg. 'Ludwig, Karl May, Hitler – three pathologic egocentrics in "recent" German history – and the link, Wagner. And this is where the idea for the other films was born.'

We were talking in his 'studio', a converted garage in the garden of his three-storey villa in the exclusive English Garden district of Munich, where he lives with his wife Helga, a dark-haired, fine-boned Viennese beauty who has worked with him for fifteen years, and their ten-year-old daughter Amelie.

The furniture in the tiny studio is simple: a desk with a cane chair, an Empire sofa and armchair. There are a few other haphazard pieces of furniture, books, mementoes and photographs from his films and, in the corner, an old-fashioned wood stove. 'I *live* in this room,' says Syberberg. 'I do all my thinking, all my writing here . . .' (All except his diary entries. He goes shooting off into corners every so often to make them. Helga shrugs: 'He's been doing that since all this awful trouble with the critics. It's a lightning conductor – otherwise he'd burst.')

Syberberg, forty-two, is slim, blond and silky-voiced, with classical North German looks. He dresses with apparent carelessness, but loves mirrors and can become ecstatic about clothes. He likes to think of himself as infinitely private, quiet and gentle, but talks about himself by the hour. It may be no accident that Amelie – a warm, big-eyed perceptive child – calls him Tiger, not father.

Born on 8 December 1935, in Pomerania, West Prussia, Syberberg is the son of an industrialist-turned-farmer, whose nineteen-year-old wife, six months after the baby's birth, tired of her husband's roving eye and left. After that came a succession of nannies ('they kept leaving because father got them into his bed') and finally a 'stepmother', the wife of the estate manager who conveniently went to war. 'She was small, plump, bosomy and emotionally intrusive. She kept wanting to paw and kiss me and have me call her mother.'

His father, while politically on the right, was anti-Hitler. 'He had worked a lot in England as a young industrialist and he always listened to the BBC. He would say, "*They* are honest about their mistakes and losses." I am sure that my father's love for fairness and for England, had a great influence on me. But, of course, Hitler was my childhood. When I researched later for background sounds for the Hitler film, they were all as familiar to me as cars, church bells and television commercials are to children now.'

Syberberg left East Germany in 1953 when he was seventeen. 'I had listened to a "show" trial on the radio and at one moment the judge broke into the defence attorney's speech and screamed: "If you say one more word in mitigation, I'll put *you* in the dock." That was "it" for me. If we had got to the point where a man was not even entitled to a fair defence, I didn't want to live there. I left, the very next day.'

By 1963, with a degree in Germanics and history of art and a job with Bavarian Television, he had met Helga, who worked as a multilingual secretary in a film office. 'Now there were two of us homeless in Bavaria.' He has felt homeless ever since leaving his Pomeranian village. 'I feel a stranger here in Munich.' He adds: 'Of course, now we have our house, and there is the family – Amelie.'

He treats Amelie as an adult and yet is infinitely protective of her. He cast her as the central figure of the Hitler film, as the child through whose eyes the whole Hitler period is seen – a decision which now torments him. 'She is deeply shy,' says Helga. 'She only agreed to be in the film for Jürgen – she did it for him because he needed her. It was a very personal thing between the two of them.'

'You are a very complicated man,' Amelie blurted out at lunch one day. 'Very hard to live with.' In weeks of knowing him, this was the only time I saw him lose control. He flushed, looked stricken, kept his eyes on his plate and allowed a totally uncharacteristic note of pleading to enter his voice. 'How can you say this? You?' Amelie flushed too. 'Not for me,' she retreated, quickly. 'You are not difficult with me. With me you are always simple.'

The smoother his voice, the more indicative it can be of anger and he is a very angry man.

'He isn't when he is abroad,' says his friend and long-time assistant, Gerhard von Halem. 'In Paris and London, where he is surrounded by appreciation, he is a different man. Do you realize that I and perhaps two others are the only people Helga and Jürgen see socially?'

'How can I meet strangers and try to make new friends?' asks Syberberg. 'With the things that are said about me in the papers – not about my *films*, about *me* – I am ashamed to go out, to look anybody in the face.'

'Of course,' says another German journalist who, significantly, asked not to be named, 'he has a right to be angry. He is a *magical* talent, a man of soaring imagination. In Germany where, since Hitler, films have been such an important part of life, we are afraid of film men with imagination. Especially if they use it to lay bare our deficiencies. Our film reviewers are a clique, men dedicated to compromise.'

A documentary about Winifred Wagner, Wagner's British daughter-in-law and Hitler's friend, was a stroke of luck. 'It fell into my lap,' says Syberberg, 'through a close relative of hers. Winifred fascinated me and, unlike all my other films, a film about her was obviously a commercial proposition – and I needed money for the Hitler film. I had finance for it, a million marks, from German, French and British television, and an art grant from the Ministry of the Interior. But it *was* clear already that – like the three other films – it would become infinitely longer than planned.'

'Despite the critics,' says Gerhard von Halem, 'up to now he has always been given money to make his films. Though nobody in the business can understand how he manages on the sums he gets.' Syberberg's production staff consists of an assistant, the cameraman and himself. 'It's all in the planning,' says von Halem. 'The day the cameras begin to run Jürgen has everything down on paper, organized to the last drawing pin.' *Ludwig*, budgeted at seventy minutes, ran 140, cost DM300,000 (£78,000) and was shot in eleven days. *Karl May*, budgeted for ninety minutes, ran three hours, cost DM1,100,000 (£276,000) and took twenty-eight days to make. *Winifred Wagner*, costing DM70,000 (£18,000) and filmed in five days, was supposed to run an hour and runs for five. And *Hitler*, financed as a 100-minute film, became 420 minutes; it cost 1 million marks and was shot in twenty studio days.

The film's first London showing – an all-night screening planned soon for the Gate 2 Cinema – will give a British audience an opportunity to assess its power and decide about the film's importance. An even wider public will see the film if, as is hoped, BBC2 shows it later this year.

Hitler, a Film from Germany is really four films of 105 minutes each: *The Grail*, *A German Dream*, *In The Night* and *We Children of Hell*. An imaginative *tour de force*, without a conventional – or logical – story-line, it is, basically, a trial without a courtroom. It takes place, as the film unfolds, in our minds – and is no film for the historically ignorant. We 'try' Hitler as we relate what is never shown – but what, after all, we *know* he did – to the voices of Goebbels, Churchill, Roosevelt and German 'freedom fighters'; to long monologues about philosophy, ethics and the most private aspects of private lives, spoken by actors representing Himmler, his masseur, and Hitler's valet, Linge. We 'try' Hitler to music by Wagner, Beethoven, Mahler and Lehar. In the background, always, is the echo of the solemn annual Nazi celebration of the dead. We see Hitler in many guises, as Caligari, Napoleon, Chaplin, Hamlet, a house-painter, a ghost rising from the grave giving the Nazi salute. He and his entourage are seen frequently as macabre puppets.

'To make a film against Hitler today – a film of atonement,' says Syberberg, 'is no trick. In Germany we are specialists in paying lip service to atonement. Everybody is against Hitler. What is different is to make films against Hitler which hurt. I don't do this to be provocative, but because there are painful totally unresolved conflicts which, until I made my films, had never been aired.

'I am an intellectual, not an instinctive film-maker,' he says. That is only true in the sense that he is a clever man who knows a lot and uses his knowledge. Perhaps more significant is that, often maddeningly arrogant, he should disparage his most important quality. For what he says, both in the film and when talking, often transcends intelligence or logic.

Some such inspiration led to his creation of the figure of the blind inward-looking child, an Alice in a Wonderland of horror, who accompanies the viewer throughout the film, providing a confused, even blurred child frame through which we see the picture, now bearable. Syberberg worked on this film from 1972. Helga recalls days of deep depression, weeks of inexplicable illness in the middle of research.

'Years of hate,' says Syberberg. 'That was the great problem. That, I think, is how I came finally upon the idea of the child and my child at that: a world into which I could inject love – and a different, more real reality than any we can glean from archives or personal accounts.'

It is the *irrational* components of the German nation, Syberberg says, which produced Hitler. This is the crux of his battle with the German film reviewers, who appear unable to budge imaginatively from their commitment to a rational, successful, materialistic Germany. Romanticism, says Syberberg in his film, produced Hitler. Imagination produced Hitler. Pride and love produced Hitler. *We*, the film screams out at us without ever actually saying so, are responsible for him, are each individually responsible for everything evil that passes.

By rejecting their part in Hitler, says Syberberg throughout his film, the Germans are rejecting their true romantic irrational selves – their real German identity – and, unless they take heed, will rob their children of their true heritage and make of Germany a dead land.

12

'The Truth Is, I Loved Hitler'

April 1996

The thickest file in the archive of ZES, the Swiss security service, belongs to an eighty-year-old businessman, François Genoud. Today, Genoud is probably, if not the last, certainly the most intransigent of Hitler's disciples. His determined secretiveness about a life spent in the passionate support of National Socialism and the (in his eyes) related Arab and Palestinian cause has earned him the title he has enjoyed for half a century: the most mysterious man in Europe.

I have known Genoud for about twenty-five of these fifty years. I met him first when I wanted to find out about a serialization of 'Hitler's Tabletalk', then running in a German magazine, in which he was identified as the copyright holder.

'I'll shoot over to Munich and tell you all about it,' he volunteered.

Five hours later, he and his wife sat with my husband and me on beds and floor of our modest hotel room. 'Action man, are you?' I asked. 'Why not,' he laughed, 'we are modern people.'

The more I looked at this attractive lively couple, the more I wanted to know how this perambulating Swiss with a permanent twinkle in his eye, came to hold these unique copyrights: of Bormann's and Goebbels's writings and, moreover, of Hitler's literary estate.

It was simple, he told me as we talked far into the night: 'I found out in 1948 that "Tabletalk" still existed [Hitler's monologues during meals, recorded on Bormann's orders] and that's what I wanted most of all. But I also heard of Bormann's letters to his wife and, as intriguing as *Tabletalk*, Goebbels's diaries. There was bound to be enormous interest in all these. But the very first thing, even before discovering where they were hidden, was to nail down the copyrights and this was to take years of arguments and court cases.'

There were three basic reasons why Genoud succeeded: one was that he was the first person to realize that there was a 'hole' in the otherwise very complete appropriation by the Allies of the property of the Nazi leaders. They had not known, or had forgotten, that these three men had written letters or diaries or, in the case of Hitler, that his conversations had been recorded. The second card he held in the negotiations he was to have with the heirs or their representatives was that, for them, Genoud's Swiss nationality and the reassurance of his manifest conviction that Hitler had been right and was being grievously wronged, were tantamount to a guarantee of integrity.

But what no doubt contributed most to his eventual success, is the force of his personality: to the surprise of many people, he invariably comes across as a sympathetic and honest man. (These are qualities also noted by Pierre Péan in the introduction to his excellent biography of Genoud, *L'Extremist*, just published in France (Fayard, 1996). 'In every man,' he writes, 'however evil . . . exists, sometimes an overwhelming, sometimes a minute measure of light. It has required a degree of obstinacy on my part to detect and admit to it in this man who has done everything to blacken his own character . . . but it is there.')

'It was never for gain that he wanted these copyrights,' said his lawyer and friend, Cordula Schacht, the completely anti-Nazi daughter of Hitler's first finance minister, acquitted at Nuremberg. 'It was primarily to hold and protect them; he is a romantic.'

Genoud is the son of a wealthy family and had four siblings. His father was a Francophile wallpaper manufacturer from Lausanne, his adored mother half-English. His happy childhood was dominated by dreams of heroes and chivalrous knights of past centuries and by contempt for the 'little old men without fire' who ruled Europe.

Even by the end of the first day we spent together – and this hasn't changed in the last twenty-five years – I realized that politically (Genoud would call it 'idealistically'), we do not agree on a single thing. I have tried over the years to argue with him and have sent him my writings, but he doesn't read them. He lays his hand gently on mine and he says: 'On n'est pas d'accord: on ne sera jamais d'accord. Mais on s'aime bien, non?' ('We don't agree: we'll never agree; but we like each other, don't we?) He has this facility for seeing, and, indeed, living life on two levels.

It has always been individuals as much as their causes who have impassioned Genoud. After his original commitment to Hitler, both the Algerian president Ben Bella, and the hijack specialist Waddi Haddad, head of the People's Front for the Liberation of Palestine, became intimate friends (these relationships stemmed from a trip in 1936, during which Genoud also met the Grand Mufti, leader of the Palestinian resistance, who would consider him a confidant until his death in 1974).

It was through Haddad that, twenty years ago, Genoud met the man he calls 'a young idealist, a wrongfully imprisoned soldier acting in the service of a noble cause' (for the Palestinians against Zionism). This man, known to the world as the terrorist 'Carlos the Jackal', is now imprisoned in France. For him, Genoud is, in the only letters he writes, his 'dearest comrade'.

François Genoud has justifiably been called a Nazi, a spy, a passionate anti-Zionist. He has also served his ideals as an editor, publisher, banker and highly effective mediator. His double life began in 1931 when his father suggested a year in a boarding school in Germany. He was to be the only foreigner among eighty boys, sons of peasants and tradesmen. 'I had read a great deal of what had been done to the Germans at Versailles and I thought they'd make me, a French-speaking boy, pay for that. But there was nothing like that at all: they were warm, friendly, eager to make me feel at home. I tell you, never would we Swiss boys have behaved like that to a visiting German. I felt shame for us, and I loved them for their generosity.'

Except in the sense that all of life in Germany in the early 1930s was contiguous to politics, the boys, he said, were not particularly political. Of course, they all knew Hitler existed and a few belonged to the newly formed Hitler Youth, but he was not much discussed. Genoud did, however, become 'very interested in him and began to read – his speeches, *Mein Kampf*, the things said by his supporters such as Goebbels'.

He realized very quickly that Hitler rejected the debilitated democracies. 'His realism was to unite his people in a classless society where everybody subscribed to one ideal,' he claims.

But had he not realized, from speeches and from *Mein Kampf*, that the 'ideal' Hitler envisioned was, above all, a racist philosophy, that had to lead to war?

'It was some time before I realized that, and he was wrong,' Genoud said with that curious naïvety one can never quite reconcile with the rest of his personality. 'But,' he smiled, 'I'm very forgiving to those I love, and the truth is, I loved Hitler.'

But how did he reconcile his affection and enduring friendship with Jews and anti-Nazis – not only then, but apparently time and again over the years – with his unconditional devotion to Hitler?

'It's a question I keep trying to answer,' sounding puzzled, again with that odd naïvety. 'My life, like that of many others, is in two parts. My ideology, my ideals, my dream for a clean and peaceful world is one: my private life, my feelings, my love for my friends is another.'

And later, when he found out what the Nazis had done?

'Although I have never believed the worst stories after the war, I keep saying that Hitler was wrong in his persecution of the Jews. And, really, not only because his policy gave the greatest boost to Zionism. I was horrified when, living in Belgium during the war, I saw the first yellow star. It is inadmissible to me to mark people by their race or colour . . . this kind of vicious racism is to me a parallel to Zionism, wrong, wrong, wrong.'

Genoud's wartime exploits covered many fields – commercial and political – but central to them was his voluntary collaboration with the *Abwehr*, German counter-espionage. 'I told them as soon as they asked me,' said Genoud, 'that I was quite prepared to provide any information I found about America and Britain; that I totally supported them in their battle, and hoped Switzerland would eventually become part of their Europe. But I also told them that, until this happened, I would under no condition do anything against my own country.'

While he refused to be paid by the Germans, he was quite happy to accept business favours: 'It was a tit for tat between me and my *Abwehr* contact [Paul Dickopf],' he told Pierre Péan. 'I was dealing in all kinds of things including currency, diamonds and gold, and Dickopf liked dealing too. So I pushed things his way and he pushed things my way . . . It was all very satisfactory; everybody was happy. We were all friends.'

By now, the Grand Mufti, in political asylum in Germany, had entrusted Genoud with the management of his enormous financial affairs. But it was to Dickopf that Genoud would provide perhaps the most dramatic proof of the value he places on friendship. With Germany's and occupied Europe's borders open to him, he had, by this time, married a seventeen-year-old girl from a distinguished and entirely anti-Nazi Belgian family, and established a residence in Brussels. And it was here, one autumn day in 1942, that Dickopf suggested that Genoud should take him to what was called the 'green frontier'; a stretch of the French-Swiss border used for illegal passage. He wanted to try it out himself, he said, with François's help.

Though puzzled, Genoud was game for anything. The two friends, driven in an *Abwehr* limousine by Dickopf's chauffeur, made their way to a village within seven miles of the border. Dickopf sent away his car and suggested a walk in the nearby woods. It was here that he, a top officer in the *Abwehr*, revealed to Genoud that he wanted out. Though still a patriotic German, he said that for a number of reasons he could no longer support the National Socialists. Genoud was staggered, but though he tried to reason with him, Dickopf wouldn't say any more except that his next assignment was to be head of the *Abwehr* in Switzerland. He didn't want to take it. Genoud was his friend and Dickopf knew he would not betray him. He was right. With Genoud's help, Dickopf went underground, first in Brussels, then eventually ending up in Switzerland. After the war, his anti-Nazi record established, he was to rise from general secretary of criminal affairs in Germany, to head of the BKA – German Intelligence – and finally to be president of Interpol.

Dickopf's desertion from the Nazi cause had been a profound shock for Genoud. Perhaps because his faith was more stubborn, perhaps because he then knew little of what the Germans were doing in the East, he could avoid drawing a moral conclusion. Over the fifty years since, almost all of which he lived in exceptional harmony with his second wife Elisabeth (who had, or developed for his sake, considerable sympathy for his ideals), Genoud's activities for Germans and Arabs have gone hand in hand. To him, it is essentially the same battle, for the poor against the rich.

In the ten years immediately after the war, he fought for the three copyrights, carefully nursing the relationships he had established with the heirs – Hitler's sister Paula, some of Bormann's nine children, and seven relatives of Goebbels.

In 1959, now even more closely linked to Arabs all over the Middle East, he set up the Arab Bank in Geneva through which enormous sums would soon wander. Though he is still reluctant to confirm such details, there is little doubt that this Arab money was the source for the help he was later to provide to individual Germans: to pay for Eichmann's legal defence, for example, and for Klaus Barbie's.

It is only now that Genoud admits to also having been on the margin of becoming 'operational' in terrorism. In 1972, he acted as Waddi Haddad's adviser on his $5 million ransom demand in the hijacking of a Lufthansa jet to Aden. He and Elisabeth drove overnight to Cologne carrying the letter with the ransom demand which he dropped into the Lufthansa postbox at dawn.

But how could he justify that, I asked. Again, that odd naïvety: 'I was helping to save lives. That is *good*, isn't it?'

And his 'work' has continued up to the present. In 1994, though much diminished in energy after Elisabeth's death from cancer – when I saw him in March he seemed to have shrunk to two thirds of his former size – Genoud came to the rescue of Carlos the Jackal, providing finance and obtaining the brilliant Jacques Verges (who also acted for Barbie) as his defence lawyer.

Last year, when Carlos wrote to him, begging him to persuade his wife, Magdalena Kopp, not to return to Europe, Genoud flew to her home in Venezuela, despite his frailty. And, as I write this, yet another radical-left, pro-Palestinian terrorist (a German, Johannes Weinrich, handed over by South Yemen and now held in Berlin) is benefiting from Genoud's generosity. 'You see, there are bad Arabs too,' he said.

Even at eighty and in poor health, he remains unrepentant. 'He will keep doing this,' said his daughter Françoise, who, like her sister Martine, fully agrees with his Palestinian sympathies but deplores the Nazis. 'He has no money, you know. Whatever he gets, he immediately passes on to somebody who needs it more. It is almost as if a man's need creates in my father a feeling of love.'

Disturbingly, far more disturbing than if he were by character violent, everything François Genoud has done – and although I am certain he has committed no acts of violence himself, I suspect he has acted on the margins and in awareness of violence throughout his adult life – has been done in and because of love.

13

Leni

September 1992

Leni Riefenstahl, one of the most gifted and notorious women of the century, was ninety years old on 22 August, a day she celebrated in a hotel on the Starnberg lake – home or weekend refuge for some of Bavaria's richest denizens – with about a hundred friends. 'I think there will only be three of the old ones,' she told me earlier this summer. 'The others are all dead. But I'm lucky. I'm surrounded by a world of wonderful younger people.'

We were talking in the living room of her chalet in Pöcking, a small village also on the lake. I first visited her there in 1986, while researching my book on Albert Speer, Hitler's favourite architect and armaments minister. On this, later, occasion she had just completed five years of 'back-breaking' work on her memoirs, and, looking worn out, was reading the proofs of the book, which was published in Germany the following year and comes out in English this week.

Writing about herself, she told me then, was not her real calling. 'I have suffered a great deal in my life,' she said, 'but perhaps in some respects never as during these five years.'

There is a curious compulsion in her not to admit – perhaps not to allow herself – happiness, except about three things: her 'real work', as she refers to her film-making in the 1930s and 1940s; her 'best friend', Horst Kettner, a tall, handsome man forty years younger than herself, with whom she has worked and lived for the past twenty-two years; and, finally, her home in a hidden little hollow near the lake, where the combination of carefully preserved 'wild' garden and the meticulously styled harmony of the interior is symbolic of both the woman and the artist.

The chalet – all glass, dark-brown wood and terraces full of flowers

– looks like a millionaire's lair. But in fact it was a prefab which she selected from a catalogue, and paid for with a loan of half a million marks from the local bank. She has never had enough money to pay it off and continues to pay the interest. She and 'Horstl' – whom she engaged as her assistant in 1970, when he was twenty-six, and who has since become her partner – moved into the house in 1979. 'I cannot imagine my life without him, or without this house,' she said.

One of the great beauties of her time, she is still beautiful now – not with the spiritual delicacy of old age, but with the challenge of a vital female. Slim and blonde, she wears a satiny white overshirt with blue designs over silk corn-blue leggings, and those legs, quite as famous in her time as those of her contemporary, Marlene Dietrich, are as fantastic as ever.

In 1923, when she was twenty-one, she appeared first as a professional dancer. 'A revelation,' wrote one of Berlin's most respected dance critics. Max Reinhardt swiftly engaged her as a solo dancer for his famous Deutsches Theater; and by 1932 – when she had not only played the lead in seven important films but had directed the last of them, *The Blue Light*, which was to win the silver medallion at the 1932 Biennale and was heralded as a great work by no less than Charlie Chaplin – her extraordinary face was known to every cinemagoer in Germany.

Including, evidently, Adolf Hitler. Her dancing was the most beautiful thing he'd ever seen, he told her when she met him for the first time in May 1932, and *The Blue Light* had been the greatest cinema experience of his life.

Sadly, given what her involvement with him later cost her, she wouldn't have needed Hitler in her life to make a success of it: just thirty years old then, she was already at a pinnacle of success. But the truth is – and, rare in Germany, she has always admitted it – that, in a sense, she loved Hitler, and, getting somewhat closer to him than most other women, loved him perhaps even more than they.

She had only this one day to talk to me. She was in the middle of taking part in a documentary about her life; after that, she and Horst planned to fly to the Maldives for what has become her greatest passion – diving.

We had a problem at the very outset: having read her autobiography, *Sieve of Time*, I noticed that she repeatedly referred to 'calendar notes' which she had used as reminders. A number of her descriptions of events on these dates, however, appeared to clash with entries in the Goebbels diaries – with which I have worked for several years for my book on Speer. I told Riefenstahl that I very much wanted to see at least some of her old 'calendars'.

'Calendars? What do you mean?'

I explained that I meant the calendars she repeatedly mentions in her book.

'Oh,' she said, manifestly taken by surprise. 'You know, it would be very difficult to find any of this. If you saw the room where we have stowed away all these papers and things . . . it would take hours to find anything specific.'

I suggested that while we talked, Horst and her secretary, Gisela, could just have a look.

'Oh, now I know what you mean . . . no, no, there aren't any "calendars" like that . . . all that has been lost long ago.'

I could have argued, of course, for it worried me: either she had told an untruth in her book, or she was being evasive now. But I let it go in favour of continuing our talk.

She wanted to know what I proposed to ask her.

Well, I said, we would have to talk about the Hitler period – there was no getting away from it. 'Of course,' she replied. 'I understand. It's what everybody wants to know.' She laughed bitterly. 'That lie about me as Hitler's bride or mistress . . .'

We were sitting quite close together, and I could almost feel her relief when I suggested we leave that subject until after supper, and talk first about her childhood, which I thought she had romanticized in her book.

She looked at me for a long moment, then nodded. 'What do you feel I didn't say?'

She had made herself sound blissfully happy, I said, but in the photographs of her as a little girl, and of her younger brother, too, they did not look like happy children. Heinz, a thin and rather wan boy who was later killed in Russia, seemed vulnerable and clinging, and she almost invariably looked sad. What I didn't say was that both these lithe children looked exceptionally unlike their father, a massive man with a blunt face.

'It is true,' she said. 'It was not a happy childhood, but good. Not happy, because my father was a despot, towards all of us – my mother, me and Heinz. I don't doubt he loved and wished to protect us, but it was an incredibly repressive love, taking away from us almost any semblance of freedom. My mother was not allowed money of her own and had to get his permission to go out for cake and coffee with her friends. I wasn't allowed out without a chaperon even at twenty. It created an incredible resistance in me, a *screaming* resistance.'

Had she screamed at him?

'At him?' She sounded astonished at the thought. 'No, of course not. But, from when I was thirteen to perhaps nineteen, every so often I'd go to my room and scream. Shall I show you?'

And, ninety years old, she put up her hands and screamed at the top of her lungs – an extraordinary sound in this wonderful quiet drawing-room full of lovely things. (I remember thinking it odd that Horst didn't rush in to see what was the matter and, although I had never seen it mentioned, wondered whether it was perhaps a not unusual part of her interviews.)

The crisis came when she was sixteen. Years before, her mother had allowed her to take dancing lessons in secret. 'That's what I meant when I said that my childhood, though not happy, was good. She was a dream mother. I loved her to distraction to the day she died.' But then one day, she danced in a school performance and her father learned of it.

'He was so horribly angry, we feared he would have a stroke. From that day on, for several weeks, he didn't speak a word with either my mother or me.'

After this, she was sent to a boarding school, with instructions to the headmistress to treat her with the utmost severity – instructions which that enlightened woman chose to ignore. 'In fact, she almost immediately allowed me to direct and act in plays. And I had packed my ballet shoes, too, and I practised every day.'

At the end of that year, her father gave in: as long as she lived at home, and obeyed his rules, she could study dancing. 'But if you ever allow your name to be seen in public, you will feel my anger,' he said. 'The funny thing was that when I then appeared on a stage for the first time, in October 1923, he cried with joy.'

She was to become famous not only for her work, but also for her love affairs. 'But not then,' she said. 'I was a very late developer. No breasts, you know, and my cycle only began when I was twenty-one. Of course, I was always in love, from heaven knows when. The first one was a boy I saw in a street near our home – for a whole year I walked along it at the same time every day, just to see him, but it was ten years until I actually met him – and by then, of course, I was quite uninterested in him.'

Her first real sexual experience was at twenty-one, with a tennis champion, eighteen years older than she. 'He was wildly handsome, the lover of Pola Negri, and I was in love with him for two years before I dared confront him.' But, although in retrospect she thinks he might have been the only man she has ever known with whom she would have liked to have a child, this first experience was disappointing.

'I think I was too innocent,' she said. 'But, you know, it taught me an important lesson – the great difference between illusion and reality. I had fallen in love with what I wanted him to be, not what he was, and although we eventually became engaged, I finally broke it off.'

When she was twenty-three, she finally moved into a flat of her own. 'Oddly enough,' she said, 'in the same building as Marlene Dietrich.'

Watching Riefenstahl, listening to her, and also reading the imaginative and romanticized account she provides in her book about many of her relationships – among them some men who had been or were to become lovers of Dietrich – one notes the early parallels and competition between them. Not for parts, which they both found easy to come by, but for attention.

'I could have gone to America,' Riefenstahl says. 'I had many invitations, many opportunities. Later I often wished I had.'

America was where Dietrich went, and where Josef von Sternberg made her into a great star. But it was not Sternberg who forced her publicly to denounce the rising Nazis, or, later, to reject Goebbels's repeated invitations to return to Germany – it was her own conviction. And although Riefenstahl didn't – couldn't – admit to it, I think it may be this stand that she now envies, a stand which she couldn't take. If I am right, then that would, after all, be an honourable afterthought.

I asked about her parents. Were they political? 'They didn't belong to any party,' she replied. 'They read the liberal newspaper, *Berliner Tageblatt*, owned by a Jew until 1933.'

Was it possible not to be interested in politics in the cauldron of Germany in the late 1920s and early 1930s?

'Of course it was,' she said. 'Now, with TV, everything is known practically the moment it happens. But then there were only local newspapers. I didn't even hear radio until 1938.'

I said that although I was a child in the early 1930s, I certainly noticed radios.

'Well, I didn't,' she said briskly. Certain circles were interested in politics, but most people weren't, she said. 'I never heard my parents speak of politics . . . only when – yes, just about that time – things were so bad, my father had to give up his business and they had to move out of our big flat into a small one. Then he did complain. But I never heard him mention a name – such as Hitler.'

But surely, I said, by 1930 that's what it had begun to be about – Hitler or not Hitler?

'What, in retrospect, it is about,' she said, 'was whether one took an active part or not. And that my father never did – he never went to any demonstration or meeting, none of us ever saw such a thing.'

But by this time, she was adult, an intelligent young woman in public life. Didn't she ever ask any questions?

'All I thought about was my small circle, my own life. I was terribly busy.'

By now she was so tense that I was afraid for her. Her voice had gone up an octave; her hand, when I touched it, was ice-cold.

During our break – smoked salmon and pâté sandwiches Horst and Gisela had prepared – we had talked about love, and her first famous affair. Louis Trenker, her partner in her early mountain films, was a skiing champion and climber with a face that looked hewn of stone and the mind of a peasant. Thirty-five years later, when he sold a fake diary of Eva Braun with horrible allegations against her to a newspaper, he would come close to ruining her for the proverbial thirty pieces of silver. Riefenstahl sued and won. 'But what's the good?' she said. 'I've fought fifty libel suits and won every one. But the lies always stick.'

The most important and long-lasting of those early relationships was with her cameraman, Hans Schneeberger. 'We were totally besotted,' she said. 'Couldn't keep our hands off each other. When he left me, I was devastated – I couldn't understand it at all. It took me five years before I even began to heal.' From 1938 to 1940 she had the quietest and gentlest of her relationships – with her sound engineer, Hermann Storr. 'He was the best in the world,' she said. 'René Clair called him to Paris for his films, too.' Their relationship broke up during the work on what essentially became the last film she made, *Tiefland*, which she produced and directed as well as starring in. 'This he couldn't take,' she said. 'He wanted to sleep with me the nights before the biggest takes . . . it was impossible.'

And then she met the man she finally married, Peter Jakob, a career officer in the German army. 'My fate,' she said, 'my greatest love and greatest emotional tragedy.'

He was, she said, a nymphomaniac (never mind the mistake in gender – it was quite clear what she meant). 'He knew it, suffered under it, loved me, but couldn't change. I was prepared to make any sacrifice, tried and tried to live with it . . . but finally couldn't. We were divorced in 1946, but really we were together until about '52. It took me sixteen years to get over him, and finally it only happened when I fell in love with Africa . . . the Nubas . . .'

When we returned to our working corner after supper it was dusk outside. It had rained and when we opened the glass doors, the garden smelled wonderfully of flowers.

'The first time I heard about Hitler,' she said, 'was after my big success with *The Blue Light* – April 1932. I noticed how emotional people became when they spoke for or against him, so I got interested and went to hear him. Well, it was like being struck by lightning. In that speech, he only spoke of peace, and work, and the evils of a class society – not a word about racism. It wasn't that I understood anything, but the simple way he said all the things I had been feeling without knowing that I did: I responded to that. I hated the class system; I hated the idea of war; and as I loved working and was sure others did, too, I deplored the sight of all the beggars in our streets.

'When I heard him, I became immediately convinced that he could save us from the abyss we seemed to face. And so, on an impulse, just before I was to leave for several months' work in Greenland, I wrote to him. Amazingly, almost immediately I had this phone call from a man who claimed to be his adjutant, Wilhelm Bruckner, who said the Führer had got my letter, was a fan of my films and would like me to come to see him the next day – the day before my departure.'

This would be the beginning of her much-discussed relationship with Hitler – which, contrary to many allegations, without doubt never became intimate. Hitler liked film stars, enjoyed being seen with beautiful women and had an almost disproportionate respect for artistic talent. Sexually, however, he responded to rather different women.

Goebbels no doubt desired her: he was compulsive in his sexual appetites, and most female film careers in those years began to bud on his office couch. Riefenstahl assures her readers over and over again of the fervency with which she loathed him. Does she protest too much? We cannot know and don't much care. But certainly in his diaries Goebbels writes very often about her over the years, confirming time and again his own and Hitler's regard for her.

Hitler's appreciation of her talents emerges clearly in her report of this first meeting in her book: knowing a good deal about Hitler, I found her description of his courtesy, his energy and his almost schoolboyish enthusiasm about films – and, indeed, about her – exactly right. Less so some of her other stories about her conversations with him after he had come to power: he was an almost compulsively private man – it is hard to believe that he would have discussed his love life with her, or that, as she claims, she would have dared reprimand him about his attitude towards the Jews. Still, while certainly unlikely, nothing in human relations is entirely impossible. A young woman as beautiful and famous as she, just might have been able to risk a naïve comment – as she quotes it – about his anti-semitism. What is impossible, however, is that Hitler would have discussed political plans and strategy with her.

Her 700-page book – which is devoid of any literary proficiency, style or, singularly, any suspicion of humour – is a wearying recital of endless betrayals by lovers, colleagues and friends (why, one wonders, did so many turn against her?); of her many nervous and physical breakdowns (hard to believe when one notes her iron constitution now); and of her 'terrible sufferings' at the hands of the Allies after the end of the war (the terrible Americans showed her pictures of concentration camps and the terrible French gave her several months' 'house arrest' in her own country house, in the company of her doting mother and loving secretary). None of it ever manages to evoke compassion, only embarrassment.

Worst of all, not unexpectedly, are her tales of being Hitler's confidante, told perhaps less for the sake of potential publicity than to satisfy still-existent needs of her own. The most indicative is probably her description of a meeting with Hitler on the night of 8 December 1932 – which, as it happened, was during the twenty-four hours of his gravest political crisis.

At lunchtime that day, Hitler had received a letter from one of his oldest friends and 'comrades', Gregor Strasser, the Nazi party's second in command, renouncing him and the party. As was his habit in those years, Hitler had spent that evening at the Goebbels home. 'We are all very depressed,' notes Goebbels in his diary, 'but we must keep our chins up . . . we will find ways and means to come through this desperate time. Dr Ley telephones: the situation is becoming more critical every hour and the Führer must return to the [Hotel] Kaiserhof [at that time the meeting place of the party chiefs]. [Soon afterwards . . .] at 2 a.m., I am called to join them; on arrival find [him with] Röhm and Himmler and we continue our deliberations till dawn . . .'

Riefenstahl had by then met Hitler briefly (so she tells us) two or three times. Here is her description of that night.

She has been to a concert, she writes, and on her way home on foot she buys the special editions of the newspapers and stops off in the 'hall' of the Kaiserhof to read them. She is discovered here by Hitler's adjutant, Bruckner, who tells her that Hitler wants to see her. Arriving in his drawing-room, she finds a 'wan' Hitler who, 'breathing heavily and clenching his hands', threatens to kill himself and then proceeds to tell her all his troubles. 'I understood,' she writes, '[that] he obviously needed someone in whom he could confide.'

It is, of course, almost grotesque to imagine that Hitler, busy with constant conferences about the handling of his worst political crisis so far, would sense a need or find the time to confide his political concerns to this film star he so far barely knew.

But, except for my question about the 'calendars', I deliberately did not discuss the book with Riefenstahl. Given the extent of my distaste for it – and my interest in talking to her about more interesting things – it seemed pointless to challenge her on its deficiencies. And finally, those eight hours of conversation seemed to justify my restraint, for she did in fact try to be honest with me: when she is honest, she is very likeable.

We discussed the film-maker Hans Jürgen Syberberg's question to Winifred Wagner, Richard Wagner's daughter-in-law: what would she have done if Hitler had survived and had knocked on her door? Frau Wagner replied that she would have opened her arms to him. Albert Speer told me *he* would have called the police. And Riefenstahl?

She thought for a long moment. 'I don't know,' she said. 'I honestly don't know. Albert, you know, was an activist; I'm a thinker, or dreamer. And of course, I'm a woman.'

And what – as a woman – *did* she feel about Hitler?

'That is difficult, too,' she said. 'I can tell you, easily, what I felt about Goebbels, who drove me crazy for years sniffing around me and begging me to be his "second wife" – disgusting. But Hitler? Certainly, I too, like so many millions, was intoxicated by him. Socially, he was charming. Very informal, unpretentious. One drank tea or coffee, sat, talked, no pressure – though no fun, either. In a way it was lucky I was not his type: he really only liked "little creatures". People like me, he liked to talk to, be seen with. But I suppose had he wanted to, I would have become his mistress; had he asked, it would have been inevitable. I'm so glad he didn't.' (This is what I mean by her trying to be honest with me: in her book, alas, she describes an entirely unbelievable occasion when he takes her into his arms, finally tearing himself away, saying that he just couldn't allow himself to love a woman . . .)

And now – did she believe that he was not a monster? 'Now I think he was schizophrenic,' she said. 'But then I knew nothing. And, you know, people simply will not believe that one knew nothing.'

It is only fair to say here that I have no doubt that she knew nothing of what was planned and of what finally happened to the Jews. But what *were* her feelings about Jews?

'Good heavens,' she said. 'I was in *films*. I had many Jewish friends and, for that matter, two doctors who were Jews and who saved my life. But it's true, all of them were lucky: none of them ended up in concentration camps . . . they went abroad. But – what my enemies will, of course, never say – every one of them remained my friend.'

This is quite true: they were loyal friends, just as she had been loyal to them when keeping faith with Jewish friends was not healthy. This emerged clearly after the war, when several of them testified in her favour. But, against that, there are dozens of remarks by Goebbels in his diaries over the years about social occasions with Riefenstahl – who, however much she assures us of her loathing for him, in fact saw a great deal of him.

On 5 February 1939, for instance, just back from a trip to America, Riefenstahl spends the evening with him. He writes: 'She reports about her trip [and] provides an exhaustive description which is anything but pleasant. We have no business over there. The Jews rule with terror and boycott. For how much longer, I wonder? Late and tired to bed.'

I asked her about this. 'Well, yes,' she said. 'He'd probably heard of the terrible time I had . . . horrible things in the press about me, posters and demonstrations in the streets. It was a nightmare.'

Had she told him it was due to 'the Jews'?

'I don't think he needed me to tell him that,' she replied drily.

We talked about the party film she was commissioned to make. Her account in the book is diametrically opposed to that of Goebbels – who, however sceptical we need to be about some of his later statements, had no reason to lie on 17 May 1933, four months after the Nazis' triumphant accession to power.

'Afternoon, Leni Riefenstahl: she tells me of her plans. I suggest she should make a Hitler film. She is over the moon about the idea . . .'

Over the next weeks the idea grows: on 12 June 1933, a happy evening 'at the Schaumburgs. Discussed with Riefenstahl her new film. She is the only one of all the stars who understands us . . .'

What is being discussed here is, in fact, two films: in September 1933 she is to film that year's party rally. She calls this *Victory of Faith*; the following year, with great preparations and enormous expertise, she makes the famous *Triumph of the Will*. Although Hitler, for a number of reasons, was eventually to transfer the responsibility for her to his deputy, Rudolf Hess, Goebbels was the initiator and the financial backer of both these projects.

On 14 June, Goebbels reports: 'Riefenstahl has spoken with Hitler: she is now starting [work on] her film.' On 16 June: 'With Hitler drive through the dusk. Later at his house [with] Philipp von Hessen and L. Riefenstahl. Very nice. Late to bed. Four hours' sleep . . .'

And so it goes on, outing after outing, all through that happy summer, and again with chats or discussions about 'the film'.

In her book Riefenstahl tells us she is invited to lunch at the Chancellery 'in the last week of August', and that Hitler, taking her to another room, asks how she is doing with the preparations for the 'party film'. She is 'dumbfounded', she tells us, hasn't heard a word of any such commission, and tells Hitler that she couldn't possibly undertake such an assignment . . . why didn't he ask someone politically more suited to such a task?

Hitler is furious. 'What? Dr Goebbels didn't convey my wishes to you?' he says. 'How is that possible?'

Indeed, how would it have been possible? Aside from the fact that Hitler's surviving schedule for that August hardly has him in Berlin, it wasn't possible anyway. But like many people writing 'imaginatively' about the past, Riefenstahl relies throughout her book on her readers' ignorance – which is how historical myths are created.

'When I was asked to make a film about the Nuremberg party day,' she said, 'I said I couldn't . . . What I did finally make when Hitler so insisted – *Triumph of the Will* – is *not* a party film; there is nothing ideological in it. It is a film of peace: He spoke only of peace . . . and work . . . against unemployment . . . not a word about Jews or anything ideological . . .'

She is defensive here, for it is not so: the Nuremberg party congress was always the most carefully planned and most powerful demonstration of Nazi ideology. And her film – doubtless the finest documentary of its kind – reflected perfectly and with enormous power the theme each speaker and Hitler, above all, hammered home: that a society based on harmony and inner 'belonging' (*Zusammengehörigkeit*) must obviously reject those who do not belong – who, because of their origins, cannot be in harmony with it. The applause which followed Hitler's unmistakable allusion to the *Untermenschen* was allowed to continue for minutes – in the film, too. And Riefenstahl's unprecedented camerawork there powerfully demonstrated the principal tenet of the Nazi faith: that beauty and order *was* harmony and as such, rather than being an aesthetic inspiration, was a moral imperative.

I think that Riefenstahl knows this now, but she cannot admit it, just as none of those close – or even not so close – to Hitler can admit to having known about his murders. ('If one admits it, one cannot go on living,' Speer's daughter said to me fifteen years ago.)

'I really don't care what people think of me at my age,' said Riefenstahl, not quite believably but now sounding very weary. 'And I really cannot bear to talk any more about what happened to the Jews. It is so dreadful, so beyond-belief awful, it even now spoils life for me. To think that I believed in something that was so corrupt, that produced this horror – for a long time I envied people who had died.

'I don't like the world any more: nature being spoiled, people killing each other everywhere . . . for nothing, it seems to me – haven't there been enough dead in our time?'

What was she happy about now?

'The happiest times of my life were my stays in Africa with the Nubas, because, though so terribly poor, their joy in being was so beautiful. They were so good to me. I wanted to stay with them and die there.

'And then, of course, I am happy that I can still have love and passion in my life. Love because I have Horsti. Passion because I can still dive: underwater I am in another world. What I see there reflects and even explains the true miracle – the genius of creation. It has allowed me, for the first time, to understand religious faith, and that is the film . . . yes, perhaps the last one . . . I want to make.'

14

Kurt Waldheim's Mental Block

February 2000

A seminar on 'the repression of memory' might have no more significance than a session in a psychiatric convention. But the seminar I attended with that title in the lovely village of Alpbach in the Austrian Tyrol in 1986 was much more than that: its subject went to the very heart of the nightmare of the past which has risen to haunt Austrians since – and in part because of – the campaign and election of Dr Kurt Waldheim as state president earlier this year.

The session was a last-minute addition to a two-week programme of the European Forum, since the war the most prestigious of the annual European think-tanks for which a thousand people – statesmen, professors and students from many countries and disciplines – come to Alpbach each August. That night the main lecture hall was full to bursting. The initiator and chairman of the occasion was the writer and publisher Fritz Molden, vice-president of the Austrian College which organizes the yearly event. He and his brother Otto Molden, co-founders (in 1945) of the Alpbach Forum, are members of an exclusive small 'club' – the genuine Austrian *Widerständler* (resisters) to the Nazis, all of whom spent time in camps and prisons and many of whom did not survive.

Fritz Molden has a special link with Waldheim: at twenty-one he became personal assistant to Austria's first post-war foreign minister, thirty-four-year-old Karl Gruber, whom he had met as a fellow resister under the Nazis. When Waldheim, then twenty-eight, applied in 1946 to enter the foreign service – presenting a curriculum vitae with excellent qualifications (and incidentally his full wartime service record in France, Russia and the Balkans from 5 August 1939 to 9 May 1945) – Fritz Molden was ordered by his minister to hurry across to the

Vienna offices of the OSS (the US Secret Service) to see if anything was known against this promising candidate. The Americans gave Waldheim a clean slate, and *that* was the beginning of his career.

It is perhaps all the more remarkable that Molden, who loyally supported Waldheim throughout the traumatic events last year – although not without severe doubts of conscience and continuous attempts (to which I can personally attest) to get Waldheim to go further in his statements – should have initiated this seminar in Alpbach.

'The blocking of memory' said psychoanalyst Professor Leupold-Löwenthal, chairman of the Vienna Society of Psychoanalysts and president of the Sigmund Freud Association, 'is very simply the inability of the mind to take issue and deal with an experience which is unacceptable to the mind or spirit. It is very dangerous,' he said, 'to block the mind: dangerous for the individual, his environment, but – also in the context that has not yet even been touched upon tonight – to the whole community.'

Austria as a community, said Fritz Molden, was handed democracy on a plate at the end of the war: it didn't work or suffer for it. 'The Moscow declaration of 1943,' he said, 'established us as the first victims of the Nazis. It was, of course a gift from heaven. We accepted it. Who wouldn't have? But very soon we used it as a justification, feeling ourselves to be – quite wrongly – a special case, and this was our first mistake which we then compounded over the months and years as the first euphoria turned into something much graver: self-deception.'

The real tragedy of Waldheim's situation is that he had a unique chance of breaking through this blockage and thereby not only saving his own integrity but more importantly, in the psychological sense the 'health' of all of Austria.

A reliable informant told me at the seminar that there was a moment a few weeks before the election when Waldheim himself was prepared for such an honest act. But his election advisers felt that he would lose hundreds of thousands of votes – all those in his own age-group – if he came out and said, 'Yes, I did know what was happening. I did see terrible things. And because I was no more a hero than most other men, I blocked these things way back into my mind and did nothing.' This is what he might and should have said, and although it might have lost him votes, he would in all likelihood still have been elected and with honour.

For the facts about Waldheim himself are quite clear by now: he was, it seems, simply the recording officer of his unit. As such, of course, he knew of all actions in his sector, reported on them and no doubt he witnessed a number of them.

The 'blocking of memory' is not restricted to those on the Nazi side. Psychiatrists have dealt with thousands of victims of the Nazis over the years who have blocked just as desperately, and there are many such cases reported too, among Allied and Third World soldiers of the Second World War and subsequent wars in Asia, Africa and Europe.

But while all wars produce isolated instances of terrible acts, the Nazi war, which used war *conditions* as pretext for much larger, more concentrated horror, was a case apart. This is the kernel of the Austrian (and German) blocking problem: that not only a few selected men, but a vast number of perfectly ordinary soldiers were forced to witness and take part in acts which – as said Professor Leupold-Löwenthal – their minds simply could not accept or deal with.

While the Germans have gone some way to take issue with the problem, the Austrians simply haven't dealt with it at all, in spite of a spate of excellent films, books and articles. 'The blocking,' said Social Democrat MP Dr Ernst Veselsky, 'means that the majority of people simply turn the knob on their TV, the page of the paper or don't buy the books.'

To return to Waldheim: in the final analysis he probably did nothing *particularly* bad; he simply knew about horrors, blocked the knowledge and when forced by circumstances into facing it, chose to deny his memories – an appalling decision, with which both he and Austria were now forced to live.

For the Austrians, strangely enough, I think this was a new chance. 'When we returned from the concentration camps in 1945,' said Fritz Molden, closing the Alpbach meeting, 'we thought that, cleared of all co-responsibility by the Allies, we could serve our country best by re-creating a beautiful Austria, a buffer between nations in Central Europe, an island of the blessed in a sea of controversy. Now at last – forty-two years later – the trauma has reached us. We have to face it that our country is not, as President Reagan tried – so kindly – to paint us, made of music, *Sachertorte*, *Lippizaner* and *Sängerknaben* (the famous boys' choir). We have to realize that we are not loved any more and perhaps will not be loved till we face ourselves. For four decades we have overrated ourselves, as did the world. The result is that when we look into the mirror now, we face an ugly visage. Only time and a new wisdom within ourselves will change this back into an honest face.'

March–April 1988

'Why do they go on so about me? Do *you* understand the reasons?' Kurt Waldheim asked me, sounding honestly puzzled rather than self-pitying, when, during the week leading up to the fifty-year *Anschluss* commemorations in Vienna, I spent several hours with him in the Hofburg, where the Emperor Joseph II's huge golden office is now his. Our meeting had been planned as an informal talk on questions of faith and morality, rather than one more inquisition, of which he had by this time undergone dozens.

His face alight, he lovingly explained a magnificent painting in the corner where we sat down to tea, of an amateur operatic performance at the Palace of Schönbrunn in 1765, to mark the Crown Prince Joseph's marriage to Maria Josepha of Bavaria. On stage were the four daughters of the Empress Maria Theresia; in the audience the huge imperial family and their suite. And had I been shown the little altar built into a bit of movable wall next door, in what had been the empress's bedroom?

'Even the British queen thought our Hofburg extraordinary,' said his personal assistant, thirty-seven-year-old Ralph Scheide, who sat in on our conversation.

'He knows more about me than I do,' Waldheim joked. Scheide, who took on this difficult job six months after Waldheim had been elected, addresses him as 'Du-Herr Bundespräsident'.

There is one interesting story that I had not seen published outside Austria before, which has to do with how the whole Waldheim saga really started.

In the run-up to the presidential elections in Austria in 1985, the

18. Heidelberg, February 1978: in conversation with Albert Speer, photographed (as so many others) by my husband, Don Honeyman.

19. Speer and his wife Margret on a little bridge (which he designed as a boy) that connected the guest cottage with the main house.

20. Gerda Bormann with their eight children: Martin, eleven, is on the left.

21. Martin Bormann's father, Hitler's secretary (*below left*).
22. Herdecke, Germany 1991: Martin Bormann Jr, priest and teacher (*below right*).

23. Cologne, 1991: Thomas Heydrich, who as singer and lyricist specializes in Jewish songs.

24. His uncle, SS General Reinhard Heydrich, assassinated in Prague in 1942, was Heinrich Himmler's principal aide in the preparation of the 'Final Solution' and chaired the infamous 'Wannsee Conference'.

25. Vienna, 1988: Kurt Waldheim, whose period as President of Austria was blighted by, I thought largely unjustified, accusations of wartime Nazi sympathies.

26. Lausanne, Switzerland, 1996: banker François Genoud, who as Nazi and Arab sympathizer was an idealist rather than ideologue. He held the literary rights to Hitler, Bormann and Goebbels and financed Eichmann's and Barbie's defence. Died in June 1996.

27. A village in the Bavarian Alps, 1982: Hans Münch, a research physician at Auschwitz from early 1943 to 1945. Dr Münch was the only accused at the Polish doctors' trial in Cracow in 1947 to be acquitted, when nineteen former prisoners testified in his favour.

28. Jerusalem, April 1988: John Demjanjuk, found guilty of having been the infamous Treblinka SS guard 'Ivan the Terrible', is sentenced to death. Almost two years later, new evidence from Russia proved him innocent of that charge.

29. Olga Danilchenko, talks to me in 1990 in Tobolsk, Siberia, about her husband, who worked with Demjanjuk, as a guard in another extermination camp.

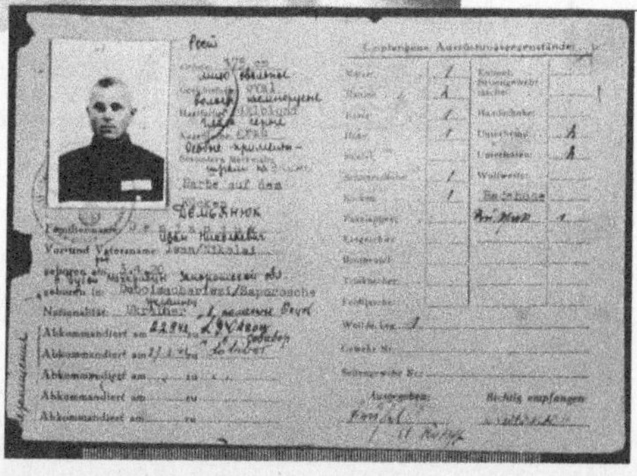

30. The 1942 SS ID card which was part of the evidence against Demjanjuk. It establishes that he was posted to Sobibor, but does not mention Treblinka.

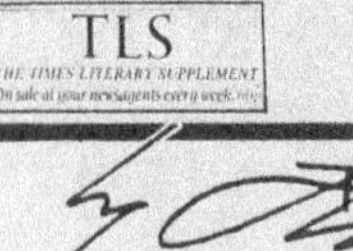

SUNDAY TIMES
review
11 DECEMBER 1983

THE HITLER DIARIES: STORY OF A SUPER-HOAX

● Last April, The Sunday Times announced a sensation: the discovery of Adolf Hitler's secret diaries, in 60 handwritten volumes, chronicling his years of power between 1933 and 1945, which had lain hidden in an East German hayloft for nearly 40 years. The diaries had been acquired, we said, by Gerd Heidemann, a reporter for the West German magazine Stern, and they had been authenticated by experts, including one of Britain's most eminent Third Reich historians, Hugh Trevor-Roper.

The announcement aroused immediate worldwide interest. But two weeks later the diaries were exposed as forgeries by the German Federal Archives. For The Sunday Times, this revelation was a severe embarrassment. But for Stern, which had given Heidemann £2.5 million to buy the diaries, it was a disaster. Not only had the magazine lost a lot of money; its reputation was badly damaged by the fact that it had apparently been deceived by one of its own journalists.

Stern knew that Heidemann had acquired the diaries from a Stuttgart dealer in military relics who went by the name of Konrad Fischer and claimed to be related to "very high-up" officials in East Germany who were his source for the diaries.

It did not take long for "Fischer's" story to unravel. His real name, it emerged, was Konrad Kujau (right). On May 25, after he gave himself up to the police, Kujau admitted: "I wrote the books." Then he made two charges: that Heidemann had been his partner in the fraud and that Heidemann had kept most of Stern's money. Heidemann denies the charges. But, like Kujau, he now sits in a Hamburg prison awaiting trial. Police investigations continue, but they are now focussed mainly on discovering what happened to the money, almost none of which has been recovered.

But The Sunday Times reveals today that the story does not stop there. For seven months, the award-winning writer GITTA SERENY has been investigating Kujau's supposedly full confession. She has criss-crossed West Germany interviewing those who were involved in the hoax. She has been where the Hamburg police could not go – to East Germany to investigate Kujau's background; and to the United States to trace Kujau's connections to the shadowy world of Nazi collectors. Finally, she has spent hours with Kujau and Heidemann in prison, testing their stories.

Her conclusion is that Kujau's "confession" to the West German police is a tapestry of lies. The real story of the hoax is much more elaborate and extraordinary than he will admit:

● Heidemann did not know the diaries were fake, though he may have kept some of Stern's money.

● The diaries were only one strand of a web of Nazi fantasies in which Heidemann had become trapped, including the belief that Martin Bormann, Hitler's deputy, was alive, well and willing to meet him.

● He was led into that web by a group of men with differing motives but a common bond: membership of the Nazi SS.

Next week we will reveal who else shared in Stern's missing millions. But we begin Sereny's report with her demolition of the "true confessions" of Konrad Kujau.

HOW THEY SPUN THE WEB

WHO'S WHO

In today's Colour Magazine: The secrets of Kujau's treasure

31. London, 1983: the *Sunday Times*'s presentation of the Hitler Diaries scandal. My subsequent investigations suggest that the real plan was not a hoax.

32. Paternion, Carinthia, May 1945: the dead man is Odilo Globocnik, SS Police Chief of Lublin and the head of the 'Aktion Reinhard', the organization responsible for the murder of the Jews in Poland. This photograph helped us disprove a web of faked documents from America which claimed that he had been helped to escape by Western intelligence.
33. Detail.

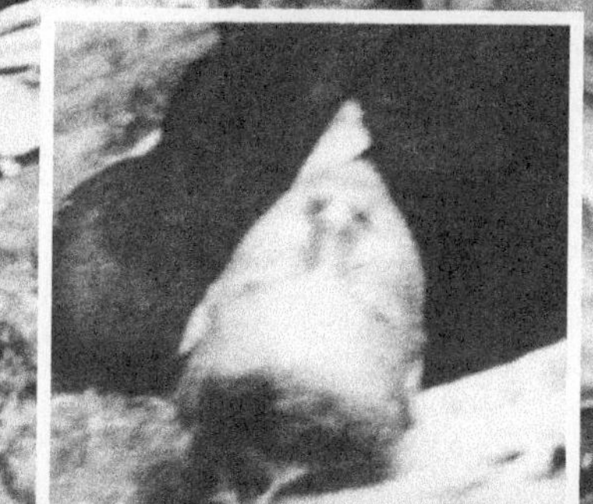

34. A summer's day in the early 1970s on the patio of Pembroke Studios in Kensington, where I wrote *Into That Darkness*

historian Georg Tidl, a Socialist, stumbled upon information in Balkan war archives to the effect that during the war Lieutenant Kurt Waldheim – who was being mentioned as a possible candidate for the conservative People's Party – had been on the staff of Army Group E in Greece, commanded by General Alexander Löhr, himself executed by the Yugoslavs for war crimes in 1947.

Personal smear campaigns are not in the tradition of Austrian politics. Also, the Socialists knew perfectly well that stirring the pot of Austria's murky Nazi past was unlikely to attract the voters' sympathy. The decision was none the less made to plant rumours about Waldheim's past abroad. If the rumours came from outside, they reasoned, they couldn't be laid at their door. One bad decision was quickly followed by another: they chose a nice man named Leon Zelman as their messenger, and sent him off to America with the news that the People's Party was about to propose for the Presidency of Austria someone with a possibly unsavoury wartime past which he was trying to hide.

Leon Zelman, a Polish Jew by birth, had come to Vienna from Auschwitz via Mauthausen in 1945, when he was still a boy. Some kind people – socialists, as it happened – provided him with a home, a country and ideals. He developed into a warm, idealistic man, dedicated to repaying the kindness shown to him in Vienna by rehabilitating his adopted city in the eyes of foreign Jews.

It was to one of the friends he had made in New York during his years of bridge-building – Israel Singer of the World Jewish Congress – that he brought the information about Waldheim. For Singer, who had little knowledge or experience of diplomacy, passion overrode all rational considerations and exposing Waldheim became a 'cause'. The disastrous result was that the accusations against Waldheim came from America and from Jews, with the predictable consequence of an election with appalling anti-semitic overtones, and a profoundly disturbing rise in anti-semitism not only in Austria but in Germany too, where it had for so long been taboo.

It is perfectly true that the one person who could have affected and altered this attitude was Waldheim himself. But for this he would have had to be either very well advised – which he wasn't – or a different man, the great statesman he longed to be.

'You ask me whether I feel bitter,' Waldheim said to me. 'I do feel bitter about what it is doing to my family. Can you imagine our lives?'

I said that surely he wouldn't claim not to feel bitter about some individual Jews? He wasn't, after all, a saint – 'St Kurt'. I was trying to lighten the atmosphere, and he gave a brief smile. But he didn't answer this, directly.

'I have a particularly good Jewish friend here to whom I talk a lot,' he said. 'He keeps saying that he is terribly afraid of the effect all this is having on Christian-Jewish understanding, the reactions perhaps yet to come against Jews. I am very concerned about this, for Austria. I am very aware of the suffering of the Jews . . .' The sentence petered out.

'You see,' he started anew, 'in order to destroy *me*, personally and politically, *Austria* is attacked – this is what most concerns me now. The international community does need to remember that it was the Allies in 1943 who decided that Austria was a "victim" – one surely cannot blame the Austrians for accepting that interpretation in 1945. In 1934 there was civil war in Austria and no possibility of co-operation between parties. Then, at war's end, out of the concentration camps, from those Austrians of all parties who were imprisoned there together, came the determination to create a "beyond-party" collaboration and this is what was done.' The result, he said, had been an unprecedented period of political harmony. 'Forty years during which Austria has made herself the stabilizing centre of Europe: that is what is now at risk.'

Leaving aside for a moment what he knew or didn't know, said or didn't say, I asked whether he felt – as, in fact, I do – that his predicament was at least in part the result of a generation gap? That a great many people now simply cannot envisage life under the Nazis?

I could almost hear his sigh of relief. 'Yes,' he said. 'You see, what happens is that people consider what happened then in terms of Western democracies now. While in fact, with just one word out of turn then, one risked not just prison but execution. I remember once coming upon my father, his ear pressed to the radio, listening to the BBC. And – I can see him still – I saw him start in stark terror as he heard my steps. How can the young today understand that kind of atmosphere? I love talking to the students who come here, although, yes, they *do* ask difficult questions. But that is only right. One boy asked me recently why I didn't just take off my uniform, throw away my weapons. He is right, it's a fundamental question. Of course, I could have. Perhaps I should have . . .'

What is a hero, I asked: the historians' commission – which the Austrians set up and paid for – seemed to think that is what he should have been. 'Yes,' he answered. 'That is a real question. I thought that the commission, who after all *I* asked for would understand. Would I really have asked for such learned men to investigate my past if I had done something wrong? Those who think me bad, do they also think me mad? But it is true, of course. I could have resisted, deserted, and I didn't.'

That was what he said now, but did he ever actually consider such a choice?

'One did think about it, of course, but . . .' He paused. 'You see, my father and my brother were both active anti-Nazis – my father lost his teaching job, was imprisoned, beaten up . . . I think,' he said slowly, 'it was because my family was so endangered that I felt . . . army life was . . . safer . . . than being a civilian. It is true. I wanted to survive.'

Did he know any Jews?

'Oh yes. I'm in touch now with three of my Jewish school friends, one in America, one here, and then of course Lord Weidenfeld – my old friend Georg – he was kind enough to give me an affidavit.' If that was a sad term for a head of state to use, he didn't notice.

Had he known about Hitler's feelings about Jews? Had he read *Mein Kampf*? He smiled – it is extraordinary in Germany and Austria, how people always smile when asked this question. That old condescension towards 'Corporal Hitler, the house-painter' still survives. 'Perhaps I should have read it,' he said then. 'I might have understood more: people say that everything was in there. One thing, though: you know, the Americans' – he means the American Jews but can't or won't say that – 'are always talking about the "Nazi *Wehrmacht*", but the staff of the *Wehrmacht* really was not Nazi – one was very carefully vetted before being taken on. In a way, you know, my problem was that I was never directly confronted with horrors: our home was in a small town, the Jews there were people one knew. I certainly never saw anyone being mistreated there in 1938. When I fought in Russia

– riding with my troop of seventy cavalrymen in front of the infantry drawing the first volleys, so to speak – I never saw a partisan. And then on the staff it was all reports, and I can assure you no troop commander reported: "Today we committed horrors." Perhaps within the SS they did – I never knew any.'

Was he saying that the reports he saw did not mention partisans?

'No, of course they'd report "encounters with *Banden*" and *Säuberungen* – clearing-out. But these were actions of war – partisan warfare was very hard, on both sides.'

But then what about *Sühnemassnahmen* – reprisals – against whole villages, women and children? Did that not appear on reports? Did he and the other young officers never talk about any of the bloodbaths in the midst of which they lived?

'It wasn't *like* that.' He sounded desperate. 'In Greece I sat in a little former American college overlooking the vineyards and the Aegean.'

But in Yugoslavia? Wasn't he in villages there which were less than twenty kilometres from the terrible Ustasha camp of Jasenovac, where countless thousands died?

'Was it really so near by?' he asked – I thought disingenuously. 'But anyway, those were Ustasha installations . . . The only thing ever brought against me was a forged telegram. The commission have looked for proof against me for six months, have read thousands of documents: nothing has been found. All they could say was: "He must have; he should have; he could have; he might have." And in spite of this, for eighteen months now one can't open a paper or turn on the radio without reading, hearing these awful things they say about me, in their appalling language. Can you imagine what this is doing to my family? My eleven-year-old grandson who comes home and asks: "Is it true that grandfather is a war criminal?" Good God, knowledge, after all, is not guilt.'

But wasn't what he had been saying precisely that he knew nothing? 'I never *saw* anything.' But he guessed, and thought? 'You mean, I'm not made of wood: I'm glad you feel that. And of course one *thought*. But in law there is a big difference between knowing and doing . . . If a report mentioned "reprisals" a few hundred kilometres away, what could one have done? Nothing. Even the commission said that even if I had given my life, it wouldn't have helped.'

But is there no moral responsibility apart from practicality, I asked. In that case, where does guilt lie?

'Not in mere knowledge,' he said. 'Only in not doing anything, if one was in a position *to* do something. I am religious – I pray. I often prayed that these horrors of war should stop.'

Didn't he feel that it was facile – not worthy of him – just to do away with the horrors by justifying them with war?

'It is good of you to say it like this. I'm prepared to go further . . . Please ask.'

'You say you prayed,' I said. '*Did* you ever go down on your knees – with the image of terrible things which happened in your mind's eye – and pray: "Please God, please stop *this*."'

'Not in that form: I prayed – as I told you – that all the horrors of the war should stop . . .'

Did he not see that in a sense he was – or is now – *using* the war?

'But it *was* war,' he said despairingly. 'Greece, Yugoslavia, Russia – savage war. But Pearl Harbor too – Hiroshima – and later, what about Vietnam, and now the West Bank, where they are breaking people's bones? In all these places the innocent died and die, women and children by the hundreds of thousands: who spoke for them, who protested there?'

I suggested that it was indeed protests in America, largely from the young – civic action by civic-minded human beings – which stopped the war in Vietnam, and I could have added, but didn't, that the Israelis are calling their soldiers to account for their conduct on the West Bank. But he did not – does not – hear this kind of argument. One gets the feeling that he can no longer (if he ever did) hear things which don't refer to his situation, and don't apply to or agree with the way he links it to other matters.

'How about horrors then which had nothing whatever to do with war?' I said. 'Can you apply the same standard to Pearl Harbor, for instance, and Treblinka? What *about* Treblinka?' I asked.

'Treblinka,' he said heavily, 'is something entirely different. You are right: it had nothing to do with war. It was a political act. It was an abomination. It was a crime. But you see, I knew nothing about these terrible places until after the war: how could a normal person imagine that anything like this *could* be done? Of course one knew about camps – concentration camps, where they sent many non-Jews too. Of course one realized that Jews were disappearing in Austria: one thought they were interned. Wiesenthal, who I helped look for Mengele when I was secretary-general of the United Nations, has been very kind to me over these last two years. He said not long ago: why didn't I just admit that I knew about the deportation of the Jews of Salonika, which my enemies say I "must have" known about? Why not just say I did – it would make it all so much easier? But I can't say that, because I didn't: I *saw* nothing. But I would have to add that even if I had "seen" something, I wouldn't have known – and had I heard rumours (which I didn't) wouldn't have believed – what was being done. I have to say too: what did the Americans do, or the British – who, as it turns out, knew more than we did? But we are back with what you said at the beginning: the inability of people now to envisage life under the Nazis. I'm being accused of "knowledge" because, in terms of the dissemination of knowledge, the level of public knowledge, today, they think one "must have known". But the fact is, one didn't. And I don't admit the thesis of "collective guilt".'

Wasn't guilt, I asked, the expression or admission of it, an inner necessity? In a way, was it not part of 'sin' in a Christian – particularly a Catholic – sense? I, for example, felt in a way guilty too – not for anything I had done but for what, perhaps because of my own deficiencies or simply because of circumstances, I had left undone. Was 'collective guilt' not acceptable or applicable in that context, in which – compared to those who suffered so gravely – we did not suffer enough?

'You feel that this sin of omission, by all of us in Austria and Germany,' said Scheide, interested in this approach, 'is really inherent in the human being – part of "original sin": is that what you mean?'

'You say *you* didn't suffer enough,' said Waldheim – he really is a pragmatist, feels at sea with abstract thought, and, compulsively and repetitively, brings all conversation back to his accusers and himself. 'I think *we* did. When, after the war, one learned about these abominations, of course one was appalled at what had been done and horrified about the iniquity, the extent of human depravity, that had made it possible. But during the war I never knew a single person who might have known about it.'

Dr Scheide said that so much that has been written is a matter of interpretation, and this applied particularly to what some of the media has made of Waldheim's role – or absence of it – in the interrogations of British commandos. I said that I myself felt uncomfortable about the attacks against the president on that score: it seemed somehow preposterous to me to condemn retroactively any young intelligence officer in the German army for not being sufficiently a hero to act against orders pertaining to commandos. Waldheim said he had enormous admiration for anyone who did so act, but thought it would have been possible only in comparative isolation and with the clear support of a superior, as was the case for the admirable staff captain Günter Kleykamp of General Felmy's 58th Army Corps in Athens, who with the knowledge of his general reported his interrogation of two British officers to the Swiss Red Cross. As a result, Captain Robert MacGregor and Lieutenant Capsis were accorded POW status, escaping the *Sonderbehandlung* – execution – of commandos which was ordered by Hitler in October 1942.

'Of course I knew about British commandos,' said Waldheim, 'only I myself never interrogated any. But you can see what happened when I said that some time ago: immediately the interpretation was that I had "admitted" something, "admission" being automatically associated with "guilt". In fact, all I did was to confirm that I was privy to information regarding commando operations. After all, that was my job, to be informed – and to pass on information to my superiors – about operations. And yes, of course I knew about the *Führerbefehl* – possibly not at that exact moment, but I certainly remember hearing about it at some point or other: everyone on the staff did. Personally, however, thank God, I had nothing to do with implementing it.'

The exhaustive research which the historical commission undertook to ascertain the precise degree of Waldheim's involvement in the interrogation of British and American commandos, and his responsibility for the subsequent *Sonderbehandlung* of so many among them, has netted the predictable results: Waldheim's intelligence unit was involved in interrogations, though as far as could be found torture and executions were reserved for the SD (SS Security Service), to whom prisoners were sent after 'ordinary' interrogations by the *Wehrmacht* within the rules of the Geneva Convention were completed.

Waldheim's initial has been found on one interrogation report only: that of James Doughty, an American medic, who as a non-combatant survived the war as a POW. Aside from this, the only documents pertaining to 'Anglo-American (Commando) missions' bearing Waldheim's signature are the daily operational reports for which he was responsible. It could be – and was being – argued that anyone who knew of Hitler's order to kill all commandos and took no individual action against it could be considered an accomplice in what the Nuremberg Tribunal would call 'war crimes'. But this is precisely the kind of mindless retroactive generalization that leads to hysteria. And it avoids essential, if uncomfortable questions. One – answered affirmatively by the commanding officer of one of the commando operations – is: were these commandos not aware that if they were caught, they were as 'expendable' as were the Germans they had come to attack? Neither commandos nor partisans could take prisoners. And the other uncomfortable question is: what is someone like Waldheim *supposed* to 'admit'?

There is a profoundly significant difference, it seems to me, between moral responsibility for the treatment of commandos, and complicity in the murder of Greek and Yugoslav civilians, including old people, women and children, in retaliation for partisan activity. But again, no proof has been adduced that as a political analyst on the army staff, Waldheim had any but the most marginal involvement in the reprisals in the Balkans, or in the crimes committed by the Croatians under the mantle of the German occupation: forced conversion of hundreds of thousands of Orthodox Serbs to Roman Catholicism, deportation of many thousands of others – including all the Jews they could find – to concentration camps and forced labour, and the murder, on the Nazi pattern, of the most helpless and 'useless' among them.

What did Waldheim actually know? There can be no doubt that he knew all about the reprisals against civilians and the deportations – into forced labour – of Yugoslavs, Greeks and, after Italy's split with Germany, Italian soldiers. Equally, of course, he knew of the deportations of Jews. But contrary to claims by American officials of the World Jewish Congress, who, one must conclude, simply don't understand wartime Europe – Waldheim would not have known about the 'Final

Solution'. The fact is that, except for civilians and soldiers in close proximity to the *Einsatzgruppen* in Russia, the gas-van murders of women and children in Serbia, or the death-camps in Poland, ordinary Germans and Austrians, including army staff, did not know about the extermination of the Jews. There were rumours and guesses. As of October 1943, after the horrible speech by Himmler in Posen, the German gauleiters knew. And three months later, in January 1944, he made accomplices of the generals by telling *them*. But until then, what would become the Nazis' greatest shame was their deepest secret.

Probably the most serious accusation against Waldheim is his alleged collaboration in the deportation of the 50,000 Jews of Salonika – in the knowledge of what was to happen to them. The precise dates of his postings have been available for some time. He was on study leave in Austria from 19 November 1942 to 31 March 1943; in Tirana from 1 April to early July; after a few days in transit at Arsakli, near Salonika, he was in Athens from 19 July to 4 October. The ghettoization and subsequent deportation of Salonika's Jews took place between February and May 1943, with one last train in August. What Waldheim knew or didn't know is impossible to prove, but he wasn't there. It is almost grotesque to reason that a young intelligence officer in the Balkans 'must have known' about this horror because a Jewish cemetery had been obliterated, and a quarter of the population of a city (Salonika) had manifestly disappeared when he returned there, two months after the sinister operation was over.

There are some very interesting thoughts, though Waldheim – who cannot now afford to 'admit' anything – will reject them too, even though they are in his favour. One is that in all probability he was an 'American asset' after the war – which would have facilitated his clearance for work at Austria's Foreign Office, and for his later election to the United Nations post. Another is that the Yugoslav 'war crime' allegation (which was never followed up, and indeed was forgotten by Tito, who years later awarded Waldheim one of his highest decorations and repeatedly entertained him for weekends on his island retreat) was a purely political move – not against Waldheim but against his then boss, Foreign Minister Karl Gruber, who was successfully lobbying the Americans and British to oppose all the territorial and financial claims which Yugoslavia was making against Austria.

Finally, there was one occasion when the twenty-four-year-old Waldheim – in an exceptional, indeed, possibly unique, initiative by a young staff officer – objected in writing to the German policy of random retaliation against civilians in Greece: '*The reprisal measures imposed in response to acts of sabotage and ambush*,' he wrote in his report to the Chief of the General Staff of Army Group E on 25 May 1944, '*have, despite their severity* [Waldheim's italics], failed to achieve any noteworthy success . . . On the contrary, exaggerated reprisal measures undertaken without a more precise examination of the objective situation have only caused embitterment and have been useful to the bands . . .' The objection, though 'not couched in moral terms', as one of his critics has said, does appear to be 'moral in inspiration'. Given the situation, no other phrasing was possible, nor would it have been in Waldheim's character to have expressed himself more boldly. The 'moral' decision was the italics.

We were now at the tail-end of a political manoeuvre that got out of hand. The truth of the Waldheim scandal, as I saw it – a truth underrated by Dr Waldheim despite his political experience – was that the real focus of bitterness was not Waldheim himself but the millions of Austrians who forty-eight years before welcomed Hitler (to his own amazement, we now know) with frenzied jubilation, and whose joy only faded with the years because he lost – not because he was evil and they had been wrong. 'I remember the first mass meeting I went to,' Waldheim told me. 'I heard screams and watched, horrified and afraid, and I said to my brother: "It's hysterical, vulgar, undignified, unnatural – it'll end badly."' No, he was not a Nazi, but had he yet to grasp that these were not the right words for what he saw?

One might have said that to a remarkable extent, 'Waldheim *was* Austria'. Like Austria he was intelligent, politically astute and ambitious in that rather special Viennese style which presupposes compromise and rejects ruthlessness. He was not imaginative, nor was he endowed with the capacity for moral excitement which is the essential prerequisite for commitment to a cause. Rather than arrogant and abrasive, as he has been described, I found him forlorn: none the less, aware that having been so close to the source of the horrors in the Balkans could affect his career, he lied, even if only marginally, for more than forty years about his war. And when one looks for signs of real feeling in him, what one finds are the ingrained prejudices of his background. Critics suspected that something embarrassing, though not a war crime, might yet be revealed about his service in the Balkans. I doubt it. I think that he was confronted by sights he didn't want to see and heard things he didn't want to know. I don't believe it was anything specific that he *did* which Waldheim was afraid might be discovered. He was afraid of the memory of what he did not do, of what he was incapable of doing. And perhaps, too, of the slow realization that while the stiff 'I regret' he repeatedly pronounced during those months was not enough, it may be all he could manage.

15

The Man Who Said 'No'

February 1982

In June 1944, when Dr Hans Münch was an SS research pathologist at a Nazi institute near Auschwitz, the camp commandant ordered him to take his turn on the ramp for the nightly selection routine which decided which new prisoners would go to the gas chambers.

Münch said no.

'Nothing was going to make me do it,' he told Austrian TV. Even more strikingly, he added: 'I don't think anyone in the SS was forced to do what they did against their will.'

He admits that his own career was ambivalent. He went to Auschwitz, he told me, more or less by accident. He had been a member of the Nazi party since university days – 'One had to be,' he says. 'Otherwise one couldn't study.' But, he says, he was not a Nazi. However, assigned early in the war to take over two older doctors' country practices, by late 1942 he was embarrassed to be safe when others were serving in the forces.

One day in Munich he bumped into a former fellow-student who was in the Waffen-SS. 'He told me he could get me something tailor-made for me pretty quickly in one of my specialities, pathology.'

What the acquaintance had not told him was that he belonged to the personal staff of the infamous SS general Reinhard Heydrich. Even if he had, it is doubtful if Münch would have been any the wiser, for he was, to put it mildly, an unusual young German of those times.

His father held the prized chair in biology at the University of Munich. 'He lived on a different planet,' says Münch. 'And my mother was in perpetual opposition.' She opposed the Prussians because they were Prussians, the French because of Alsace-Lorraine, and the Nazis because they were louts. Young Münch himself had chosen to practise quietly in the country from the time he qualified. In the context of Hitler's Germany, the whole family lived in cloud-cuckoo land.

The chance meeting with the helpful young doctor on Heydrich's staff got Münch into uniform within weeks. After a quick briefing in SS etiquette, he was posted to Rajsko, a medical institute near Auschwitz.

'But I was so ignorant about Auschwitz. I let my wife accompany me for the train journey. We had a meal at the station on arrival, then I saw her off for the return home, still neither of us knowing anything.'

Rajsko, like most of the other thirteen sub-camps, was some miles from the huge labour camp, Auschwitz I. Equally, it was a long way from Birkenau, the extermination part of the complex.

Did he know that Jews were being gassed there? I asked him. 'Not when I came there,' he said. 'I only knew it was a labour camp, and my own part of it a purely scientific installation. But after a few days I found out it was happening.'

Apart from one other SS pathologist, his staff were prisoners at Auschwitz, many of them eminent scientists. Ninety per cent of them were Jews. 'I wouldn't have known the difference,' he claims. Certainly, he got on with them well enough. 'He treated us as human beings,' one survivor said in a recent West German TV documentary. 'He shook hands with us in the mornings, and addressed us as Herr Doktor and Herr Professor. It was unheard of.'

By June 1943, typhoid and typhus epidemics were ravaging the 100,000 slave workers in Auschwitz, and had also begun to endanger their 7,000 SS guards. The primary task of Münch's institute was to find effective mass immunization methods. He does not deny that twice a week he carried out immunization experiments on prisoners at Auschwitz's infamous Block 10 – the sterilization barracks. 'But they were totally harmless,' he says. 'On the contrary, the patients got supplementary rations.'

But was he not fully aware of the other experiments being carried out in Auschwitz? 'Yes, I was,' he said. 'And a lot of people died, Jews and others. One was always aware of the smell of burning. Everyone for miles around knew about it.' He refused to watch the gassing process, but he had, he said, seen victims being pushed into gas chambers and, on one occasion, he had heard their death moans. 'A sound like no other,' he said. 'Very soft.'

In a strange echo from my conversations with Stangl many years before, he said that all the SS officers, particularly the doctors, talked endlessly about the Final Solution – 'more openly, much more freely, than on the outside.' Many of them, he said, 'while aware of the necessity to remove the Jews from Western European society, deplored the gassings, and would have preferred resettlement in remote areas, such as Madagascar.' But Münch does not hesitate to quote Joseph Mengele, the chief doctor at Auschwitz, known to have gone to hide in South America. 'He was the only SS doctor there really worth talking to.' Mengele, he says, 'saw the gassings, with no hate or fanaticism, as the only rational solution, and argued – equally rationally – that as the prisoners were going to be gassed anyway, there was simply no reason *not* to use them first for medical experiments.'

The extraordinary thing is that this intelligent man with a manifestly tortured conscience can quote such monstrosities without batting an eyelid as proof of Mengele's integrity.

So how did he himself live in Auschwitz for over a year? What were his days like?

'A very famous psychiatrist from America came to talk to me,' he says. 'I was glad.* I thought he could help me. He asked me that same question. Do you know what happened? I sat there and couldn't remember. What *were* my days? Just days . . . I could find no words to explain them. And do you know why? Because all of it is inexplicable except within the context of our unique situation there. 'It is no excuse,' he adds. 'I'm just not able to explain why one can't explain.'

It was in mid 1944 that he finally felt forced to take a stand. A new camp commandant decided that as all the SS doctors at Auschwitz were being overworked, the two Rajsko research physicians had been sufficiently coddled, and would now have to take part in the selection. 'I travelled to Berlin and told my department chief that doing that was

* Robert Lifton, who though identifying him only by initials reported on their conversation in his book *The Mercy Doctors*.

against all my ethical principles and that I refused. He asked who had ordered me to do it, and said that certainly I didn't have to.'

A few weeks later, Münch's young assistant, Dr Delmod, also refused. 'But they tricked him into it,' says Münch, 'quite gently and quite subtly.' At first, the authorities agreed to excuse him – if he took double term on the camp roster aside from his institute work. Then, when he was exhausted by these triple shifts, he was talked around, with the help of his young wife, who was invited to come and stay at the camp and in the end, Münch says, he took part in the selections. Delmod committed suicide as soon as the war ended, and one senses in Münch a deep sense of guilt at Delmod's fate.

The trial of forty SS doctors at Auschwitz ended in Cracow on 22 December 1947. Twenty-three were sentenced to death, six to life imprisonment, ten to prison sentences of between three and fifteen years. Münch alone was acquitted: nineteen former prisoners had testified in his favour.

Since then he has not ceased to question himself and to lay himself open to questioning, a process which – his wife told me – has ruined their family life and his relationship with his children. 'And is that of no relevance?' she asked me, in front of him. But he did not appear to hear her.

'How could I stand it?' he said. 'I could have left. I could have deserted, gone to Switzerland, it would not have been difficult. True, I would have had to leave my family behind: my wife would never have left our two children behind, even with her parents – it was impossible. But even so, how could I, as a human being, bear to stay? I cannot understand myself. And I need to before I die.'

16

Albert Speer

February 2000

It was at the beginning of 1946 that a friend of mine, George Vassilchikov, one of the first two simultaneous interpreters in the world, obtained a visitor's pass for me to attend the Nuremberg trials.

This was the first time I saw Albert Speer. I knew nothing about him and only noticed him among the twenty-one accused because, then forty years old, he looked young and, with his smooth face and strangely shaped, bushy black eyebrows, startlingly handsome. In contrast with many of the other defendants, who pretended to be bored or asleep, or who read or fidgeted endlessly, he always sat very still, listening intently, his face immobile except for those dark, intelligent eyes.

'Who is Speer?' I asked Georgie one night at the Grand Hotel where we were dining and dancing.

'The second most important man in Germany,' he said, leading me, a rather bad dancer, expertly around the floor. 'It was because of his requests for evermore workers that the people you are looking after now were shipped to Germany as forced labour.'

I remember feeling an odd sense of surprise. It was hard to reconcile the terrible treatment of the slave labourers with the interesting, chiselled face I had become aware of in the dock.

'You mean, he was responsible for the way they were treated?' I asked.

Georgie was always precise in his answers. 'We can't really know yet about the nature and extent of people's individual responsibility,' he said. 'But of course, he had to *know*.'

Later, I learned that if it hadn't been for Speer, Hitler would have had to give up at least a year earlier than he did. A year. How many people died in that year? It was then, I think, that Speer entered my subconscious. The next two times I attended the trial, I looked harder, focused more on that silent figure, that attractive face in the dock.

It was – it seems incredible – thirty-one years later, in the second half of July 1977, that I received a letter from Speer, who had been sentenced to twenty years in Spandau prison and released in 1966. He was writing, he said, because he wanted to thank me for an article I had written for the London *Sunday Times*. He felt he needed to express his appreciation of the manner in which we had approached the subject.

The article Speer had read was written in collaboration with a *Sunday Times* colleague, Lewis Chester. After publication of my book about Stangl, *Into That Darkness*, I promised myself that I would stop exposing myself to Nazi horrors. But I never quite succeeded in suppressing my involvement with the Third Reich and its aftermath. I often succumbed when editors asked me to undertake commissions in or about Germany. It was one such commission which resulted in my letter from Speer. The article's subject was a book, *Hitler's War*, written by the British revisionist David Irving. Irving claimed to have discovered that Hitler had not known about the genocide of the Jews until October 1943 at the earliest. On first reading, his arguments were plausible – just; his proof, in the form of quotes from Hitler, Himmler and others, was intriguing. Revisionists all over the world had for years been trying desperately to clear Hitler of the gas-chamber murder of the Jews. If they could prove that Hitler had not been involved in the order for genocide and indeed had not known for years that such genocide was happening, then they would have succeeded in changing Hitler's image and, with it, the history of the Third Reich.

Our method of investigating Irving's claims was to follow the trail he himself had laid. Irving was surprisingly helpful: 'This is my Jew file,' he said, pointing to a long box filled with meticulously cross-indexed cards. 'Everything is in it; you can borrow it.' He was so generous and persuasive that I almost thought he might have something.

I spent just under two months talking to survivors from Hitler's circle and checking in German archives every document Irving had registered in his 'Jew file'. By the end of our research, we understood the devices Irving had employed to support his thesis, and our long article completely discredited his claims.

In his letter, Speer wrote that it was 'ludicrous' for anyone to claim that the genocide of the Jews could have been anyone's idea but Hitler's: 'It shows a profound ignorance of the nature of Hitler's Germany, in which nothing of any magnitude could conceivably happen, not only without his knowledge, but without his orders.' The fact that there was no documentary evidence of such an order from the Führer meant nothing, he said. He knew from personal experience that many of Hitler's most critical orders were issued only verbally. 'From the historical point of view,' he wrote, 'the matter has now, thanks to your exposé, been dealt with. None the less, unfortunately, Irving has provided fodder for the abominable efforts of those whose aim is to create a new *Dolchstoss Lüge* (war-guilt lie), as it was called after 1918, in order yet again to deceive the German people. It appals me.'

Although I knew a great deal about Speer, had read his two books and had seen him many times on television, I had never wanted to meet him. I had admired his books, the second one, *Spandau: the Secret Diaries*, even more than the first. This story of his twenty years' imprisonment – his bitter relationships with at least four of his six co-prisoners; his extraordinary personality change under the tutelage of the French chaplain Georges Casalis; his transformation of the prison yard into a flowering park; the thousands of letters he wrote to his best friend the architect Rudolf Wolters and his children; his organized reading and study programme (he read 5,000 books, taught himself English and French and by the end of his imprisonment could probably have obtained degrees in literature, ethics and even theology); and, finally, his 'walk around the world', carefully measured hikes he took daily around his 'park', supported in his imagination by maps and descriptions Rudi Wolters supplied him with, walking from country to country and city to city over deserts, plains and mountains until, twelve years after he had started, he had walked just under 32,000 kilometres – all this made it the most extraordinary prison memoir I had ever read; he had been, it was obvious, an extraordinary man.

But none of this had emerged from what I saw of him over the years on television after his release and read in countless interviews where, too glib, too smooth, too sure, he appeared only to repeat himself endlessly, above all in denying that he had ever known anything about the Nazi crimes. He made me uncomfortable; I didn't like him; I didn't want to know him. Then, the day after receiving his first letter, another one arrived. He had forgotten to mention, he wrote, that a year or two previously, he had read *Into That Darkness*, which had caused him sleepless nights. If I was ever in the vicinity of Heidelberg, would I perhaps care to come and talk?

I telephoned him after receiving this second letter, partly to thank him and partly because the letters didn't sound the way I imagined him. His voice came as a great surprise, and was partly responsible for me changing my mind about meeting him. In the interviews I had read – perhaps because the questions and answers had essentially always been the same – his replies and obvious evasions had irritated me; on television, particularly when he spoke in his heavily accented English, he had almost always sounded arbitrary and arrogant. But on the telephone, speaking German, he sounded hesitant, shy – not of me, specifically, but as a person. What intrigued me most, however, was that unexpectedly I sensed sadness in him.

At the beginning of 1978, the editor of the *Sunday Times* magazine agreed that I could do a profile of Speer, and that my husband, Don, could take the pictures. By the time we went to Heidelberg in April, Speer had telephoned me many times – we had already talked for hours, and my feelings about him had changed: I no longer regarded him with active dislike, though I could not say that I liked or, above all, trusted him. Even if he had been truthful about everything else in his books and interviews, he was, I was sure, lying about not having known until Nuremberg about the murder of the Jews. But I had no idea what he felt, admitted or denied about Hitler's other crimes; nor did I know about his family, about his friends and enemies during the Third Reich and since, about what his life had been like before the Nazis came to power and when he was a child.

To find out about the background, motivations and feelings of Franz Stangl was one thing. To try to discover how a man of Speer's talent and immense intelligence could have been convinced by the arguments of National Socialism and become – as far as was possible – Hitler's friend, how he could have stood by him until the very end and probably through his efforts prolonged the war by a considerable period, was quite another. But my main feeling, as we drove up to the Speer house in time for tea, was curiosity.

Over the years, I have established a way of dealing with these professional encounters. When I am talking to someone whose past is immensely controversial, my rule is to tell him at the very start how I feel about him. I do not pretend to come as his friend, to help or console him. If he has murdered, I want to find out what has made him do it; if he has cheated, I want to find out why; if he is a ruler of an industrial empire or a country, and I find his rule suspect, I tell him so. In the case of people involved with the Third Reich, I tell them what I feel about the Nazis and how I feel about them personally.

For me, this is a kind of insurance policy: I want none of them to be able to say afterwards that, in order to get them to talk, I pretended to be other than I am. And quite aside from feeling that this is for me, morally, the right approach, I have also found that making such a statement creates a special atmosphere: people respond to it, speaking more openly, saying, perhaps, things they would not otherwise have said. This was certainly the case with Speer.

Speer's house was large and comfortable but, except for his study, which was full of papers and books about the Third Reich and was dominated by a large painting of his mother, it was curiously impersonal: 'good' furniture, carpets and paintings; ornaments on the tables; expensive curtains and lots of flowers. It could have been the home of any upper-class German family. It conveyed no sense of Speer, or even of his wife, who had lived in it throughout his imprisonment and raised their six children there. It was later, at their house in the mountains, that I got more of a sense of him; he had created it himself, from an old farmhouse. It was very simple, almost spartan, but everything it contained – the old pieces in the bedrooms and the kitchen, and the new ones Speer had designed for the huge living room, converted from the former stables – was beautiful.

By the end of that first evening, Speer had made friends with my husband. He had almost immediately suggested that they call each other by their Christian names, which is very unusual in Germany. With me, he was, not reticent, but much cooler. It would be some time before we too called each other by our first names, though of course never the intimate '*Du*'.

By the time we left that night, though knowing no details, I knew that Speer had had a miserable childhood and hated the Heidelberg house because it reminded him of it, and that he and his wife and he and his children were and always had been miles apart. I knew that he was deeply nostalgic for Spandau, though I didn't know why; and I knew that he had loved Hitler, though not to what extent. What I didn't yet know, and wasn't to learn until much later, was that he was consumed with guilt about the murder of the Jews. It was a long time before I grew to like Speer, but by the end of our first three weeks together, I fully believed, and loved, that feeling of guilt in him.

Albert Speer died in 1981. By then, we had talked a great deal, and I have often asked myself how I really felt about him. Perhaps my reaction to his death goes some way towards providing an answer: I was shaken, because it happened so unexpectedly, in London, while we were away, and because there was a message from him on our answerphone when we returned, by which time he was already dead. But I was not sad. He had given me a great deal of himself, of knowledge and of understanding, and I was grateful to him for that. No one else could have given me what he did; there was no one else who knew and understood as much as he did. But when he died, I thought that his death was right and, in a terrible way, overdue; fate had given him thirty-five years after the Nuremberg trials, at which he should probably have been sentenced to death, as were others perhaps less guilty than he.

What Speer gave me was a new perspective on Hitler, on his personality, his actions and his goals; a new understanding of the significance, in political events, of human emotions. The book I subsequently decided to write was the book that I had wanted to write ever since finding the imprisoned children at Dachau and the stolen children in southern Germany, ever since learning about the dead children in Treblinka, Sobibor and Belzec. Speer had given me the gift of himself, against whom I could place, consider, deplore and mourn all those events, and all those human beings who had lived and died in my time.

September 1978

The morning I arrived in Heidelberg in the early spring of 1978, for the beginning of the first two and a half weeks I was to spend talking with Albert Speer,* he had received a letter signed 'Heil Hitler' notifying him that the writers intended killing him – and soonest.

You pig of a traitor [it started]. We have looked for you for a long time. You, who as our Führer's architect profited when he went from victory to victory. You, who planned to gas him and his staff when he defended our Berlin.

You pig played the penitent, and betrayed us . . . barricaded yourself in a villa guarded by dogs. Your lying scribbles show your true character. By sending your money to Jewish immigrant organizations in the USA, with speeches and toadying of all kinds, you are trying to get readmitted to society . . . Rudolf Hess, our Führer's deputy, sits in Spandau, because he is and always will be, until death, a loyal National Socialist, while you never were or ever will be anything but a money-grabbing pig! . . . When we put an end to you, no one will care. No one will shed a single tear. And we *will* put an end to you. Rely on it!

The signature was the initials 'L.P.'; the SS rank *Sturmführer* (captain). On the back of the envelope, the sender was noted as 'The victims of Oct. 16, 1946' (the date ten major war criminals were hanged in Nuremberg). And the letter heading, below a stamped eagle with the swastika and the letters: NSDAP AO (standing for National Socialist Party, Foreign Section) was 'Odessa 15', all imaginative touches but by no means the only ones. For Speer's 'barricaded villa' in Heidelberg, where I was sitting with him and his wife that day, has belonged to his family for three generations; the name SPEER is plainly displayed – some might think in unnecessarily large letters – on the post next to the permanently open gates; and the 'guard dogs' is one ridiculously soppy St Bernard who loves nothing more than tenderly wet-kissing

* Another four days would follow a month later when we checked through the draft of the finished piece for possible errors. After that, except for a few breaks of two, three months, when he was ill or abroad, we remained in almost constant touch until he died on 1 September 1981.

visitors and is the playmate of two Speer grandchildren who live in a cottage on the estate.

Speer doesn't entirely dismiss these threats which, he says, 'come quite frequently' – he did inform the police – but he takes them philosophically. What is however significant, is that all the points in this diatribe are familiar from reproaches made against him for years by many reputable critics. 'It is interesting, isn't it?' he says, with the half-ironic detachment many people find so disconcerting, 'that I should be so identically berated by former friends and former enemies?'

Speer and his wife, Margret, both now seventy-three, occupy two floors of a patrician family property on the hill above the Heidelberg castle. 'I hate this house,' he said, looking around the lovely drawing-room. 'Margret loves it; it's where she brought up the children. But for me it is a constant reminder of the miseries of my childhood.'

Two years ago, he found an old farmhouse in the mountains where they now spend more and more of their time. 'There, hardly anyone has our address and we can walk and ski for hours without meeting a soul,' he said.

There is an aura of intense loneliness about these two people. His preoccupation with the past has alienated him from his six children and from most of his few friends, who are eager to deny *all* responsibility for the Nazi era. 'They call what I do "soiling one's own nest",' he said. He shrugged – he shrugs often – 'I can see their point. I don't blame them. It's just, because I've never had many friends, with one or two of them, it hurts.'

His relationship with the children who, all successful, are mostly married and living all over Germany, seems formal to a degree. He stands up when they arrive or leave; they shake hands without otherwise touching. 'Well, hello,' or 'Well then, goodbye,' he says.

'Good evening; goodbye,' they reply – it seems hard for them even to pronounce the word 'Father'.

The first evening of my eleven days at Heidelberg, some of them came to spend the night. It was the first time in three years that several were there together.

'After you left,' he told me the next morning, 'we sat down to supper. Margret had made it quite festive. She can be so gay, so girlish: did you notice, when she was with the children? It was pleasant enough; we chatted until, about 11.30, I went up to bed. As soon as I got upstairs, I could hear them laugh like anything. There had been no laughter while I was there; there never is. I weigh upon them.' He was stating a fact, not accusing anyone or manifesting self-pity.

Margret's face closed up when I repeated some of this to her later. 'What can you expect?' she said flatly. 'It was too long. When he first came out of Spandau, he talked quite a bit about it, and the children were interested. But then they would try to tell him about things that had happened to *them* in those years – he'd listen for an instant and then he'd just get up and go away. So, soon they didn't try any more.'

'The problem was insuperable,' said Speer. 'My Spandau rhythm, the pattern of twenty years, my need for solitude, thinking – it could not, cannot change. You see,' he paused, 'Spandau eventually was not so much a prison for me, as a refuge.'

Like others who have talked with Speer, I was taken aback at first by his easy charm, by his surprising sense of humour, by his enduring good looks – which seem to belie his claims of penitence and despair – and by an almost glib readiness to admit guilt, concede wrongs and discuss equably any subject one brings up. Could he – I wondered – be a particularly subtle fake? Or was he, within familiar limitations he set a long time ago, a peculiarly honest man?

'You often mention that you prayed,' I said. 'Do you still?'

'In a way,' he said. Whenever he speaks of anything really private – always difficult for him – his face changes completely: the smoothness, blandness disappears; he looks older, less obviously handsome, and his voice sounds tentative. 'I am not conventionally religious,' he finally said. 'But I have come to believe.'

'I hadn't understood that he would never be able to rid himself of the past,' said Margret. She is small, slender, and shy with strangers, but her face looks oddly hungry for communication and warmth. Always encouraged by him, she sat in on many of our talks.

But what lies like a spectre over their lives, continually haunting both their minds, is Hitler's most abominable crime – the extermination of the Jews, knowledge of which Speer has denied for over three decades. 'I should have known,' he has always said. 'I could have known. But I didn't know.'

Margret cannot bear to mention it at all; he, on the contrary, cannot leave it alone. On our first day together, after eight hours of concentrated conversation, he had suddenly seemed irritable, nervous, and with it came that curious change to an older, less self-assured man. 'You seem tired,' I said. 'Shall we stop?'

'No,' he answered, 'I know you are holding back on the essential question: everything always leads up to it.' He sounded suddenly angry, 'Why don't you just ask it and get it over with?' I said it was too soon.

The foundations for the fall of Albert Speer, as I would paradoxically call his meteoric rise to power, were laid in his earliest childhood, spent in Mannheim and Heidelberg and filled with fears and loneliness. His pretty mother was sixteen years her husband's junior; his serious architect father despised overt emotion: 'Love was not part of the marriage arrangement,' Speer said drily. His maternal grandmother was as cold and socially pretentious as his mother, 'And stingy to boot,' he said. 'She used to count the sugar cubes,' added Margret.

Then there were his two brothers. 'They used to gang up on me and beat me up. I fainted quite a bit – psychosomatic, no doubt. I was always trying to get them to love me.'

'And your mother?' I asked.

'She was very busy with her social life. The only warmth I remember came from Mademoiselle Blum, our French governess – she was Jewish, as a matter of fact.* And from my father's office staff. I was their favourite.'

He also loved his grandfather, a man who was born a forester's son and became one of Germany's leading industrialists. 'I think it's from him I inherited my talent for organization,' he said. 'But he was a very modest man. I loved his simplicity.' He died when Albert was sixteen.

He and Margret met when they were seventeen. 'I fell as much in love with her family as with her,' he said. 'They were much simpler people than we; but they were warm and close. Once I met her, I was

* Much later, this former governess, now living in New York, would inform me he had been mistaken; she was not Jewish.

down at her house all the time. Our best times were punting and hiking in the mountains.'

His photo album, covering the years 1922–7, is equally a statistical record of their hikes: '1926, year's summary: nine touring days, total height climbed, 6,223m; daily average: 691.4m; longest climb in one day: 1,458m; longest descent: 1,689m.'

'But we never *talked*,' he said. 'Even when we hiked for days; nor did I write to her about feelings in my letters. There is a curtain between me and others,' he said. 'There always has been.'

As our understanding developed, I came to comprehend the solitary nature of Speer and the three relationships which determined his fate: with his father; his architect teacher; and finally – the heart of the problem – the extraordinary love between him and Adolf Hitler.

His pre-Nuremberg life falls easily into three phases, each dominated by a strong relationship. The first was his love and desperate need to please his father. The word 'love' – in whatever context – is uncomfortable for him: 'I respected – no, I suppose more than that – I revered him. I wanted to be a mathematician. I *loved* mathematics and statistics. But my father thought it unsuitable. "No money, no standing, no future", he said.'

So Speer chose the one profession his architect father would have to approve – architect. 'Though I didn't think I had any talent.'

The architect who accepted him as a student, Heinrich Tessenow, became the second man he revered. And when Tessenow in 1928 – Speer now twenty-three – made him his first assistant ('He must have felt an affinity for me; it can't have been for my talent: all I did was copy him'), he and Margret married, rented a tiny house in Berlin, and served rice and noodles to dozens of impoverished friends. 'It was the purest, the happiest time we ever had.'

His third and decisive attachment was to Hitler, with whom, over the years, he developed one of the fateful relationships of our time. It was not a homosexual one, 'But certainly' – wrote Professor Alexander Mitscherlich, one of Germany's leading social psychologists – 'it was, like many relationships between people of the same sex, an erotic one.' And Speer says: 'Mitscherlich is on the right track.'

Speer, at twenty-seven, had already been a party member for four years, 'From the instant I heard Hitler speak.' He was then a junior member of the team rebuilding the old Reichs Chancellery. 'I had often been one of the group showing Hitler around the site, but only as the most subaltern of subalterns. And then suddenly one day, he turned to me and said, "Come up and have lunch".

'I thought I'd faint. I was immediately worried about my suit – I'd got some plaster on my sleeve that morning. "We'll fix that upstairs," Hitler said, and took me into his private suite and told his valet to fetch his dark blue jacket.

'Before I knew it, here I was, walking back into the dining-room behind him, wearing his jacket. "What on earth are you doing?" asked Goebbels – he had noticed right away Hitler's golden party badge, the only one of its kind. "He's wearing my jacket," said Hitler.

'Can you conceive how I felt? Here was the greatest man in the world, and here was I, twenty-seven years old, totally insignificant in my own eyes, sitting next to him at lunch, wearing his clothes and elected – at least that day – to be virtually his sole conversational partner.'

To Hitler, the tall, handsome, well-spoken Speer was a German ideal, from a background that Hitler, as a lower-middle-class Austrian, had always worshipped from afar. And architecture – the dream of his youth – was Speer's discipline.

It was certainly not Hitler's passion for architecture that compelled Speer, nor, at the beginning, success: it was the man.

Amazed at first at what Hitler saw in him, astonished at what it led to, as time went on and he became increasingly blinded to reality, Speer convinced himself – at least on the surface – that he was indeed what Hitler ordained him to be, and desperately drove himself to be it.

Although it had been a year before Hitler found out Speer was married, he and Margret – childless until 1936, after which the children came in rapid succession – soon were never far from Hitler. 'We went wherever he went; had houses, flats, studios near him.' Even so, alone of all of Hitler's circle, Speer challenged, resisted – later even dominated Hitler to some extent, as if he knew that Hitler sought that too.

'I suppose that strange incident at tea on the Berghof in 1936 showed that up very clearly,' he said. 'When he suddenly fixed me with his eyes, obviously challenging me – you know the children's game – to hold or give way. I made myself hold on. It felt like for ever. But it was he who looked away first. I had won.'

During those earlier years, no other relationship mattered, except, marginally, the friendship he had developed with Eva Braun, with whom he shared a total commitment to their hero.

Although she went skiing and abroad with both the Speers, it was he who became her special confidant. (It was to him she came, years later, in tears, to tell him that, 'The Führer has just told me to find someone else; he can no longer fulfil me as a man!')

'She has been much maligned,' he said. 'She was very shy, modest. A man's woman: gay; gentle and kind, incredibly undemanding . . . a restful sort of girl. And her love for Hitler – as she proved in the end – was beyond question.'

By the beginning of the war, Speer had carried out dozens of enormous commissions. 'You are the greatest architect in Germany,' enthused Göring. Yet underneath Speer knew he was totally out of his depth. He abandoned without a backward glance Tessenow's principles of architectural simplicity; his father's approval too had become irrelevant.

At one time his father had boasted to friends of young Speer's success. But when the old man was shown the model of the new Berlin – the capital of the 1,000-year Reich that was to be completed by 1950 – 'he stood and looked at it for a long moment. Then he said, "You've all gone insane," and walked out. I just thought he was too old to understand our time.'

The next day, at Hitler's request, Speer introduced his father. 'As soon as he stood facing Hitler, I saw him go white and his whole body shuddered. He didn't even seem to hear Hitler's hymns of praise about me; he just bowed without a word, and left . . . Now I understand that he somehow detected that other self of Hitler which I had never sensed.'

By the early summer of 1939 Speer says he had every reason to know what Hitler was planning. 'In 1937 I showed him the model for the giant Nuremberg Stadium. I was worried that it didn't conform to Olympic regulations. I remember his tone of voice when he answered, "This doesn't matter. In 1940, the Olympic Games will be in Tokyo.

After that they will take place in Germany for evermore. And *we* will decide on proper measurements." All I felt was pride.'

And in the early summer of 1939, Hitler, dreaming over Speer's detailed Berlin model, saw the eagle, a swastika in its claws, that was to crown the enormous dome of the new *Reichshalle*: 'He said: "Instead of the swastika, have the eagle hold a globe." Of *course* I realized that this meant he intended to rule the world. But that's what I wanted then: I *wanted* this man to rule the world.'

In February 1942 Hitler appointed Speer Minister for Armaments. Until then, German industry had been functioning virtually on its peacetime basis. To mobilize it for victory, 'Hitler required a genius,' wrote Professor Hugh Trevor-Roper. 'Genius selects genius intuitively. Hitler chose Speer.'

'I didn't want it,' said Speer. 'I told him I knew nothing about munitions or armaments.' Some critics now denigrate Speer's achievements, but the historical record proves they were enormous.

Immediately following this appointment, although they continued to meet daily, Hitler became distant and cold. 'I found this almost unbearably painful,' said Speer. 'I had been so used to what had become an almost easy familiarity. But after a few days I understood: he kept me at a distance until he was sure I had learned the lesson of how a minister behaves. When he thought I knew, we returned to a somewhat easier relationship.'

By then, Speer had already lost the innate sense of morality which had shown up so clearly in a collection of schoolboy essays he had shown me, a series of analyses of plays and operas, always concerned with aspects of right and wrong.

Already by 1938 he did not react to the pogroms, except with disapproval at disorder in the streets. He knew about the euthanasia programme. 'I remember Hitler describing mental patients, and feeling, from his awful descriptions, that they *would* perhaps be happier dead.' He knew about the arrest of Pastor Niemöller and the executions of the student resisters, Hans and Sophie Scholl, beheaded in February 1943. 'I don't think I would have approved of their being executed. But for me they were traitors who *had* to be put where they couldn't do any more harm.'

Geoffrey Barraclough, the historian, also accused Speer of having inserted passages on his remorse about the Final Solution which were not in the German edition, *ex post facto* into the American edition as a 'sop to American susceptibilities'.

Speer's German publisher, Wolf Jobst Siedler, says to this: 'In the first draft of *Inside the Third Reich* the question of the Jews and his guilt came up in every third paragraph. We argued for days. Finally he gave up and let me get on with cutting it. Then Macmillan in New York disagreed with me, so I gave them 200 pages I had taken out, and they put some of them back in. That was how it happened.'

Often, over the days, Speer had brought up the subject of the Jews, and I had time and again deflected it. It was the ninth morning of our talks when I suggested devoting that day to it. He was intensely relieved, almost frisky, when I told him. 'At last!' he exclaimed. But this soon gave way to increasing tension.

If he was going to maintain his claim of ignorance about the Final Solution, I asked him how *could* he explain a man of his intelligence not realizing what Hitler's constant raving had to lead up to?

'First of all,' he said sharply, 'there was no possible way to predict that *this* was the horror on his mind: nobody could have guessed that. But it is difficult to explain my reaction to his anti-semitic tirades; mainly I felt embarrassed: to me it was an expression of his vulgar side – an aspect of him I simply didn't want to admit.'

In January 1942, assigned to sorting out the winter chaos of the transport system in the Ukraine, he joined his team in Dnepropetrovsk where Einsatzgruppe C, Commando 5, had been machine-gunning the 30,000 Jews of the city for weeks.

'Didn't anyone tell you of these public murders?' I asked. 'Even if you didn't witness anything yourself.'

'No,' he said. 'They wouldn't have dared: I was much too close to Hitler. The higher one was, the less one knew.'

Over the years, the 'Speer Ministry', as it was called, ended up employing 28 million workers, 6 million of them foreign, and about 60,000 of them concentration camp prisoners. Even if he never saw secret documents pertaining to 'extermination' camps, as the employer of 60,000 concentration camp inmates, was he really unaware? He would not answer this question.

In May 1942, when the whole Eastern railway system broke down, he (and General Milch) had briefly been appointed 'Traffic Czars'. At that time three death-camps were operating within sixty miles of Warsaw, with up to 10,000 people a day being shipped there in trains. How could he have not known this?

'We were responsible for 145,000 railway cars,' he said. 'Even if 2,000 of them were used to transport these victims, don't you think it is reasonable that the men in charge in Berlin wouldn't know the details of 2,000 cars?'

None the less, he *should* have known, he said, as he had said so often, and volunteered another incident: in the spring of 1943, Hitler, talking to a small group, said, 'Gentlemen, the bridges behind us are broken.' 'When he said that,' said Speer, 'cold shivers ran down my back – I remember it well. I had a presentiment of something terrible.'

'Terrible in what way?' I asked.

'I thought . . . I did think . . . I think now I did connect it with the Jews. He was threatening, warning us, telling us that there was no way back.'

(We had been talking then for five consecutive hours: he looked grey. I have a note on my block: 'He has beads of sweat on his chin and lips. The room isn't hot, but I turned down the thermostat and opened the window.')

I told him that unless Hitler had explained the 'bridges' – or, more likely, could expect them to know – there was little sense in the remark. 'Surely the threat could only find its mark if you were fully in the picture?' He didn't answer.

In October 1943 he either heard, or learned about it hours later, Himmler tell a conference of gauleiters in Posen about the extermination of the Jews.

After that October there was a sharp change in his relationship with Hitler. 'He used to telephone me regularly . . . the telephone calls gradually ceased.'

And in December he visited 'Dora', the caves in the Harz Mountains where 10,000 slave workers, living under unspeakable conditions ('the hell on earth', as it was described at Nuremberg), produced the V2 rockets. 'It was the worst place I had ever seen,' Speer said. 'I feel ill even now when I think of it.' He ordered the immediate construction of a barracks camp on the surface and radical improvement in the prisoners' diet and hygiene.

After Christmas with the troops in Lapland in 1943 (thereby, significantly I thought, for the first time avoiding the family Christmas), Speer returned to furious confrontations with Hitler. Speer wanted to stop the deportations from Western Europe which were turning those populations increasingly against Germany, and instead put the large labour reserve of Germans to work, especially hundreds of thousands of women who (unlike British women) had never been conscripted for war work. 'But I lost,' he said. 'Bormann [lobbying with Hitler] had done his work well, and 4 million more workers were to be dragged in from conquered territories.'

As his mind accumulated evermore knowledge, his body once again refused to serve him. On 18 January 1944 he entered hospital with 'exhaustion, depression and a swollen knee'. He nearly died – he had a 'death-experience' he describes as 'the happiest moment of my life', but was brought back to life.

Hitler visited him during his convalescence. 'The first time I saw him again, after ten weeks, was quite extraordinary,' Speer says. 'When he walked through the door, it was as if thick scales had fallen off my eyes. "My God," I thought, "he is so ugly." It was such an overwhelming discovery, I could hardly keep my countenance.'

By May 1944, Speer was firmly entrenched with the generals as against the most vicious party men: Bormann, Himmler, Ley. Was Speer saying that his military friends too didn't tell him a thing?

'At that time I hadn't been around for months,' he said wearily. 'I was on sick leave.'

This was true; he did fall ill. And because we now know that Speer's rare illnesses were always connected with work, consequences of intolerable pressures, we can reasonably assume that from 1942 on he had known about the killings in Russia, but, in common with many Germans, was able to attribute them to the harsh necessities of war and thereby put them out of his mind. Further, as we see, in the spring of 1943, he had suspected that Hitler's 'The bridges are broken' referred to the Jews.

In the spring of 1944 Speer nearly resigned, but was persuaded by his industrialist friends to stay. There is a great deal he wishes now he had done or left undone. He briefly toyed with the idea of killing Hitler. 'It was only a brief impulse of despair,' he said, sounding tired, 'which nobody was supposed to hear of later. A friend gave it away to the Allies and then they asked me about it at Nuremberg.'

This may not have happened as innocently as he now claimed: Speer always knew where his interests lay. But certainly it was at great risk to himself that as of early 1945 he openly opposed Hitler's scorched-earth policy. 'If you weren't my architect,' Hitler said to him in the course of an extraordinary meeting on 27 March 1945, 'I would insist you take the consequences.'

Speer replied that he was prepared for the consequences; all that mattered now, he said, was their duty to the people. 'If you consider me unsuitable as your minister, fire me,' he said.

As for months past, Speer's instinct proved correct. Hitler ended up pleading with him to give in: to show conviction that the war could still be won. If not that, at least to show *faith*. And finally, 'If at least you could say that you *hope* we have not lost. You must surely be able to hope . . . that would satisfy me.' He was given twenty-four hours to decide.

That midnight, firmly determined to repeat his refusal, Speer says, 'I stood in front of him, saw this broken old man and – I assure you against my volition – heard myself say, "My Führer, I stand unconditionally behind you." And Hitler gave me his hand and began to cry.'

Speer's powers were restored and, travelling day and night all over the country, he used them to stop the scorched-earth measures wherever he could, until, on 24 April, he flew back to Berlin for a last goodbye. 'The gesture of a madman,' he says now.

'It was a strangely quiet talk,' he said. Hitler spoke to him gently about his planned suicide, asked his opinion, and, in a way reassured him that he was not afraid, but glad to die. 'To my own surprise, I found myself confessing to him that I had countermanded his orders. He said nothing.'*

Speer thought the hold Hitler had over him – the magic – had ended with his death. But in Spandau he dreamt constantly about him.

* This later turned out to be a lie: he had never 'confessed' to Hitler.

'Incredibly clear and vivid dreams.' Then, for a long time, the dreams ceased. 'And now they have come back,' he said. 'They are always the same. About his knowing what I was doing against him, including my wanting to kill him. Sometimes he isn't in the picture, but the dream is still about him . . .'

'I think I know what you knew about the Jews,' I told Speer on our last day, 'but could you not yourself go a little further?'

Again he had known I would ask this final question.

'I can say,' he said slowly, 'that I . . . had a . . . sense that some dreadful things were happening with the Jews . . .'

This was no longer the same man I had found glib, and almost theatrically charming when we first met. He was personal, resigned, exhausted and serious.

'But if you suspected then you knew: you cannot "sense" into a void: you knew.'

He was silent for a long moment, then got up, went down to his study and came back with several sheets of paper. 'Read this,' he said. 'Do as you wish with it; and then let us speak of other things.'

It was a letter from the South African Jewish Board of Deputies, asking him to assist the board in a legal action against the publishers and distributors of the pamphlet *Did Six Million Die?*, to prevent its distribution in South Africa.

The three questions they asked him, in essence required him to affirm that he could testify from his own knowledge that there had been a plan to exterminate the Jews and that this plan was implemented. It is perhaps a tribute to the board's percipience that they thought he might now answer these incriminating questions, and to their sensitivity that they have never publicized his reply.

Speer's affidavit consists of three pages in which, point after point, he describes the background to the exterminations, and the devastating admissions of the accused at Nuremberg. 'I still recognize today,' he writes, 'that the grounds on which I was convicted by the International Military Tribunal were correct. More than this: I still consider it today essential to take upon myself the responsibility and thus the blame in general, for all crimes which were committed after I became part of the Hitler government on 7 February 1942 . . . My main guilt however,' he ends, 'I still see today in my tacit acceptance [*Billigung*] of the persecution and the murder of millions of Jews.'

'Why did you finally say this now,' I asked, 'after denying it for so long?'

He had been sitting, motionless, not watching while I read. 'For this purpose,' he answered, 'with these people, I wouldn't . . . I couldn't . . . hedge [*handeln*].'

Certainly, had he said these words in Nuremberg, he would have hanged. He didn't say them, partly because he wanted to live; partly because the truth – so deeply imbedded in his unconscious – was unbearable. If he has said them now, it is because, I think, he has come beyond – and wearied of – the evasion.

Albert Speer is no martyr. But nor is he a fraud. He is a haunted man who has battled for three decades to recapture his lost morality. Unless we deny all men the potential for regeneration, this man, I believe, must now be allowed peace.

17

Children of the Reich

February 2000

It is now fifty-five years since the end of the Third Reich, yet in Germany the past seems always present. It is no longer (as it certainly was for a long time) that as a foreigner one provokes this awareness: it is just there.

It was in large measure due to that awareness that in October 1998 I spent two extraordinary days in the Ruhr city of Bochum where the Schauspielhaus, one of Germany's leading repertory theatres, was rehearsing Harold Pinter's *Ashes to Ashes*. A few months previously, in May, Henriette Thimig, a brilliant actress I had known since she was a child – she is Helene Thimig's niece and the last of Austria's greatest theatre family to have become an actress – called me to say that the Bochum theatre wanted to invite me to come in October to talk to them about how Pinter had started to write this play 'after reading your book'.

I have to admit that I didn't know anything I had written had contributed to Pinter's play – in 1996–7, when it was first produced in London, my mind was on violence done to children, not to victims of brutal politics. But that May (which with the terrible tabloid reaction to the announcement of my book on Mary Bell, *Cries Unheard*, had not been a happy time for me), the idea of such a change of pace, the smell of the stage, the ready minds of actors, the work on interpretation of a wonderful playwright's thoughts, was very attractive and I said yes without even knowing what they really wanted. (In fact, until I talked to Pinter just before leaving early in October, I thought the figure who might have interested him was Franz Stangl, commandant of Treblinka, the subject of *Into That Darkness*. But, 'No, no,' he said, 'it was your book on Speer.' And he sent me Michael Billington's *The*

Life and Work of Harold Pinter which explains it all. The play is about a man and a woman who both care for and hate one another, and explores the way in which force and coercion can produce sexual magnetism.)

On the way to Bochum, I stopped in Frankfurt for the presentation at the book fair of the German edition of *Cries Unheard*. The past was glaringly alive there. On the dozens of small white buses, which are the only (and free) transport allowed in the almost unwalkable three and a half square miles of the *Messe* area, three-foot-high black letters proclaimed publication of the first volume of HITLER: DIE NEUE BIOGRAPHIE VON IAN KERSHAW. Because it is illegal in Germany now to reproduce Hitler's image in a public place, to Kershaw's considerable surprise, the photograph on the buses was that of the author of the book rather than the subject.

My German publisher for *Cries Unheard* was Karl Blessing who, though (then) merely a youthful fifty-three, is considered one of the great elder statesmen of German publishing. He had invited 200 people to his sumptuous annual buffet lunch at Frankfurt's newest hotel, the Maritim, to which 280 guests came. And as I grazed from table to table, all the talk seemed to be about people and politics rather than books (publishers are nice to authors at the Frankfurt fair, but we are quite superfluous there).

That night, at Blessing's 'bistro' dinner for six authors and five of his staff, politics of the past and present entirely ruled the occasion, the three eminent writers present expressing their endless misgivings about their then newly elected chancellor Gerhardt Schröder: he was too bland, too handsome, too often divorced – Germany needed a *man*. And the next morning, when former West German president Richard von Weiszäcker came by Blessing's stand to say hello, an applauding crowd collected. 'The only man of stature in Germany,' a man next to me said, sadly.

The sixty-odd actors, directors, designers, musicians and dramaturgs in Bochum who, astonishingly for that comparatively small city, maintain a repertory of twenty productions, are mostly young but of mixed provenance. I've been in Germany many times since reunification, but I've never felt quite so strongly the differences between West and East. Perhaps it is because theatre is among other things, the art of physically exposing emotions, the line between professional necessity and personal need often becomes very fine. Also, the particularly raw emotions of Pinter's *Ashes to Ashes* carried over, for me too, from rehearsals to hours of talk about the universal issues Pinter raises, of submissive and possessive relationships, of cruelty committed, permitted, suffered and remembered, all of which seemed horribly close to this group, especially to those from the East. One red-haired actress of about forty said both her grandfathers and her father had been in the SS. 'When I was fifteen, I decided to make them tell me the truth. I know everything they did. And I still can't sleep at night.'

The director, Dimiter Gotscheff, a hugely talented and moody Bulgarian, loves the play but was angry about the conversations it provoked, angry I think even about the fact that what provided the first spark for it for Pinter, was what the Nazis did, what Speer saw and felt.

'What about *us*?' he said. 'I have to live *my* biography; do you Westerners even *know* what Stalin did; do you read *anything* about us?' Another actor who had grown up in East Germany said, 'What do they know here [in West Germany]? They talk democracy: what they really want is authority and order, the German tragedy.' Its two parts were miles apart, this reunified Germany.

History remained inescapable on Sunday, my last day on this trip, when my friends Martin and Cordula Bormann who live near by came to lunch with me. He is Bormann's oldest son, Hitler's godson. In May 1945, then fifteen, he very nearly killed himself. But he decided to live, became a Catholic, a priest, a missionary in Africa, then, leaving the priesthood, became a teacher and married Cordula, whose moral and spiritual development had strangely paralleled his. Nobody could know more, feel more than Martin does against what the Nazis were and did. And at last – yet again, the pervasiveness of this history in the lives of the young – German and Austrian schools and colleges are asking him to speak to their children. 'I don't have to invent or even describe,' he said. 'I just read them bits from Hitler's speeches, about the teaching of the young. ' "I want no intellectual education," Hitler said. "Knowledge will spoil the young for me. It is control they must learn; it is the fear of death they must conquer: this is what creates true freedom, creativity and maturity for the young . . ." When I read this to boys and girls now,' Martin said, 'and tell them how Hitler owned us from the age of ten, and how, he said, going from *Pimpf* [a junior Hitler Youth] to "Hitler Youth", to "Workers Front", into the SS, SA and *Wehrmacht* would make us his for ever, they can identify with what it was. They can relate it to their own so very different lives and understand the absolute arbitrariness of this one-man dictatorship which we, who were all his and never free, never could.'

I looked at Martin's open ascetic face. He is shining proof of the capacity of mind and spirit to overcome genetic inheritance and childhood influences to become mature, human and, yes, free.

July 1990

The setting is the quiet, comfortable living room of a house in a small town nestled in the gentle hills of the Ruhr; the occasion, a seemingly innocuous gathering of middle-aged men and women, grouped around a table laden with coffee and cookies. Yet the Germans here today have come to relive a nightmare, to dredge up events that occurred forty-five years ago, during the Second World War. Some bear household names, and the stories they tell, the pain they convey, seem almost irreconcilable with their apparent 'ordinariness'.

They are, one might say, Hitler's children – the sons and daughters of those who accomplished his terrible work. For half a century they have been unable to talk to anyone about their feelings, their knowledge, their relationships with their parents. And as one listens to them, as one sees their loneliness, a single thought keeps recurring: How many more like them are there?

Gunild, now fifty-seven, hasn't slept without sedatives for decades. She is small, round, charming, with a smile that seems permanently painted on her face. In 1924, one of Gunild's brothers died; he was three months old and had a club-foot. She thinks – though she can barely bring herself to say it – that her father (a doctor, now dead), who served a prison sentence for having been in charge of the euthanasia programme in the Rhineland and for 'clearing' the Cologne area of Jews, had his handicapped son killed.

Others in her family – siblings, cousins and one of her own children

– have since died. Only her twenty-four-year-old daughter is left. 'Is God exacting payment from us?' Gunild asks, and trembles for her daughter's life.

Dirk turned fifty this year. His father – head of the Gestapo in Braunschweig, where thousands of forced labourers died at the Göring plant – was hanged in 1948. Twenty years later, Dirk married Lena, a Russian girl from Israel. 'Children?' he says. 'No, we have no children. How could we?' And Lena cries. 'I would have liked a child,' she says.

Though now nearing fifty, Gonda, who is Dutch, still belongs, in the eyes of the older generations in Holland, to a group of children described since the end of the war as 'the Wrong Ones'. Her father collaborated with the Nazis during the occupation. 'I was only two and a half when the war ended,' she says, 'and throughout my childhood, we were isolated – I never knew why.'

Forty-nine-year-old 'Monika' (an assumed name) was an illegitimate child and never met her father, though he has dominated her thoughts for years. She spent the first three years of her life in a Children's Home of the *Lebensborn*, the organization set up by the SS to encourage the breeding of 'perfect' Aryan children. Monika remembers the nurses there as kind, even tender. Life after the war was more difficult. She lived with her mother, a lonely, secretive woman, who claimed Monika's wonderful father was missing in action. Monika believed that her father, like so many others, was a POW of the Soviets and that he, like other fathers, would eventually come home. In the meantime, she tried to make her mother love her. '*Now* you are happy to have a girl, aren't you?' she asked after a spectacular scholastic success at the age of eight. 'No,' her mother answered, 'I am not.' In this cold environment, all of Monika's childish dreams and longings were focused on the loving and warm father her mother constantly cried for. Every time someone came to the door, she would run to watch her mother open it, hoping to catch her parents' first words to each other; every time her mother baked a cake, Monika would put a bit of hers aside for him.

In fact, she would later learn, by that time her father was already dead – executed for war crimes. He had been an early member of the SS and an organizer of the first nationwide pogrom, the *Kristallnacht* ('Night of Broken Glass'), in November 1938, when carefully synchronized violence against Jewish people and their property erupted in major German cities. As the commanding SS general of the *Einsatzgruppen* (the Special Action Groups) in the Soviet Union and the Baltics in 1941, he had been in charge of the murder of half a million or more Jews and tens of thousands of non-Jewish Russians. He was hanged in Riga in February 1946.

'I only discovered the details about eight years ago,' says his daughter, 'and I think it's true that as of then I always wanted to punish, hurt myself; if I had this father, I told myself . . . I must pay for it.'

Thomas Heydrich, very young-looking at fifty-nine, is a well-known actor who reads and sings all over Germany, mostly from works by Jewish poets. He has many memories of his uncle, Reinhard Heydrich, who was also his godfather, but never knew him as head of the Gestapo, creator of the 'Final Solution', and 'Protector of Bohemia-Moravia', where he was assassinated on 6 June 1942.

Thomas was eleven years old at the time. For him, Reinhard Heydrich was his father's much-loved older brother, with whom his parents had regularly played bridge; he was also a fine musician, and on Thomas's birthday and for Christmas he would send his chauffeur with extravagant presents.

'I was angry when he was killed,' says Thomas, 'because I was, of course, at that time a "fire and flame" *Pimpf*.' He stops and shakes his head. 'Well,' he continues, 'he was a kind of hero to us; we didn't know anything about politics: we only knew that he was a fantastic sportsman – fencing champion, I think . . . and, of course, always in the papers, standing next to the Führer, our idol. Well, you know . . . And I was sad when he was assassinated because I knew my father would be very sad. My uncle was a very good, tender father,' he says thoughtfully. 'It's almost a cliché now, isn't it, about these appalling men? But that doesn't make it any less true – one just doesn't like to think of it. Can you imagine? Tender?' He repeats the word bitterly.

Martin Bormann, now sixty, was Hitler's favourite godson. Like Thomas, Martin was a passionate Nazi child, immensely proud of his important father, who was Hitler's personal assistant. (The author Hugh Trevor-Roper has described the elder Martin Bormann as 'the most powerful, the least public, and the most mysterious of all the Nazi leaders . . . In Hitler's last years . . . Bormann reigned undisputed over the court . . . he built around the Führer "a Chinese wall" impenetrable except by his favour.')

Bormann co-signed Hitler's last will and took part in the bizarre burning of the bodies after the double suicide of Hitler and his wife of one day, Eva Braun, during the afternoon of 30 April 1945. He then escaped from the bunker two nights later with the remaining members of Hitler's circle. For twenty-eight years afterward, the secret services of the Western powers were inundated with reports of sightings of Martin Bormann: in South America, in Switzerland, in Spain. In 1973 the Frankfurt police issued a statement that a skeleton discovered in Berlin was Bormann's. 'But I have never been sure of that,' says his oldest son. 'Their proof was unconvincing.'

For fifteen-year-old Martin, the shock of 'the end' was enormous. The night he learned that Hitler had died, eight people in the group with which he was hiding – high officials of the party chancery – committed suicide. 'I, too, was close to killing myself,' he says. 'But I do think that, as time went on, the children of people who had not been at the very top had a much more difficult time than we had: they were left surrounded by silence and lies. In our world, lies were impossible after the war – we knew where our fathers had stood. All we had to do was watch and read and listen, and accept the truth.'

Martin Bormann learned the truth while living under a false name with devoutly Catholic Austrian peasants. 'I learned from them what is a good man,' he says. In 1947 he was received into the Catholic Church. For years afterwards, he lived in fear: his father hated Jews – but he hated Catholicism even more. Convinced that he was still alive and in hiding, 'I was afraid he would have me liquidated because I had become a Catholic.'

It took an outsider of sorts to bring together Hitler's children – all of them, I'm bound to say, exceptional people – and encourage them to take issue with the past. Six years ago, a forty-six-year-old Israeli psychologist, Dan Bar-On, on a visiting professorship at the West German University of Wuppertal, realized that not only had the relationships between Hitler's aides and their children never been thoroughly researched, but four decades after the end of the 'thousand-year' Reich the subject was still taboo in Germany.

In 1985, Bar-On had ads inserted in the local papers asking for 'persons whose parents were in the SS or took an active part in ... persecution and extermination' to contact him. A surprising number of people replied. Bar-On, the Israeli-born son of assimilated German Jews who fled Hamburg in 1933, spent the next two years interviewing forty-nine children of perpetrators in Germany. His book, *Legacy of Silence*, tells (anonymously in all but one case) the stories of thirteen children.

They, who had never spoken to anyone of their terrible legacy, except perhaps to their life partners, agreed to talk to Bar-On, they told me, primarily for two reasons: he was not only an Israeli and a descendant of their fathers' victims, as they were the descendants of the victimizers, but also an academic, a scientist belonging to a 'caring' discipline, who, by 'caring' about them and their feelings, might ease the terrible weight of transferred guilt they carried.

Bar-On's original interest was complicated by a built-in resistance to all things German and although he knew it to be irrational, especially to the children of the Germans who had killed or been instrumental in the murder of his people. The most moving aspect of his undertaking, I found, was the change that gradually took place in him. The pain and the manifest honesty of those he interviewed slowly allowed Bar-On to drop some of his own reserve and lower the barriers of his prejudices. Slowly he came to see them as individuals in dire need, rather than as Germans tainted by their parentage – so much so that his real triumph was perhaps not the publication of the book itself but a conference a year earlier in Wuppertal, which many of the 'children' attended in a show of mutual support. It was there that Bar-On initiated the notion of a self-help group, which would continue the healing process.

Nine 'children' joined this group – the first and only such undertaking in Germany to date. Eight of these, several now under their real names, agreed to be interviewed for this article, a decision they courageously made so that others in the same position might feel able to 'come out' of the isolation their parents had imposed on them.

The guiding German spirit behind the group is Konrad Brendler, a professor of education at the University of Wuppertal and a good friend of Bar-On. His own, Catholic parents – bakers by profession – were not Nazis. 'But I, too, a few years ago, found myself looking into their past with different eyes: not, you see, for what they did, but for what – despite their religious commitment – they did *not* do.'

Brendler's family lived in Breslau when he was a child. He recently provoked a confrontation by asking his parents what they remembered about the *Kristallnacht*. 'My father said that the shop next door had been plundered that night and that the owners disappeared – he assumed they had emigrated. He had bought their piano for 300 marks. He added that he had told the movers to drive around the block and bring it from the opposite side so that people wouldn't know he'd bought it from Jews. I asked him whether he knew what happened to Jews when they were removed.

'"Well, they just left," he said, implying it was all voluntary. And my mother – who had been in the habit of slipping unauthorized bread and rolls to Jews she knew – said, "No, don't you remember that transport of Jews we saw in the Klosterstrasse, and on it were our two young doctors – the ones who looked after the children? They weren't on it by choice." And she started to cry. And my father made the sort of disparaging gesture I remember well from my childhood, when he regularly mocked and beat me for the sin of sensitivity. '"Nonsense," he said to my mother, just as he had always said to me. "You are quite wrong. Those doctors weren't among those people at all – they had long been gone." You see, even now, he couldn't face the truth. He had to look away now just as he had looked away then.

'I have come to ask myself whether the guilt of our parents' generation isn't finally much more encompassing than we thought, with those who "merely" did nothing only fractionally less guilty than those who were actively involved. But, facing that, I also have to look at myself: if my father was basically a coward, and, in his attitude towards me, his least assertive son, a bully, what am I? What – I say it deliberately, as a German – are my potentials under pressure?'

To Brendler, the taboo that parents of the Hitler generation have imposed on their children – whether actively or passively – is not due to shame or feelings of guilt. 'More than anything else, our actions and reactions in Germany – then as now – are due to our mania for *Anständigkeit* (respectability, propriety). It both dictates and exalts conduct at the price of conscience.'

He cites as the most glaring and appalling demonstration of this inverted sense of values Himmler's speech to SS leaders and gauleiters on 4 and 6 October 1943 in Posen, in which he explained in detail the reasons and methods behind the extermination of the Jews. Himmler said he had not considered it justified to exterminate men while permitting their potential avengers – women and children – to live. Logic dictated that the women and children be eliminated, too. 'I think I can say that this – the most difficult order we have been issued so far – was executed without allowing our men . . . to suffer any damage in mind or in spirit,' Himmler told his audience. 'The danger was very real: the line between the two potentials – to become cruel and heartless and to lose respect for human life, or else to turn soft and break down – is incredibly fine . . . To have persisted and at the same time . . . to have remained decent men . . . this is a page of glory in our history which has never been written and is never to be written . . . We must take this secret with us to the grave.

'May I invite you to join us for refreshments next door,' Bormann said when Himmler had finished.

'What I cannot understand,' says Bormann's son, talking about the far-right elements now surfacing in East Germany, 'is how anyone can still defend National Socialism, when – quite aside from living witnesses – the records of these speeches exist in the archives.'

Martin Bormann is tall and thin, with close-cropped grey hair and an ascetic face which belies the humour and warmth that become quickly apparent when he is with people he trusts. The group, I found, treats him gingerly. Although most are children of high-level Nazis, the son of Hitler's closest assistant – who in addition carries his father's name – stands out. Why didn't he ever change his name? 'For two years after the war,' he replies, 'I lived under another name, Martin Bergmann. But as I learned to understand what had happened and became my own person, I decided my name was part of me, as my father and the past were part of me, and I had to live with it.

'My father was very strict,' he continues, 'and strictest with me, because I was the oldest.' In 1940, when Martin was ten, his father heard of a notation in his son's report card from the Berchtesgaden school he attended: 'Lazy; could do better.' Bormann ordered that the boy be sent at once to Feldafing, an élite military-type boarding school of which he himself was chairman. 'Well, that was difficult,' Martin says. 'You see, all the others had been selected specifically for their academic qualifications or else for excellence in sports; I was just *put* there.' Would he say, looking back, that the school brainwashed the students? He smiles. 'They didn't have to brainwash us – there was no boy there who wasn't pre-conditioned. It was quite as strict as my father wanted for me. I never resented it. Well, almost never.'

There was one occasion, he says, when he did feel bitter. He was thirteen, and, as had become the custom for him as Hitler's godson, when he came home on leave he was summoned to a special audience. Wearing his Feldafing uniform he stood at attention and raised his arm in the formal salute. 'But I made a mistake,' he says. 'Instead of the prescribed "Heil, mein Führer," I said, "Heil Hitler, mein Führer," and before I knew it, my father slapped my face so hard I thought my jaw had cracked, and tears came to my eyes – that too was taboo. I was mortified. Why did he have to do that, right in front of the *Chef*?'

His father periodically inspected the school. 'I was proud of him,' Martin remembers. At one point, when there seemed to be irregularities in the school provision accounts, his father ordered him 'to watch certain members of the kitchen staff. No, I didn't think he was using me as a spy, only that he trusted me enough to confer a difficult job on me.'

From 1941, when Martin was eleven, until the war's end, he spent summers working on the land, and saw his father only rarely. 'It was then very special,' he says. 'Once in 1943, on an estate in the Rhineland, I was allowed to go riding with him. I had a Russian pony, which, of course, couldn't keep up with his big horse, but he'd wait for me. It was a wonderful summer.'

The field hands he worked with there were Polish POWs. 'There were no guards, no problems; they ate with the German staff.'

If the Polish POWs at the farm fared well, were he and his school friends aware that this was not the norm? 'Well, yes,' he says. 'Our school, you see, was quite near Dachau, and there was a prisoner detachment that worked in construction just next to our school. And they were really ill-treated by their Kapos. But that meant that we hated the Kapos, who were prisoners too, you see, not the SS.'

On 23 April 1945, with the Allied forces advancing, Feldafing school was abruptly closed; the other boys were given 100 marks each and told to find their own way home. Martin was taken to join some of his father's staff at a village inn near Salzburg. 'It was very small,' he remembers of the inn's saloon, where the group had gathered. 'We were tightly packed together. It's impossible now to convey the atmosphere. The worst moment was when, at two o'clock in the morning of 1 May, the news of Hitler's death came through. I remember it precisely ... but I can't describe the stillness of that moment, which lasted ... for hours. Nobody said anything, but people started to go outside, first one ... then there was a shot ... then another, and yet another ... Not a word inside, no other sound except those shots from outside, but one felt that all of us would have to die.'

And so finally Martin, too, took the gun he had been given and stepped outside. 'My world was shattered; I couldn't see any future at all. But there was another boy out there – he was 18 – a good bit older than I. We sat down on some logs. The air smelled good, the birds sang, and we talked ourselves out of it. If we hadn't had each other at that moment, both of us would have gone – I know it.'

Unsure what to do, he fell in with a column of the Führer-Leibstandarte, Hitler's personal guard regiment. On 8 May, as they were debating forming 'Werewolf' groups to fight as partisans in the mountains, he and some others came down with food poisoning. 'It was destiny, I think, that made me collapse outside a mountain farm,' he says. 'The peasants had no idea who I was, but they took me in as if I were their own son.'

Every day that summer, the farmers sent him up to the *Alm* – the mountain pasture – with the cattle. 'It was quiet and beautiful; I was alone and could think, and later also read books I borrowed from the nearest library. In the evening, when I came down, the peasant gave me his paper to read. It was a liberal paper, the *Salzburger Nachrichten*, which factually and unemotionally – the only way I could bear to read about it – told the truth about what the Nazis had done.'

A year later, Martin found a small announcement of his mother's death. 'By that time a great deal had happened, not so much *to* but *in* me. I had seen how good men live, how good men *are*. Querleitner, the peasant, was what I wanted to become: a real Christian.'

In January 1947 a priest accepted him for instruction, and on 4

May, his real name now revealed to the peasant who became his godfather, Martin Bormann was received into the church. What had Querleitner said when the boy told him he was Bormann's son? 'He said, in his broad Austrian accent, that being my godfather was the only thing he shared with Hitler.' After that a priest found his eight brothers and sisters for him; they had been taken in by different families in the South Tyrol. 'At Easter 1950 I was able to go and see them for the first time.'

In September 1947 he had been accepted by the Trappists to begin his religious training, and in 1951 he joined the order of the Heart of Jesus. Until 1971 Martin Bormann was a priest, much of the time as a missionary in Africa. Then, having decided that he was no longer suited to the essential narrowness of religious life, and also having seriously injured his legs in a car accident which threatened to leave him entirely dependent on his order, he was granted a dispensation to leave the priesthood. A year later he was given permission to continue to teach religion and Germanics. By that time, he had been working for several years with a missionary nun who had had similar doubts about her vocation and, prior to his decision and independent of it, had asked her order to release her from her vows.

It had been Cordula who had nursed him back to health. They have now been married for nineteen years and live a quiet and modest life in a small modern flat overlooking a hilly village in the Ruhr. It is filled with hundreds of minutely organized books, many of them theological works, and reference materials. Contrary to a first impression of reserve, they turn out on closer acquaintance to be gentle people, openly tender with each other and concerned about the world.

Martin Bormann has not always been sure of his commitment to the therapy group, however. During one meeting, he announces that, after a year and a half of attending, he might drop out – he didn't feel he had much more to contribute.

'You always speak of contributing *to* the group,' Lena tells him. 'Has the group not given you anything?'

Martin doesn't respond to this challenge, and the talk continues around for a while, almost as if he weren't there. And then, as sometimes happens when people sit together for a long time, there is a sudden silence and, just as suddenly, Martin's quiet, grave voice speaks into this silence. He begins to tell a story he has never told to anyone before, a story he has evidently hidden even from himself in that part of the mind where human beings store intolerable memories.

It happened, he says, late in the war, when he was at home on the Berghof (in Berchtesgaden) during a school holiday. Himmler's secretary and mistress, Frau Pothast, who had borne him two children, then about two and three years old, invited Martin's mother to bring him and his thirteen-year-old sister, Eike, over for tea.

The old farmhouse where Himmler had installed her only a few months before was about a twenty-minute drive in one of the special large black Mercedeses at the disposal of Hitler's top echelon and their families. 'Our chauffeur waited outside and we walked in through a nice wild sort of garden,' Martin says as the memory takes shape. 'And she gave us hot chocolate and cakes. It was nice.' Later, Frau Pothast said she would show them something interesting, a special collection Himmler kept in the house. She led the way up to the attic.

'When she opened the door and we flocked in, we didn't understand at first what the objects in that room were – until she explained, quite scientifically, you know. Tables, and chairs, made of parts of human bodies. There was a chair . . .' Martin's voice becomes toneless as he describes it; the people around the table have frozen into stillness, and I feel my body go prickly. 'The seat was a human pelvis, the legs human legs – on human feet. And then she picked up one of a stack of copies of *Mein Kampf* – all I could think of was that my father had told me not to bother to read it, as it had been outdated by events. She showed us the cover, made of human skin, and explained that the Dachau prisoners who produced it used the *Rückenhaut* – the skin of the back – to make it.'

The children fled, he says, his mother pushing them ahead of her down the stairs. 'Eike was terribly upset, and I was, too,' he tells us. 'About a year later, when I saw photographs of the horrors of the camps, and people said they must be faked, having seen this, I knew it was all true: I had no doubts at all, ever . . .' His face is red with stress.

'The swine,' says Dirk.

'To call those people swine,' says Martin Bormann's son, 'is an insult to swine.'

'I loved my father,' he tells me weeks later when we come back to this story late one spring evening at his home. 'I certainly didn't identify this horror with him.' Yet he realizes that for years he entirely suppressed one of the most traumatic experiences of his life. 'I just buried it. It proves the usefulness of the group, doesn't it?' (Eventually he will decide to remain a member.) Does he think Hitler ordered these atrocities performed? 'All big decisions were made only by him, but I doubt that he would have initiated anything like this. Why should he?' Martin says. 'He had others for that. He hated details. He was a great vacillator – I heard my father say this to someone when he didn't know I was around.'

What weighs most heavily on him, he says, is that it was mainly his father who built the protective wall around Hitler that in the final months kept the reality of the war at bay. 'The war was never mentioned at home – perhaps it was his way of protecting us. But I remember one occasion, late in the war, when he told us about a train trip with Hitler. For the first time, Hitler – and my father too – saw the terrible consequences of the bombings. My father was not only appalled himself, but really shaken by Hitler's despair. He said he was convinced that Hitler had to be totally insulated from knowledge about these events if he was to continue to function. Perhaps,' says Martin sadly, 'if he hadn't so insulated him, it would have been stopped sooner.'

In deciding to take issue with their family history, the 'children' have risked alienating their relatives and friends.

'Several of the people I talked with found themselves virtually ostracized as a result of talking,' says Dan Bar-On. 'Not because they talked to *me*, but because they talked at all. Once they started, of course, they couldn't stop; they talked at home, to their partners, to their friends – their children too. There are marriages that broke up under the strain, children who left home, friends who withdrew. But then again, it brought others to the point of realizing they had to speak out.'

'Last night,' Gunild says during one meeting, 'my sister, hearing that I was coming here today, suddenly told me that *she* couldn't stand living with this past any more. She has been a doctor all her life, took over my father's practice twenty years ago, and has just retired. For all these years, the authorities have managed to keep secret that medical schools in the Federal Republic have been using specimens for the past forty-five years that were obtained from the corpses of the people the Nazis murdered. Now it has come out, and they are having to remove them from the university pathology labs. For my sister, sixty-six years old, the realization that she learned her profession – which our father so fatally abused – using specimens obtained under those conditions is bringing her close to suicide. Is it surprising that she is suicidal and that I, despite a wonderful husband and child, live in despair, addicted to tranquillizers?'

Some partners resent this return to the past by those they love; some fear it; some are just impatient with it. Cordula Bormann – against her better judgement, she tells me – accompanied Martin to a recent session. 'I got horribly irritated with their emotional self-indulgence,' she says, 'and I didn't think it was good for Martin at all.' Like Konrad Brendler's parents, Cordula's family were devout Catholics, but put their principles into practice by providing a home to a young Jewish girl for the duration; she survived. 'I feel totally out of place here,' she tells the group at one point. 'I was shocked when one of you described the intense mourning she was experiencing. Is mourning so important to you that it must remain a living part of your life? If you had said that, having taken issue with the problem of your parentage, you can begin to reduce your mourning, then this, it seems to me, would indicate progress. But the feeling I get is that you revel in the mourning, and it makes me very uncomfortable, so I won't come again.'

Resentments such as this – familiar to all therapists – are mutual: people in the 'working-through' process often react badly to criticism from outside.

'In Holland,' says Gonda, 'we get it from both sides. The young, like my children, for instance, resent our preoccupation with the past – partly because it bores them, partly because they feel emotionally deprived by it. Then there is the other side of the coin, the children of the Resistance, who tell us, "It's very difficult to talk to you – just think, perhaps your father betrayed mine during the occupation." And I answer, "Yes, that's quite possible, but don't you think it might be difficult for *me* to talk to *you*, given that perhaps my father betrayed yours?" They look at me with amazement – it has never occurred to them.'

Monika – the daughter of the *Einsatzgruppen* general – feels ambivalent about the sessions. 'When the date for the next meeting approaches, I'm invaded by anxiety. Am I right to go on exposing myself to this pain? On the other hand, I know that I *have* to take issue with it. I've been doing it intensively for three years now. For a long time, if anyone asked me about my past, I lost my voice. Now it's the opposite – if I don't answer, I suffocate.'

Even so, she doesn't attend the next meeting. 'There was something wrong with my car,' she tells me a few days later at her apartment in Cologne, a beamed attic full of colour, with low furniture, lots of cushions and plants. 'But I suppose I *could* have found a way to go if I had really wanted to.' Why didn't she?

'I think it is because I sense a fascination with evil in the group. I understand it; I had this, too.' A few years ago, Monika took a year's unpaid leave from her teaching job and devoted it to research about her father. She was driven by the need to find answers to a host of questions: 'What happened inside these men once they were shorn of their power and confronted with their crimes? Did they admit their awful guilt to themselves? Above all' – and this is the question that preoccupies all of them – 'were they sorry? Did they repent before they died?'

But Monika no longer feels the urgency of such questions. 'Having so long sought absolution for the evil that might have been transferred to me from him, I feel I'm beyond that now,' she says. 'I have read everything, I have worked in all the archives; I went to Riga to talk to his victims and others who attended the trial.' She even persuaded her mother – who had never in so many words admitted realizing what the man she loved had done – to come to Riga with her. 'I need for her to accept it,' Monika says, 'not, for heaven's sake, in order to see her suffer, or even to make her share my suffering, but for herself, as an individual, as a woman.'

No, her mother has not come along to any of the group meetings. 'But you know, I honestly think she understands, almost by a kind of osmosis.'

All of the children – in keeping with Konrad Brendler's '*Anständigkeit*' observation – have struggled against the determined blocking mechanisms that continue to suppress or distort the truth about the war years. 'My mother was very poor,' says Monika, 'so all I had to wear were the cast-offs from her relatives, who were terrible to me. But it wasn't because of what my father had done – I don't think they cared any more than any of that generation in Germany did. They punished me for being illegitimate – it wasn't "proper". When they gave me something for my birthday or Christmas, they always left the price tag on it: it was never for more than fifty or ninety-eight pfennig – that's what I was worth.'

'Of all the men who were tried,' says Gonda of the Dutch collaborators, 'only two admitted what they did – my parents to this day don't admit to any wrongdoing. My father was not a politician or a physician or a military officer. He was a ship designer who was ideologically a collaborator. Feeling as strongly as I do, I can understand that if my parents admitted the extent of their commitment to this terrible ideology – and its consequences – they would have to commit suicide. So, as they couldn't, and can't, confrontation with the truth has been left to their children.'

Another participant describes to the group the goodbye letter her father wrote before his execution. 'He spoke only of God. In 1936, expediency dictated that they leave the Church. In 1946, propriety made it advisable to rejoin. And when, finally, he is sentenced to death for deeds which go against every law and concept of God, he babbles on about finding his consolation and assurance of eternal life in God. Isn't it enough to make you sick?'

'Wouldn't you think,' says Dirk, whose father was also executed, 'that if a father is about to take his final walk he would have the courage to say, "My son, I did terrible things and am now paying for it with my life – you must learn from it never to do anything so bad." If he'd written that, it would really have helped. But they were incapable of shame or repentance and therefore left us alone with nothing but the heritage of their awful guilt.'

Virtually all of the children of Nazis told me of their contempt for elders who insisted, to the end of their lives, that they knew nothing, saw nothing, and even suspected nothing reprehensible during the Nazi time, while their children remembered with amazing clarity not only events but also their reactions to those events.

Thomas Heydrich's family lived on the exclusive Prinzregentenstrasse in Berlin when he was small. The large house next door – 'It had lovely big steps on which I played as a child' – belonged to Jews. 'It was burned down during the *Kristallnacht*,' he says. 'I watched furniture being thrown out of a window, including a piano – imagine, a *piano*. I remember wondering why anybody would do this rather than calling the fire brigade. I mean, our family was musical and I knew those neighbours were, too. I asked, but was told to hush.' Very shortly after that he noticed placards on shops and park benches: JEWS NOT PERMITTED. 'I remember them, and they do, too,' he says. 'They are liars – a generation of liars.'

In 1941 his father, a journalist, suddenly asked for a posting to the Eastern Front as a private in an army information unit. 'He was by nature a very happy, jolly sort of man – I adored him,' Thomas says. 'I think now that his reason for wanting to get away from Berlin was that he had begun to have doubts. What I remember very clearly is that every time he came home on leave he was more depressed. My mother often asked why he was so sad, and he would invariably answer, "We'll talk about it after the war." I think,' Thomas says, 'there is to this day a mass denial in Germany about what millions of German soldiers witnessed in the East. It is a very important part of our unresolved pathology, which – by lies and silence – has created a historical falsehood: a myth of an "ordinary war". These millions of men saw – and some marginally participated in – the murder of literally hundreds of thousands of men, women and children, Jews and non-Jews. This is not what all the films and tens of thousands of newspaper articles have been about, which is the killings in gas chambers in the camps in occupied Poland. This is what happened in hundreds of cities and towns in Russia as soon as the Nazis captured them: they drove all the Jews, men, women, and children – and also all local communist administrators, teachers, priests and intellectuals of all kinds – to the outskirts of the towns, and they shot them. The gassings in Poland were done behind walls, barbed wire, secretly; but these murders – the official orders for which anyone can see in our historical archives – were committed openly. Nobody could avoid knowing about them. Afterwards, these soldiers, out of their own need, walled these horrors into recesses of their minds, where they festered and may well have affected all their subsequent feelings and actions. *That* is our country,' says Thomas.

He doesn't think his father knew the worst things his uncle had been responsible for until after Reinhard Heydrich's assassination. 'There is a photograph of my father at my uncle's state funeral in June 1942, standing in his sergeant's uniform between Hitler and Göring. Later that day an officer came bringing my father a thick letter from my uncle that had been found in his safe. He took it and went to his study. Hours later he came out, ashen-faced, with this sheaf of pages. He went into the kitchen, which still had an old wood stove, and burned them, one by one, very slowly, almost like a ceremony. There must have been a hundred pages. We all stood there watching and at the end, when he looked about to drop and my mother put her arms around him and asked him what was in the letter, he said, "Don't ever ask: I can't talk about it, ever – not until it's all over."'

Thomas now feels sure that in the letter his uncle explained to his father everything he was planning and justified everything he had done in the cause of Nazism. Thomas's conviction stems from the fact that his father, extraordinarily enough, then became an active anti-Nazi, using the printing facilities available to him to produce passports and other papers to spirit people – most of them Jews – out of Germany. In late 1944, believing himself discovered, he wrote a goodbye letter to his family and shot himself.

'I think that by this time he was so disillusioned, so hurt,' Thomas says, 'he thought that if the Gestapo had found out about him his death would be our best protection. We never knew whether he'd really been discovered – a prosecutor had come that evening and they'd spent all night in his study, talking. Shortly after that he killed himself.' Thomas didn't learn of his father's anti-Nazi activities until years later; at the time, he remembers, the family felt deserted and resentful. 'I understand him now, of course,' he says. 'But if he had stayed alive, it would have helped me very much: he would have shouldered the guilt I carried for twenty years. I would have been free . . .

'I began to feel this guilt when, only weeks after the war, I saw the photographs and read what had been done,' Thomas says. 'This feeling of responsibility only intensified over the next twenty years. I was, if you like, deputizing for all the others: my aunt [Reinhard Heydrich's widow], who felt proud of her husband; his three children, who – I cannot understand why – felt and feel nothing; my mother, who, having always instinctively disliked my uncle, was able to hide comfortably behind that early rejection. My father, of course, was no longer there. *Somebody* had to feel guilt for the devilish things my uncle had done.'

It is probably of psychological significance that Martin Bormann's son – referred to as 'Krönzi' for 'Kronprinz' (crown prince) at home and by his father's associates – sought his freedom after the fall of the Reich in the spiritual discipline of the Catholic Church. From the way he tells his story, there can be no doubt that the priests who took over the care of this desperately lonely boy saved his sanity, even his life, and taught him the quiet husbanding of his innate strength. He is perceptive, not only about others, but also about himself. 'It really was providential,' he says, 'that I found myself on my own when it all ended. I was such a passionate young Nazi, if I had been with my mother and siblings, I might well have got in the way of their development.'

As it is, all of Bormann's nine children came to reject their father's beliefs, though perhaps, on a moral and intellectual basis, none struggled as Bormann's firstborn did.

'My youngest brother – born in 1943 – opted out of it altogether,' Martin tells us. 'He says that he had nothing whatsoever to do with "that man." The fact of his having fathered him, he says, was merely a biological accident which doesn't commit him as a person to any connection with our father: as far as he is concerned, he is non-existent.'

There were several reasons, Martin says, why he and his siblings doubted that their father had died, as the Frankfurt prosecutors certified in 1973. 'The corpse they produced lacked any sign of an injury we knew – and the prosecutors didn't – our father had suffered just before the war. He had fallen off a horse and broken his collarbone. Pathologists told us it was impossible for this not to be visible on a skeleton, however long afterward. The Frankfurt prosecutors told me they had pursued over 4,000 trails. Perhaps they tired of it and this was a political burial.'

The many alleged sightings of Bormann over the years were very disturbing for his children, Martin says. And there was one they were inclined to believe. 'It came from a pre-war member of our parliament, Paul Hesslein, who had known him well for years. He says he met up with three riders on the Chilean border in the early 1970s and was pretty sure one of them was my father, particularly as he heard him say, "Wasn't that Hesslein?"'

Martin shrugs. 'If he *did* manage to save himself, I don't think he could have afforded to seek contact with us. Certainly, learning of the path I had taken, I would have been the very last person he would have communicated with. I think if he stayed alive he just went his own way, created a new life for himself.'

Martin is executor of Bormann's estate, or what survives of it – mainly his writings, letters to and from his wife, Gerda, and the complete record (later published as *Hitler's Tabletalk*) of Hitler's monologues during meals on the Berghof, in Berlin, and at his field headquarters, which upon Bormann's orders were taken down to be preserved for posterity. The material itself is almost entirely in the hands of the former Swiss banker, François Genoud, who immediately after the war managed to persuade both Hitler's and Bormann's then executors to sell him the copyrights. Although Genoud has had to fight many lawsuits to maintain his rights over the papers, there is general agreement that they were properly obtained and remain his. Genoud and Martin Bormann now [1990] find themselves in a stalemate over further publication of the documents. 'I deeply distrust Genoud's politics,' says Martin, 'and I would prevent at any price that anything over which we have control is used to whitewash National Socialism. My brothers and sisters agree with me.'

The crimes against the Jews under Hitler were of course the worst, 'and it is indeed because they *were* so awful that the world has concentrated so exclusively on them,' he says. 'But in a terrible way that makes it too easy on the Nazis. I think to identify Nazism exclusively with anti-semitism is very short-sighted. Our plans for the world were so wide-reaching, and so terrible, that we can only thank God we lost the war.'

Predictably, the group's most recent meeting, in late April, revolved around the developments in East Germany and the prospect of imminent reunification. 'When the issue first exploded last October,' said

Konrad Brendler, 'I suppose everybody in Germany – and the world – was euphoric. But since then other aspects have emerged.'

'The danger in East Germany,' Martin Bormann had observed earlier, 'is that while we in the West were able to develop slowly, through a fairly long process of apprenticeship, they have had fifty-seven years of unremitting, unrelenting life under dictatorships – it is naïve to think that the removal of a wall can automatically remove their blinkers.'

'Everybody,' Brendler says of the April gathering, 'was aware of, sensitive to, and afraid of the manifestations of nationalism we now perceive in East Germany.' The group was concerned about right-wing radicals popping up 'like mushrooms in the rain': worried about the tremendous antagonism displayed against foreigners; apprehensive about the resentments already building between the eastern and western portions of a still-divided nation: and, of particular relevance to the 'children', alarmed by the apparent search for individuals or groups on which to pin blame.

'The decision we have come to now,' said Dirk, 'is to *come out* altogether: to tell others what we are doing, and, on the basis of what we have learned over the past two years, to offer our help in setting up and running other groups around the country – Munich, Bonn, Hamburg . . .'

'And eventually,' added Brendler, 'also in Leipzig and East Berlin.'

'But I think we have to be very vigilant,' Martin Bormann said. 'We have to stop the rot wherever we find it. The moment one hears somebody say something offensive to human dignity in any way, whether against foreigners – as happens only too often now in West Germany – or people of other faiths or colour, one must protest and argue. These individual attitudes must never go unchallenged.

'Some fifty years ago,' he continued, 'a few people created horror, but far too many, knowing about it, tolerated it. It started then just as now – with graffiti, vulgar jokes, and knowing winks. Then it was the Jews, now it is the Turks and the Vietnamese. The obscenity of discrimination will only be stopped if we accept individual responsibility for never, in a single instance, allowing it to go unchallenged. That, I think, is our task – yes, as our parents' children.'

18

The Case of John Demjanjuk

February 2000

The trials of John Demjanjuk, accused first in Cleveland, Ohio, in 1981, and then in Israel from February 1987 to April 1988, of having been the dreaded Ukrainian guard at the extermination camp Treblinka known as 'Ivan the Terrible', were of great significance in several ways.

First because the by then forty-year-long tension between the United States and the Soviet Union, where Demjanjuk was born and bred (and whose documentation on him was essential for the 1987 American denaturalization trial) transformed a civil proceeding against a Ukrainian immigrant into an essentially political trial. The huge American and Canadian Ukrainian community who provided financial backing for him from the beginning to the very end, defended a man not because they did not believe he had done what he was accused of doing, but as one of their own who – so they had been persuaded by a well-organized support campaign – was being attacked by their traditional enemies, the communists and the Jews.

Secondly it was significant because the American Department of Justice, unable by law to conduct a criminal trial in such cases and in need of further congressional support to maintain their Office for Special Investigations (OSI), needed a show trial of such a case abroad to justify the OSI's expensive denaturalization proceedings. In order to achieve this, they used political pressure to force the Israelis to extradite Demjanjuk for a criminal trial in Israel on a charge which – doubts which they did not mention to the Israelis – they knew from early evidence from Germany and the Soviet Union was at the very least questionable.

Thirdly (though only indirectly touching that case) in Rome, in July 1998, 120 UN member states signed an undertaking towards the creation of an international court to prosecute 'Crimes against Humanity' and 'Genocide', but twenty-one countries abstained and tragically, seven – among them the United States, China and Israel – voted against the resolution, thereby almost fatally diminishing the authority of the potential court. (The United States also insisted that 'War Crimes' be deleted from the competence of the proposed court which without doubt had it existed, *should* have been the remit for Demjanjuk's trial.)

Lastly – probably the most important points for all future trials of this kind – the Demjanjuk case demonstrated, as no other case had done or has done since, on the one hand the difficulty for the accused in such cases to admit the truth, even if it might save them, and on the other the fragility of survivor eyewitness testimony.

I first heard about Demjanjuk in 1978 when I received a letter from a government agency in Washington asking whether I would assist them with information about former SS men in the extermination camp Treblinka who had figured in my book *Into That Darkness*. The letter said they might be required as witnesses in a denaturalization case of a former Ukrainian at present under investigation, and some knowledge of their personalities would be helpful.

I told them what I knew. Seven years earlier, in 1971, I had talked at length with the two men in question, SS Sergeant Franz Suchomel, a hefty man for whom Treblinka had manifestly been the high point of his life; and the small wispy Corporal Otto Horn, a one-time male nurse who told me he had only survived it by quite literally closing his eyes. 'I slept whenever I could,' he said. Well, maybe. Both men – no doubt to impress me with the harmlessness of their own conduct in Treblinka – had spoken about the savagery of the *Hiwis*, as the Ukrainian and Baltic SS auxiliaries were called.

They had mentioned no names, but Suchomel, with quite disgusting relish, told tales that made my blood run cold, of whippings and other violent pastimes the *Hiwis* liked to engage in. And they spoke, too, with contempt of the primitiveness of these 'volunteers from the East' who had never heard of modern lavatories or showers, or forks, knives and spoons at table, until introduced to these marvels of Western civilization by their German masters. Suchomel mentioned a Ukrainian who enjoyed mutilating women and forcing boys and men into sexual acts on their way to the gas chamber, but (until years later) never provided a name. 'If you saw such things,' I asked him, 'didn't you try to stop them?' He himself, he replied severely, worked in another part of the camp where such things didn't happen; otherwise, yes, of course he would have stopped them. Of course. And Otto Horn, who was stationed in the part of the camp that held the gas chambers – 'the upper camp' it was called – where he was in charge of supervising the burning of the bodies, said he had never seen anything like that. Indeed, how could he? He slept.

Further evidence from Suchomel and another SS guard I knew, Gustav Münzberger, who had been sentenced to twelve years in prison at the West German Treblinka trial for having been in charge of the gassings there, was to confuse the Israeli judges during the trial but came to be of considerable importance for the appeal.

By 1975 – two years before the Demjanjuk family was apprised of the US Department of Immigration's doubts about them – two things had happened: John Demjanjuk (he had changed his first name from Ivan), by then a well-established American citizen with three children, a good job and a nice house of their own, had written to his mother in the Ukraine, who had believed him dead, and told her he was alive and well in Cleveland, Ohio, USA. A conscientious woman, she promptly informed the Soviet authorities, who had for many years been paying her an allowance as the mother of a dead soldier. And Demjanjuk's wife, Vera, safe under the protection of her American passport, went on a visit home to the Ukraine with wonderful American presents for all her relatives.

It is uncertain whether it was the mother's honesty or the wife's sentimental visit that caused the Soviet authorities to check Demjanjuk's record. But whichever it was, they found two things: one, a statement made at a war crimes trial in Kiev in 1949 by a Ukrainian, Ignat Danilchenko, who had been a guard at the Sobibor extermination camp in Poland from March 1943, in which he mentioned Ivan Demjanjuk as his friend there. When Sobibor was closed, he had told the court, he and Demjanjuk were transferred as guards to the concentration camp of Flossenburg (and then to Regensburg) in

Germany to guard political prisoners until the end of the war. (Even though there is no reason to believe these two men were directly involved, it is worth remembering in this context that it was in Flossenburg, only weeks – in some cases days – before the war ended, that the Nazis hanged some of the most remarkable resisters in Germany, including Admiral Canaris, chief of the *Abwehr*, General Oster, his chief of staff, Count von Moltke, founder of the Christian resistance group, the 'Kreisau Circle', and the great theologian and pastor Dietrich Bonhoeffer.)

The Soviet war crimes court sentenced Danilchenko to twenty-five years in a gulag. After his release, Danilchenko married a Siberian girl and settled there. When, as I recount in the following pages, I flew there in 1990 to meet him, I was able to clarify a number of discrepancies in his statement to the war crimes court. It was only on my return through Moscow that the prosecutor who had been in charge of his case told me that following a request of the US government she had obtained a second statement from Danilchenko in 1979 without telling him the reason for it. This time he had described Demjanjuk in detail, and the description fitted exactly a 1942 photograph the Soviets had found of him. As Danilchenko had long completed his sentence by then and there was no reason for him to lie, she was sure he had spoken the truth.

The photograph the prosecutor mentioned was on the second item the Soviets had found in 1975, an identity card, No. 1393, from the SS training centre Trawniki in Poland, made out to Ivan Demjanjuk. On it he was wearing the habitual black uniform of SS auxiliaries. The ID placed him after his training at Trawniki first at Okszów in Poland, as a guard on a farm worked by Jewish women, and then, just as Danilchenko had said, in Sobibor in March 1943. Treblinka did not figure on the ID.

The Soviets sent this information to the United States in the late summer of 1975 after having had it printed in a Soviet weekly (which was also published in Ukrainian and English in the United States six months later), adding the information that Demjanjuk had fled to America and giving his Cleveland address.

The Demjanjuk family and his defenders would always claim that both the Danilchenko statement and the Trawniki card were fakes and that the whole thing was a Soviet plot against him in which the

American authorities 'controlled by communists and Jews' had joined. And there is no doubt that the Soviets did not like people who had emigrated to the West and that they enjoyed showing America up as a haven for war criminals. There is little doubt either that once their attention had been drawn to Demjanjuk by the family's communication with relatives in the Ukraine, they decided to use him in their propaganda games. What was always unlikely, and very damaging to his case, was the megalomaniac insistence of his defenders that the Americans' case against him was the result of a plot with – and faked documentation from – the Soviet Union.

My accounts of the unfolding story over seven years in *The Times*, the *Sunday Times*, the *Independent*, the *Sunday Correspondent*, and the *New York Review of Books*, which I have drawn together for this book, covered all aspects of the Demjanjuk case. As far as I know, this is now the fullest account of it to have appeared in print. With the preparations for the trials, the case stretched over seventeen years.

1986–1993

'Are you that terrible man, Ivan from Treblinka?' asked the defendant's American counsel. The large temporary courtroom in Jerusalem, normally a 350-seat theatre in a huge modern conference centre overlooking the city, was filled to capacity on that blisteringly hot day. The question, simultaneously translated into Hebrew and, in a just audible murmur, Ukrainian by the interpreter sitting next to the man in the dock, was followed by a kind of hiss of indrawn breaths, and then dead silence.

The audience in that hall – and the three judges on the dais – knew well that this was the high point at the end of the examination of John Demjanjuk. But the man on trial seemed oblivious of drama. And his answer – almost mechanical, he had said it so often – sounded, if anything, weary. 'I have never been in Treblinka, Sobibor, or Trawniki. I was a prisoner of war of the Germans.'

Three extermination camps – Belzec, Sobibor, and the largest and most efficient, Treblinka – were set up in 1942 in a sparsely populated forest area of occupied Poland (the first, in Chelm, was established in December 1941). The operation was code-named *Aktion Reinhard*. The staff for this operation – 92 German SS and 3,500 Ukrainian, Baltic and ethnic German auxiliaries – supervised the ghettos and transports in addition to their tasks as guards and executioners in the camps. Recruited in the terrible German POW camps in Russia, they were schooled, beginning in the winter of 1941, in the SS training camp Trawniki.

Between March 1942, when the operation began, and October 1943, when it ended, about 2,250,000 human beings were gassed in these three camps. In contrast to the huge labour camps like Auschwitz and Majdanek, no records were kept in the *Aktion Reinhard* camps – created solely for killing – and nothing tangible was allowed to remain. The corpses were burned on huge iron racks called 'roasts'; the bones not consumed by the fire were pounded until all that remained was grey ash and whitish powder which, mingled with the pale brown earth of the region, years later could not be told apart.

Of the more than a million Jews who entered Treblinka, barely sixty escaped death after a heroic revolt on 2 August 1943. Two months later – the buildings demolished, lupins and pine trees planted over the site, and a small farmhouse constructed from the bricks of the gas chambers, with an ethnic German farmer installed to deceive the approaching Russians – Treblinka was obliterated. The documentary record is scanty; our knowledge of it depends, in the final analysis, on human memory.

For months much of Israel had been glued to radio and television for seven and a half hours a day, four days a week, listening to the prosecution witnesses' tragic accounts and the historical and scientific testimony of the experts.

For a whole people one of the most terrible events of human history, which many of the old had refused to discuss for half a lifetime, and which their Israel-born children, most of them seasoned fighters now in their thirties and forties, had rejected as part of their heritage, was once again being brought to life. Within days of the beginning of the trial on 16 February last year, queues of many hundreds formed in the pink light of the Jerusalem dawn, many of them those tanned slender young for whom the Nazi murder of their people is no less 'just history' than for children everywhere. They watched and listened, and many cried, and yet, extraordinarily enough, for many months the predominant feeling among Israelis of all classes, young, middle-aged and old, remained one of doubt and unease.

For this big hunk of a man, in his one ill-fitting brown suit, sitting day after day flanked by two armed élite regiment soldiers, seemed oddly miscast as an arch-villain. We looked for indications in his face, his bearing and his conduct that would show that he was capable of the horrors he was accused of. On two fleeting occasions some of us thought we saw glimpses of latent brutality. But was it? Or was it only pent-up frustration at his own inability to influence events?

What we saw much more often was an East European peasant who, by no means unintelligent though unschooled, seemed unaware of possible animosity. He gaily, even boisterously, waved his manacled hands to the crowd on entering; as soon as the handcuffs were off, embraced his twenty-two-year-old son John who, by special permission of the court, sat behind him on the platform throughout the trial; blew kisses to his wife Vera on the rare occasions when she came to Israel, and to his two daughters Lydia, thirty-eight, and Irene, twenty-eight, who sat, increasingly distraught as the trial progressed, tense and pale in the front row; and tried time and again to joke with his guards and interpreters in his bits of prison-learnt Hebrew.

Watching him arrive in court every morning, one had almost to force oneself to remember the appalling acts of brutality and torture this apparently warm and simple man was charged with having committed – not on command but of his own free will: '. . . the Accused used to select individual victims among those going to their deaths for his torments . . . would stab [them] in various parts of the body, tore pieces of flesh from their limbs . . . used to beat "work-Jews" [and] shoot those who cried out or erred in counting the strokes of the whip [which was the rule] . . . [He] sliced off noses or ears thus condemning the prisoners to death as being "marked" or "stamped" . . . One day [he] ordered a prisoner to lie face down on the ground and . . . took a tool for drilling wood and drilled a hole into the prisoner's buttocks . . .'

Is it possible for men and women who witnessed such deeds happening in front of them for months on end ever to forget the face of the man who committed them? Or could a half-century of agonizing need for retribution against the figure of 'Ivan' – the personification of the monstrosity that was Treblinka – have drawn them unconsciously into identifying a physically similar but different man, as a symbol of that horror?

'I dream about him every night,' said Pinhas Epstein, still fine-drawn and slim, who was a strong, blond seventeen-year-old when he and his family arrived at Treblinka in 1942. His family was gassed immediately, but he was selected to live on as a 'work-Jew', burning bodies in the small 'upper camp', where the gassings took place and the corpses were disposed of.

'I find it difficult to compare Ivan to animals: when a lion is sated, a gazelle can go by and not be attacked. Ivan was never satisfied. The others, too, are in my nightmares, but Ivan most of all I could never forget. For eleven months I saw him, was near him every day . . . Now he is in this hall . . .' He cried, and was gently comforted by the judge. 'It is he,' he said, and buried his head in his arms.

The issue of testimony by traumatized survivors is central to the ongoing debate all over the Western world, including Britain, about the legitimacy of such trials decades after the events. It has plagued the West Germans who, despite bitter public opposition, have carried on Nazi crime (NS) trials for four decades, and has been the main impediment there to more convictions and tougher sentences.

Because of the lack of documentary evidence on the extermination camps, the validity of survivor testimony will have been the gravest question confronting the Israeli judges when they reviewed the 14,000 pages of the trial manuscript. For twelve years Demjanjuk has maintained that it is simply a case of mistaken identity. Never had he volunteered for any service with the Germans, worn their uniform, or used a whip, club, knife, or gun on their behalf. 'Ivan,' he says, 'was another man.'

Ivan and Wira Demjanjuk, then thirty-one and twenty-six, and their baby daughter Lydia, arrived in the United States on 9 February 1952, carrying all their possessions in two cardboard boxes. The IRO (International Refugee Organization) paid for their passage and found a farmer in Indiana who guaranteed them work and lodging.

For five lonely months Ivan tended pigs and sheep, and Wira kept house in their little room. But good friends from the old country, William and Anne Lishchuk, had settled into the large Ukrainian community in Cleveland, Ohio, and in July the Demjanjuks moved into their first proper home in a Cleveland suburb. On 1 August 1952, Ivan joined William at the Ford Motor Company, where – an excellent mechanic (he was trained by the US Army as a DP in Germany after the war) – he was to remain for over thirty years.

Now began their real American immigrant life – hard-working, money-saving, church-attending, child-bearing and, within four years, house-owning. Their social life centred on the St Vladimir Orthodox Church; they moved with the church, as it too became richer, to the white-collar suburb of Parma. And on 14 November 1958, Ivan and Wira – now John and Vera – with a minimum of English but a maximum of dedication to the stability and freedom of their new existence, became American citizens. 'The happiest day of our lives,' said Vera. A year later they had their second daughter, Irene, and their youngest child, John, arrived in 1965.

This was a close family, with few conflicts. 'We laughed a lot,' Irene told Michele Lesie, of the Cleveland *Plain Dealer*, after her father had been extradited to Israel. 'Now, it's almost like death: he's not here, so I find myself thinking of all the things I always loved about him.' Her parents, she says, rarely talked about the past. 'They wanted us to be American, not be burdened. Maybe they should have . . .'

The 'Demjanjuk case', unbeknown to the person most concerned, officially started in the winter of 1975. Since the early 1970s, members of Congress, Jewish organizations and the media had questioned the US government with increasing urgency about war criminals hiding out in the United States. Reacting to the pressure, the Department of Justice and the INS, their Immigration and Naturalization Service, put together a 'master list' of 205 names, mainly East Europeans, who had emigrated to the United States in the early 1950s and were suspected of lying about their wartime activities. Ivan Demjanjuk was No. 116 on this list because of crucial information he himself had supplied, almost thirty years earlier.

On 3 March 1948, in the IRO office in Landshut, southern

Germany, a Ukrainian-speaking interviewer had taken down Ivan and Wira Demjanjuk's particulars for their Displaced Persons eligibility forms. It was a vitally important occasion for the young couple, twenty-seven and twenty-two years old and married for six months. Everybody in the DP camps – where they had spent three years – knew the importance of these forms which determined not only their immediate future – the continuation of their DP benefits – but their suitability for emigration overseas. Most of them came well prepared, having exchanged information and tips on how to avoid possible dangers. Indeed, they were advised, by DP camp officials sympathetic to their plight, to find – that is to *invent* – suitable places in Poland or Czechoslovakia to put on the forms.

For the Yalta Agreement promised safety from repatriation if they were living outside Russia on 1 September 1939: the eligibility forms therefore – virtually forcing them into lies – had to show that they had left Russia before that date.

The questions on the all-important form were simple: date and place of birth, education and any useful skills, desired destinations and – a critical question – places of residence for the past twelve years. In Demjanjuk's case, his answers in 1948 would have to cover his life back to 1937.

He said on the form that from 1937 to 1943 he had lived and worked as a farmhand in Sobibor, in Poland. But Sobibor, little more than a railway halt in the forest, hardly appeared on pre-war Polish maps. What had made him think of Sobibor? How indeed had he found it as the place he wished to cite as his 'invented' pre-1939 residence?

It was only in 1942 that Sobibor had become noteworthy, when it was chosen as the site of one of the four extermination camps of the *Aktion Reinhard*. Even in 1948 its existence was still so clouded that its name on a form would not exclude Demjanjuk from DP status or emigration to the United States. But twenty-seven years later that name had become a monument of shame: its appearance on his official DP and immigration forms put him on the American 'master list' and together with other information, placed him eventually in the Jerusalem courtroom.

'*Why* did you put Sobibor?' asked Judge Dov Levin, president of the Israeli court, as mystified as the rest of us. 'If you needed a place of residence in Poland,' added Judge Dalia Dorner, 'why didn't you choose an anonymous city – Warsaw, Cracow – nobody would have known the difference. How could Sobibor, of all places, possibly come into your mind?'

Demjanjuk, red-faced and sullen, said that when he arrived at the International Refugee office that day, he 'had no idea' what he would put on the form. Another DP in the waiting-room had an atlas, he said, and he asked him for help. The man pointed at a map and said, 'Put down Sobibor – it's a good place – there were many Ukrainians there.' Judge Levin sharply quelled the titters in the audience. But scepticism was justified: the only Ukrainians in Sobibor were the guards at the extermination camp.

How then does he stand accused of being 'Ivan the Terrible' from Treblinka?

In 1975 the association of Demjanjuk with Sobibor was strengthened by information from Russia supplied through an American communist of Ukrainian descent, Michael Hanusiak, who publishes a Ukrainian-language paper in New York. He brought a list of Ukrainians the Russians claimed had committed war crimes: Demjanjuk, with the notation 'Sobibor' next to his name, was on the list. In addition Hanusiak claimed to have seen the Trawniki identity card in Demjanjuk's name, showing a posting to Sobibor.

In 1976, therefore, the US Immigration and Naturalization Service made up a spread of photographs taken from visa applications in the 1950s, including Demjanjuk and another Ukrainian, Feodor Federenko (also on both lists), who was suspected of having been a perimeter guard at Treblinka. The photographs were shown to twelve Sobibor survivors in the United States, none of whom recognized either man. They were then sent to Israel, where most Treblinka survivors have settled, to try for an identification of Federenko – not Demjanjuk. The two Israeli officials showing the photospread were thus startled when one Treblinka survivor, then another, and within two days a third, though recognizing Federenko too, excitedly picked out Demjanjuk's picture as 'Ivan from Treblinka'. John Horrigan, the US Attorney responsible for the investigation of suspects in the Cleveland area, was in Germany when he heard about the Israeli identifications, and drove the length of the country to reach the only Treblinka survivor living there, before there was any chance of his being tipped off from Israel – with which he had in fact no known association. But he, too, immediately identified Demjanjuk as Ivan.

Over the next two years eight survivors described the 1951 visa photograph of Demjanjuk as 'exactly' or 'very much' like Ivan the Terrible, though 'fatter', 'broader' or 'more mature'. Then Horrigan obtained from the Russians in 1978 a photocopy of the ID card from Trawniki, bearing Demjanjuk's name, personal details and a photo. This and seven other photographs of young men in black German uniforms they also sent were used for another round of identifications: all with the same result. Eventually ten people were positive that the photos were 'Ivan': all but one of them had worked near the infamous 'Ivan' in the upper camp at Treblinka – the 'death camp' – for many months. Interestingly, however, three other survivors of the upper camp – two in Israel and one in Australia – did *not* see a resemblance.

In August 1977, Demjanjuk received a formal letter from the US Department of Justice, charging that he was 'Ivan from Treblinka'. Unless he could explain the lies on his visa application his citizenship would be revoked. It requested a detailed reply within two months.

The news of the government charges broke the next day, and that afternoon the couple, distressed to the point of hysteria, allowed themselves to be interviewed on television.

'No, no,' Demjanjuk says when asked if the charges are true, 'I don't know nothing about it. I was no any place they writing. I was German prisoner . . .'

'Is not true, is not true,' Vera cries and faints against her husband, who jumps up, clasps his hands and begins to cry . . .

The Demjanjuks' plans for an untroubled future were now shattered. In 1975 they had bought their retirement home, a brick ranch house on a leafy street in the middle-class suburb of Seven Hills. Inside is a bit of the Ukraine: hand-carved animals, decorated vases, a portrait of the Ukrainian poet and nationalist hero, Taras Shevchenko, in the living room. The sun porch, which was the centre of the family's life when there was a family life, overlooks the two-acre garden which

Demjanjuk had made into a showpiece – a fine vegetable patch, fruit trees, rich red geraniums and rose bushes in all colours.

'They come to this country same as us – deaf and dumb,' says their friend Anne Lishchuk. 'But they learn . . . work hard . . . and now their life should be good. It isn't fair.'

'For as many years as we've known Johnny,' she went on, 'he never once said anything about all this. Even when we are sitting around with the vodka and telling stories, he never says anything about the war years.'

Demjanjuk's first defenders, as his case developed with ever-increasing publicity, were the Ukrainian community, particularly the members of his own church.

Bishop Antony Scharba, from the New Jersey headquarters of St Vladimir's, would later twice go to Israel for pastoral visits to Demjanjuk. 'In all the years we've talked with priests and parishioners about him, I haven't heard a single bad word against him.' He shook his head and searched for words. 'I cannot bring together the man I know, who really only wants to talk about matters of faith, and cries the moment his family is mentioned . . . and the man he is accused of being.' He raised his hands in helpless bewilderment. 'How *can* it be?'

Bishop Scharba very soon veers away from Demjanjuk, to talk about the aspect of these cases which makes the whole Ukrainian community feel unjustly attacked. 'Why do their witnesses, the moment they mention SS guards or the horrors they are alleged to have committed, invariably say "the Ukrainians"? Don't they know how many other nationalities were forced to work for the Germans?'

The considerable financial support the Ukrainians, both in the United States and in Canada, have given for the Demjanjuk defence over the years (by the end, amounting to about $1¾ million) is primarily due to the outrage they feel at having all Ukrainians tarred with this same appalling brush of collaboration and anti-semitism. It seems that their tragic history of conquest and oppression, and their awareness of the desperate circumstances under which some of their people assisted the Germans, has blinded them to the necessity for a clear distinction between three categories of Ukrainians under the Nazis: the millions forced into slave labour; the Ukrainian nationalists who, choosing what they thought was a lesser evil, took up German arms against the hated Soviets; and those few who readily – some indeed eagerly – assisted the Nazis in their worst crimes. Their fear of the consequences of both true and false accusations (there have been bombs, suicides and at least one assassination in the wake of charges) has forced them into an indiscriminate solidarity which extends even to individuals whose attitudes and conduct most of them would normally deplore.

By the late 1970s a number of trials against immigrants from Eastern Europe accused of lying about their wartime activities had gone through the US courts. Feodor Federenko had been convicted, and would be deported to Russia, where, in June 1987, it was announced that he had been tried and executed. Some were acquitted, some left the US before trial, some appealed against denaturalization.

The most controversial case was that of Frank Walus, a Polish resident of Chicago, who was accused by eleven survivors of the Kielce ghetto of being a member of the Gestapo there, with detailed accounts of his barbaric deeds. He was convicted, but his appeal demonstrated that the eyewitnesses were wrong: he had been a forced farm labourer in Germany as of 1940. His health insurance records and other documentation were produced in court, and his former employers, fondly referring to him as 'our Franzl', gladly gave evidence for him.

The Walus case, continuously held up by opponents of the trials as proof of the fallibility of survivor testimony forty years on, has haunted the American judiciary ever since. And by the late 1970s the Demjanjuk case, which John Horrigan had been investigating all over Europe for years, took shape not only as the trial of one individual, but as a tool for confrontation between powerful forces.

In 1979 the US Department of Justice, at the urging of several highly vocal members of Congress, set up the Office for Special Investigations, the OSI, which would take over from the INS the prosecution of suspect immigrants. The support of Congress was principally obtained through the zealous lobbying of organizations such as the World Jewish Congress and the Simon Wiesenthal Center, who are obsessively committed to rooting out and prosecuting anyone involved in the Nazi murders of the Jews.

The crimes, however, had been committed in the Eastern territories captured by the Russians and any documentary evidence was in Russian hands.

The Soviets were ready to help, up to a point. They had three aims: to show up the West as harbourers of Nazi criminals, to sow dissension between the new ethnic populations and other Americans, and to discredit the prosperous emigrants in the West, whose political and religious propaganda beamed to their homelands was increasingly troublesome.

To tackle this problem Ukrainians such as John Demjanjuk, against whom monstrous charges could be found – or produced – were a gift for the Soviets. For the American prosecutors, however uneasy they felt about the Russians' underlying motives, their co-operation was essential to their investigations.

Ranged against the OSI and its supporters is an alliance which stretches from respectable conservatives, with honest misgivings about war crimes trials and the Russian evidence supplied for them, to individuals of the radical right who not only passionately loathe the Soviets but also the Jews, and refuse to accept that genocide and above all gassings ever took place.

So in 1981 when John Horrigan, a Catholic, and Harvard-educated Norman Moskowitz, a Jew, prosecuted the denaturalization case in Ohio, the Demjanjuk case, with its 'Ivan the Terrible' label, had taken on the shape of a US Eichmann trial, even though it was only a civil case: US law does not allow prosecution for crimes committed abroad.

By this time, the Russians had delivered by courier the original Trawniki ID card bearing Demjanjuk's name and picture, and Horrigan had not only several Treblinka survivors on the witness stand, but also the videoed testimony of Otto Horn, the seventy-seven-year-old German SS sergeant who had been in charge of burning the bodies at Treblinka. He was the only SS man acquitted at the 1965 Treblinka trial in Düsseldorf: he turned state's evidence, and was described by the survivors as 'inoffensive'. His identification of Demjanjuk as Ivan was important: he had no axe to grind.

Demjanjuk's story was hard to believe from the start. He had written 'Sobibor' on his DP questionnaire as his residence from 1937 to 1943 after 'finding the name of this village on a map'. On his visa application in 1951, he said, he had repeated it merely 'to be consistent'. But he had never been in Sobibor: he had lied because a residence outside Russian territory on 1 September 1939 would save him from repatriation to Russia and almost certain death.

He said he was conscripted into the Russian army in 1940, wounded and taken prisoner in the Crimea in 1942, and ended up as a prisoner of war in Rovno in the Ukraine and (though he only remembered this after months of interrogation) in a terrible camp in Chelm in Poland until October 1944. To have been taken prisoner alive was already treason in Stalin's eyes, but worse was to come. From there, he claimed, now dressed 'in clean but old Italian uniform', he was co-opted into two anti-Soviet units, the Galician (Waffen-SS) Division in which he 'was given the SS blood-group tattoo', and then – he would add in 1984 – into the Vlasov Army. (The 'Galician' and the 'Vlasov Army' were military units set up by the Germans with anti-Soviet volunteers from the USSR.)

'I was uncertain for a long time how strong the case was,' said John Horrigan, 'until during pre-trial examination I interrogated Demjanjuk myself many times. He works hard at playing the simpleton, but it isn't true: he is actually very intelligent. Not intellectual, of course, but very canny . . .' It was the name 'Ivan the Terrible' (virtually unknown in Treblinka but snapped up by the US media) that had caught the imagination of the public. 'But none of this was important,' said Horrigan. 'What mattered was that Demjanjuk was a liar. His alibi was a lie. He kept adapting it as new information emerged. By the time we went to trial, in February 1981, I had no doubt whatever that he was Ivan from Treblinka, a truly terrible man. Prosecuting him, for all of us, became an obsession.'

The judge's decision too, was that Demjanjuk had lied. The prosecution case was found proved by the documentary evidence plus the survivors' testimony, and he was denaturalized for having falsified his visa application.

Four years later, with all appeals exhausted and his extradition to Israel getting ever closer, the support for Demjanjuk turned into a carefully orchestrated attack on those considered responsible for his plight. William Turchyn, a self-styled 'archivist' who has been a mainstay of the Demjanjuk defence for years, made a speech in 1985 to

North American ethnic leaders which was widely distributed under the title 'Victory Without Fear'. He addressed himself to what he and many others saw as the four main issues of such cases: the 'alliance' between the Jewish-dominated OSI and 'the evil KGB'; the pervasive influence of Jews in American public life; the danger to Christianity arising from these 'Nazi-hunting' activities, and the 'fraud and corruption' which produced such fabricated cases. He found the testimony against Demjanjuk 'contradictory . . . self-serving . . . questionable . . . and very fraudulent, probably due to the profit motive'.

John Demjanjuk arrived in Israel on the morning of 28 February 1986. Wearing that same brown suit and open-necked white shirt he would be seen in ever since, he asked permission upon getting off the plane to kiss the ground of the Holy Land. Permission was refused.

It was to a great extent to unite their divided generations and national elements that Israel twenty-five years ago kidnapped and tried Eichmann, that quintessential 'desk-murderer'. And now again, though with enormous reluctance and misgivings, they had accepted Demjanjuk for trial, perhaps less from a sense of justice than in order to make history serve to unify their people and strengthen their resolve.

Specifically, it was the Americans who persuaded them to stage their second war crimes trial. By 1984 the US government was anxious to justify the enormous expenditures incurred for 350 investigations and 50 civil trials, with 300 more cases still in the pipeline. They tried to get first the West Germans and then the Israelis to accept a deportee for a criminal trial. The West Germans, who since 1958 have investigated tens of thousands of cases and brought several hundred to trial (among them the *Einsatzgruppen*, Auschwitz, Majdanek, Sobibor, Treblinka and Trawniki trials, each lasting for years), still have a large backlog of their own. The Israelis had always felt, rightly or wrongly, that the Eichmann trial satisfied their country's need for a symbolic act. But under continuing American pressure, they finally agreed, subject to three conditions: the accused had to be healthy and reasonably young, indictable for murder, and credible witnesses had to be available. John Demjanjuk fulfilled the conditions.

The prospect of the trial aroused the most contrary emotions in Israel. First and foremost the discomfort (which would persist to the end of the trial) of trying someone whose identity was in doubt. Then, remembering the Eichmann trial, there were reservations about the 'show trial' aspect, and fears that it would reopen appalling wounds. Set against that was the hope that it would be a catharsis – that by learning to understand what it took for a Jew to survive Treblinka, and that by airing the horrible dilemma and complex guilt-feelings of the 'work-Jews' of the death camps (and by extension of the Jewish councils and police of the ghettos), the generations might at last be reconciled.

While the prosecution team of thirty continued the worldwide search for documentation and witnesses which resulted in the almost encyclopaedic knowledge they later displayed, the Demjanjuk circle in America was busy, too. Ed Nishnic, Demjanjuk's son-in-law, left his job to take over fund-raising and co-ordination. He acquired with demonic energy over the years a vast store of historical, political and legal information. 'We have a baby,' his wife Irene said sadly, 'but no life.'

'I know what you are doing,' Demjanjuk whispered to her once on a prison visit, 'but please, live – live your life.'

It was not possible: Lydia's marriage broke up and the defence team, including Turchyn and another ready helper, James McDonald, who had connections with *Spotlight*, a leading publication of the radical right, established their headquarters in the basement of the Demjanjuk house.

One of Demjanjuk's earliest supporters was Jerome Brentar, a travel agent of Croatian extraction who after the war had worked in Germany as an IRO screening officer. He is still proud today, he told us with engaging frankness, of the help he gave to 'suitable' immigrants. 'We managed to get thousands of Waffen-SS over here and helped them get established. And we got advice on just what people had to say to get their visas.'

His agency specializes in 'visits home' for the area's huge immigrant population. He also heads the Cleveland chapter of the St Raphael Society (Motto: 'To aid the traveller in need'). In Rome after the war the society, true to its motto, was instrumental in getting Adolf Eichmann, among others, out of Europe.

Brentar, at his own expense, travelled widely on Demjanjuk's behalf, getting statements from three Polish villagers near Treblinka that Demjanjuk's photograph in no way resembled the 'Ivan' they had known: a 'giant' approaching his forties, with greying hair. He then visited Kurt Franz, Treblinka's deputy commandant, in his German prison where this most awful of the SS men [then] still alive was serving a life sentence, and got an affidavit with an identical description.

Later, two of Demjanjuk's present defence lawyers travelled to Poland to interview the villagers – 'unaccompanied and not interfered with in any way', they told us – and, although Israeli visas and Polish travel permits had been provided, decided not to call them. And the same lawyers would decide, too, to dispense with the testimony of Kurt Franz.

Brentar and other lobbyists for Demjanjuk see no reason for embarrassment at their methods: to them the end justifies the means. Their aim is to *use* men such as Demjanjuk in their holy war against communism, to make them into symbols for their battle against the hated Soviets. In this battle the fanatical right was soon joined by respectable conservatives and liberals, who also warned against putting any trust in Soviet-supplied evidence.

The biggest gun in Demjanjuk's support came from the heart of the White House when Patrick Buchanan, then President Reagan's Chief of Communications, came to his defence. Writing in syndicated columns in the *Washington Post*, the Cleveland *Plain Dealer* and other papers around the country, he attacked the treatment of Demjanjuk, who (he wrote) was clearly innocent. He was 'a decent and honest family man whose life has been destroyed by Soviet malice and American gullibility'. Quite understandably, said Buchanan, he had lied on his visa application to avoid being repatriated to Russia and executed 'as a traitorous member of the Vlasov Army'; his name was not on any of 'the Trawniki rosters or Treblinka transfer lists now in possession of the defence'; the only documentary evidence – the Trawniki ID card – had been 'proved a fake' by two experts; Polish witnesses who had 'definitely' established 'Ivan' as being twice Demjanjuk's age and half again his size had been 'prevented from coming to testify'; and, most important of all, various people had recorded the fact that the monstrous 'Ivan' had been killed in 1943, in the Treblinka uprising.

All this made impressive reading for millions, coming as it did from such an authoritative spokesman. But unfortunately, as we will see, whatever the truth about Demjanjuk was, none of Buchanan's 'facts' was true.

Buchanan's information, as he told us when we went to see him at his beautiful mansion near Washington, came from Mark O'Connor, who was Demjanjuk's chief counsel from 1982 until June 1987, when the family finally sacked him.

In a way O'Connor, too, was a symbolic figure, for he had been provided as a sort of legacy by a man highly placed in US public affairs, who as a passionate anti-communist became a staunch supporter of Demjanjuk, and appeared as a witness for the defence in his US trial in 1981.

This was Ed O'Connor, Mark's father, an Irish-American of considerable charm and ability who was the most active of three Commissioners of Displaced Persons appointed by President Truman. Like Jerome Brentar – a close friend in Germany in the 1950s – he was very early convinced of the Russian menace, and helped half a million DPs to enter the US, and a million and a half more to find homes in other countries. He later in a special report described these immigrants as '. . . active seeds of Russian disaffection'.

In 1982 this powerful man recommended that his forty-year-old son Mark, who had taken a law degree in Buffalo after his Vietnam service as a captain but had never pleaded a major case in court, should take over the Demjanjuk case.

It would be difficult to overstate the harm which Mark O'Connor's inexperience and naïvety, coupled with an almost mystical anti-Soviet ideology, did to his client. After the deportation hearing and two appeals had failed, knowledgeable sympathizers in the American Ukrainian community (which by then had already funded the defence to the tune of $750,000) suggested replacing O'Connor with either of two well-known trial lawyers of Ukrainian descent. But the Demjanjuks, remembering Ed O'Connor's help and dazzled by his son's charm and promises of eventual victory over the conspiracy of the KGB and the OSI, didn't listen.

For three years Ed O'Connor had stood behind his son with advice and political connections. But when he died, in 1985, Mark O'Connor was on his own.

Until a few days before the extradition to Israel, he had assured the family it would never happen. When it did, he was still cheerful. 'There's nothing to worry about,' he kept telling the Demjanjuks in chatty overseas phone calls from Jerusalem. 'The prosecution hasn't got a case: they're getting ready to drop it.'

He complained bitterly to whoever would listen that his attempts to prepare the case were blocked by the impossibility of finding an Israeli lawyer to assist him, and by the refusal of the Israelis 'who had financed Eichmann's defence' to do the same for Demjanjuk.

However, when Gershon Orion, a distinguished Israeli lawyer and expert on identification, at the request of the Israeli Bar Association offered his services free of charge (except for the minimal legal aid which Eichmann's defence received), O'Connor was deeply suspicious. Within a week he had firmly stamped down on Orion's proposal for a different approach to the case: to begin with a 'mini-trial' purely on the question of identity. Such a procedure, if allowed by the judges, would cut out the dangers of a show-trial. If the prosecution could *not* prove his identity, the trial would be over.

But this did not appeal to O'Connor at all: he sacked Dr Orion before there was time to sign a contract [told Ed Nishnic to go and get more money] and hired a quiet Cleveland lawyer, John Gill [for a 50:50 split of the fees after the first $250,000, of which he would keep 70 per cent.]

Then [for a modest fee] he enlisted as adviser on Israeli law an intelligent thirty-eight-year-old native-born Israeli of Ukrainian descent, Yoram Sheftel, who speaks seven languages and shared his detestation of the Russians. Also, like many Israelis of his generation, Sheftel had ambivalent feelings about the survivors, and gloried in impossible tasks. 'I wouldn't have taken it on if I thought Demjanjuk was "Ivan",' he told me. 'But that's the indictment, and legally nothing else he might have done counts' – an observation which, however cynical it appears, was to prove to be prophetically accurate.

O'Connor, happy in the security of heading a team, and with money streaming in from generous American and Canadian Ukrainians, was full of optimism. 'We'll fly John home in triumph,' he announced to the Demjanjuks. 'The Senate will quash the denaturalization and we will have struck the greatest blow for freedom in this century.' And he quoted to all and sundry Buchanan's final literary flourish: '... John Demjanjuk may be the victim of an American Dreyfus case.'

Less exuberant as the trial drew nearer, he talked time and again about the lack of credibility of the survivors. 'If the Israelis persist in going ahead,' he told me two months before it started, 'I'm going to turn their witnesses inside out and show them up for what they really are.'

The discrediting of witnesses' memories is a legitimate strategy in cross-examination. But, appearing entirely insensitive to the emotional minefield he was entering, O'Connor seemed oblivious to the fact that he was taking on the Jews' greatest taboo, the nightmare which has pursued the survivors asleep and awake for forty-five years ... that they, Jews, helped to kill Jews.

Once the trial started, it took him hardly any time to get to this point. His primary target was Treblinka survivor Eliyahu Rosenberg, who was twenty when he arrived at Treblinka in 1942 and was posted to the 'upper camp' – the worst assignment for any 'work-Jew'. He has testified in many trials and was the strongest and most controversial Israeli witness.

'Is it not true that ... taking out the lifeless bodies was one part of your work?' O'Connor opened his attack.

'True.'

'... and ... cleaning of the gas chambers once the lifeless bodies were removed?'

'Yes ... and to clean the stains ...'

O'Connor pounced. 'Was *sealing* the gas chambers also part of your duties?'

There were angry murmurs in the hall, and Judge Levin intervened, as he would often have to do, in an effort to stem O'Connor's emotive approach. 'So the components of the work were (1) to take out the corpses, (2) clean up, and (3) seal the doors?' he asked.

'Yes ... [When] there was a shout from an SS, "*Rampe raus*" [Ramp detail on the double], we knew ... we had to lower the doors and fill the gaps in with sand ...'

'Are you now saying that with the innocent naked men, women and children [sealed] in the gas chambers, you stood on the *Rampe* while they died in agony?'

'To my great sorrow, yes.'

Rosenberg was a strong, massive figure of a man, rather like Demjanjuk, with a stubborn working-man's voice and a cragged angry face. When they were both twenty – one a blond Ukrainian, one a dark-haired Polish Jew – their essential East European resemblance may have been less obvious, but now it was astounding.

Whether Rosenberg's personal confrontations with Demjanjuk date back to Treblinka forty-five years ago or only began at the Cleveland trial, it became increasingly evident over the months of the trial that a strong and rather frightening current existed between the two men – one in the dock on trial for his life, the other his most vocal and practised accuser.

Demjanjuk much of the time gave the impression of being a spectator at his own trial. But if one observed closely, he did of course show tension: he continually stretched his jaws, sipped water, clenched his hands and pulled at his fingers.

'If he is really innocent, though,' said Israeli psychologist Dan Bar-On, 'then however often he has heard these accusations, he would *have* to show anger.'

That afternoon, too, Eliyahu Rosenberg related a unique occasion when a group of Polish Jews, being driven through the 'tube' – the fenced-in path to the gas chambers – pitched themselves *en masse* against the barbed wire, toppling one section of it, and ran out into the 'upper camp'.

'How were they able to break out of the "tube,"' asked O'Connor.

'It wasn't a problem for people who knew they were going to their death to push down a fence,' said the witness drily. 'They could have pushed down a wall.'

O'Connor led Rosenberg – his purpose only apparent at the end – through a minute description of these victims' abominable suffering when they were locked into one of the small gas chambers, chlorine was poured in through an opening in the roof and they took all night to die.

'Good heavens,' he exclaimed, as he reached the point he had been aiming for. 'What did you feel when you saw them so heroically rebel? Did you not find it in your heart to help them?'

The prosecutor shot to his feet but the judge stopped him. 'No,' he said. 'The defence has a hard task. I will give them the chance to explore even this avenue.'

Rosenberg was trembling now. 'How could I help?' he said. 'There was no possibility of contact. I couldn't even shout at them. If I had . . .' He paused and then gave vent to his fury and the despair O'Connor had proved incapable of understanding.

'What could I say to them? Not to go? The worst anti-semites never asked me such a question.' Then he turned to the dock and – it was impulsive, not theatrical – stretched out his arm stiffly, pointed at Demjanjuk. 'Ask *him* why I didn't try to help,' he shouted hoarsely. 'I would have been thrown into a pit of blood.'

It was at that moment that Demjanjuk, flushed to the roots of his hair, said in Hebrew, 'You are a *liar*.'

Was this, as I certainly felt at the time, the anger of an innocent man that Dan Bar-On had predicted? But O'Connor could never leave well enough alone. Time and again, his 'blind' questions led to calamity.

Thus, another day he asked Pinhas Epstein, 'When you saw John Demjanjuk get off the plane, did that man fit the "memory you couldn't forget"?' (He had spoken of his daily nightmares.)

'We were in that place – together, one might say – for almost a year,' replied Epstein, a man of considerable dignity. 'He was twenty-two or twenty-three, I was seventeen. He was tall, thick-necked, with those protruding ears . . . and the way he walked – shall I show it?' he asked the judge. He produced an uncanny likeness of the way we had all seen Demjanjuk walk. 'Heavily,' Epstein said, as he demonstrated, 'his weight on his left foot, just as he did when he stepped off the plane arriving in Israel . . . "Oh, my God, my God," I said to my wife. "Look at the walk. That's just how I saw him walking every day in Treblinka."' His wife, sitting just in front of me, nodded vigorously. 'Exactly,' she whispered, 'that's exactly what he said.'

It was one of those moments when one's doubts dissolve: this was no horror story, no prepared scenario by a professional witness. He could not have known this question would be asked – just as O'Connor had not expected the answer: the memory of how a man walked, a characteristic that is said not to change with age.

*

It was, not surprisingly perhaps, the survivors' testimony which provoked the strongest comments in America's and Germany's hate-journals, showing that the shadow of the 'gas chambers never existed' cabal hovered over the trial.

David McCalden (aka Lewis Brandon) in the extreme right magazine *Truth Mission*:

Absent from the Israel case is its basics: no murder weapon nor any forensic evidence to show there ever was one . . . no corpse or corpses, nor any . . . evidence that such ever existed . . . (and no) documentation (that) such an enormous programme was ever presented . . . only recycled hearsay . . .

And the broadsheet *Ostdienst* in Hamburg warned its public:

If Demjanjuk can be convicted on . . . manufactured evidence . . . it opens the door wide to the 'Auschwitz-lie' thesis. In Germany discussion is rife: why is there new anti-semitism in a country with almost no Jews? It is trials such as this one against Ivan Demjanjuk which are responsible.

And William Turchyn, to Ukrainian leaders:

The real 'Ivan' was killed by the inmates . . . in 1943 . . . I did not invent this fact . . . The death of 'Ivan' was reported by a Treblinka survivor . . . in a *sworn affidavit* in Vienna . . . This (same) survivor . . . testified . . . against John Demjanjuk. I leave the conclusion for you.

'Ivan is dead' became the cornerstone of O'Connor's public relations in Israel as it had been in America. He expected to prove it through Eliyahu Rosenberg, who had made the Vienna statement in 1947.

'Did you say there,' he asked, 'that people in the "upper camp" *including Ivan* were killed in the uprising?'

'I said that comrades from the "lower camp" said they had *beaten to a pulp* some Ukrainians, including Ivan.'

'Did you think then that everything [you said then] was the truth?'

'. . . I certainly knew that certain parts of it were true . . .'

'What was not true?'

'I found out later . . . that some of the acts of heroism I described were not true.'

This was a success for O'Connor – a survivor had admitted that he had lied – and he could have left it at that. Instead he triumphantly announced to the world's press that the man who had taken down Rosenberg's statement in 1947 – 'an Israeli for whom I have the highest regard' – would appear as a defence witness 'to testify about what Rosenberg had *really said* in Vienna, which would establish once and for all that Ivan was dead.' 'IVAN DEAD' appeared in headlines all over the world next day.

But O'Connor's witness did not appear (he hurriedly left for America). And worse, whether or not O'Connor was aware of it, a 1965 statement from the Düsseldorf Treblinka trial had been entered in the trial record – by SS sergeant Gustav Münzberger, Ivan's immediate boss at the gas chambers. He was asked, 'What happened to Ivan?' 'Ivan?' he had said. 'He came with my group to Trieste. Towards the end he cleared off into the partisans.'

That statement – which could have accounted for the 'Italian uniform' Demjanjuk had said he ended the war in – is supported by additional information which did not come before the court. The director of the Adriatic Institute for Research into Partisan Warfare, Dr Giuliano Fogar, told us in 1986 in Trieste, 'A lot of people got away from the Germans in those last weeks . . . The partisans took anybody; they put them into some sort of Italian uniform and put them where they could shoot at Germans.'

O'Connor's last cross-examination at the end of the prosecution's case, before the Demjanjuks finally dismissed him in June, produced yet another catastrophe for the defence.

The three judges had travelled to West Berlin (unprecedented for an Israeli court) for a 'rogatoire' (the hearing of a witness who cannot travel) of Otto Horn, the SS man who, as a non-victim, was a key witness for the identification of 'Ivan'.

Questioned not at all gently by Israeli prosecutor Michael Horowitz, who loathed being in Germany and loathed Horn too, the old man described 'Ivan' with precision: 'I saw him all the time,' he said, 'except when I was on night duty or on leave. He was light-haired, 1.75 or 1.80 tall, strong, solid, about twenty-three years old. He wore a black uniform, cap and boots . . . carried a pistol and a whip . . .'

O'Connor understandably was desperate to discredit in some way this witness whose description of 'Ivan' was so close to that on the

Trawniki ID card. He asked, 'And you did nothing yourself, only watched? . . . But still . . . you consider yourself innocent?'

'Morally,' said Horn slowly, with unexpected dignity, 'it was my responsibility too. But that's what all of us did: we just stood by . . .'

A little later, O'Connor asked weightily, 'Do you know that John Demjanjuk is on trial for his life?'

'What? What?' asked Horn, who is now rather deaf. 'His life?'

'Yes. Do you realize that what you say here, now, can hang this man?'

'Now really, Mr O'Connor,' interposed Judge Levin, with an apology to the presiding German judge, Hans Jürgen Müller. 'Nobody has said yet that anyone is going to hang.'

Horn, his mind working a little slowly, had missed this exchange. 'I didn't know anybody was still hanged,' he said, sounding sad. 'In 1979 I recognized the photograph as Ivan. I now also think – [he compromised] there is a resemblance.' He paused. 'I cannot help it,' he said regretfully. 'The resemblance is there.'

And Otto Horn delivered a final blow to the defence's most important claim, that 'Ivan' was killed in the Treblinka revolt.

'I was on leave when it took place,' Horn said. 'When I came back the barracks had been burned down. Only the gas chambers remained standing. Afterwards, they still gassed people.' Then he added, unasked, 'Ivan was there – I saw him.'

Back in Israel, the judges were said not to be entirely happy with the sacking of O'Connor, 'really because a change in midstream is usually bad for the defendant', said someone close to the court. Demjanjuk, no doubt brainwashed into accepting O'Connor as his saviour, seemed depressed for days. His family, by contrast, were relieved, especially when a desperate search for a senior lawyer produced Canadian-Ukrainian Paul Chumak, a highly regarded former chief prosecutor.

The responsibility for leading Demjanjuk through his evidence when he appeared as the first witness for the defence (as required by Israeli law), would now fall on John Gill. 'Would you believe that in five years he did not find a single witness we could use, and nobody ever worked with Demjanjuk?' he fumed two weeks later, while Demjanjuk was on the stand. 'Mark wouldn't let us go near him; he was his property. After he finally left, I went to the prison to prepare Demjanjuk for his testimony. "What you doing, John?" he said to me. "What's all these questions? You a prosecutor now?"'

Certainly, with O'Connor gone, the defence would be conducted in a far more expert manner, and Sheftel, now acting as chief counsel, a fact which appalled most Israelis, succeeded too in finding reputable expert witnesses in England and Holland. Nevertheless the case was extremely difficult, the fundamental problem being Demjanjuk's alibi.

Demjanjuk's account of his life until 1942 was generally accepted: with four years' schooling, he became a tractor driver on a collective farm in the Ukraine. He was conscripted in 1940, wounded in action, taken prisoner in the Crimea in late 1941, and briefly held in a POW camp in Rovno. There the disputes begin.*

The prosecution claimed he then volunteered as a foreign auxiliary in the SS, and, not later than July 1942, was trained for the *Aktion Reinhard* at Trawniki. Though sent for brief periods to Okszów, a farm worked by Jewish women, and Sobibor, his main posting, they said, was Treblinka, where survivors claim he spent most of the year between July 1942 and September 1943 servicing the gas chambers.

* Documents presented during the Israeli trial would show that Demjanjuk was indeed recruited by the SS in the awful POW transit camp of Rovno in July 1942. Years later, Streibel, the camp commander, recounted proudly at his trial in Hamburg, how he himself selected the candidates. First, ethnic Germans because of the language; then young strong men of 'Aryan' appearance. If there was proof of anti-Soviet background in their families, or if they had some technical training – as mechanics, electricians or drivers – those were bonuses. Demjanjuk, simple and uneducated, with a mere four years of schooling (often barefoot as there was only one pair of shoes between his father and him), qualified admirably: he had the required Aryan looks; his family had always been religious and thus anti-Soviet; and before he was called up for the Soviet army, he had driven a tractor on a collective farm, and it is quite likely that he was anti-semitic: most rural Ukrainians blamed their dire poverty on Jews, the only 'wealthy' people they ever saw being Jewish traders, and some of the communist officials who made their lives a misery being Jews, too.

The young men Streibel selected at Rovno and in other POW camps, would not have known what they would be trained to do. They only knew that they would have fine German uniforms, good food, money and extra rations and privileges for their families back home.

One might feel there is despair, and even a kind of courage in the degree of mendacity Demjanjuk displayed in order to protect his new American life and those he loved.

Demjanjuk says that this is not true: from Rovno he was sent to a terrible camp at Chelm, where he stayed for eighteen months.

Historians called by the prosecution said it was impossible: no prisoners stayed in the Chelm POW camp for eighteen months. The first 100,000 Russian POWs died in the appalling conditions that winter, except for those transferred to work in Germany. Early in 1943, with the camp now empty, new lots arrived but stayed only for short periods. In September 1943, with the Italian surrender to the Allies, 13,000 Italians, now POWs, came to Chelm: Demjanjuk never mentioned their presence.

Demjanjuk first told the Americans he left the camp in late 1944, but when evidence was presented that Chelm was captured by the Russians in July 1944, he revised his departure from Chelm. His next story was that he left the camp in the spring with 350 other Ukrainians, to join the Galician (Waffen-SS) Division in Graz, Austria. There he said he was given the SS blood-group tattoo. (This, too, was considered impossible: only SS and *Western* Waffen-SS frontline troups plus a few exceptions such as the *Aktion Reinhard* men on anti-partisan duty in Trieste received this medical precaution.)

According to Demjanjuk's story in the US court, maintained later in Israel, he was transferred a few weeks later to the Vlasov Army in Heuberg, Germany, where he was assigned to a unit 'guarding the generals'. He stayed there for a year, 'not doing anything much', and wound up in various DP camps after the war. In Heuberg, he said, he 'scraped off' the tattoo 'because only the SS had it, and the Vlasov Army wasn't SS'. The mark that remained was tiny, and – extraordinarily again – Demjanjuk himself had drawn the attention of the Americans to it.

But this, too, was impossible according to the experts. The Galician Division was training in north Germany until July 1944, 1,000 kilometres from Graz. The Vlasov Army did not exist until November 1944, thus was not at Heuberg – and there were certainly no generals to guard at the time he claimed. Besides, the Galician Division never received the SS blood-group tattoo.

Chelm was to haunt Demjanjuk throughout the Israeli trial. How was it, the chief prosecutor asked, that over the first eight months of American interrogation, when he remembered so clearly everything else about his life, he had 'forgotten' just one place – the 'most terrible place he had ever been to'? For just the period when the prosecution said he was at Trawniki and Treblinka, he had 'forgotten' Chelm?

'I guess only God knows how it happened,' said Demjanjuk.

'You are saying,' asked Judge Dalia Dorner, 'that when the prosecution says you were at Treblinka, you were actually at Chelm. Is that right?' 'Yes.' 'And *this*,' she shook her head in disbelief, 'this you didn't remember when you appeared before the American investigators?'

'Mr Demjanjuk,' said Judge Levin. 'Please listen to me very carefully. I want to explain to you what an alibi is . . . *Chelm, Chelm is your alibi.*'

'Honourable Judges,' he answered, 'I'm an honest person and have always told the truth. Have you never forgotten anything in *your* life?'

Judge Dorner said sadly, 'Yes, yes . . . but *this* . . .'

The court was dead quiet. Demjanjuk's face was glistening with sweat and his voice trembled when he replied, 'Your Honour, it was read out [from the US transcripts] that I said I had been in two camps, one of which I forgot the name of. I wish to be shown [those statements].'

The judge stopped Prosecutor Blattman as he rose. 'Don't object,' he said. 'He is on a grave charge and in a predicament. Let us show him. Maybe it will help him. Justice must be seen as well as done.'

The court was silent while Demjanjuk, his English reading ability minimal, slowly read the transcript. 'I have read it,' he said then, stiffly. 'It says I was in Rovno and another place and I forgot the name. I can't say why I forgot: I just did.'

'Maybe there is a different reason,' said Blattman in his severe, measured voice. 'You weren't *at* Chelm.'

Demjanjuk's answer came back in a flash – no trembling now, or primitivity either: 'That's what *you* say. *I* say I was at Rovno and Chelm, two camps. If you say I was at Sobibor and Treblinka, you'll have to *prove* it.'

In the end there is only one piece of documentary evidence: the bitterly contested Trawniki ID card [though more would be discovered years later]. For, contrary to what Patrick Buchanan wrote, neither the prosecution nor the defence have any Treblinka or Trawniki staff documentation: there is nothing left except one Trawniki duty roster, with fourteen names.

The Russians say they found the ID in one of their war archives. Demjanjuk's backers say, how convenient – they faked it.

The controversial document in the Demjanjuk case is the 'Service ID No. 1393' from the SS training camp Trawniki where between 1941 and 1943 about 3,500 foreign auxiliaries, most of them from the Baltic countries and the Ukraine, were prepared for work connected with the *Aktion Reinhard.*

If the document is genuine, it proves that the account Demjanjuk gave of his life between May 1942 and the end of 1943 is a lie and that – even if he was not the monstrous 'Ivan' – he was a member of this infamous unit. Its authenticity was hotly disputed since its appearance, first in the United States and then in Israel, by Demjanjuk's defence and backers, who are passionately convinced that it is a KGB fake.

Their belief that it is a fake stems mainly from its Soviet provenance. And certainly, it is an untidily spelt – and printed – document. The defence cite three substantial points to back their claim: there is (very curious for an ID) no date either of issue or of validity. Strange, too, Demjanjuk's two postings are written in by hand, so that the bearer could, theoretically, have written in, and transferred himself to, any place he wished.

Even more peculiar, the SS quartermaster, Teufel, who signed Demjanjuk's card No. 1393 as *Rottenführer* (private), was promoted to *Unterscharführer* (corporal) on 19 July 1942. But Teufel signed a lower-numbered card, No. 1211 (one of three the Russians sent to Israel last August) with his *new* rank.

And the most important witness Sheftel found, Dr Julius Grant, one of Britain's most distinguished forensic scientists, considered Demjanjuk's signature, in Cyrillic writing, 'unlikely' to be genuine. All these were considerable flaws in a document on which the life of a man partly depended. And the Russians *could* have learnt in 1975 that Demjanjuk's name was on the American 'master list' linked with Sobibor, making him an ideal tool for their political machinations.

But if that was in fact their game, why stop at Sobibor? Why not place him firmly at Treblinka? His identification by the Treblinka survivors was known long before the first photocopy of the document arrived in the West in 1978. It thus seems hard to believe that, if the Soviets had really faked the document in order to create a *cause célèbre*, they would not have added a posting to Treblinka.

But if Demjanjuk's case was gravely imperilled by his own mention of the blood-group tattoo and Sobibor, the prosecution case hung on a less-than-satisfactory ID card, plus photo-identifications which many people felt were carried out with less than impeccable procedures.

The original identifications in Israel in May 1976, were preceded by multilingual advertisements in the Israeli press, asking any survivor who had known a 'war criminal' Feodor Federenko at Treblinka, or Ivan Demjanjuk at Sobibor, to come forward. No one did, but the defence points out that the ads could have provided an unconscious conjunction of 'Ivan' with Treblinka, so that when its survivors, only a few days later, were confronted with the photospreads (with a photograph perhaps *resembling* 'Ivan'), a suggestion could have remained in their minds. Although few of the SS and normally none of the Jewish workers knew the surnames of the auxiliaries (who in a way were 'non-persons' too, to the Nazis), the very first man to identify 'Ivan', Mr Eugene Turowski (now deceased), said he knew Demjanjuk's family name.

The defence further said that the arrangement of the visa photos, with Demjanjuk's and Federenko's pictures next to each other, was suggestive. Besides, Demjanjuk's full-faced photograph on that page was bigger than the others. They felt, too, that after two of the first three survivors had described 'Ivan' as 'short-necked' and 'broad-faced', the gallery should have included a majority of faces of that description. As a CBS reporter from Cleveland remarked, 'If you go to a service at St Vladimir's, heads like Demjanjuk's are a dime a dozen.'

Finally, almost two years were to elapse before all of the ten survivors who would eventually testify in America had been shown the photospreads. The five who testified in Israel (four have died, and one was too fragile to take the stand) all said they did not discuss the *identification among themselves*. Although unlikely even those many years before, this could not possibly be true eleven years later.

The Treblinka survivors – by that time only about thirteen remained alive in Israel – knew each other intimately, had for years travelled together to testify at a number of trials, lived together on those occasions for long weeks, and met every August in a Tel Aviv cemetery to commemorate the Treblinka revolt in August 1943 during which they escaped. Was it humanly possible that they would not have mentioned to each other on 2 August 1976, 1977 or 1978 the incredible survival of Ivan? Or, even quite aside from those August encounters, that those who were friends never discussed this shattering development as soon as it was known? On that day, my doubts began. My friend Alfred Spiess, the German prosecutor of the Treblinka trial and the trial of Franz Stangl, considered the original identification procedure in Israel which produced the identification of Demjanjuk as Ivan the Terrible to be unacceptable. He had told the Israelis when they invited him to testify at the trial, that he would have to say so in court, at which point the invitation, not surprisingly, was withdrawn. Spiess had told me repeatedly over the months, 'They must concentrate on Sobibor; if they don't, it is going to be a catastrophe.'

A few weeks into the trial, I invited Demjanjuk's three children, Lydia, Irene and John Jr to lunch. They were genuinely charming young Americans.

I talked to them about Sobibor and told them that there seemed to be little doubt that their father had been there. Was it not possible, I asked, that his story was an attempt to protect their peace of mind? And couldn't they find it in themselves to release him from this protective silence? I told them that legal opinion I had gathered was that if he admitted to Sobibor, for which there was documentary evidence from the start, such an admission could have precedence over eyewitness testimony for Treblinka. (On one of the last days of the trial, the president of the court, Judge Dov Levin offered Demjanjuk's counsel that very defence.) The main thing though, I told them, according to all the information I had, was that he could not have been in both places at the same time.

They listened very quietly, but the truth was that, however well informed I was, nothing I could say could shake their conviction of his innocence. They did not believe for one minute, they told me, that their father could have been that terrible man. 'My father,' Irene finally said softly, 'I just can't believe that he ever had anything to do with such a place.' 'Wait until he takes the stand,' said young John, 'then you'll understand.' Lydia was silent.

The last week of the trial produced the angriest confrontation between judges and defence. Canadian lawyer Paul Chumak, who during his six months on the team had won the court's respect for his professional demeanour, denounced the ID card as part of the 'KGB conspiracy' which had put Demjanjuk in the dock. The Russians, he said, were punishing Demjanjuk for defecting, all Ukrainians for not wanting to live in the Soviet Union, and causing dissension between Jews and Ukrainians everywhere. Picking up Patrick Buchanan's 'Dreyfus case' description, he warned the judges to 'be careful': Israeli justice was 'on trial'.

'Are you threatening this court?' asked Judge Dorner ominously.

It was not he who threatened anyone, Mr Chumak replied. (He would 'unreservedly' apologize the next day.) It was the Soviets with their plans for world domination. He said that a few years from now the KGB might do to Israel, with their large numbers of Russian immigrants, exactly what they had done to Ivan Demjanjuk.

But I felt he was wrong: it was not the KGB or the Americans who put Demjanjuk in the situation he finds himself in. It is Demjanjuk himself.

Why had he claimed, on not one but two official documents, to have lived in Sobibor? The mystery remains where it started thirty years ago. Time and again he has been asked the same question by investigators, and by judges.

'Your Honours,' he said despairingly, in Israel, 'if I had really been in that terrible place, would I have been stupid enough to say so?'

Israeli prosecutor Michael Shaked, the most elegant legal mind addressing the court, believed that, needing a residence outside Russia, he chose a place he knew, in case he was ever questioned. Knowing only Sobibor, Treblinka, and a few neighbouring villages, he chose the lesser of two evils, hoping no one would be left to identify him.

Demjanjuk bolstered that explanation in pre-trial interrogation. 'Superintendent Russek asked you on 4 April 1986,' said Shaked, 'were you ever in either of the following places: Kossow or Miedzyrze-Podleski? You said you didn't want to answer. He asked the same question again and you said, "No comment – you are pushing me towards Treblinka." What I want to know is, how did you know this was pushing you towards Treblinka?' Blushing deeply, Demjanjuk said, 'It wasn't a question I wanted to reply to.'

The judge tried to help him. 'Did you feel [looking at the map] these two places being near Treblinka meant you were being pushed towards Treblinka?' Demjanjuk didn't notice the helping hand. 'No,' he said. 'I didn't know where those places were.'

In February this year the prosecution's final arguments were interrupted by the defence, who brought Eliyahu Rosenberg back to the stand to confront him again with the statement he had made in 1945, implying that he had seen someone named 'Gustav beating [Ivan] to death with a spade'.

Rosenberg admitted that the statement had been untrue. Many things were said and done in the euphoria of surviving Treblinka, he said, which were the result of wishful thinking and the desire to be part of a heroic deed.

'Liar, liar, you are a *liar*!' Demjanjuk again shouted hoarsely at Rosenberg in Hebrew.

It is hard to estimate how Rosenberg's untruths will affect the judges' view of him. Their questions during the prosecution's final arguments, many on dubious points in the original photo-identifications, clearly demonstrated that they were troubled by gaps in the evidence.

What did the prosecution claim had happened to Demjanjuk after Treblinka? Were they saying that he went to Trieste, or that he was transferred to concentration camps as a guard?

Where he went afterwards, said the chief prosecutor, was not the question before the court: he was indicted for Treblinka, and the prosecution had concentrated their evidence on Treblinka.

But was it not true, asked Judge Levin, that the accused could have used the ID card as an alibi, as proof that he was in Sobibor, not at Treblinka?

Confirming now the German prosecutor Alfred Spiess's warning years before, he offered the same point to the defence. 'You need to be very clear in your mind,' he said. 'As his counsel, should you not advise him to change his alibi?' The judges, of course, had not yet come to any decision, he said, 'but if we conclude that the ID is authentic, and that his alibi is *not* true, this could create major cumulative weight as far as the identification is concerned.

'Identifications are never fool-proof,' Judge Levin warned, 'and if the alibi is accepted it outweighs the identifications. But if it is refuted, there *is* a problem, and we will have to weigh the identifications all the more.'

The defence was unmoved: Demjanjuk would stick with his alibi. But in their final arguments they no longer defended the contested points of the alibi. 'We submit,' said Sheftel, 'there are three Ivans: Ivan from Treblinka, Ivan on the ID photograph, which is *not* Demjanjuk, and Ivan Demjanjuk.' It was up to the prosecution to prove that the three are one man, he said: in the absence of clear proof, his client should be set free.

Then, on the last day of the trial, Sheftel was given exceptional permission by the court to introduce the Danilchenko statement into evidence. He said that he had only just received it from the Americans, as the result of an application under the Freedom of Information Act. But the introduction of the statement, at a point when no more arguments were admissible, was in fact a gesture of despair, manifestly directed at an appeal. After rejecting the Trawniki ID card as a fake throughout the trial, the defence now appeared to accept its evidence of Demjanjuk's presence at Sobibor as *claimed* by Danilchenko, which they and their client had assiduously denied for thirteen years, in the US and Israel.

This was what Danilchenko said: 'I served as an SS guard in the Sobibor concentration [*sic*] camp in Poland from March 1943 until March or April 1944, I cannot exactly remember when. The camp was located near a small railway station called Sobibor, near the edge of a forest, and was designed for the mass killing of Jews from the Soviet Union, Poland, Holland and other nations occupied by the Nazis. There was a company of 120 [auxilliary] SS guards in the camp. Four platoons with approximately thirty men in each were formed according to height. Guards at least 180cm tall served in the first platoon. At that time I was 184cm tall. Of the guards with me in the first platoon, I remember Ivan Ivchenko, who was our cook, and Ivan Demjanjuk. Demjanjuk and I were sent from Sobibor to the city of Flossenburg in Germany, where we guarded an aircraft factory and a concentration camp for political prisoners. In late autumn of 1944, October or November, Demjanjuk and I [among other guards] were sent to escort 200 political prisoners to Regensburg. Until April 1945, we guarded the prisoners in this camp [until] due to the approaching front, the camp was evacuated and the prisoners marched towards Nuremberg. I escaped along the way [and] suggested to Demjanjuk to escape with me, but he refused. I have never seen Demjanjuk since, and his fate is unknown to me.'

There remained the possibility that Demjanjuk was 'Ivan' – he might have worked at Treblinka from the summer of 1942 to February 1943, the most intense period of gassings there, and that he had been transferred to Sobibor in March when there was a lull in the Treblinka gassings for two months. Had this been the case, however, it seemed to me and to many others highly unlikely, that his main posting would not have been recorded on the Trawniki ID. It had been confirmed by the Central Agency for Investigations into NS Crimes in Ludwigsburg that the Trawniki ID was almost certainly genuine; they had handled hundreds of them. But they had never seen one which lacked a guard's alleged main posting.

The judges decided to ignore both this likelihood and the Danilchenko statement, and on 18 April 1988 brought a guilty verdict against John Demjanjuk. Seven days later he was sentenced to hang.

Although I had admired the three judges, whose balanced severity and kindness to both sides throughout those difficult and heart-rending proceedings had been astonishing, their guilty verdict seemed tragically flawed. Incomprehensibly, it entirely ignored the recorded testimony of Suchomel and Münzberger, the former SS guards, that five of them, all non-commissioned German SS officers, and five Ukrainian SS auxiliaries, among them 'Ivan', had been transferred in September 1943 to Trieste, where they worked first at the San Sabba concentration camp for Jews, and then in anti-partisan warfare. Equally, it ignored Danilchenko's statement which placed Demjanjuk at Flossenburg during the same period. Even worse, it explicitly stated that Demjanjuk as 'Ivan the Terrible' could have commuted the sixty-five miles of bad Polish roads to function simultaneously at Sobibor and Treblinka in 1943.

February 2000

I was convinced that a terrible mistake was being made. I was certain that the truth could only be found in Russia, through Danilchenko and the judicial authorities in Kiev and Moscow. And as luck would have it, as Demjanjuk's appeal was slowly taking its course, Tina Brown at *Vanity Fair* in New York accepted my proposal of a profile of Vladislav Starkov, the founder and editor of *Argumenti i Fakti*, a comparatively liberal weekly which he had developed to become the largest circulation newspaper in the world. (In 1990 it had a readership of 100 million and, although now slimmed down, it continues as healthy and politically independent as ever.)

I was determined that once I finished the work in Moscow, I would go to Siberia. Before leaving London, I asked Starkov, through his deputy Alexander Mershevsky (who spoke fluent English) to find out for me through their Siberian sources whether Ignat Danilchenko was still alive and living in Tobolsk. The reply came the day before I left: *Argumenti i Fakti*'s distributor in Tobolsk had confirmed that Danilchenko was still there – the local rationing board had said he had picked up his sugar ration card that very week.

Starkov, to whom of course I had told the whole story, was at once fascinated and bewildered by my wish to fly thousands of miles to freezing Siberia in January, in order to help a man who forty-eight years earlier had killed Jews in Poland. Why, he asked, did I want to go to all that trouble for that man in Israel, who whether he was in Treblinka or not had doubtlessly been a bad man? 'One man,' he said. 'I cannot understand you Westerners. You go on and on about the Nazis' killing of the Jews, but nobody writes about the 30 million Russians who were killed first by Stalin and then by Hitler.'

Still – and that of course was why his paper is so good – he was open to my argument that justice for one man, whatever he was, was the only way to assure justice for all. And journalistically, my quest, he agreed, was certainly a 'story'. So he would send a reporter and a photographer to Siberia with me – they could assist me and write about us crazy Westerners afterwards.

May 1990

Olga Petrovna is sixty-two. She is small – perhaps five feet tall – and very heavy, with hugely swollen legs, bundled, even at home, in thick woollen stockings. She lives alone in a two-room flat in Tobolsk, on the first floor of one of those huge blocks of concrete which dominate all Soviet cities.

Olga Petrovna came to Siberia from her home town of Lesakovka in the Urals in 1955, when she was twenty-seven. It was the period of Khruschev's drive for 'mobility', when millions of people were moved all over the Soviet Union. 'I was posted as an assistant station master to the 58th Halt,' she says.

This small railway station was near a camp – we know them as gulags – in which long-term prisoners, men and women, served their sentences. 'It was called Terekhty,' she says. Within a few days – before she understood anything about these places – Olga, a slim young beauty, met the man of her dreams.

He was tall, blond, with a 'good face', as she puts it, and right away 'a good smile' for her. She was intrigued, because he wore what seemed to her like very good clothes, of good thick material. She thought he was elegant. 'A funny thing,' she tells us and laughs as she recalls her own naïvety, 'on the lapel of his suit, on the back of his jacket and, funniest of all, on both knees of his trousers, were big white patches with the number 25 written in black. "What can it mean?" I thought.'

This was Ignat Terentyevich Danilchenko who in 1949, in a trial in his home republic – the Ukraine – had been sentenced to twenty-five years' hard labour in Siberia (significantly enough, as we shall see, not to death).

By the time Danilchenko left school and was called up for the army at seventeen, he had a certificate in animal husbandry and was put to work looking after the army horses. In early 1942 he was wounded in the famous battle of Kerch and, with 40,000 others, became a prisoner of the Germans at the infamous Rovno camp in the western Ukraine. But Danilchenko, despite the starvation diet of 'only one issue of disgusting thin soup a day', as Olga puts it, and 'backbreaking work digging trenches from dawn to night', managed to recover from his injury. 'After a few weeks – or maybe months', he and an army friend – a Ukrainian too whose name she never knew – decided to escape from the terrible camp.

'Listen well,' she says, 'because this man becomes very important in Ignat's story. They managed to escape, but they were soon recaptured.' The Germans took them 'to a terrible punishment camp where they were beaten and tortured by dogs; and then they were sent to another camp. Much later, some farmers came from Germany and recruited them to work in Germany and that's where they stayed to the end of the war.' This was her story, the fable that Danilchenko had told her.

'When the war ended,' she said, 'they were under the Americans, who tried to recruit him as a spy. But he refused – he would never have betrayed his country. But his friend appeared in an American officer's uniform – a terrible shock: he must have been a spy all along.'

This determined Ignat to go home, she said, and when he got out of the army, he went back to being a veterinary technician. In 1949, she says, he was put on trial.

'And did he tell you why he had been put on trial?' I asked, and her face still reflecting the love she had felt for the tall Ignat with his 'good face', she recited the fairy tale he had told her.

'Oh, he explained it all to me. You see, in his job he had to issue certificates on animal health – you know, that cows were all right to be milked, and pigs and other animals all right to be slaughtered for food. So on one bad occasion, as there was a shortage of hay, he authorized that 300 sheep could graze in the fields and they all died. So he was put on trial and given twenty-five years in Siberia for sabotage.'

We had, of course, come to see Danilchenko himself. But when we had knocked on the door of that third-floor flat only a few days later, it transpired that the 'official sources' my Moscow friends had been told about, as happens only too often in Soviet bureaucracy, were mistaken. Danilchenko was dead. It was Olga Petrovna who had continued to draw the sugar ration. He had died in December 1985, and she gave us a photograph of his funeral showing his family standing by the bier.

I asked her whether she didn't think that twenty-five years was a very long sentence for having made a mistake over a flock of sheep. For the first time, Olga Petrovna, who until now appeared to feel a kind of comfort in speaking about the past, became evasive. It was as if she knew a moment of truth was approaching, which she sought, yet wanted to put off a few moments longer. 'All the prisoners at Terekhty had been given twenty-five years,' she said. 'Most of them for nothing else than for having been prisoners of the Germans. Ignat Terentyevich didn't like to talk about all this – he always felt he suffered for nothing.'

I sensed something as yet unsaid. I said I wanted to ask her a very personal question and hoped she would forgive me the intrusion. She nodded and looked at me attentively. 'Did you and your husband love each other very much?'

The smile she had so determinedly kept on her face disappeared. 'I don't know,' she said slowly. 'Till 1975 my husband was a good man. We lived in my home town then, Lesakovka; we had a nice flat, a small dacha, he had a good job in a factory. But then my son went to Tobolsk to study and I didn't think he should be alone. I said, let us all go there. It is a good place to live too, with good schools. But he wouldn't go. He said, "You go, I stay and Tamara" – our fifteen-year-old daughter – "she stays with me". So I went and not all that long afterwards he came, bringing "Tamara" back.'

She stood up heavily, opened a drawer and pulled out a small flat paper package. She sat down, unfolded it and showed us, almost with reverence, a little heap of torn-up bits of paper inside. 'That was our marriage certificate,' she said. 'He tore it up and he said, "Now we are no longer married." And after that he went back to Lesakovka alone, told everybody there I had died, and married another woman. After not too long he divorced her and married again. Over the ten years, 1975 to 1985, he married – or just lived with – three other women.'

All this time I had felt there was something unsaid, something she wanted or needed to ask or talk about but didn't dare.

'Would you like to know the truth about your husband?' I finally asked.

'Yes,' she said, after a long silence. 'I did begin to wonder when, in 1974 I think, they took away his war-veteran card.'

Had she asked him why this had happened?

'Yes, he said it was just a mix-up. They would issue him a new one by and by. Even after he married these other women, you know, he kept coming back to us when he had trouble with his lungs, and we looked after him. And then he was called to Tyumen in 1979 and stayed there for three days. Well, when he came back he told me that a prosecutor had told him that his conviction would be quashed, his honour restored.'

'And did you believe this?'

'I was suspicious and I felt ashamed for feeling like this. In the early 1980s – I'm not sure of the year – he was called to Tyumen again, just for one day this time. He told me they had confronted him with that man – you know, his former army friend. They told him not to tell anyone, so I have never spoken of it to this day. Then in 1985, two KGB men came to speak to him. He was back in Lesakovka but I said I didn't know where he was. They asked what he had told me about what he had done during the war, and I told them. And when they left, they said "Do not ever speak of him, or even think of him, as a war veteran".'

So she really knew, didn't she, I asked, that he had lied to her all their lives together. She nodded. Was she sure? Again she nodded and briefly laid her hand on mine. Would she like to know more? She nodded. Had she ever heard the name Ivan Demjanjuk?

She said their daughter Tamara had a notebook which contained the names of two people. 'I think, but can't be absolutely sure, this was one of them. I must look at the notebook. I could go to see Tamara at Surgut.'

On 21 November 1979, I said, her husband had told Procurator Kolesnikova in Tyumen that he and Demjanjuk had been together in a place called Sobibor, in Poland.

'He never mentioned that place, I am sure.'

I showed her the English copy of Danilchenko's statement and, my young Russian colleague translating, read the three crucial paragraphs to her. Olga Petrovna covered her face with both hands and slowly began to rock to and fro. The room remained silent for a long time.

She took her hands away from her face. It was bathed in tears. I said I was sad to cause her unhappiness. 'No,' she said, 'thank you for telling me the truth. I'm very glad it is at last out in the open,' and she continued to sob as if she couldn't stop.

I tried to comfort her. You know, I said, they were very young men; they were in a terrible POW camp where their comrades were dying all around them. So when the Germans offered them a chance of survival – good food, good pay, warm uniforms and extra rations too for their hungry families at home – they grabbed it. I didn't think, I said, that until they actually arrived in the SS training camp they knew that they had been recruited to murder Jews. They were told they would be police auxiliaries, and they accepted because they wanted to save their lives.

'Honest people,' she said, her voice hard through her sobs, 'did not try above all else to save their lives. One of my uncles was burned alive by the Nazis. Another was in the resistance – they kept him hanging, alive, for three days before he died. Two other boys in my family died fighting the Germans and I . . . had a husband who did this.'

Later, when we said goodbye, she said she would try to get the notebook which she thought had Demjanjuk's name in it. Yes, she understood, she said: if Demjanjuk was with her husband in Sobibor and then in Germany, he could not have been the Ivan who was in Treblinka and then in Trieste.

February 2000

When we consider Danilchenko's story to his wife in the context of his statement to the procurator, plus what we know of Demjanjuk's past, what really happened becomes clear.

They were prisoners together in Rovno in early 1942, chosen together to train at Trawniki in the summer, and by March 1943 were both guards at Sobibor (the 'terrible prison camp' where they were 'tortured by dogs' in his story to Olga: Sobibor was where the monstrous Kurt Franz, briefly commandant there too, had trained his dog Bari to attack prisoners' genitals). There are some missing months here, only partly explained in Demjanjuk's case by an entry on his Trawniki identity card: the assignment on 22 September 1942 to Okszów, which in all likelihood ended as the winter approached.

Danilchenko's statement that they were at Sobibor until March or April 1944 was also in one respect manifestly false, because the camp was demolished in November 1943.

His statement that they went to Flossenburg, staying in southern Germany until the end of the war, on the other hand, compares well with the evidence – decades apart – of the two German SS men that Ivan of Treblinka spent that same period in Trieste in Italy. It is the clinching proof that Demjanjuk cannot have been *that* Ivan. Danilchenko's description to his wife of his friend trying to recruit him as an American spy was presumably a story which he first told in 1947 at his own trial. To have spurned such an offer, in order to return loyally to his motherland – which under the circumstances then was an act of courage as well as faith – may well have saved his life, and left him in a position to be given amnesty a few years later. He could cheerfully accuse his friend of being an American spy without betraying him, as Demjanjuk was safe by that time in the West.

When I returned to Moscow, Natalia Kolesnikova, the senior procurator and judicial adviser who had interrogated Danilchenko in 1979 and 1982, told me that although she didn't now recall details of his statement, she did remember clearly that she had been sure that he had told the truth about his relationship with Demjanjuk. 'We had no interest in Demjanjuk, and Danilchenko's case too was finished for us,' she said. 'He had been convicted and served his sentence. We only questioned him as a courtesy to the American prosecutors who wanted to know more about his connection with Demjanjuk and with Sobibor.'

Could he have lied to her? 'He was warned of the severe penalties he would incur if it was found he had not told the truth, as were the four other men questioned by other prosecutors in the Ukraine,' she said. (According to Office for Special Investigations records, three of these identified Demjanjuk, one of whom was 'the cook', Ivchenko, who had served with him and Danilchenko at Sobibor.) 'Of course all these men had almost invariably done worse things than they would admit, and they tried to protect themselves – sometimes by accusing others to reduce the risk to themselves.'

She knew nothing of my conversation with Olga Petrovna, but

added that, when she had talked to Danilchenko she had found it interesting that he had volunteered the information that he had not told his wife or family about his real past.

'Later, when we had to see him again, we took account of this and instead of going to Tobolsk, as we might have done, called him again to Tyumen: we had no reason to cause unhappiness to his family.'

She did not know whether Danilchenko had mentioned Demjanjuk at his original trial by name, or if it would be possible for anyone from outside to gain access to the trial records (which could settle the 'Soviet conspiracy' claim once and for all). When I asked why the Americans had not been permitted to see Danilchenko themselves, she replied that it was 'a government decision'. She did not know either why Danilchenko had been given twenty-five years rather than being executed, nor why he was freed after serving only eight years: 'These were decisions of the courts and the courts knew what they were doing.'

This applied also to the court in Israel – she couldn't understand why a British journalist should concern herself with Danilchenko. 'The Israeli trial is over. I saw some of it on TV and thought the witnesses were convincing. The prosecutors (she thought, mistakenly) had all the information from the Soviet Union. Whatever happens now is only the business of the court – journalists cannot understand these matters. Only lawyers can.'

Over the two years following my journey to Siberia, Demjanjuk's appeal was delayed time and again. The first postponement was when on 29 November 1988, one week before the appeal was to be heard, Dov Eitan, a happily married, experienced lawyer Yoram Sheftel had engaged to help him with the appeal, jumped out of a fifteenth-floor window of a hotel lobby in the centre of Jerusalem. The mystery of this alleged suicide would never be solved but the court agreed to put off the appeal for six months. Two days later, during Eitan's funeral on 1 December, a madman threw acid into Yoram Sheftel's face, which, had it not been for a complicated operation in Boston a few months later, would have cost him the sight of his left eye.

However tragic the reasons, the delays in the appeal proved providential for Demjanjuk. For over the next two years, both Sheftel and prosecutor Michael Shaked travelled all over Russia and found in various court files statements by twenty-one Soviet citizens who had been tried for war crimes after serving as SS auxiliaries during the war. Sheftel also obtained under the US Freedom of Information Act 100 further pages from Soviet court records which included statements from six former Treblinka guards the Russians had sent to the US Department of Justice in August 1978, but which, significantly, had not been sent on to Israel.

Both lots of evidence identified a man who was *not* Demjanjuk as having been the gas-chamber guard 'Ivan the Terrible' in Treblinka. His name was Ivan Marchenko and his photograph (not unlike that of Demjanjuk except that Marchenko was brown haired and wide shouldered and Demjanjuk had been slim and blond) was included in yet another group of statements from the Soviet Union which – again not handed on to Israel later – reached the OSI in 1979.

In addition, Michael Shaked found in the enormous concentration camp section of the West German Federal Archives in Koblenz, records from the offices of the Flossenburg camp dated October 1943 (when Sobibor ceased to exist). Duty rosters, daily work schedules and lists of weapon distribution bear dozens of Ukrainian (as well, of course, as German) names, each followed by a number. 'W. [*Wachmann* = guard] Demianiuk' [*sic*] and W. Daniltschenko [*sic*] figure on both lists. Demjanjuk's name is followed by his Trawniki Training Centre ID No. 1939; Danilchenko's by 1016 – *his* ID number. Contrary to all the defence claims, this confirmed the Trawniki card as being authentic. And exactly as Danilchenko had said in 1949 and again in 1979 – Demjanjuk had served both in Sobibor and Flossenburg.

These then were the documents Israel's five top judges had before them when they assembled on 1 June 1992 – by then four years since Demjanjuk's death sentence – for the nine-day appeal hearing everyone hoped would be the last. Legally – in most courts in the world – the accused can only be convicted of the crime he is charged with. From that point of view the new evidence from Russia established beyond a shadow of a doubt that another man, clearly identified by well over a dozen witnesses in formal court hearings, had been the dreaded 'Ivan', and that therefore Demjanjuk had been falsely accused. The problem was that the Israelis could not bear to declare him innocent. The United

States, after investigations of their own Department of Justice, had by then announced that Demjanjuk, if acquitted in Israel, was free to return to his home in Cleveland (and he had also been invited to go and live in the Ukraine).

There can be little doubt that if this trial had taken place in Germany, Britain or any other country in Western Europe – or indeed in an International Court – this would have been the end of the case. But this was Israel and they were in a desperate emotional dilemma. For acquitting Demjanjuk was not only tantamount to the country's highest court calling the survivors liars, but meant furthermore that he would never be called to account for his undoubted presence in Sobibor – and Flossenburg.

And so, the case dragged on for month after month, while groups or individuals, trying to delay what was by now for most of us Demjanjuk's inevitable acquittal by seeking a legal loophole that would permit him to be tried for other crimes, brought charges against him in other courts, each of which the appeal court had to consider and dismiss. No survivors of Sobibor could be found who could describe any crimes he might have committed. None were sought from Flossenburg. It was finally only on 23 September 1993, by which time Demjanjuk had been in prison in Israel for seven and a half years, that, finally released, he boarded a 1 a.m. El Al flight to New York.

There is of course no question that he had to be acquitted. Whatever else Demjanjuk was guilty of, he was not 'Ivan the Terrible' of Treblinka. There is no question either that however admirably on the whole the Israelis conducted themselves throughout despite the flawed verdict, he should never have been tried there: this is a lesson for us, invaluable it seems to me for the future, that no one accused of crimes against humanity or war crimes should ever again be tried by their victims. In cases where men – or indeed women – are accused of terrible offences against other human beings, detachment – by those who prosecute, defend or judge (or indeed those who report on such cases, whether they be about world-shaking events, or individuals in everyday life who treat others, adults *or* children with cruelty and abuse) is extremely difficult to achieve. For victims of such crimes or, later, their relatives, it is impossible.

However, whatever the complexities of this case, the psychological problems of the US judicial authorities or – much discussed in the literature – the malfunction of memory in survivors, it cannot be said often enough that the key problem of the case was always Demjanjuk himself.

By April 1988 when the Israeli District court sentenced him to be hanged, he had lived a life of falsehood for forty-three years. He lied about what he did during the war to gain entry to the United States; he lied to his children and his church, and he lied his way through two trials. I do not underrate the appalling difficulties of a twenty-two-year-old Ukrainian peasant taken prisoner by the Germans in early 1942. Hundreds of thousands of Russians died from starvation and exposure in the horrific German POW camps in the conquered areas of the Soviet Union that winter, and from thirst and disease the following summer – the hottest in living memory. How many young men such as Demjanjuk would have rejected the Germans' suggestion that they should live rather than die?

Demjanjuk is doubtlessly one of many to have lived such a lie since May 1945; we have seen it happen, not only in post-Hitler Germany and then repeatedly in Africa over the past thirty years, and in the 1990s in the Balkans, but, closer to us perhaps and our way of life and vision of morality, in America as a consequence of Vietnam and in Britain too, after the Gulf War. And, yes, we can understand the lies, the denials, the blocking of memory. But what is important to establish, for the past, the present and the future when without doubt other men will be tempted to tolerate, sanction, take part in or commit similar crimes, is that contrary to the old saying, to understand does not mean to condone, or to forgive.

But although the crimes are now and must remain a part of history, the Nazi-crime trials must cease. The alleged criminals, the survivors and the witnesses are too old: these are now men and women in their eighties; memories and evidence become flawed. Prosecutions are not safe. The survivors of that terrible period, with a pain of the soul that none of us can imagine, and their children who inevitably had to share it, must be allowed and indeed allow themselves to let go of it – to rest.

If, however, a case such as this is to teach us anything, it must be that crimes against humanity, whether on a collective or individual basis, must no longer be tolerated. It is no doubt an illusion to believe that wars will cease to exist. But it is entirely rational to decide as a civilized world community, that any man, or woman, who – outside the strict limitations of formal warfare, whether it be by orders, by consent or by individual will, for reasons of race, religion, ideology or vengeance – offends, abuses or injures another human being, whether adult or child, will be tried by due process by an international court.

19

A Last Witness to Hitler

September 2000

Traudl Junge is eighty now, slim, elegant, whitehaired but smooth-skinned, and quite beautiful. Which is why one can very easily imagine what she must have been like at twenty-two (her name then Gertraud Humps) when Hitler chose her, in December 1942 from a shortlist of nine from hundreds of young applicants, to become his fourth and youngest secretary.

When I went to see her a few weeks ago in her flowerfilled studio flat in Munich, her birthplace and home, the German edition of Ian Kershaw's *Nemesis* – the second volume of his Hitler biography – was lying on her table. It had only arrived the day before but she had already read the last six chapters. 'I don't understand much about military things,' she said, 'but these pages are about the time I worked for him, from January 1943 to the end.' She has become weary of reading Nazi history 'There is so much of it, so much of the same or wrong.' But she is deeply impressed with Kershaw's objectivity.

'He is different, perhaps because he is of a different generation. The way he presents what the "red threat" was to us in the early years, and how Hitler used it, is quite extraordinary. It isn't that he defends or justifies us in any way, but he appears to understand, better than others have done, how it ended up in the Germans being – not oppressed of course as later the Poles and Russians, but psychologically subjugated by Hitler. That terrible, terrible charisma of his, all of it serving, as we know now but didn't know then, his ultimate megalomaniac goal, a race-selected United Europe under German domination.'

'Of course,' she says, 'only a foreign historian can look at Hitler like this; no German could have this "*Distanz*", not even the younger ones, not yet. That is probably why, except for Joachim Fest's twenty years ago, there is barely a Hitler biography written by a German.'

She is now one of the last survivors of Hitler's inner circle and there are many details of her two and a half years with him which she can no longer recall 'And anyway, all the facts are known' she said. 'What I can . . . well . . . perhaps still contribute, is the atmosphere around him, the different man we knew . . .' she is not given to hyperbole and hesitated for a moment '. . . the two men he was.'

Frau Junge and I were not strangers. Over the past fifty years, every historian and every journalist who wrote about the Third Reich, including me repeatedly, has tried to pick her brains, about the people who were part of this intimate group, and about Hitler himself whom she knew so differently than others did. To her he had always been kind, concerned about her welfare 'very paternal' she says. She still doesn't like to talk about these feelings. 'It embarrasses people,' she said. 'They don't understand and how can they? But I can't and I won't deny how I felt about him.'

A little like Albert Speer (whom she respected and sympathized with after he left Spandau prison, in contrast to most of Hitler's circle who, loyal to Hitler to their deaths, rejected him as a traitor) she went through a long period of reflection and deep disillusionment after the war and to this day has periods of depression. She is convinced that Hitler basically had two separate personalities of which she and all the 'ladies' of his close circle – his mistress, and for just twenty-four hours at the end his wife, Eva Braun, his four secretaries, the wives of his personal physician (Annie Brandt), his favourite military aide (Maria von Below) and Albert Speer's wife Margret – only saw the human, often charming side.

'We never saw him as the statesman; we didn't attend any of his conferences. We were only summoned when he wanted to dictate and he was as considerate then as he was in private. And our office, both in the Reichschancellery and in the bunkers, was so far removed from the Fuhrer area, we never saw or even heard any of his rages we heard whispers about. We knew his timetable, whom he received, but except for the few men he sometimes had to meals we attended, such as Speer, the other architect Giesler, or his photographer, Hoffmann, we rarely saw any of them. (After Stalingrad the two older secretaries shared his lunch, the younger ones his supper and one was always detailed to host the post-midnight tea.)

What was really missing in Hitler's life, she said, and they were aware of this, was an equal, a peer. 'My colleagues told me that in the earlier years he would talk incessantly, about the past, and the future, but after Stalingrad, well . . . I don't remember many monologues. We all tried to distract him, with talk about films, or gossip, anything that would take his mind off the war. He loved gossip. That was part of that other side of him, which was basically the only one we ever saw.'

And she recalls the first dictation she took from him, the test which was to decide her future, at the 'Wolfsschanze', his East Prussian field HQ, in December 1942. 'Later I realized what a dreadful time that was for him, just before Stalingrad. But you wouldn't have guessed it: the only thing he seemed to have on his mind was to make me comfortable and reassure me.' Hitler hated heat, she said 'His working quarters were kept at eleven degrees and, imagine, he had them bring in a heater for me. (Three years later, in the Berlin Bunker, hours before his suicide, she would have a similar experience, ' "How are you, my dear (mein Kind)?" he asked me. "Have you had a bit of rest? I want to dictate to you. Do you think you are up to it?" ' She only realized what he wanted to dictate when he said the title 'My Testament.')

His voice when dictating – always straight into the machine – was usually quiet, but at times, when working on speeches, it would suddenly became raucous, his gestures studiedly expansive.

'It happened from one moment to the next, and he was clearly acting, rehearsing, performing,' she said. This 'performance' would include the use of awful words which he never used in private. 'His speeches all had these words in them (about the Jews and the Slavs) and I now know that one simply got used to them, didn't really hear them, blocked them, I suppose, in the sense that otherwise they would . . . surely . . . have been unacceptable. And an instant later, he would be quiet again, professorial with his steel-rimmed glasses.'

She has been convinced for years now that genocide, of whole populations as well as the Jews, was on his mind from the start. And she is bewildered to this day how it could be that despite the fact that these dictations of speeches, orders and *aides-memoire*, continually revised as he spoke and thus obviously containing his ideas and plans, remained so completely unindicative both to her and her three colleagues of that other – that second man. 'What with having to be available to him day and night and at the same time sharing most of his private life, meals and leisure, we too, I now know, led a dual existence,' she said. 'But I don't think that ever occurred to us at the time, and isolated from the experiences of other Germans, we accepted as normal our not only very privileged but entirely abnormal life.'

Was she aware of Hitler's impulsiveness? 'Kershaw's biography reminded me how unsystematic everything was, his political and military decisions, his life, really. Putting together what this book now shows us and what I probably felt in my bones then, but only understand consciously now, the essential thing about Hitler probably was that his mind and his actions were ruled not by knowledge, but by emotion. I had never understood until now how he, who supposedly so loved the Germans, was prepared to sacrifice them so cold-bloodedly at the end. I have never understood the effect he had on all of us, including the generals. It was more than charisma, you know. Sometimes when he went off somewhere without us, the moment he was gone, it was almost as if the air around us had become deficient. Some essential element was missing: electricity, even oxygen, an awareness of being alive. There was a vacuum.'

'What was decisive, perhaps from the start I think, was that – different I now know, even from other dictators – he had no peer: there was no one whom he could or indeed would consult for advice, or who would have dared question his decisions. Speer was basically the only one he felt emotion for, listened to and could really talk with, but not about politics. Goebbels could have filled that other role except that – we knew this, though Goebbels never did – Hitler didn't feel anything for him; he was in a way too intellectual. It sounds absurd, but I think he intimidated him. Of course, Goebbels would have done anything for him, and of course in the end he, his wife and their children died for him.'

In the last days in the Bunker, they felt like automatons: 'We had no normal feelings anymore; we thought of nothing except death. Hitler and Eva, when they would die, when the six children would be killed, when and how we would die.'

All feelings of rank had gone. 'I asked Magda Goebbels, who looked like a ghost, whether there wasn't something that could be done to get the children out. And she answered that she preferred for her children to die than for them to live in the disgrace of the Germany that would be left.'

When, two hours before Hitler killed himself, she found herself alone with him in the conference room, waiting to take down his last will, she suddenly felt quite intensely that this was the moment of truth.

'I thought that now I would be the first person on earth to know why all this happened. He would say something that explained . . . that justified it all, that would teach us something, leave us with something. But then, as he dictated, my God, that long list of ministers he so grotesquely appointed to succeed his Government, I thought – yes, I did think then – how undignified it all was. Just the same phrases, in the same quiet tone and then, at the end of it, those terrible words about the Jews. After all the despair, all the suffering, not one word of sorrow, of compassion. I remember thinking, he has left us with nothing. A nothing. (*Ein Nichts*).'

20

Final Reflections

April 2001

He had, of course, not left them with nothing. For, surely unexpectedly for Germany itself and the world, the horror he wrought in their name has changed the Germans, has made them into different people.

In any discussion of the problems in our world today, racism must rank high. Not because we are soft-minded liberals obsessed with countless crimes throughout history induced by colour, religion, tribalism or chauvinism of one kind or another. But because the poison which we hoped and believed had been eradicated in our own time by the knowledge of the ultimate evil – the gaschamber murders committed by the Nazis – is in fact still present, not in any one area of discrimination or racism, or in a restricted number of specific rulers or governments, but in all humankind. I call it 'Inner Racism'.

Germany, always vulnerable to charges of xenophobia, has been forced by history to be Europe's most open society. Statistics of racial offences are therefore more readily available there than elsewhere. But given what we know about key cases in Britain, such as the police brutality in the Stephen Lawrence case; or about the incapacity of Central and Eastern European governments to find a solution for the appalling age-old discrimination against Romanies which is now being extended to the West, as, learning of economic and welfare advantages in the West, they try to slip illegally over West European borders; or about the disproportionate number of blacks on death row in America, many of them convicted as minors; or about the appalling cruelties between warring African tribes, often committed by brainwashed child-soldiers; or about the hate-filled civil war between Israelis and Palestinians which is killing children every day; or finally about the apparent unwillingness of the rich white West to supply poor black

Africa with the sophisticated medicines they must have if a third of their continent's population is not to die of AIDS within the next few years – all of these iniquities force us to admit that the evil of racism is far more deeply embedded in the human psyche than we hoped.

In the four decades following the demise of the Third Reich, Germany appeared to have largely overcome these perils. But the reunification of East and West Germany in 1989 demonstrated the deep differences which had been created in the two parts of Germany over forty-five years and the fragility of the country's inner harmony.

While diametrically opposed politically, these two post-war Germanies were not unlike in their determination to instil the ideologies of their mentors – in East Germany the heavy-handed imposition of Soviet communism, in West Germany the spoonfeeding of American style democracy. East Germany was a police state until 1989 where anything except pro-communist views was prohibited. West Germany's wealth to this day owes much to America's financial backing in the 1950s, support which would not have been given without the willingness of post-war West German governments to institute severe anti-discriminatory legislation under which any public display of neo-Nazism or anti-semitism was heavily penalized. In both parts of the country, because of a shortage of non-Nazi teachers, re-education of the young limped along for years, but from the very start ideology played a large part in the press, the film media and in the publishing industry, which, above all in West Germany (as I hope I have demonstrated in earlier pages of this book), determinedly kept alive the lessons of Germany's by now not so 'recent history'. In one way or the other, however, throughout those years, three young generations were provided with a forty-year period of stability, in East Germany through the ideological but artificially effective 'from the cradle to the grave' security imposed by communism, in West Germany by allowing them to feel included in the Western Alliance.

This seemed to come to an end when the Berlin Wall came down in 1989. The western part of Germany has had to carry the financial burden of re-making the East. But while life has not markedly changed for young West Germans, eastern Germany and particularly the young there have reeled for over a decade now under the consequences of reunification.

Under the discipline of the communist system, East Germany felt safe, never aware that this 'safety' would one day turn out to have been another serfdom. The capacity for independent thinking and mobility required of them when they were joined to the West's market society, was strange and disturbing for them. Because of insufficient teaching staff then and still now, a percentage of them are still virtually unemployable in our technology orientated world: re-education was slow to be offered and slow to be accepted. Condescended to by their rich and sophisticated West German compatriots, they consider themselves second-class citizens. The inevitable consequence has been that over the years frustration and resentment developed into anger and violence against those even further down the social scale – the foreign workers who fill jobs which otherwise might have been and might be now available to native Germans.

The year 2000, for the first time since the Second World War, produced a series of attempted murders of foreigners and blacks in thirteen cities, most of them in former East Germany. 746 cases of assault resulting in severe injuries across the country were mostly committed by East Germans, all of them against people of colours other than white. Hostels for Turkish '*Gastarbeiter*' (guestworkers) have been burned down, and swastikas smeared on walls and Jewish gravestones. But the swastika is now for most simply an expression of aggression, not necessarily a symbol of neo-Nazi beliefs. So the question asked now in Germany is not only whether the laws West Germany originally created to protect society against neo-Nazism and anti-semitism, are applicable to these acts by angry young East Germans, but how long it will take to recreate from these two so deeply contrasting halves of the country a single economically thriving German society which acknowledges the fatal effects of racism, and rejects it.

This question was high on the agenda at the International Forum on Intolerance and Xenophobia held in Stockholm in January 2001. In his address there, the German journalist Toralf Staud, born in East Germany in 1972 and now writer on East German youth for the influential Hamburg weekly *Die Zeit*, said that while prior to reunification political violence was virtually non-existent in the strictly policed communist East Germany, and although only 17 per cent of

Germany's total population now live there, an overwhelming proportion of the acts of right-wing violence now increasing in Europe are perpetrated in the five formerly East German '*Länder*' by disaffected youths. While in previous decades, right wing radicalism didn't exist in East Germany and in West Germany was largely confined to older generations, he said, the extremist camp in the East now has a much younger following. As they are heavily exposed to extremist influences, the victims, besides foreigners and non-whites, increasingly include traditional right-radical targets: homosexuals, the handicapped and the homeless. And right-wing extremists have an easy time appealing to values cultivated by the communist regime, authoritarianism, collectivism, anti-individualism and anti-pluralism, which still flourish or are nostalgically remembered in the East today. What he finds of greatest concern is that right-wing or racist ideology, expressed in music, dress codes and idiom, has in recent years turned into a kind of social movement. In many rural regions and smaller towns, he says, it is no longer a minority phenomenon but a dominant pattern of youth culture. Skinhead bands are widely popular and German runes, pagan mythology and racist expressions, recalling Nazi practices, are used by right-wing extremists to construct a bogus cultural tradition. Startlingly, NPD activists (from the extreme-right National Democratic Party) have succeeded in creating so-called 'nationally liberated zones': no-go areas for non-believers, aliens, dark-skinned Germans and anybody else who does not conform to their racist ideology.

The existence in various German cities of such areas, where it is now not safe for coloured people to go, was confirmed to me in January 2001 when I spent much of a day in Munich with graduating 'Gymnasium' history students. But although several of them commented on stories they had read, heard or seen about this on TV, none of them emphasized or even mentioned that these things were happening in eastern rather than western Germany. Their knowledge of life, or problems in eastern Germany was patchy, but then – and this seems to the observer a very positive development – for them, who were seven years old when the Berlin Wall came down, it seemed that the word re-unification has become merely another historical term. And if they thought it terrible that such things should be happening in their country, they meant all of Germany, not half of it.

But young people's feelings about the Nazi past, they said, differed widely. They depended almost entirely on the one hand on family attitudes, and on the other on the willingness of teachers to teach Nazi history. In academic schools like theirs, said seventeen-year-old Anna, 'modern history is, of course, part of the curriculum, but it is entirely up to the teachers which part of it they will teach. If she or he isn't interested, or [again there was that shrug – the educated German young, I found, are very knowing about their elders] if they have personal reasons not to want to go into Third Reich history, they can easily just touch upon it superficially, sort of glide past it.' Also, as in England, where the curriculum differs widely depending on the location of the school, it is a question of social group. 'I have a lot of friends who go to a "Hauptschule" [secondary school],' said an eighteen-year-old boy who lived in a working-class district of the city. 'They don't get modern history at all.' He shrugged 'So you see, instruction in Nazi history has become a matter of class.'

What, I asked could teachers' reasons be for not wanting 'to go into' Nazi history?

It was swiftly emphasized that they were not talking about their own history teacher, a woman in her late thirties who having invited me into her class was manifestly open to discussion, and indeed pointedly left the room when this subject arose so as not to intimidate her students' by her presence. For them, talking about Nazi history was closely linked to a problem that preoccupied them just as it had the German students I had talked with thirty or more years earlier – the old German propensity to authoritorianism. In their own school, they said, there was only one teacher, a sixty-year old, who was both openly authoritarian and suspected of feeling nostalgic for Nazi discipline. But there were 'quite a few who carried the leftovers of authoritarianism within them. One can't argue with them. One can't admit weakness: they make fun of it'.

It is impossible to estimate how widespread that characteristic still is, but even if, as I suspect, it now only applies to a small percentage, it echoes disturbingly the remarks made to me in the 1970s by their parents' generation, about their own parents (these childrens' grandparents) who, authoritarian themselves, urged awareness upon them that good marks, good exam results, and chances for further education depended on not having independent ideas and certainly on not expressing them to teachers. Their teachers now, said these students, are now only one generation older than themselves, and had family problems not unlike their own, though the teachers' were with parents and grandparents, while their own were with grand- and great-grandparents.

'My father is a good example,' said Sabine, who intended to study history at university. 'He is cool, not a bit authoritarian, and he understands me. But he can't manage with his parents, my grandparents, who, quite old when he was born, were formalistic, strict and enthusiastic Nazis and can't forget it. His solution to the problem is that he hardly sees them, and we barely know them, and that is sad, isn't it?'

Interestingly however, in this group of about twenty-five, only six knew of, or admitted to, Nazi sympathies by grand- or great-grandparents. Interesting too, that those who had close relationships with these older generations, enjoyed pointing out how frank (no doubt in contrast to others) these grandparents were about their feelings, however controversial the subjects. Jan said that his 82-year old grandfather had been perfectly ready to talk about the Nazis for years, but now thinks enough is enough. 'He thinks that we have to go on remembering what happened to the Jews – that we owe it. But as to the teaching of German history in general, he thinks we should go on to more recent events, that what happened in Eastern Europe since the war – Russia above all – is just as important for us to learn about.'

Another boy, also called Jan, said his grandfather feels differently. 'He says we need to think more about the Nazis, not less, that everything negative now in the thinking and feeling of Germans, had its origins in Nazi philosophy. He thinks that there is very little difference between what the Nazis felt about the '*Fremdarbeiter*' (foreign workers) and what we now feel about the '*Gastarbeiter*' (guest-workers) – that one and the other reaction is condescending, xenophobic and wrong.'

'We don't only feel that about guestworkers, but about East Germans too,' another girl said. 'If I were an East German, I'd rather stay there, unemployed, than come over here, even to take a good job, and be treated as an '*Ostler*' made to feel that I'm less than the '*Westis*' are and that everything in the East was always bad.' Almost all of them agreed immediately that older West Germans are arrogant, 'not toward foreigners, but very much toward East Germans'.

'And towards foreigners,' said sixteen-year-old Uwe, 'we are bloody servile. I'm German and I feel German. My father won't go shopping in France because he feels ashamed of being German. I'm furious when Germans misbehave abroad, but I have no problem with feeling good about being German. Why should I have?'

All of them, it turned out, had travelled abroad, several of the girls as au pairs in France and England during summer holidays, and all of them had had problems, 'Especially in England,' said Anna, with an embarrassed smile for me, the visitor from Britain. 'It isn't that they aren't nice to us,' she said, 'but you know, there are all these old films on TV about the Nazis, it seemed like every night. England's the only place where I felt embarrassed about being German – I mean, you can't blame them if they identify everything German with the Nazis when it's rubbed into them on TV all the time. I was taking care of some small children there and even though everybody was nice to me, the older kids kept saying "Hun" to me, and "Nazi" if I told them off when they misbehaved.'

Also, several of them said, they became very careful about expressing pride in Germany or anything that was achieved there. 'The French and the British are very proud of their countries,' one said, 'and I am proud of us, too. But I came to feel I mustn't be: if I expressed it they wouldn't like it, they wouldn't like me.' One girl had travelled in America with her parents. 'We couldn't go anywhere, it seemed, without somebody bringing up the Jews. In my family, the terrible things the Nazis did to the Jews have always been talked about, openly, but suddenly it felt as if we were the ones who had done it. One night I heard my father, who had always said we mustn't forget, say to my mother, "When is it all going to end; the damned Jews." He didn't mean it: he feels so strongly against the Nazis. But I understood him; I felt that too, in America. I still feel badly now about having felt it, even for a moment.'

Thirty years ago, young people in Germany also talked about the extent foreigners were preoccupied with Nazis, but they felt then it was justified. If they deplored their families' or their teachers' continued authoritarianism, they saw no way of eliminating it from their lives, or even opposing it. None of them admitted to pride in Germany, only shame. And, however justified or understandable it might have been, I don't think many of them would have expressed irritation with 'Jews' or for that matter any foreigners. Whether in an intellectual discussion, or in a momentary impulse, however innocent, criticism was taboo.

Modern Germany, more than any other Western country, has achieved a fundamental change since the Second World War. Although continuing, quite rightly, to be aware of what for decades was referred to as 'Germany's recent past', young generations can now, as they should, see it from a proper perspective as part of Germany's history without being weighed down by it, and pride in their country's achievements is returning. It is true that the recent revival of xenophobia and racism in the old East, the product of frustration and exclusion, is a real cause for concern and must be watched with extreme care. But it is also true that the majority of Germany's younger generation is freer of racism than much of the rest of Europe, where the 'inner racism' is never far below the surface. The nature of the interest intelligent young Germans manifest now in the Nazi past, is different from the pain and anger of their parents and grandparents. Although still baffled that this could happen in their country, the involvement of the young now is more intellectual than emotional. The seriousness and the moral nature of the questions they ask about the past however, and the concerns they voice for the present, remain the same.

Note on the Text

All the essays in this collection have been revised for this edition, and were first published in their original form as below:

1. 'Beginnings' was first published in *Granta*, Autumn 1995
2. 'My Friend, a Heroine of France' was first published in the *Sunday Times*, March 1997
3. 'Stolen Children' was first published in *Talk*, November 1999
4. 'Generation without a Past' was first published in the *Daily Telegraph* magazine, September 1967
5. 'Colloquy with a Conscience' was first published in the *Daily Telegraph* magazine, October 1971
6. 'Men Who Whitewash Hitler' was first published in the *New Statesman*, November 1979
7. 'The Hitler Wave' was first published as 'Facing up to the New "Hitler Wave" in Germany', in the *New Statesman*, May 1978
8. 'Fakes and Hoaxes: The Hitler Diaries' was first published in the *Sunday Times*, December 1983
9. 'The Great Globocnik Hunt' was first published as 'A Nazi Hunter Run to Earth' in the *Sunday Independent*, July 1992
10. 'Private Lives' was first published in this edition, September 2000
11. 'The Three Sins of Syberberg' was first published in the *Sunday Telegraph* magazine, May 1978
12. '"The Truth Is, I Loved Hitler"' was first published in the *Observer*, April 1996
13. 'Leni' was first published as 'Loving Hitler' in the *Sunday Independent* Review, September 1992

14 'Kurt Waldheim's Mental Block' was first published in the *New Statesman*, September 1986

15 'The Man Who Said "No"' was first published as 'The SS Man Who Said "No"' in the *Sunday Times*, February 1982

16 'Albert Speer' was first published as 'The New Speer Controversy: Did he tell all?' in the *Sunday Times* Magazine, September 1978

17 'Children of the Reich' was first published in *Vanity Fair* (New York), July 1990

18 Parts of 'The Case of Demjanjuk' are taken from 'Is this Ivan of Treblinka?' in the *Sunday Times* magazine, March 1989 and articles first published in the *Times*, *Sunday Correspondent*, the *Independent* and *New York Review of Books*

19 'The Right to Say "No"' was first published as 'The Courage to Say "No"' in the *Independent*, December 1989

Index